JOHN WESLEY'S JOURNAL

JOHN WESLEY'S JOURNAL

AS ABRIDGED BY

Nehemiah Curnock

PHILOSOPHICAL LIBRARY
NEW YORK

PUBLISHED, 1951, BY
THE PHILOSOPHICAL LIBRARY, INC.
15 EAST 40TH STREET, NEW YORK 16, N.Y.

ALL RIGHTS RESERVED
PRINTED IN GREAT BRITAIN

PRINTED AND BOUND IN ENGLAND BY
HAZELL WATSON AND VINEY LTD
AYLESBURY AND LONDON

PREFACE

THE Journal of John Wesley was originally published in a series of small volumes, each named "An Extract." It has since been republished in many forms. The present reissue is an attempt to condense into one volume of moderate size the more interesting features of the standard four-volume edition. The aim has been to preserve in a continuous narrative the main facts that illustrate the rise and progress of Methodism as described by John Wesley himself. This edition of the Journal differs from the original only in its omissions. The quaint phraseology has been preserved, and even the old spelling of names. In Wesley's own words, without alteration or comment, the story is told.

Of set purpose the earlier chapters have suffered less from the pruning knife than the second half of the book. This it is hoped will render the work all the more valuable to Wesley Guild and other students who require a handbook to assist them in their systematic study of the "Roots of Methodism." At the same time the general reader will find all that is most thrilling in the story of early

Methodism, and will naturally turn with whetted appetite to that complete Journal which in our own day has been recognised as one of the most remarkable literary products of the eighteenth century.

N. C.

CONTENTS

CHAP.		PAGE
	THE HOLY CLUB	1
I.	A MISSIONER TO GEORGIA	7
II.	A SOCIETY IN ALDERSGATE STREET	38
III.	A VISIT TO HERNHUTH	55
IV.	THE UNITED SOCIETIES	61
V.	A TIME OF CONFLICT	90
VI.	BUILDING OF THE ORPHAN HOUSE	116
VII.	PERILS AND PERSECUTIONS	157
VIII.	TRIUMPHANT PROGRESS	197
IX.	CALM AFTER STORM	234
X.	THE PREACHER	269
XI.	INCREASING LABOURS	289
XII.	AMONG THE SOCIETIES	315

Contents

CHAP.		PAGE
XIII.	REAPING THE HARVEST	333
XIV.	THE HONOURED GUEST	347
XV.	NEW PREACHING HOUSES	363
XVI.	THE PASSING OF THE OLD METHODISTS	376
XVII.	"MY REMNANT OF DAYS"	388
	INDEX	425

THE HOLY CLUB

In November 1729, at which time I came to reside at Oxford, your son, my brother, myself, and one more, agreed to spend three or four evenings in a week together. Our design was to read over the classics, which we had before read in private, on common nights, and on Sunday some book in divinity. In the summer following, Mr Morgan told me he had called at the gaol, to see a man who was condemned for killing his wife; and that, from the talk he had with one of the debtors, he verily believed it would do much good, if anyone would be at the pains of now and then speaking with them. This he so frequently repeated, that on the 24th of August, 1730, my brother and I walked with him to the castle. We were so well satisfied with our conversation there, that we agreed to go thither once or twice a week; which we had not done long, before he desired me to go with him to see a poor woman in the town, who was sick. In this employment, too, when we came to reflect upon it, we believed it would be worth while to spend an hour or two in a week; provided the minister of the parish, in which any such person was, were not against it. But that we might not depend wholly on our own judgments, I wrote an account to my father of our whole design; withal begging that he, who had lived seventy years in the world, and seen as much of it as most private men have ever done, would advise us whether we had yet gone too far, and whether we should now stand still or go forward.

Part of his answer was this:—

"And now, as to your own designs and employments, what can I say less of them than *Valde probo*:[1] and that I have the highest reason to bless God, that He has given me two sons together at Oxford, to whom He has given grace and courage to turn the war against the world and the devil, which is the best way to conquer them. They have but one more enemy to

[1] I greatly approve.

combat with, the flesh; which if they take care to subdue by fasting and prayer, there will be no more for them to do, but to proceed steadily in the same course, and expect 'the crown which fadeth not away.' You have reason to bless God, as I do, that you have so fast a friend as Mr Morgan, who, I see, in the most difficult service, is ready to break the ice for you. You do not know of how much good that poor wretch who killed his wife has been the providential occasion. I think I must adopt Mr Morgan to be my son, together with you and your brother Charles; and when I have such a ternion to prosecute that war, wherein I am now *miles emeritus*,[1] I shall not be ashamed when they speak with their enemies in the gate.

"Go on then, in God's name, in the path to which your Saviour has directed you, and that track wherein your father has gone before you! For when I was an undergraduate at Oxford, I visited those in the castle there, and reflect on it with great satisfaction to this day. Walk as prudently as you can, though not fearfully, and my heart and prayers are with you."

Soon after, a gentleman of Merton College, who was one of our little company, which now consisted of five persons, acquainted us that he had been much rallied the day before for being a member of *The Holy Club*; and that it has become a common topic of mirth at his college, where they had found out several of our customs, to which we were ourselves utter strangers. Upon this, I consulted my father again, in whose answer were these words:—

"For my part, on the present view of your actions and designs, my daily prayers are, that God would keep you humble; and then I am sure that if you continue 'to suffer for righteousness' sake,' though it be but in a lower degree, 'the Spirit of glory and of God' shall, in some good measure, 'rest upon you.' Be never weary of well-doing: never look back; for you know the prize and the crown are before you: Though I can scarce think so meanly of you, as that you would be discouraged with 'the crackling of thorns under a pot.' Be not high-minded, but fear. Preserve an equal temper of mind under whatever treatment you meet with from a not very just or well-natured world. Bear no more sail than is necessary, but steer steady."

The outcry daily increasing, we proposed to our friends, or opponents, these or the like questions:—

[1] A soldier past service.

I. Whether it does not concern all men of all conditions to imitate Him, as much as they can, "who went about doing good"?

Whether all Christians are not concerned in that command, "While we have time let us do good to all men"?

Whether we shall not be more happy hereafter, the more good we do now?

Whether we can be happy at all hereafter, unless we have, according to our power, "fed the hungry, clothed the naked, visited those that are sick, and in prison"; and made all these actions subservient to a higher purpose, even the saving of souls from death?

Whether it be not our bounden duty always to remember, that He did more for us than we can do for Him, who assures us, "Inasmuch as ye have done it unto one of the least of these my brethren, ye have done it unto Me"?

II. Whether, upon these considerations, we may not try to do good to our acquaintance? Particularly, whether we may not try to convince them of the necessity of being Christians?

Whether of the consequent necessity of being scholars?

Whether of the necessity of method and industry, in order to either learning or virtue?

Whether we may not try to persuade them to confirm and increase their industry, by communicating as often as they can?

Whether we may not mention to them the authors whom we conceive to have wrote the best on those subjects?

Whether we may not assist them, as we are able, from time to time, to form resolutions upon what they read in those authors, and to execute them with steadiness and perseverance?

III. Whether, upon the considerations above mentioned, we may not try to do good to those that are hungry, naked, or sick? In particular, whether, if we know any necessitous family, we may not give them a little food, clothes, or physic, as they want?

Whether we may not give them, if they can read, a Bible, Common-Prayer Book, or Whole Duty of Man?

Whether we may not, now and then, inquire how they have used them; explain what they do not understand, and enforce what they do?

Whether we may not enforce upon them, more especially the necessity of private prayer, and of frequenting the church and sacrament?

Whether we may not contribute what little we are able, toward having their children clothed and taught to read?

Whether we may not take care that they be taught their catechism, and short prayers for morning and evening?

IV. Lastly: Whether, upon the considerations above mentioned, we may not try to do good to those that are in prison? In particular, Whether we may not release such well-disposed persons as remain in prison for small sums?

Whether we may not lend smaller sums to those that are of any trade, that they may procure themselves tools and materials to work with?

Whether we may not give to them who appear to want it most, a little money, or clothes, or physic?

Whether we may not supply as many as are serious enough to read, with a Bible, and Whole Duty of Man?

Whether we may not, as we have opportunity, explain and enforce these upon them, especially with respect to public and private prayer, and the blessed sacrament?

I do not remember that we met with any person who answered any of these questions in the negative; or who even doubted, whether it were not lawful to apply to this use that time and money which we should else have spent in other diversions. But several we met with who increased our little stock of money for the prisoners and the poor, by subscribing something quarterly to it. Almost as soon as we had made our first attempts this way, some of the men of wit in Christ Church entered the lists against us; and, between mirth and anger, made a pretty many reflections upon the Sacramentarians, as they were pleased to call us. Soon after, their allies at Merton changed our title, and did us the honour of styling us, The Holy Club. But most of them being persons of well-known characters, they had not the good fortune to gain any proselytes from the sacrament, till a gentleman, eminent for learning and well esteemed for piety, joining them, told his nephew that if he dared to go to the weekly communion any longer, he would immediately turn him out of doors. That argument, indeed, had no success; the young gentleman communicated next week: upon which his uncle, having again tried to convince him that he was in the wrong way by shaking him by the throat to no purpose, changed his method, and by mildness prevailed upon him to absent from it the Sunday following; as he has done five Sundays in six ever since. This much delighted our gay opponents, who increased their number apace; especially when, shortly after, one of the seniors of the college, having been with the Doctor, upon his return from him sent for two young gentlemen severally, who had communicated weekly for some time, and was so successful in his exhortations that for the future they promised to do it only three times a year. About this time there was a meeting of several of the officers and seniors of the college, wherein it was consulted what would be the speediest way to stop the progress of enthusiasm in it. The result we know not, only it was soon publicly reported that Dr. —— and the censors were going to blow up The Godly Club. This was now our common title; though we were sometimes dignified with that of The Enthusiasts, or The Reforming Club. As for the names of Methodists, Supererogation-men, and so on, with which some of our neighbours are pleased to compliment us, we do not conceive ourselves to be under any obligation to regard them, much less to take them for arguments.—JOHN WESLEY.

[*An extract from a letter written by John Wesley, on Oct. 18th, 1732, to Mr Morgan, father of the first member of the Holy Club.*]

JOHN WESLEY'S JOURNAL

CHAPTER I

A MISSIONER TO GEORGIA

FROM OCTOBER 14, 1735, TO FEBRUARY 1, 1738

Tuesday, October 14, 1735.—Mr Benjamin Ingham, of Queen's College, Oxford, Mr Charles Delamotte, son of a merchant in London, my brother Charles Wesley, and myself, took boat for Gravesend, in order to embark for Georgia. Our end in leaving our native country was not to avoid want (God having given us plenty of temporal blessings), nor to gain the dung or dross of riches or honour; but simply this,—to save our souls; to live wholly to the glory of God. In the afternoon we found the *Simmonds* off Gravesend, and immediately went on board.

Fri. 17.—I began to learn German, in order to converse with the Germans, six-and-twenty of whom we had on board. On Sunday, the weather being fair and calm, we had the morning service on quarter-deck. I now first preached extempore, and then administered the Lord's Supper to six or seven communicants.

Mon. 20.—Believing the denying ourselves, even in the smallest instances, might, by the blessing of God, be helpful to us, we wholly left off the use of flesh and wine, and confined ourselves to vegetable food—chiefly rice and biscuit.

Tues. 21.—We sailed from Gravesend. Our common way of living was this:—From four in the morning till five, each of us used private prayer. From five to seven we read the Bible together, carefully comparing it with the writings of the earliest ages. At seven we breakfasted. At eight were the public prayers. From nine to twelve I usually learned German, and Mr Delamotte, Greek. My brother writ sermons, and Mr Ingham instructed the children. At twelve we met to give an account to one another what we had done since our last meeting, and what we designed to do before our next. About one we dined. The time from dinner to four, we spent in reading to those whom each of us had taken in charge, or in speaking to them severally, as need required. At four were the evening prayers; when either the second lesson was explained (as it always was in the morning), or the children were catechised and instructed before the congregation. From five to six we again used private prayer. From six to seven I read in our cabin to two or three of the passengers (of whom there were about eighty English on board), and each of my brethren to a few more in theirs. At seven I joined with the Germans in their public service; while Mr Ingham was reading between the decks, to as many as desired to hear. At eight we met again to exhort and instruct one another. Between nine and ten we went to bed, where neither the roaring of the sea, nor the motion of the ship, could take away the refreshing sleep which God gave us.

Fri. 24.—Hitherto it has pleased God, the sea has not disordered me at all; nor have I been hindered one quarter of an hour from reading, writing, composing, or doing any business I could have done on shore.

Fri. 31.—We sailed out of the Downs. At eleven at night I was waked by a great noise. I soon found there was no danger. But the bare apprehension of it gave me a lively conviction what manner of men those ought to be who are every moment on the brink of eternity.

Sat. Nov. 1.—We came to St. Helen's harbour, and the next day into Cowes road. The wind was fair, but we waited for the man-of-war which was to sail with us. This was a happy opportunity of instructing our fellow-travellers.

Sun. 16.—Thomas Hird, and Grace his wife, with their children, Mark, aged twenty-one, and Phebe, about seventeen, late Quakers, were, at their often-repeated desire, and after careful instruction, admitted to baptism.

Fri. 21.—One recovering from a dangerous illness, desired to be instructed in the nature of the Lord's Supper. I thought it concerned her to be first instructed in the nature of Christianity; and, accordingly, fixed an hour a day to read with her in Mr Law's *Treatise on Christian Perfection*.

Sun. 23.—At night I was awaked by the tossing of the ship and roaring of the wind, and plainly showed I was unfit, for I was unwilling, to die.

Tues. Dec. 2.—I had much satisfaction in conversing with one that was very ill and very serious. But in a few days she recovered from her sickness and from her seriousness together.

Sun. 7.—Finding nature did not require so frequent supplies as we had been accustomed to, we agreed to leave off suppers; from doing which, we have hitherto found no inconvenience.

Wed. 10.—We sailed from Cowes, and in the afternoon passed the Needles. Here the ragged rocks, with the waves dashing and foaming at the foot of them, and the white side of the island rising to such a height, perpendicular from the beach, gave a strong idea of "Him that spanneth the heavens, and holdeth the waters in the hollow of His hand!"

To-day I spoke closely on the head of religion, to one I had talked with once or twice before. Afterwards she said, with many tears, "My mother died when I was but ten years old. Some of her last words were, 'Child, fear God; and though you lose me, you shall never want a friend.' I have now found a friend when I most wanted and least expected one."

Thur. 18.—One who was in a high fever, and almost wasted away with a violent cough, desired to receive the holy communion before she died. At the hour of her receiving she began to recover, and in a few days was entirely out of danger.

Thur. Jan. 15, 1736.—Complaint being made to Mr Oglethorpe of the unequal distribution of the water among the passengers, he appointed new officers to take charge of it. At this the old ones and their friends were highly exasperated against us, to whom they imputed the change.

Sat. 17.—Many people were very impatient at the contrary wind. At seven in the evening they were quieted by a storm. It rose higher and higher till nine. About nine the sea broke over us from stem to stern; burst through the windows of the state cabin, where three or four of us were, and covered us all over, though a bureau sheltered me from the main shock. About eleven I lay down in the great cabin, and in a short time fell asleep, although very uncertain whether I should wake alive, and much ashamed of my unwillingness to die. Oh how pure in heart must he be, who would rejoice to appear before God at a moment's warning! Toward morning, "He rebuked the winds and the sea, and there was a great calm."

Fri. 23.—In the evening another storm began. In the morning it increased, so that they were forced to let the ship drive. I could not but say to myself, "How is it that thou hast no faith?" being still unwilling to die. About one in the afternoon, almost as soon as I had stepped out of the great cabin door, the sea did not break as usual, but come with a full, smooth tide over the side of the ship. I was vaulted over with water in a moment, and so stunned, that I scarce expected to lift up my head again, till the sea should give up her dead. But thanks be to God, I received no hurt at all. About midnight the storm ceased.

Sun. 25.—At noon our third storm began. At four it was more violent than before. Now, indeed, we could say, " The waves of the sea were mighty, and raged horribly. They rose up to the heavens above, and " clave " down to hell beneath." The winds roared round about us, and (what I never heard before) whistled as distinctly as if it had been a human voice. The ship not only rocked to and fro with the utmost violence, but shook and jarred with so unequal, grating a motion, that one could not but with great difficulty keep one's hold of anything, nor stand a moment without it. Every ten minutes came a shock against the stern or side of the ship, which one would think should dash the planks in pieces. At this time a child, privately baptized before, was brought to be received into the Church. It put me in mind of Jeremiah's buying the field, when the Chaldeans were on the point of destroying Jerusalem, and seemed a pledge of the mercy God designed to show us, even in the land of the living.

At seven I went to the Germans. I had long before observed the great seriousness of their behaviour. Of their humility they had given a continual proof, by performing those servile offices for the other passengers, which none of the English would undertake ; for which they desired, and would receive no pay, saying, " it was good for their proud hearts," and " their loving Saviour had done more for them." And every day had given them occasion of showing a meekness which no injury could move. If they were pushed, struck, or thrown down, they rose again and went away ; but no complaint was found in their mouth. There was now an opportunity of trying whether they were delivered from the spirit of fear, as well as from that of pride, anger, and revenge. In the midst of the psalm wherewith their service began, the sea broke over, split the mainsail in pieces, covered the ship, and poured in between the decks, as if the great deep had already swallowed us up. A terrible screaming began among the English. The Germans calmly sung on. I asked one of them afterwards, " Was you not afraid ? " He answered, " I thank God, no." I asked, " But were not your women and children afraid ? " He replied mildly, " No ; our women and children are not afraid to die."

Thur. 29.—About seven in the evening, we fell in with the skirts of a hurricane. The rain as well as the wind was extremely violent. The sky was so dark in a moment, that the sailors could not so much as see the ropes, or set about furling the sails. The ship must, in all probability, have overset, had not the wind fell as suddenly as it rose. Toward the end of it, we had that appearance on each of the masts, which (it is thought) the ancients called Castor and Pollux. It was a small ball of white fire, like a star. The mariners say, it appears either in a storm (and then commonly upon the deck), or just at the end of it, and then it is usually on the masts or sails.

Fri. 30.—We had another storm, which did us no other harm than splitting the foresail. Our bed being wet, I laid me down on the floor, and slept sound till morning. And, I believe, I shall not find it needful to go to bed (as it is called) any more.

Sun. Feb. 1.—We spoke with a ship of Carolina; and Wednesday, 4, came within soundings. About noon, the trees were visible from the masts, and in the afternoon from the maindeck.

Thur. 5.—Between two and three in the afternoon, God brought us all safe into the Savannah river. We cast anchor near Tybee Island, where the groves of pines, running along the shore, made an agreeable prospect, showing, as it were, the bloom of spring in the depth of winter.

Fri. 6.—About eight in the morning, we first set foot on American ground. It was a small uninhabited island, over against Tybee. Mr Oglethorpe led us to a rising ground, where we all kneeled down to give thanks. He then took boat for Savannah.

Sat. 7.—Mr Oglethorpe returned from Savannah with Mr Spangenberg, one of the pastors of the Germans. I soon found what spirit he was of; and asked his advice with regard to my own conduct. He said, "My brother, I must first ask you one or two questions. Have you the witness within yourself? Does the Spirit of God bear witness with your spirit, that you are a child of God?" I was surprised, and knew not what to answer. He observed it, and asked, "Do you know Jesus Christ?" I paused, and said, "I know He is the Saviour of the world." "True," replied he; "but do you know He has saved you?" I answered, "I hope He has died to save me." He only added, "Do you know yourself?" I said, "I do But I fear they were vain words.

Fri. 13.—Some of the Indians sent us word of their intention to come down to us.

Sat. 14.—About one, Tomo Chachi, his nephew Thleeanouhee, his wife Sinauky, with two more women, and two or three Indian children, came on board. As soon as we came in, they all rose and shook us by the hand; and Tomo Chachi (one Mrs Musgrove interpreted) spoke as follows :—

"I am glad you are come. When I was in England, I desired that some would speak the great Word to me; and my nation then desired to hear it; but now we are all in confusion. Yet I am glad you are come. I will go up and speak to the wise men of our nation; and I hope they will hear. But we would not be made Christians as the Spaniards make Christians; we would be taught, before we are baptized."

Sun. 15.—Another party of Indians came; they were all tall, well-proportioned men, and had a remarkable softness in their speech, and gentleness in their whole behaviour. In the afternoon they all returned but three.

Mon. 16.—Mr Oglethorpe set out for the new settlement on the Alatamahaw river. He took with him fifty men, besides Mr Ingham, Mr Hemsdorf, and the three Indians.

Thur. 19.—My brother and I took boat, and, passing by Savannah, went to pay our first visit in America to the poor heathens. But neither Tomo Chachi nor Sinauky was at home. Coming back, we waited upon Mr Causton, the chief magistrate of Savannah.

Sat. 21.—Mary Welch, aged eleven days, was baptized according to the custom of the first church, and the rule of the Church of England, by immersion. The child was ill then, but recovered from that hour.

Tues. 24.—Mr Oglethorpe returned. In the evening I went to Savannah again, whence Mr Spangenberg, Bishop Nitschman, and Andrew Dober, went up with us to Mrs Musgrove's, to choose a spot for the little house, which Mr Oglethorpe had promised to build us. Being afterward disappointed of our boat, we were obliged to pass the night there.

At our return the next day (Mr Quincy being then in the house wherein we afterwards were), Mr Delamotte and I took up our lodging with the Germans. We had now an opportunity, day by day, of observing their whole behaviour. They were always employed, always cheerful themselves, and in good humour with one another; they had put away all anger, and strife, and wrath, and bitterness, and clamour, and evil-speaking; they walked worthy of the vocation wherewith they were called.

Sat. 28.—They met to consult concerning the affairs of their Church; Mr Spangenberg being shortly to go to Pennsylvania, and Bishop Nitschman to return to Germany. After several hours spent in conference and prayer, they proceeded to the election and ordination of a bishop. The great simplicity, as well as solemnity, of the whole, almost made me forget the seventeen hundred years between, and imagine myself in one of those assemblies where form and state were not ; but Paul the tent-maker, or Peter the fisherman, presided ; yet with the demonstration of the Spirit and of power.

Sun. 29.—Hearing Mr Oglethorpe did not come any more to Savannah, before he went to Frederica, I was obliged to go down to the ship again, and receive his orders and instructions on several heads. From him we went to public prayers ; after which we were refreshed by several letters from England. About four I returned to Savannah.

Sun. Mar. 7.—I entered upon my ministry at Savannah, by preaching on the Epistle for the day, being the thirteenth of the first of Corinthians. In the second lesson (Luke xviii.) was our Lord's prediction of the treatment which He Himself (and, consequently, His followers) was to meet with from the world ; and His gracious promises to those who are content, *nudi nudum Christum sequi.*[1]

Sun. 14.—Having before given notice of my design to do so, every Sunday and holiday, according to the rules of our Church, I administered the holy communion to eighteen persons.

Mon. 15.—Mr Quincy going for Carolina, I removed into the minister's house. It is large enough for a larger family than ours, and has many conveniences, besides a good garden.

Tues. 30.—Mr. Ingham, coming from Frederica, brought me letters, pressing me to go thither. The next day Mr Delamotte and I began to try, whether life might not as well be sustained by one sort as by variety of food. We chose to make the experiment with bread, and were never more vigorous and healthy than while we tasted nothing else.

Sun. April 4.—About four in the afternoon I set out for Frederica in a pettiawga,—a sort of flat-bottomed barge. The next evening we anchored near Skidoway Island, where the water, at flood, was twelve or fourteen feet deep. I wrapped myself up from head to foot in a large cloak, to keep off the sand-flies, and lay down on the quarter-deck. Between one and two I waked under water, being so fast asleep that I did not find where I was till my mouth was full of it. Having left my cloak, I know not how, upon deck, I swam round to the other side of the pettiawga, where a boat was tied, and climbed up by the rope without any hurt, more than wetting my clothes.

The winds were so contrary, that on Saturday, 10, we could but just get over against Doboy Island, twenty miles from Frederica, but could not possibly make the creek, having a strong tide also against us. Here we lay beating off till past

[1] Naked to follow a naked Christ.—ED.

one, when the lightning and rain, which we had long seen at a distance, drove down full upon us; till, after a quarter of an hour, the clouds parted, some passing on the right, and some on the left, leaving us a clear sky, and so strong a wind right after us, as in two hours brought us to Frederica

A little before we landed, I opened my Testament on these words: " If God be for us, who can be against us?" Coming on shore, I found my brother exceeding weak, having been for some time ill; but he mended from the hour he saw me. This also hath God wrought!

Sun. 11.—I preached at the new storehouse on the first verse of the Gospel for the day: "Which of you convinceth me of sin? And if I say the truth, why do ye not believe me?"

In every one of the six following days, I had some fresh proofs of the absolute necessity of following that wise advice of the apostle: " Judge nothing before the time; until the Lord come, who both will bring to light the hidden things of darkness, and will make manifest the counsels of the hearts."

Sat. 17.—We set out for Savannah, and reached it on Tuesday evening.

Not finding, as yet, any door open for the pursuing our main design, we considered in what manner we might be most useful to the little flock at Savannah. And we agreed—1. To advise the most serious among them to form themselves into a sort of little society, and to meet once or twice a week, in order to reprove, instruct, and exhort one another. 2. To select out of these a smaller number for a more intimate union with each other, which might be forwarded, partly by our conversing singly with each, and partly by inviting them all together to our house; and this, accordingly, we determined to do every Sunday in the afternoon.

Wed. May 5.—I was asked to baptize a child of Mr Parker's, second bailiff of Savannah; but Mrs Parker told me, " Neither Mr P. nor I will consent to its being dipped." I answered, " If you 'certify that' your 'child is weak, it will suffice (the rubric says) to pour water upon it.'" She replied, " Nay, the child is not weak, but I am resolved it shall not be dipped." This argument I could not confute. So I went home; and the child was baptized by another person.

Sun. 9.—I began dividing the public prayers, according to the original appointment of the Church (still observed in a few places in England): the morning service began at five; the Communion Office (with the sermon), at eleven; the evening service, about three; and this day I began reading prayers in the court-house,—a large and convenient place.

Mon. 10.—I began visiting my parishioners in order, from house to house; for which I set apart (the time when they cannot work, because of the heat), viz., from twelve till three in the afternoon.

Sun. 16.—We were surprised in the evening by my brother, just come from Frederica. After some conversation we consulted how the poor people there might be taken care of during his absence: and it was at last agreed that Mr Ingham and I should take our turns in assisting them; and the first was allotted me. Accordingly, on Tuesday, 18th, I walked to Thunderbolt; whence the next afternoon we set out in a small boat. In the evening we touched at Skidoway, and had a small, but attentive, congregation to join with us in evening prayer.

Sat. 22.—About four in the afternoon we entered upon Doboy Sound. The wind, which was right ahead, was so high, when we were in the middle of it, and the sea so rough, being driven in at the inlet, that the boat was on the point of sinking every moment. But it pleased God to bring us safe to the other side in half an hour, and to Frederica the next morning.

Thur. June 3.—Being Ascension Day, we had the holy communion; but only Mr Hird's family joined with us in it. One reason why there were no more was, because a few words which a woman had inadvertently spoken had set almost all the town in a flame.

Thur. 10.—We began to execute at Frederica what we had before agreed to do at Savannah. Our design was, on Sundays, in the afternoon, and every evening, after public service, to spend some time with the most serious of the communicants, in singing, reading, and conversation. This evening we had only Mark Hird. But on Sunday, Mr Hird and two more desired to be admitted. After a psalm and a little conversation, I read Mr Law's *Christian Perfection*, and concluded another psalm.

Sat. 19.—Mr Oglethorpe returned from the south, and gave orders on Sunday, the 20th, that none should profane the day (as was usual before) by fishing or fowling upon it. In the afternoon I summed up what I had seen or heard at Frederica, inconsistent with Christianity, and, consequently, with the prosperity of the place. The event was as it ought: some of the hearers were profited, and the rest deeply offended.

Tues. 22.—Observing much coldness in Mr ——'s behaviour, I asked him the reason of it. He answered, "I like nothing you do. All your sermons are satires upon particular persons, therefore I will never hear you more; and all the people are of my mind, for we won't hear ourselves abused.

"Beside, they say, they are Protestants. But as for you, they cannot tell what religion you are of. They never heard of such a religion before. They do not know what to make of it. And then your private behaviour: all the quarrels that have been here since you came, have been 'long of you. Indeed, there is neither man nor woman in the town who minds a word you say. And so you may preach long enough, but nobody will come to hear you."

He was too warm for hearing an answer. So I had nothing to do but to thank him for his openness, and walk away.

Wed. 23.—About eleven at night we took boat; and on Saturday, 26th, about one in the afternoon, came to Savannah.

Sun. 27.—About twenty joined with us in morning prayer. An hour or two after, a large party of Creek Indians came; the expectation of whom deprived us of our place of public worship, in which they were to have their audience.

Wed. 30.—I hoped a door was opened for going up immediately to the Choctaws, the least polished, that is, the least corrupted, of all the Indian nations. But upon my informing Mr Oglethorpe of our design, he objected, not only the danger of being intercepted or killed by the French there; but much more, the inexpediency of leaving Savannah destitute of a minister. These objections I related to our brethren in the evening, who were all of opinion, "We ought not to go yet."

Thur. July 1.—The Indians had an audience: and another on Saturday, when Chicali, their headman, dined with Mr Oglethorpe. After dinner, I asked the greyheaded old man, what he thought he was made for. He said, "He that is above knows what He made us for. We know nothing. We are in the dark. But white men know much. And yet white men build great houses, as if they were to live for ever. But white men cannot live for ever. In a little time, white men will be dust as well as I."

Tues. 20.—Five of the Chicasaw Indians (twenty of whom had been in Savannah several days) came to see us, with Mr Andrews, their interpreter. They were all warriors, four of them headmen. The two chief were Paustoobee and Mingo Mattaw.

Mon. 26.—My brother and I set out for Charlestown, in order to his embarking for England; but the wind being contrary, we did not reach Port Royal, forty miles from Savannah, till Wednesday evening. The next morning we left it. But the wind was so high in the afternoon, as we were crossing the neck of St Helena's Sound, that our oldest sailor cried out, "Now everyone must take care for himself." I told him, "God would take care for us all." Almost as soon as the words were spoken, the mast fell. I kept on the edge of the boat, to be clear of her when she sunk (which we expected every moment), though with little prospect of swimming ashore against such a wind and sea. But "how is it that thou hadst no faith?" The moment the mast fell, two men caught it, and pulled it into the boat; the other three rowed with all their might, and "God gave command to the wind and seas"; so that in an hour we were safe on land.

Mon. Aug. 2.—I set out for the Lieutenant-Governor's seat, about thirty miles from Charlestown, to deliver Mr Oglethorpe's letters. It stands very pleasantly on a little hill, with a vale on either side, in one of which is a thick wood; the other is planted with rice and Indian corn. I designed to have gone back by Mr Skeen's, who has about fifty Christian negroes. But my horse tiring, I was obliged to return the straight way to Charlestown.

I had sent the boat we came in back to Savannah, expecting a passage thither myself in Colonel Bull's. His not going so soon, I went to Ashley Ferry on Thursday, intending to walk to Port Royal. But Mr Belinger not only provided me a horse, but rode with me himself ten miles, and sent his son with me to Cumbee Ferry, twenty miles farther; whence, having hired horses and a guide, I came to Beaufort (or Port Royal) the next evening. We took boat in the morning; but, the wind being contrary and very high, did not reach Savannah till Sunday, in the afternoon.

Finding Mr Oglethorpe was gone, I stayed only a day at Savannah; and leaving Mr Ingham and Delamotte there, set out on Tuesday morning for Frederica. In walking to Thunderbolt I was in so heavy a shower that all my clothes were as wet as if I had gone through the river. On which occasion I cannot but observe that vulgar error, concerning the hurtfulness of the rains and dews of America. I have been thoroughly wet with these rains more than once, yet without any harm at all. And I have lain many nights in the open air, and received all the dews that fell; and so, I believe, might anyone, if his constitution was not impaired by the softness of a genteel education.

At Thunderbolt we took boat; and on Friday, August 13th, came to Frederica, where I delivered Mr O. the letters I had brought from Carolina. The next day he set out for Fort St George. From that time I had less and less prospect of doing good at Frederica; many there being extremely zealous and indefatigably diligent to prevent it; and few of the rest daring to show themselves of another mind, for fear of their displeasure.

Sat. 28.—I set apart (out of the few we had) a few books towards a library at Frederica. In the afternoon I walked to the fort on the other side of the island. About five we set out homeward; but, my guide not being perfect in the way, we were soon lost in the woods. We walked on, however, as well as we could, till between nine and ten, when, being heartily tired and thoroughly wet with dew, we laid down, and slept till morning.

About daybreak, on Sunday, the 29th, we set out again, endeavouring to walk straight forward; and soon after sunrise found ourselves in the Great Savannah, near Frederica. By this good providence I was delivered from another fear—that of lying in the woods; which experience showed was, to one in tolerable health, a mere "lion in the way."

Thur. Sept. 2.—I set out in a sloop, and about ten on Sunday morning came to Skidoway, and to Savannah in the evening.

Tues. Oct. 12.—We considered if anything could yet be done for the poor people of Frederica; and I submitted to the judgment of my friends; which was, that I should take another journey thither: Mr Ingham undertaking to supply my place at Savannah, for the time I should stay there. I came hither on Saturday, the 16th, and found few things better than I expected.

I was at first a little discouraged, but soon remembered the word which cannot fail: "Greater is He that is in you than he that is in the world." I cried to God to "arise and maintain His own cause"; and after the evening prayers were ended, invited a few to my house; as I did every night while I stayed at Frederica. I read to them one of the exhortations of Ephraim Syrus: the most awakening writer, I think, of all the ancients.

Mon. 18.—Finding there were several Germans at Frederica, who, not understanding the English tongue, could not join in our public service, I desired them to meet me at my house; which they did every day at noon from thence forward. We first sung a German hymn; then I read a chapter in the New Testament; then explained it to them as well as I could. After another hymn, we concluded with prayer.

Mon. 25.—I took boat, and, after a slow and dangerous passage, came to Savannah on Sunday, the 31st.

Tues. Nov. 23.—Mr Oglethorpe sailed for England, leaving Mr Ingham, Mr Delamotte, and me at Savannah; but with less prospect of preaching to the Indians than we had the first day we set foot in America. Whenever I mentioned it, it was immediately replied, "You cannot leave Savannah without a minister." To this indeed my plain answer was, " I know not that I am under any obligation to the contrary. I never promised to stay here one month. I openly declared both before, at, and ever since my coming hither, that I neither would nor could take charge of the English any longer than till I could go among the Indians." But though I had no other obligation not to leave Savannah now, I could not resist the importunate request of the more serious parishioners, " to watch over their souls yet a little longer, till someone came who might supply my place." And this I the more willingly did, because the time was not come to preach the gospel of peace to the heathens ; all their nations being in a ferment.

Wed. Dec. 23.—Mr Delamotte and I, with a guide, set out to walk to the Cowpen. When we had walked two or three hours, our guide told us plainly, he did not know where we were. However, believing it could not be far off, we thought it best to go on. In an hour or two we came to a cypress swamp, which lay directly across our way : there was not time to walk back to Savannah before night ; so we walked through it, the water being about breast high. By the time we had gone a mile beyond it, we were out of all path ; and it being now past sunset, we sat down, intending to make a fire, and to stay there till morning ; but finding our tinder wet, we were at a stand. I advised to walk on still ; but my companions, being faint and weary, were for lying down, which we accordingly did about six o'clock : the ground was as wet as our clothes, which, it being a sharp frost, were soon froze together ; however, I slept till six in the morning. There fell a heavy dew in the night, which covered us over as white as snow. Within an hour after sunrise, we came to a plantation ; and in the evening, without any hurt, to Savannah.

Tues. 28.—We set out by land with a better guide for Frederica. On Wednesday evening we came to Fort Argyle, on the bank of the river Ogeechy. The next afternoon we crossed Cooanoochy river, in a small canoe ; our horses swimming by the side of it. We made a fire on the bank, and, notwithstanding the rain, slept quietly till the morning.

Sat. Jan. 1, 1737.—Our provisions fell short, our journey being longer than we expected : but having a little barbecued bear's flesh (that is, dried in the sun), we boiled it, and found it wholesome food. The next day we reached Darien, the settlement of the Scotch Highlanders : a sober, industrious, friendly hospitable people; whose minister, Mr M'Leod, is a serious, resolute, and, I hope, a pious man.

On Monday evening we left Darien, and on Wednesday, the 5th, came to Frederica. Most here were, as we expected, cold and heartless: we found not one who retained his first love.

After having beaten the air in this unhappy place for twenty days, on January 26th I took my final leave of Frederica. It was not any apprehension of my own danger, though my life had been threatened many times, but an utter despair of doing good there, which made me content with the thought of seeing it no more.

Mon. 31.—We came to Savannah. Tuesday, February 1, being the anniversary feast, on account of the first convoy's landing in Georgia, we had a sermon and the holy communion. Thursday, 24. It was agreed Mr Ingham should go for England, and endeavour to bring over, if it should please God, some of our friends to strengthen our hands in His work. Saturday, 26. He left Savannah.

Fri. Mar. 4.—I writ the Trustees for Georgia on account of our year's expense, from March 1, 1736, to March 1, 1737; which, deducting extraordinary expenses, such as repairing the parsonage house, and journeys to Frederica, amounted, for Mr Delamotte and me, to £44 4s. 4d.

From the directions I received from God this day, touching an affair of the greatest importance, I could not but observe, as I had done many times before, the entire mistake of those who assert, "God will not answer your prayer, unless your heart be wholly resigned to His will." My heart was not wholly resigned to His will. Therefore, not daring to depend on my own judgment, I cried the more earnestly to Him to supply what was wanting in me. And I know, and am assured, He heard my voice, and did send forth His light and His truth.

Thur. 24.—A fire broke out in the house of Robert Hows, and in an hour burned it to the ground: a collection was made for him the next day, and the generality of the people showed a surprising willingness to give a little out of their little for the relief of a necessity greater than their own.

Sun. April 3, and every day in this great and holy week, we had a sermon and the holy communion.

Mon. 4.—I began learning Spanish, in order to converse with my Jewish parishioners; some of whom seem nearer the mind that was in Christ than many of those who call Him Lord.

Tues. 12.—Being determined, if possible, to put a stop to the proceedings of one in Carolina, who had married several of my parishioners without either banns or licence, and declared he would do so still, I set out in a sloop for Charlestown. I landed there on Thursday, and related the case to Mr Garden, the Bishop of London's Commissary, who assured me, he would take care no such irregularity should be committed for the future.

Tues. 19.—We left Charlestown; but meeting with stormy and contrary winds, after losing our anchor, and beating out at sea all night, on Thursday, the 21st, we with some difficulty got back into Charlestown harbour.

Fri. 22.—It being the time of their annual visitation, I had the pleasure of meeting with the clergy of South Carolina; among whom, in the afternoon, there was such a conversation for several hours on "Christ our righteousness," as I had not heard at any visitation in England, or hardly on any other occasion.

Sat. 23.—Mentioning to Mr Thompson, minister of St Bartholomew's, near Ponpon, my being disappointed of a passage home by water, he offered me one of his horses, if I would go by land, which I gladly accepted of. He went with me twenty miles, and sent his servant to guide me the other twenty to his house. Finding a young negro there, who seemed more sensible than the rest, I asked her how long she had been in Carolina: she said, two or three years; but that she was born in Barbadoes, and had lived there in a minister's family from a child. I asked whether she went to church there: she said, "Yes, every Sunday,—to carry my mistress's children." I asked, what she had learned at church: she said, "Nothing; I heard a deal, but did not understand it."

The attention with which this poor creature listened to instruction is inexpressible. The next day she remembered all, readily answered every question; and said, she would ask Him that made her, to show her how to be good.

Wed. 27.—I came to Mr Bellinger's plantation at Chulifinny, where the rain kept me till Friday. Here I met with an half-Indian (one that had an Indian mother and a Spanish father), and several negroes, who were very desirous of instruction.

Mr Bellinger sent a negro lad with me to Purrysburg.

This lad too I found both very desirous and very capable of instruction. And perhaps one of the easiest and shortest ways to instruct the American negroes in Christianity, would be, first, to inquire after and find out some of the most serious of the planters. Then, having inquired of them which of their slaves were best inclined and understood English, to go to them from plantation to plantation, staying as long as appeared necessary at each. Three or four gentlemen in Carolina I have been with, that would be sincerely glad of such an assistant, who might pursue his work with no more hindrances than must everywhere attend the preaching of the gospel.

Sat. 30.—I came to Savannah, and found my little flock in a better state than I could have expected; God having been pleased greatly to bless the endeavours of my fellow-labourer, while I was absent from them.

Wed. May 18.—I discovered the first convert to Deism that, I believe, has been made here. He was one that for some time had been zealously and exemplarily religious. But indulging himself in harmless company, he first made shipwreck of his zeal, and then of his faith.

Wed. 25.—I was sent for by one who had been several years of the Church of Rome; but was now deeply convinced (as were several others), by what I had occasionally preached, of the grievous errors that Church is in, and the great danger of continuing a member of it. Upon this occasion I could not but reflect on the many advices I had received, to beware of the increase of Popery; but not one, that I remember, to beware of the increase of infidelity. This was quite surprising when I considered: 1. That in every place where I have yet been, the number of the converts to Popery bore no proportion to the number of the converts to infidelity. 2. That as bad a religion as Popery is, no religion is still worse; a baptized infidel being always found, upon the trial, twofold worse than even a bigoted Papist. 3. That as dangerous a state as a Papist is in, with regard to eternity, a Deist is in a yet more dangerous state, if he be not, without repentance, an assured heir of damnation. And, lastly, That as hard as it is to recover a Papist, it is still harder to recover an infidel: I myself having known many Papists, but never one Deist, reconverted.

May 29.—Being Whitsunday, four of our scholars, after having been instructed daily for several weeks, were, at their earnest and repeated desire, admitted to the Lord's Table.

Indeed, about this time we observed the Spirit of God to move upon the minds of many of the children. They began more carefully to attend to the things that were spoken both at home and at church, and a remarkable seriousness appeared in their whole behaviour and conversation.

June 25.—Mr Causton, the store-keeper and chief magistrate of Savannah, was seized with a slow fever. I attended him every day (as I did any of my parishioners who were in any painful or dangerous illness), and had a good hope, from the thankfulness he showed, that my labour was not in vain.

Sun. July 3.—Immediately after the holy communion, I mentioned to Mrs Williamson (Mr Causton's niece) some things which I thought reprovable in her behaviour. At this she appeared extremely angry; said, she did not expect such usage from me; and at the turn of the street, through which we were walking home, went abruptly away. The next day Mrs Causton endeavoured to excuse her; told me she was exceedingly grieved for what had passed the day before, and desired me to tell her in writing what I disliked; which I accordingly did the day following.

But first, I sent Mr Causton the following note:—

"SIR,—To this hour you have shown yourself my friend: I ever have and ever shall acknowledge it. And it is my earnest desire, that He who hath hitherto given me this blessing would continue it still.

"But this cannot be, unless you will allow me one request, which is not so easy an one as it appears: *do not condemn me for doing, in the execution of my office, what I think it my duty to do.*

"If you can prevail upon yourself to allow me this, even when I act without respect of persons, I am persuaded there will never be, at least not long, any misunderstanding between us. For even those who seek it shall, I trust, find no occasion against me, 'except it be concerning the law of my God.'— I am, etc.

"*July* 5, 1737."

Wed. 6.—Mr Causton came to my house, with Mr Bailiff Parker, and Mr Recorder, and warmly asked, "How could you possibly think I should condemn you for executing any part of your office?" I said short, "Sir, what if I should think it the duty of my office to repel one of your family from the holy communion?" He replied, "If you repel me or my wife, I shall require a legal reason. But I shall trouble myself about none else. Let them look to themselves."

Sat. 23.—Reflecting on the state I was now in, I could not but observe in a letter to a friend, "How to attain to the being crucified with Christ, I find not, being in a condition I neither desired nor expected in America,—in ease, and honour, and abundance: a strange school for him who has but one business, Γυμναζειν εαυτον προς ευσεβειαν."[1]

---

[1] To exercise himself unto godliness.

Wed. 27.—I rejoiced to meet once more with that good soldier of Jesus Christ, August. Spangenberg, with whom, on Monday, August 1, I began my long-intended journey to Ebenezer. On the way, I told him, the calm we had so long enjoyed was now drawing to an end; that I hoped he would shortly see I was not (as some had told him) a respecter of persons; but was determined (God being my helper) to behave indifferently to all, rich or poor, friends or enemies. I then asked his advice as to the difficulty I foresaw; and resolved, by God's grace, to follow it.

In the evening, we came to New Ebenezer, where the poor Salzburghers are settled. The industry of this people is quite surprising. Their sixty huts are neatly and regularly built, and all the little spots of ground between them improved to the best advantage. One side of the town is a field of Indian corn; on the other are the plantations of several private persons; all which together one would scarce think it possible for a handful of people to have done in one year.

Wed. Aug. 3.—We returned to Savannah. Sunday, 7, I repelled Mrs Williamson from the holy communion. And Monday, 8, Mr Recorder, of Savannah, issued out the warrant following:—

"Georgia. Savannah ss.
"*To all Constables, Tithingmen, and others, whom these may concern:*

"You, and each of you, are hereby required to take the body of John Wesley, Clerk:

"And bring him before one of the Bailiffs of the said town, to answer the complaint of William Williamson and Sophia his wife, for defaming the said Sophia, and refusing to administer to her the sacrament of the Lord's Supper, in a public congregation, without cause; by which the said William Williamson is damaged one thousand pound sterling: and for so doing, this is your warrant, certifying what you are to do in the premises. Given under my hand and seal the 8th day of August, *Anno Dom.* 1737.

"Tho. Christie."

Tues. 9.—Mr Jones, the constable, served the warrant, and carried me before Mr Bailiff Parker and Mr Recorder. My answer to them was, that the giving or refusing the Lord's Supper being a matter purely ecclesiastical, I could not acknowledge their power to interrogate me upon it. Mr Parker told me, "However, you must appear at the next court, holden for Savannah." Mr Williamson, who stood by, said, "Gentlemen, I desire Mr Wesley may give bail for his appearance." But Mr Parker immediately replied, "Sir, Mr Wesley's word is sufficient."

Wed. 10.—Mr Causton (from a just regard, as his letter expressed it, to the friendship which had subsisted between us till this affair) required me to give the reasons in the court-house, why I repelled Mrs Williamson from the holy communion. I answered, " I apprehend many ill consequences may arise from so doing : let the cause be laid before the Trustees."

Thur. 11.—Mr Causton came to my house, and among many other sharp words, said, " Make an end of this matter : thou hadst best. My niece to be used thus ! I have drawn the sword, and I will never sheathe it till I have satisfaction."

Soon after, he added, "Give the reasons of your repelling her before the whole congregation." I answered, "Sir, if you insist upon it, I will; and so you may be pleased to tell her." He said, "Write to her, and tell her so yourself." I said, " I will ; " and after he went, I wrote as follows :—

" *To Mrs Sophia Williamson.*

"AT Mr Causton's request, I write once more. The rules whereby I proceed are these :—

"'So many as intend to be partakers of the holy Communion shall signify their names to the curate, at least some time the day before.' This you did not do.

"'And if any of those . . . have done any wrong to his neighbours, by word or deed, so that the congregation be thereby offended, the curate . . . shall advertise him, that in any wise he presume not to come to the Lord's Table, until he hath openly declared himself to have truly repented.'

" If you offer yourself at the Lord's Table on Sunday, I will advertise you (as I have done more than once) wherein you have done wrong. And when you have openly declared yourself to have truly repented, I will administer to you the mysteries of God.

" JOHN WESLEY.

"*August* 11, 1737."

Mr Delamotte carrying this, Mr Causton said, among many other warm sayings, "I am the person that am injured. The affront is offered to me ; and I will espouse the cause of my niece. I am ill-used ; and I will have satisfaction, if it be to be had in the world."

Which way this satisfaction was to be had, I did not yet

conceive. But on Friday and Saturday it began to appear: Mr Causton declared to many persons, that " Mr Wesley had repelled Sophy from the holy communion, purely out of revenge; because he had made proposals of marriage to her, which she rejected, and married Mr Williamson."

I could not but observe the gracious providence of God, in the course of the lessons all this week. On Monday evening God spake to us in these words : " Call to remembrance the former days, in which ye endured a great fight of afflictions ; partly, whilst ye were made a gazing-stock, both by reproaches and afflictions ; and partly, whilst ye became companions of them that were so used.—Cast not away therefore your confidence, which hath great recompense of reward. For ye have need of patience, that, after ye have done the will of God, ye might receive the promise" (Heb. x. 32-36).

The evening lesson on Tuesday was the eleventh of the Hebrews ; in reading which I was more particularly encouraged by his example, who " chose rather to suffer affliction with the people of God, than to enjoy the pleasures of sin for a season ; esteeming the reproach of Christ greater riches than the treasures of Egypt."

The lesson on Wednesday began with these words : " Wherefore seeing we are compassed about with so great a cloud of witnesses, let us lay aside every weight,—and run with patience the race that is set before us : looking unto Jesus, the author and finisher of our faith ; who for the joy that was set before Him endured the cross, despising the shame, and is set down at the right hand of the throne of God " (Heb. xii. 1, 2).

In the Thursday lesson were these comfortable words : " I will never leave thee, nor forsake thee. So that we may boldly say, The Lord is my helper, and I will not fear what man shall do unto me" (Heb. xiii. 5, 6).

The words of St. James, read on Friday, were, " Blessed is the man that endureth temptation " ; and those on Saturday, " My brethren, have not the faith of our Lord Jesus Christ—with respect of persons" (Jas. ii. 1).

I was only afraid, lest those who were weak should "be turned out of the way" ; at least so far as to forsake the public "assembling of themselves together." But I feared where no fear was. God took care of this also. So that on Sunday, the 14th, more were present at the morning prayers than had been for some months before. Many of them observed those words in the first lesson, " Set Naboth on high among the people ; and set two men, sons of Belial, before him, to bear witness against him."

Tues. 16.—Mrs Williamson swore to and signed an affidavit, insinuating much more than it asserted; but asserting, that Mr Wesley had many times proposed marriage to her; all which proposals she had rejected. Of this I desired a copy; Mr Causton replied, "Sir, you may have one from any of the newspapers in America."

On *Thursday* or *Friday* was delivered out a list of twenty-six men, who were to meet, as a grand jury, on Monday, the 22nd. But this list was called in the next day, and twenty-four names added to it. Of this grand jury (forty-four of whom only met), one was a Frenchman, who did not understand English, one a Papist, one a professed infidel, three Baptists, sixteen or seventeen others Dissenters; and several others who had personal quarrels against me, and had openly vowed revenge.

To this grand jury, on Monday, the 22nd, Mr. Causton gave a long and earnest charge, "to beware of spiritual tyranny, and to oppose the new, illegal authority which was usurped over their consciences." Then Mrs Williamson's affidavit was read: after which, Mr Causton delivered to the grand jury a paper, entitled,—

"A list of grievances, presented by the grand jury for Savannah, this — day of August, 1737."

This the majority of the grand jury altered in some particulars, and on Thursday, September 1, delivered it again to the court, under the form of two presentments, containing ten bills, which were then read to the people.

Herein they asserted, upon oath, "That John Wesley, Clerk, had broken the laws of the realm, contrary to the peace of our Sovereign Lord the King, his crown and dignity.

"1. By speaking and writing to Mrs Williamson, against her husband's consent.

"2. By repelling her from the holy communion.

"3. By not declaring his adherence to the Church of England.

"4. By dividing the morning service on Sundays.

"5. By refusing to baptize Mr Parker's child, otherwise than by dipping, except the parents would certify it was weak, and not able to bear it.

"6. By repelling William Gough from the holy communion.

"7. By refusing to read the burial service over the body of Nathaniel Polhill.

"8. By calling himself Ordinary of Savannah.

"9. By refusing to receive William Aglionby as a godfather, only because he was not a communicant.

"10. By refusing Jacob Matthews for the same reason: and

baptizing an Indian trader's child with only two sponsors." (This, I own, was wrong; for I ought, at all hazards, to have refused baptizing it till he had procured a third.)

Fri. Sept. 2.—Was the third court at which I appeared since my being carried before Mr P. and Mr Recorder.

I now moved for an immediate hearing on the first bill, being the only one of a civil nature: but it was refused. I made the same motion in the afternoon; but was put off till the next court-day.

On the next court-day I appeared again; as also at the two courts following: but could not be heard, because (the judge said) Mr Williamson was gone out of town.

The sense of the minority of the grand jurors themselves (for they were by no means unanimous) concerning these presentments, may appear from the following paper, which they transmitted to the Trustees:—

"*To the Honourable the Trustees for Georgia.*

"WHEREAS two presentments have been made, the one of August 23, the other of August 31, by the grand jury for the town and county of Savannah, in Georgia, against John Wesley, Clerk.

"We, whose names are underwritten, being members of the said grand jury, do humbly beg leave to signify our dislike of the said presentments; being, by many and divers circumstances, thoroughly persuaded in ourselves, that the whole charge against Mr Wesley is an artifice of Mr Causton's, designed rather to blacken the character of Mr Wesley, than to free the colony from religious tyranny, as he was pleased, in his charge to us, to term it. But as these circumstances will be too tedious to trouble your Honours with, we shall only beg leave to give the reasons of our dissent from the particular bills.

"With regard to the first bill, we do not apprehend that Mr Wesley acted against any law, by writing or speaking to Mrs Williamson, since it does not appear to us, that the said Mr Wesley has either spoke in private, or wrote to the said Mrs Williamson, since March 12 (the day of her marriage) except one letter of July 5th, which he wrote at the request of her uncle, as a pastor, to exhort and reprove her.

"The second we do not apprehend to be a true bill; because we humbly conceive Mr Wesley did not assume to himself any authority contrary to law: for we understand, 'every person intending to communicate should signify his name to the curate, at least some time the day before,' which Mrs Williamson did not do; although Mr Wesley had often, in full congregation, declared, he did insist on a compliance with that rubric, and had before repelled divers persons for non-compliance therewith.

"The third we do not think a true bill; because several of us have been his hearers when he has declared his adherence to the Church of England in a stronger manner than by a formal declaration, by explaining and defending the Apostles', the Nicene, and the Athanasian Creeds, the Thirty-nine Articles, the whole Book of Common Prayer, and the Homilies of the said Church; and because we think a formal declaration is not required, but from those who have received institution and induction.

"The fact alleged in the fourth bill we cannot apprehend to be contrary to any law in being.

"The fifth we do not think a true bill; because we conceive Mr Wesley is justified by the rubric, viz. 'If they (the parents) certify that the child is weak, it shall suffice to pour water upon it.' Intimating (as we humbly suppose) it shall not suffice, if they do not certify.

"The sixth cannot be a true bill; because the said William Gough, being one of our members, was surprised to hear himself named, without his knowledge or privity; and did publicly declare, it was no grievance to him, because the said John Wesley had given him reasons with which he was satisfied.

"The seventh we do not apprehend to be a true bill; for Nathaniel Polhill was an Anabaptist, and desired in his lifetime that he might not be interred with the office of the Church of England. And further, we have good reason to believe, that Mr Wesley was at Frederica, or on his return thence, when Polhill was buried.

"As to the eighth bill we are in doubt, as not well knowing the meaning of the word 'Ordinary.' But for the ninth and tenth, we think Mr Wesley is sufficiently justified by the canons of the Church, which forbid 'any person to be admitted godfather or godmother to any child, before the said person has received the holy communion'; whereas William Aglionby and Jacob Matthews had never certified Mr Wesley that they had received it."

This was signed by twelve of the grand jurors, of whom three were constables, and six more tithingmen; who, consequently, would have made a majority, had the jury consisted, as it regularly should have done, of only fifteen members, viz. the four constables and eleven tithingmen.

Fri. 30.—Having ended the Homilies, I began reading Dr Rogers's eight sermons to the congregation: hoping they might be a timely antidote against the poison of infidelity, which was now with great industry propagated among us.

October 7.—I consulted my friends, whether God did not call me to return to England. The reason for which I left it had now no force; there being no possibility, as yet, of instructing the Indians; neither had I, as yet, found or heard of any Indians on the continent of America, who had the least desire of being instructed. And as to Savannah, having never engaged myself, either by word or letter, to stay there a day longer than I should judge convenient, nor ever taken charge of the people any otherwise than as in my passage to the heathens, I looked upon myself to be fully discharged therefrom, by the vacating of that design. Besides, there was a probability of doing more service to that unhappy people in England, than I could do in Georgia, by representing, without fear or favour, to the Trustees the real state the colony was in. After deeply considering these things, they were unanimous, "that I ought to go; but not yet." So I laid the thoughts of it aside for the present; being persuaded, that when the time was come, God would "make the way plain before my face."

Sat. 15.—Being at Highgate, a village five miles from Savannah, consisting of (all but one) French families, who, I found, knew but little of the English tongue, I offered to read prayers there in French every Saturday in the afternoon. They embraced the offer gladly. On Saturday, the 22nd, I read prayers in German likewise, to the German villagers of Hampstead; and so continued to do, once a week. We began the service (both at Highgate and Hampstead) with singing a psalm. Then I read and explained a chapter in the French or German Testament, and concluded with prayers and another psalm.

Sat. 29.—Some of the French of Savannah were present at the prayers at Highgate. The next day I received a message from them all, "that as I read prayers to the French at Highgate, who were but few, they hoped I would do the same to those of Savannah, where there was a large number who did not understand English." Sunday, the 30th, I began so to do; and now I had full employment for that holy day. The first English prayers lasted from five till half an hour past six. The Italian (which I read to a few Vaudois) began at nine. The second service for the English (including the sermon and the holy communion) continued from half an hour past ten, till about half an hour past twelve. The French service began at one. At two I catechised the children. About three began the English service. After this was ended, I had the happiness

of joining with as many as my largest room would hold, in
reading, prayer, and singing praise. And about six, the service
of the Moravians, so called, began : at which I was glad to be
present, not as a teacher but a learner.

Thur. Nov. 3.—I appeared again at the court, holden on
that day ; and again, at the court held Tuesday, Nov. 22nd.
On which day Mr Causton desired to speak with me. He then
read me some affidavits which had been made September 15th,
last past ; in one of which it was affirmed, that I then abused
Mr Causton in his own house, calling him liar, villain, and
so on. It was now likewise repeated before several persons,
which indeed I had forgot, that I had been reprimanded at the
last court, for an enemy to, and hinderer of, the public peace.

I again consulted my friends, who agreed with me, that
the time we looked for was now come. And the next morning,
calling on Mr Causton, I told him, I designed to set out
for England immediately. I set up an advertisement in the
Great Square to the same effect, and quietly prepared for my
journey.

Fri. Dec. 2.—I proposed to set out for Carolina about noon,
the tide then serving. But about ten, the magistrates sent for
me, and told me, I must not go out of the province ; for I had
not answered the allegations laid against me. I replied, " I
have appeared at six or seven courts successively, in order to
answer them. But I was not suffered so to do, when I desired
it time after time." Then they said, however, I must not go,
unless I would give security to answer those allegations at
their court. I asked, " What security ? " After consulting
together about two hours, the Recorder showed me a kind of
bond, engaging me, under a penalty of fifty pounds, to appear
at their court when I should be required. He added, " But
Mr. Williamson too has desired of us, that you should give bail
to answer his action." I then told him plainly, " Sir, you use
me very ill, and so you do the Trustees. I will give neither
any bond, nor any bail at all. You know your business, and I
know mine."

In the afternoon, the magistrates published an order, requiring all the officers and sentinels to prevent my going out of
the province ; and forbidding any person to assist me so to do.
Being now only a prisoner at large, in a place where I knew by
experience, every day would give fresh opportunity to procure
evidence of words I never said, and actions I never did ; I saw
clearly the hour was come for leaving this place : and as soon
as evening prayers were over, about eight o'clock, the tide then
serving, I shook off the dust of my feet, and left Georgia, after

having preached the gospel there (not as I ought, but as I was able) one year and nearly nine months.

Sat. Dec. 3.—We came to Purrysburg early in the morning, and endeavoured to procure a guide to Port Royal. But none being to be had, we set out without one, an hour before sunrise. After walking two or three hours, we met with an old man, who led us into a small path, near which was a line of blazed trees (that is, marked by cutting off part of the bark), by following which, he said, we might easily come to Port Royal in five or six hours.

We were four in all; one of whom intended to go to England with me; the other two to settle in Carolina. About eleven we came into a large swamp, where we wandered about till near two. We then found another blaze, and pursued it, till it divided into two: one of these we followed through an almost impassable thicket, a mile beyond which it ended We made through the thicket again, and traced the other blaze till that ended too. It now grew toward sunset; so we sat down, faint and weary, having had no food all day, except a gingerbread cake, which I had taken in my pocket. A third of this we had divided among us at noon; another third we took now; the rest we reserved for the morning; but we had met with no water all the day. Thrusting a stick into the ground, and find-the end of it moist, two of our company fell a-digging with their hands, and, at about three feet depth, found water. We thanked God, drank, and were refreshed. The night was sharp: however, there was no complaining among us; but after having recommended ourselves to God, we lay down close together, and (I at least) slept till near six in the morning.

Sun. 4.—God renewing our strength, we arose neither faint nor weary, and resolved to make one trial more, to find out a path to Port Royal. We steered due east; but finding neither path nor blaze, and the woods growing thicker and thicker, we judged it would be our best course to return, if we could, by the way we came. The day before, in the thickest part of the woods, I had broken many young trees, I knew not why, as we walked along: these we found a great help in several places, where no path was to be seen; and between one and two God brought us safe to Benjamin Arieu's house, the old man we left the day before.

In the evening I read French prayers to a numerous family, a mile from Arieu's; one of whom undertook to guide us to Port Royal. In the morning we set out. About sunset, we asked our guide, if he knew where he was; who frankly answered, "No." However, we pushed on till, about seven, we came to a plantation ; and the next evening, after many difficulties and delays, we landed on Port Royal Island.

Wed. 7.—We walked to Beaufort ; where Mr Jones, the minister of Beaufort, with whom I lodged during my short stay here, gave me a lively idea of the old English hospitality. On Thursday Mr Delamotte came ; with whom, on Friday, the 9th, I took boat for Charlestown. After a slow passage, by reason of contrary winds, and some conflict (our provisions falling short) with hunger as well as cold, we came thither early in the morning, on Tuesday, the 13th. Here I expected trials of a different kind, and far more dangerous. For contempt and want are easy to be borne : but who can bear respect and abundance ?

Wed. 14.—Being desired to read public prayers, I was much refreshed with those glorious promises, contained both in the seventy-second Psalm, and in the first lesson, the fortieth chapter of Isaiah.

In the afternoon, visiting a dying man, we found him still full of the freshest advices ; and busy in settling the affairs of the Czarina, Prince Thamas, and the Ottoman Porte.

Fri. 16.—I parted from the last of those friends who came with me into America, Mr Charles Delamotte, from whom I had been but a few days separate since Oct. 14, 1735.

Sun. 18.—I was seized with a violent flux, which I felt came not before I wanted it. Yet I had strength enough given to preach once more to this careless people ; and a few " believed our report."

Thur. 22.—I took my leave of America (though, if it please God, not for ever), going on board the *Samuel*, Captain Percy, with a young gentleman who had been a few months in Carolina, one of my parishioners of Savannah, and a Frenchman, late of Purrysburg, who was escaped thence with the skin of his teeth.

Sat. 24.—We sailed over Charlestown bar, and about noon lost sight of land.

The next day the wind was fair, but high, as it was on Sunday, 25, when the sea affected me more than it had done in the sixteen weeks of our passage to America. I was obliged to lie down the greatest part of the day, being easy only in that posture.

Mon. 26.—I began instructing a negro lad in the principles of Christianity. The next day I resolved to break off living delicately, and return to my old simplicity of diet ; and after I did so, neither my stomach nor my head much complained of the motion of the ship.

Wed. 28.—Finding the unaccountable apprehensions of I know not what danger (the wind being small, and the sea smooth), which had been upon me several days, increase, I cried earnestly for help; and it pleased God, as in a moment, to restore peace to my soul.

Sun. Jan. 1, 1738.—All in the ship, except the captain and steersman, were present both at the morning and evening service, and appeared as deeply attentive as even the poor people of Frederica did, while the Word of God was new to their ears.

Mon. 2.—Being sorrowful and very heavy (though I could give no particular reason for it), and utterly unwilling to speak close to any of my little flock (about twenty persons), I was in doubt whether my neglect of them was not one cause of my own heaviness. In the evening, therefore, I began instructing the cabin-boy: after which I was much easier.

I went several times the following days, with a design, to speak to the sailors, but could not. I mean, I was quite averse from speaking; I could not see how to make an occasion, and it seemed quite absurd to speak without.

Fri. 6.—I ended the *Abridgment of Mr de Renty's Life*.

Sat. 7.—I began to read and explain some passages of the Bible to the young negro. The next morning, another negro who was on board desired to be a hearer too. From them I went to the poor Frenchman, who, understanding no English, had none else in the ship with whom he could converse. And from this time, I read and explained to him a chapter in the Testament every morning.

On *Monday*, 9, and the following days, I reflected much on that vain desire, which had pursued me for so many years, of being in solitude, in order to be a Christian. I have now, thought I, solitude enough. But am I, therefore, the nearer being a Christian? Not if Jesus Christ be the model of Christianity.

Fri. 13.—We had a thorough storm, which obliged us to shut all close; the sea breaking over the ship continually. I was at first afraid; but cried to God, and was strengthened. Before ten, I lay down: I bless God, without fear. About midnight we were awakened by a confused noise of seas and wind and men's voices, the like to which I had never heard before. The sound of the sea breaking over and against the sides of the ship, I could compare to nothing but large cannon, or American thunder. The rebounding, starting, quivering motion of the ship much resembled what is said of earthquakes. The captain was upon deck in an instant. But his men could not hear what he said. It blew a proper hurricane; which beginning at south-west, then went west, north-west, north, and, in a quarter of an hour, round by the east to the south-west point again. At the same time the sea running, as they term it, mountain-high, and that from many different points at once, the ship would not obey the helm; nor indeed could the steersman, through the violent rain, see the compass. So he was forced to let her run before the wind, and in half an hour the stress of the storm was over.

About noon the next day it ceased. But first I had resolved, God being my helper, not only to preach it to all, but to apply the word of God to every single soul in the ship; and if but one, yea, if not one of them will hear, I know "my labour is not in vain."

I no sooner executed this resolution, than my spirit revived; so that from this day I had no more of that fearfulness and heaviness, which before almost continually weighed me down.

Tues. 24.—We spoke with two ships, outward-bound, from whom we had the welcome news of our wanting but one hundred and sixty leagues of the Land's End. My mind was now full of thought: part of which I writ down as follows:—

"I went to America, to convert the Indians; but oh! who shall convert me? who, what is he that will deliver me from this evil heart of unbelief? I have a fair summer religion. I can talk well; nay, and believe myself, while no danger is near: but let death look me in the face, and my spirit is troubled."

Sun. 29.—We saw English land once more; which, about noon, appeared to be the Lizard Point. We ran by it with a fair wind; and at noon, the next day, made the west end of the Isle of Wight.

Toward the evening of Jan. 31 was a calm; but in the night a strong north wind brought us safe into the Downs. The day before, Mr Whitefield had sailed out, neither of us then knowing anything of the other. At four in the morning we took boat, and in half an hour landed at Deal: it being Wednesday, February 1, the anniversary festival in Georgia for Mr Oglethorpe's landing there.

It is now two years and almost four months since I left my native country, in order to teach the Georgian Indians the nature of Christianity: but what have I learned myself in the meantime? Why (what I the least of all suspected), that I who went to America to convert others, was never myself converted to God.[1] "I am not mad," though I thus speak,

[1] I am not sure of this.

but "I speak the words of truth and soberness"; if haply some of those who still dream may awake and see, that as I am, so are they.

Are they read in philosophy? So was I. In ancient or modern tongues? So was I also. Are they versed in the science of divinity? I too have studied it many years. Can they talk fluently upon spiritual things? The very same could I do. Are they plenteous in alms? Behold, I gave all my goods to feed the poor. Do they give of their labour as well as of their substance? I have laboured more abundantly than they all. Are they willing to suffer for their brethren? I have thrown up my friends, reputation, ease, country; I have put my life in my hand, wandering into strange lands; I have given my body to be devoured by the deep, parched up with heat, consumed by toil and weariness, or whatsoever God should please to bring upon me. But does all this make me acceptable to God? Does all I ever did or can know, say, give, do, or suffer, justify me in His sight? By no means. If the oracles of God are true, all these things, though, when ennobled by faith in Christ,[1] they are holy and just and good, yet without it are "dung and dross," meet only to be purged away by "the fire that never shall be quenched."

This, then, have I learned in the ends of the earth : that I "am fallen short of the glory of God": that my whole heart is "altogether corrupt and abominable"; and, consequently, my whole life, seeing it cannot be that an "evil tree" should "bring forth good fruit": that "alienated as I am from the life of God, I am "a child of wrath,"[2] an heir of hell: that my own works, my own sufferings, my own righteousness, are so far from reconciling me to an offended God, so far from making any atonement for the least of those sins, which "are more in number than the hairs of my head," that the most specious of them need an atonement themselves, or they cannot abide His righteous judgment: that, "having the sentence of death" in my heart, and having nothing in or of myself to plead, I have no hope, but that of being justified freely, "through the redemption that is in Jesus"; I have no hope, but that if I seek I shall find Christ, and "be found in Him, not having my own righteousness, but that which is through the faith of Christ, the righteousness which is of God by faith" (Phil. iii. 9).

If it be said that I have faith (for many such things have I heard, from many miserable comforters), I answer, So have the devils,—a sort of faith; but still they are strangers to the

[1] I had even then the faith of a servant, though not that of a son.
[2] I believe not.

covenant of promise. So the apostles had even at Cana in Galilee, when Jesus first "manifested forth His glory"; even then they, in a sort, "believed on Him"; but they had not then "the faith that overcometh the world." The faith I want is,[1] "A sure trust and confidence in God, that, through the merits of Christ, my sins are forgiven, and I reconciled to the favour of God." I want that faith which St Paul recommends to all the world, especially in his Epistle to the Romans; that faith which enables everyone that hath it to cry out, " I live not; but Christ liveth in me; and the life which I now live, I live by faith in the Son of God, who loved me, and gave Himself for me." I want that faith which none can have without knowing that he hath it (though many imagine they have it, who have it not); for whosoever hath it, is "freed from sin, the" whole "body of sin is destroyed" in him; he is freed from fear, "having peace with God through Christ, and rejoicing in hope of the glory of God." And he is freed from doubt, "having the love of God shed abroad in his heart through the Holy Ghost which is given unto him"; which "Spirit itself beareth witness with his spirit, that he is a child of God."

[1] The faith of a son.

CHAPTER II

A SOCIETY IN ALDERSGATE STREET

FROM FEBRUARY 1, TO JUNE 6, 1738

Wednesday, Feb. 1.—After reading prayers and explaining a portion of Scripture to a large company at the inn, I left Deal, and came in the evening to Feversham.

I here read prayers, and explained the second lesson to a few of those who were called Christians, but were indeed more savage in their behaviour than the wildest Indians I have yet met with.

Fri. 3.—I came to Mr Delamotte's, at Blendon, where I expected a cold reception. But God had prepared the way before me; and I no sooner mentioned my name, than I was welcomed in such a manner, as constrained me to say, " Surely God is in this place, and I knew it not !"

In the evening I came once more to London, whence I had been absent two years and near four months.

Many reasons I have to bless God, though the design I went upon did not take effect, for my having being carried into that strange land, contrary to all my preceding resolutions. Hereby I trust He hath in some measure " humbled me and proved me, and shown me what was in my heart." Hereby I have been taught to " beware of men." Hereby I am come to know assuredly, that if " in all our ways we acknowledge God, He will," where reason fails, " direct our path," by lot, or by the other means which He knoweth. Hereby I am delivered from the fear of the sea, which I had both dreaded and abhorred from my youth.

Hereby God has given me to know many of His servants; particularly those of the Church of Hernhuth. Hereby my passage is opened to the writings of holy men in the German, Spanish, and Italian tongues. I hope too some good may come to others hereby. All in Georgia have read the Word of God. Some have believed, and began to run well. A few steps have been taken towards publishing the glad tidings both to the African and American heathens. Many children have learned "how they ought to serve God," and to be useful to their neighbour. And those whom it most concerns have an opportunity of knowing the true state of their infant colony, and laying a firmer foundation of peace and happiness to many generations.

Sat. 4.—I told my friends some of the reasons which a little hastened my return to England. They all agreed it would be proper to relate them to the Trustees of Georgia.

Accordingly, the next morning I waited on Mr Oglethorpe, but had not time to speak on that head. In the afternoon I was desired to speak at St John the Evangelist's. I did so on those strong words, "If any man be in Christ, he is a new creature." I was afterwards informed, many of the best in the parish were so offended, that I was not to preach there any more.

Mon. 6.—I visited many of my old friends, as well as most of my relations. I find the time is not yet come when I am to be "hated of all men." Oh may I be prepared for that day!

Tues. 7.—(A day much to be remembered.) At the house of Mr Weinantz, a Dutch merchant, I met Peter Böhler, Schulius Richter, and Wensel Neiser, just then landed from Germany. Finding they had no acquaintance in England, I offered to procure them a lodging, and did so near Mr Hutton's, where I then was. And from this time I did not willingly lose any opportunity of conversing with them, while I stayed in London.

Wed. 8.—I went to Mr Oglethorpe again, but had no opportunity of speaking as I designed. Afterwards I waited on the Board of Trustees, and gave them a short but plain account of the state of the colony.

Sun. 12.—I preached at St Andrew's, Holborn. Here too, it seems, I am to preach no more.

Wed. 15.—I waited on the Trustees again, and gave them in writing the substance of what I had said at the last board.

Fri. 17.—I set out for Oxford with Peter Böhler, where we were kindly received by Mr Sarney, the only one now remaining here, of many who, at our embarking for America, were used to "take sweet counsel together."

Sat. 18.—We went to Stanton-Harcourt, to Mr Gambold, and found my old friend recovered from his mystic delusion, and convinced that St Paul was a better writer than either Tauler or Jacob Behmen. The next day I preached once more at the castle, in Oxford.

All this time I conversed much with Peter Böhler.

Mon. 20.—I returned to London. On Tuesday I preached at Great St Helen's.

Wed. 22.—I was with the Trustees again ; to whom I then gave a short account, and afterwards delivered it to them in writing, of the reasons why I left Georgia.

Sun. 26.—I preached at six, at St Lawrence's ; at ten, in St. Katherine Cree's church ; and in the afternoon, at St John's, Wapping. I believe it pleased God to bless the first sermon most, because it gave most offence ; being indeed an open defiance of that mystery of iniquity which the world calls " prudence."

Mon. 27.—I took coach for Salisbury, and had several opportunities of conversing seriously with my fellow-travellers. But endeavouring to mend the wisdom of God by the worldly wisdom of prefacing serious with light conversation, all I had said was written on the sand.

Tues. 28.—I saw my mother once more. The next day I prepared for my journey to my brother at Tiverton. But on Thursday morning, March 2nd, a message that my brother Charles was dying at Oxford, obliged me to set out for that place immediately.

With regard to my own behaviour, I now renewed and wrote down my former resolutions.

1. To use absolute openness and unreserve with all I should converse with.

2. To labour after continual seriousness, not willingly indulging myself in any the least levity of behaviour, or in laughter ; no, not for a moment.

3. To speak no word which does not tend to the glory of God ; in particular not to talk of worldly things. Others may, nay, must. But what is that to thee ? And,

4. To take no pleasure which does not tend to the glory of God ; thanking God every moment for all I do take, and therefore rejecting every sort and degree of it, which I feel I cannot so thank Him in and for.

Sat. Mar. 4.—I found my brother at Oxford, recovering from his pleurisy ; and with him Peter Böhler ; by whom, in the hand of the great God, I was, on *Sunday*, the 5th, clearly convinced of unbelief, of the want of that faith whereby alone we are saved.[1]

Immediately it struck into my mind, " Leave off preaching. How can you preach to others, who have not faith yourself ? " I asked Böhler, whether he thought I should leave it off or not. He answered, " By no means." I asked, " But what can I

---
[1] With the full Christian salvation.

preach?" He said, "Preach faith till you have it; and then, because you have it, you will preach faith."

Accordingly, *Monday*, 6, I began preaching this new doctrine, though my soul started back from the work. The first person to whom I offered salvation by faith alone, was a prisoner under sentence of death. His name was Clifford. Peter Böhler had many times desired me to speak to him before. But I could not prevail on myself so to do; being still, as I had been many years, a zealous asserter of the impossibility of a deathbed repentance.

Tues. 15.—I set out for Manchester, with Mr Kinchin, Fellow of Corpus Christi, and Mr. Fox, late a prisoner in the city prison. Between five and six we called at Chapel-on-the-Heath, where lived a poor man, sometime prisoner in the castle of Oxford. He was not at home; but his wife came to us, to whom Mr Kinchin spoke a few words, which so melted her heart, that she burst out into tears, and we went on rejoicing and praising God.

About eight, it being rainy and very dark, we lost our way; but before nine, came to Shipston, having rode over, I know not how, a narrow foot-bridge, which lay across a deep ditch near the town. After supper I read prayers to the people of the inn, and explained the second lesson.

The next day we dined at Birmingham; and, soon after we left it, were reproved for our negligence there, in letting those who attended us go, without either exhortation or instruction, by a severe shower of hail.

In the evening we came to Stafford. The mistress of the house joined with us in family prayer. The next morning, one of the servants appeared deeply affected, as did the ostler before we went. Soon after breakfast, stepping into the stable, I spake a few words to those who were there. A stranger who heard me said, "Sir, I wish I was to travel with you"; and when I went into the house, followed me, and began abruptly, "Sir, I believe you are a good man, and I come to tell you a little of my life." The tears stood in his eyes all the time he spoke; and we hoped not a word which was said to him was lost.

At Newcastle, whither we came about ten, some to whom we spoke at our inn were very attentive; but a gay young woman waited on us, quite unconcerned: however, we spoke on. When we went away, she fixed her eyes, and neither moved nor said one word, but appeared as much astonished as if she had seen one risen from the dead.

Coming to Holms-Chapel about three, we were surprised at

being shown into a room where a cloth and plates were laid. Soon after two men came in to dinner. Mr Kinchin told them, if they pleased, that gentleman would ask a blessing for them. They stared and, as it were, consented ; but sat still while I did it, one of them with his hat on. We began to speak on turning to God, and went on, though they appeared utterly regardless. After a while their countenances changed, and one of them stole off his hat, and laying it down behind him, said, all we said was true; but he had been a grievous sinner, and not considered it as he ought; but he was resolved, with God's help, now to turn to Him in earnest. We exhorted him and his companion, who now likewise drank in every word, to cry mightily to God, that He would "send them help from His holy place."

Being faint in the evening, I called at Altringham, and there lit upon a Quaker, well skilled in, and therefore, as I soon found, sufficiently fond of, controversy. After an hour spent therein, perhaps not in vain, I advised him to dispute as little as possible; but rather follow after holiness, and walk humbly with his God.

Late at night we reached Manchester. *Friday*, the 17th, we spent entirely with Mr Clayton. Mr Hoole, the rector of St Ann's church, being taken ill the next day, on *Sunday*, 19th, Mr Kinchin and I officiated at Salford chapel in the morning, by which means Mr Clayton was at liberty to perform the service of St Ann's ; and in the afternoon I preached there on those words of St Paul, " If any man be in Christ, he is a new creature."

Early in the morning we left Manchester, taking with us Mr Kinchin's brother, for whom we came, to be entered at Oxford. We were fully determined to lose no opportunity of awakening, instructing, or exhorting any whom we might meet with in our journey. At Knutsford, where we first stopped, all we spake to thankfully received the word of exhortation. But at Talk-on-the-hill, where we dined, she with whom we were was so much of a gentlewoman, that for near an hour our labour seemed to be in vain. However, we spoke on. Upon a sudden, she looked as one just awaked out of a sleep. Every word sunk into her heart.

About five, Mr Kinchin riding by a man and woman double-horsed, the man said, " Sir, you ought to thank God it is a fair day ; for if it rained, you would be sadly dirty with your little horse." Mr Kinchin answered, "True ; and we ought to thank God for our life, and health, and food, and raiment, and all things." He then rode on, Mr Fox following : the man said, "Sir, my mistress would be glad to have some more talk with that gentleman." We stayed, and when they came up, began to search one another's hearts. They came to us again in the evening, at our inn at Stone, where I explained both to them and many of their acquaintance who were come together, that great truth,—godliness hath the promise both of this life and of that which is to come.

Tues. 21.—Between nine and ten we came to Hedgeford. Just then, one was giving an account of a young woman, who had dropped down dead there the day before. This gave us a fair occasion to exhort all that were present, "so to number" their own "days," that they might apply their "hearts unto wisdom."

In the afternoon one overtook us, whom we soon found more inclined to speak than to hear. However, we spoke, and spared not. In the evening we overtook a young man, a Quaker, who afterwards came to us to our inn at Henley, whither he sent for the rest of his family, to join with us in prayer; to which I added, as usual, the exposition of the second lesson. Our other companion went with us a mile or two in the morning; and then not only spoke less than the day before, but took in good part a serious caution against talkativeness and vanity.

An hour after, we were overtook by an elderly gentleman, who said he was going to enter his son at Oxford. We asked, "At what college?" He said, he did not know; having no acquaintance there on whose recommendation he could depend. After some conversation, he expressed a deep sense of the good providence of God; and told us he knew God had cast us in his way, in answer to his prayer. In the evening we reached Oxford, rejoicing in our having received so many fresh instances of that great truth, "In all thy ways acknowledge Him, and He shall direct thy paths."

Thur. 23.—I met Peter Böhler again, who now amazed me more and more by the account he gave of the fruits of living faith,—the holiness and happiness which he affirmed to attend it. The next morning I began the Greek Testament again, resolving to abide by "the law and the testimony"; and being confident that God would hereby show me whether this doctrine was of God.

Sun. 26.—I preached at Witham, on "the new creature," and went in the evening to a society in Oxford, where (as my manner then was at all societies), after using a collect or two and the Lord's Prayer, I expounded a chapter in the New Testament, and concluded with three or four more collects and a psalm.

Mon. 27.—Mr Kinchin went with me to the castle, where,

after reading prayers and preaching on, "It is appointed unto men once to die," we prayed with the condemned man, first in several forms of prayer, and then in such words as were given us in that hour. He kneeled down in much heaviness and confusion, having "no rest in" his "bones, by reason of" his "sins." After a space he rose up, and eagerly said, "I am now ready to die. I know Christ has taken away my sins; and there is no more condemnation for me." The same composed cheerfulness he showed, when he was carried to his execution; and in his last moments he was the same, enjoying a perfect peace, in confidence that he was "accepted in the Beloved."

Sat. April 1.—Being at Mr Fox's society, my heart was so full that I could not confine myself to the forms of prayer which we were accustomed to use there. Neither do I purpose to be confined to them any more; but to pray indifferently, with a form or without, as I may find suitable to particular occasions.

Sun. 2.—Being Easter Day, I preached in our college chapel on, "The hour cometh, and now is, when the dead shall hear the voice of the Son of God, and they that hear shall live." I preached in the afternoon, first at the castle, and then at Carfax, on the same words. I see the promise; but it is afar off.

Believing it would be better for me to wait for the accomplishment of it in silence and retirement, on *Monday*, 3, I complied with Mr Kinchin's desire, and went to him at Dummer, in Hampshire. But I was not suffered to stay here long; being earnestly pressed to come up to London, if it were only for a few days. Thither, therefore, I returned, on Tuesday, 18th.

Sat. 22.—I met Peter Böhler once more. I had now no objection to what he said of the nature of faith: namely, that it is (to use the words of our Church) "a sure trust and confidence which a man hath in God, that through the merits of Christ his sins are forgiven, and he reconciled to the favour of God." Neither could I deny either the happiness or holiness which he described, as fruits of this living faith. "The Spirit itself beareth witness with our spirit that we are the children of God;" and, "He that believeth hath the witness in himself," fully convinced me of the former: as "Whatsoever is born of God, doth not commit sin;" and, "Whosoever believeth is born of God," did of the latter. But I could not comprehend what he spoke of an instantaneous work. I could not understand how this faith should be given in a moment; how a man could at once be thus turned from darkness to light, from sin and misery to righteousness and joy in the Holy Ghost. I searched the Scriptures again, touching this very thing, particularly the Acts of the Apostles ; but, to my utter astonishment, found scarce any instances there of other than instantaneous conversions ; scarce any so slow as that of St Paul, who was three days in the pangs of the new birth. I had but one retreat left ; namely, "Thus, I grant, God wrought in the first ages of Christianity ; but the times are changed. What reason have I to believe He works in the same manner now ? "

But on *Sunday*, 23, I was beat out of this retreat too, by the concurring evidence of several living witnesses ; who testified, God had thus wrought in themselves, giving them in a moment such a faith in the blood of His Son, as translated them out of the darkness into light, out of sin and fear into holiness and happiness. Here ended my disputing. I could now only cry out, " Lord, help thou my unbelief ! "

I asked P. Böhler again, whether I ought not to refrain from teaching others. He said, "No ; do not hide in the earth the talent God hath given you." Accordingly, on *Tuesday*, 25, I spoke clearly and fully at Blendon to Mr Delamotte's family, of the nature and fruits of faith. Mr Broughton and my brother were there. Mr Broughton's great objection was, he could never think that I had not faith, who had done and suffered such things. My brother was very angry, and told me, I did not know what mischief I had done by talking thus. And, indeed, it did please God then to kindle a fire, which I trust shall never be extinguished.

Mon. May 1.—The return of my brother's illness obliged me again to hasten to London. In the evening I found him at James Hutton's, better as to his health than I expected ; but strongly averse from what he called "the new faith."

This evening our little society began, which afterwards met in Fetter Lane.

Wed. 3.—My brother had a long and particular conversation with Peter Böhler. And it now pleased God to open his eyes ; so that he also saw clearly what was the nature of that one true, living faith, whereby alone, "through grace, we are saved."

Thur. 4.—Peter Böhler left London, in order to embark for Carolina.

Sun. 7.—I preached at St Lawrence's in the morning ; and afterwards at St Katherine Cree's church. I was enabled to speak strong words at both ; and was therefore the less surprised at being informed, I was not to preach any more in either of those churches.

Tues. 9.—I preached at Great St Helen's, to a very numerous congregation. My heart was now so enlarged to declare the love of God to all that were oppressed by the devil, that I did not wonder in the least when I was afterwards told, "Sir, you must preach here no more."

Wed. 10.—Mr Stonehouse, vicar of Islington, was convinced of the "truth as it is in Jesus." From this time till Saturday, 13, I was sorrowful and very heavy, being neither able to read, nor meditate, nor sing, nor pray, nor do anything. Yet I was a little refreshed by Peter Böhler's letter.

Sun. 14.—I preached in the morning at St Ann's, Aldersgate; and in the afternoon at the Savoy chapel, free salvation by faith in the blood of Christ. I was quickly apprised, that at St Ann's, likewise, I am to preach no more.

Fri. 19.—My brother had a second return of his pleurisy. A few of us spent Saturday night in prayer. The next day, being Whitsunday, after hearing Dr Heylyn preach a truly Christian sermon, and assisting him at the holy communion (his curate being taken ill in the church), I received the surprising news, that my brother had found rest to his soul. His bodily strength returned also from that hour.

I preached at St John's, Wapping, at three, and at St Bennett's, Paul's Wharf, in the evening. At these churches, likewise, I am to preach no more. At St Antholin's I preached on the *Thursday* following.

Monday, *Tuesday*, and *Wednesday*, I had continual sorrow and heaviness in my heart.

What occurred on *Wednesday*, 24, I think best to relate at large, after premising what may make it the better understood.

1. I believe, till I was about ten years old I had not sinned away that "washing of the Holy Ghost" which was given me in baptism; having been strictly educated and carefully taught, that I could only be saved "by universal obedience, by keeping all the commandments of God"; in the meaning of which I was diligently instructed. And those instructions, so far as they respected outward duties and sins, I gladly received, and often thought of. But all that was said to me of inward obedience, or holiness, I neither understood nor remembered. So that I was indeed as ignorant of the true meaning of the law, as I was of the gospel of Christ.

2. The next six or seven years were spent at school; where, outward restraints being removed, I was much more negligent than before, even of outward duties, and almost continually guilty of outward sins, which I knew to be such, though they were not scandalous in the eye of the world. However, I still read the Scriptures, and said my prayers, morning and evening.

And what I now hoped to be saved by, was: 1. Not being so bad as other people. 2. Having still a kindness for religion. And, 3. Reading the Bible, going to church, and saying my prayers.

3. Being removed to the University for five years, I still said my prayers, both in public and in private, and read, with the Scriptures, several other books of religion, especially comments on the New Testament. Yet I had not all this while so much as a notion of inward holiness; nay, went on habitually and, for the most part, very contentedly, in some or other known sin: indeed, with some intermission and short struggles, especially before and after the holy communion, which I was obliged to receive thrice a year. I cannot well tell what I hoped to be saved by now, when I was continually sinning against that little light I had, unless by those transient fits of what many divines taught me to call repentance.

4. When I was about twenty-two, my father pressed me to enter into holy orders. At the same time, the providence of God directing me to Kempis's *Christian's Pattern*, I began to see, that true religion was seated in the heart, and that God's law extended to all our thoughts as well as words and actions. I was, however, very angry at Kempis, for being too strict; though I read him only in Dean Stanhope's translation. Yet I had frequently much sensible comfort in reading him, such as I was an utter stranger to before: and meeting likewise with a religious friend, which I never had till now, I began to alter the the whole form of my conversation, and to set in earnest upon a new life. I set apart an hour or two a day for religious retirement. I communicated every week. I watched against all sin, whether in word or deed. I began to aim at, and pray for, inward holiness. So that now, "doing so much, and living so good a life," I doubted not but I was a good Christian.

5. Removing soon after to another college, I executed a resolution which I was before convinced was of the utmost importance,—shaking off at once all my trifling acquaintance. I began to see more and more the value of time. I applied myself closer to study. I watched more carefully against actual sins; I advised others to be religious, according to that scheme of religion by which I modelled my own life. But meeting now with Mr Law's *Christian Perfection* and *Serious Call*, although I was much offended at many parts of both, yet they convinced me more than ever of the exceeding height and breadth and depth of the law of God The light flowed in so mightily upon my soul, that everything appeared in a new view. I cried to God for help, and resolved not to prolong the time

of obeying Him as I had never done before. And by my continued endeavour to keep His whole law, inward and outward, to the utmost of my power, I was persuaded that I should be accepted of Him, and that I was even then in a state of salvation.

6. In 1730 I began visiting the prisons; assisting the poor and sick in town; and doing what other good I could, by my presence, or my little fortune, to the bodies and souls of all men. To this end I abridged myself of all superfluities, and many that are called necessaries of life. I soon became a byword for so doing; and I rejoiced that my name was cast out as evil. The next spring I began observing the Wednesday and Friday fasts, commonly observed in the ancient Church; tasting no food till three in the afternoon. And now I knew not how to go any farther. I diligently strove against all sin. I omitted no sort of self-denial which I thought lawful: I carefully used, both in public and in private, all the means of grace at all opportunities. I omitted no occasion of doing good: I for that reason suffered evil. And all this I knew to be nothing, unless as it was directed toward inward holiness. Accordingly this, the image of God, was what I aimed at in all, by doing His will, not my own. Yet when, after continuing some years in this course, I apprehended myself to be near death, I could not find that all this gave me any comfort, or any assurance of acceptance with God. At this I was then not a little surprised; not imagining I had been all this time building on the sand, nor considering that "other foundation can no man lay, than that which is laid" by God, "even Christ Jesus."

7. Soon after, a contemplative man convinced me still more than I was convinced before, that outward works are nothing, being alone; and in several conversations instructed me, how to pursue inward holiness, or a union of the soul with God. But even of his instructions (though I then received them as the words of God) I cannot but now observe: 1. That he spoke so incautiously against trusting in outward works, that he discouraged me from doing them at all. 2. That he recommended (as it were, to supply what was wanting in them) mental prayer, and the like exercises, as the most effectual means of purifying the soul, and uniting it with God. Now these were, in truth, as much my own works as visiting the sick or clothing the naked; and the union with God, thus pursued, was as really my own righteousness, as any I had before pursued under another name.

8. In this refined way of trusting to my own works and my own righteousness (so zealously inculcated by the mystic

writers), I dragged on heavily, finding no comfort or help therein, till the time of my leaving England. On shipboard, however, I was again active in outward works; where it pleased God of His free mercy to give me twenty-six of the Moravian brethren for companions, who endeavoured to show me "a more excellent way." But I understood it not at first. I was too learned and too wise. So that it seemed foolishness unto me. And I continued preaching, and following after, and trusting in, that righteousness whereby no flesh can be justified.

9. All the time I was at Savannah I was thus beating the air. Being ignorant of the righteousness of Christ, which, by a living faith in Him, bringeth salvation "to every one that believeth," I sought to establish my own rightousness; and so laboured in the fire all my days. I was now properly "under the law"; I knew that "the law" of God was "spiritual; I consented to it, that it was good." Yea, "I delighted in it, after the inner man." Yet was I "carnal, sold under sin." Every day was I constrained to cry out, "What I do, I allow not: for what I would, I do not; but what I hate, that I do. To will is" indeed "present with me: but how to perform that which is good, I find not. For the good which I would, I do not; but the evil which I would not, that I do. I find a law, that when I would do good, evil is present with me:" even "the law in my members, warring against the law of my mind," and still "bringing me into captivity to the law of sin."

10. In this vile, abject state of bondage to sin, I was indeed fighting continually, but not conquering. Before, I had willingly served sin; now it was unwillingly; but still I served it. I fell, and rose, and fell again. Sometimes I was overcome, and in heaviness: sometimes I overcame, and was in joy. For as in the former state I had some foretastes of the terrors of the law, so had I in this, of the comforts of the gospel. During this whole struggle between nature and grace, which had now continued about ten years, I had many remarkable returns to prayer; especially when I was in trouble: I had many sensible comforts; which are indeed no other than short anticipations of the life of faith. But I was still "under the law," not "under grace" (the state most who are called Christians are content to live and die in); for I was only striving with, not freed from, sin: neither had I the witness of the Spirit with my spirit, and indeed could not; for I "sought it not by faith, but as it were by the works of the law."

11. In my return to England, January, 1738, being in imminent danger of death, and very uneasy on that account, I was strongly convinced that the cause of that uneasiness was

unbelief; and that the gaining a true, living faith was the "one thing needful" for me. But still I fixed not this faith on its right object: I meant only faith in God, not faith in or through Christ. Again, I knew not that I was wholly void of this faith; but only thought I had not enough of it. So that when Peter Böhler, whom God prepared for me as soon as I came to London, affirmed of true faith in Christ (which is but one), that it had those two fruits inseparably attending it, "dominion over sin, and constant peace from a sense of forgiveness," I was quite amazed, and looked upon it as a new gospel. If this was so, it was clear I had not faith. But I was not willing to be convinced of this. Therefore I disputed with all my might, and laboured to prove that faith might be where these were not; especially where the sense of forgiveness was not: for all the scriptures relating to this, I had been long since taught to construe away; and to call all Presbyterians who spoke otherwise. Besides, I well saw, no one could, in the nature of things, have such a sense of forgiveness, and not feel it. But I felt it not. If, then, there was no faith without this, all my pretensions to faith dropped at once.

12. When I met Peter Böhler again, he consented to put the dispute upon the issue which I desired, namely, Scripture and experience. I first consulted the Scripture. But when I set aside the glosses of men, and simply considered the words of God, comparing them together, endeavouring to illustrate the obscure by the plainer passages; I found they all made against me, and was forced to retreat to my last hold, "that experience would never agree with the literal interpretation of those scriptures. Nor could I therefore allow it to be true, till I found some living witnesses of it." He replied, he could show me such any time; if I desired it, the next day. And accordingly, the next day he came again with three others, all of whom testified, of their own personal experience, that a true, living faith in Christ is inseparable from a sense of pardon for all past, and freedom from all present, sins. They added with one mouth, that this faith was the gift, the free gift, of God; and that He would surely bestow it upon every soul who earnestly and perseveringly sought it. I was now thoroughly convinced; and by the grace of God, I resolved to seek it unto the end: 1. By absolutely renouncing all dependence, in whole or in part, upon my own works or righteousness; on which I had really grounded my hope of salvation, though I knew it not, from my youth up. 2. By adding to the constant use of all the other means of grace, continual prayer for this very thing, justifying, saving faith, a full reliance on the blood of Christ shed for me;

a trust in Him as my Christ, as my sole justification, sanctification, and redemption.

13. I continued thus to seek it (though with strange indifference, dulness, and coldness, and unusually frequent relapses into sin), till Wednesday, May 24. I think it was about five this morning, that I opened my Testament on those words, "There are given unto us exceeding great and precious promises, even that ye should be partakers of the divine nature" (2 Peter i. 4). Just as I went out, I opened it again on those words, "Thou art not far from the kingdom of God." In the afternoon I was asked to go to St Paul's. The anthem was, "Out of the deep have I called unto Thee, O Lord: Lord, hear my voice. O let Thine ears consider well the voice of my complaint. If Thou, Lord, wilt be extreme to mark what is done amiss, O Lord, who may abide it? For there is mercy with Thee; therefore shalt Thou be feared. O Israel, trust in the Lord: for with the Lord there is mercy, and with Him is plenteous redemption. And He shall redeem Israel from all his sins."

14. In the evening I went very unwillingly to a society in Aldersgate Street, where one was reading Luther's preface to the Epistle to the Romans. About a quarter before nine, while he was describing the change which God works in the heart through faith in Christ, I felt my heart strangely warmed. I felt I did trust in Christ, Christ alone, for salvation: and an assurance was given me, that He had taken away my sins, even mine, and saved me from the law of sin and death.

15. I began to pray with all my might for those who had in a more especial manner despitefully used me and persecuted me. I then testified openly to all there, what I now first felt in my heart. But it was not long before the enemy suggested, "This cannot be faith; for where is thy joy?" Then was I taught, that peace and victory over sin are essential to faith in the Captain of our salvation; but that, as to the transports of joy that usually attend the beginning of it, especially in those who have mourned deeply, God sometimes giveth, sometimes withholdeth them, according to the counsels of His own will.

16. After my return home, I was much buffeted with temptations; but cried out, and they fled away. They returned again and again. I as often lifted up my eyes, and He "sent me help from His holy place." And herein I found the difference between this and my former state chiefly consisted. I was striving, yea, fighting with all my might under the law, as well as under grace. But then I was sometimes, if not often, conquered; now I was always conqueror.

17. *Thur.* 25.—The moment I awaked, "Jesus, Master," was in my heart and in my mouth; and I found all my strength lay in keeping my eye fixed upon Him, and my soul waiting on Him continually. Being again at St Paul's in the afternoon, I could taste the good word of God, in the anthem, which began, "My song shall be always of the loving-kindness of the Lord: with my mouth will I ever be showing forth Thy truth from one generation to another." Yet the enemy injected a fear, "If thou dost believe, why is there not a more sensible change?" I answered (yet not I), "That I know not. But this I know, I have 'now peace with God.' And I sin not to-day, and Jesus my Master has forbid me to take thought for the morrow."

18. "But is not any sort of fear," continued the tempter, "a proof that thou dost not believe?" I desired my Master to answer for me; and opened His Book upon those words of St. Paul, "Without were fightings, within were fears." Then, inferred I, well may fears be within me; but I must go on, and tread them under my feet.

Fri. 26.—My soul continued in peace, but yet in heaviness, because of manifold temptations. I asked Mr Telchig, the Moravian, what to do. He said, "You must not fight with them, as you did before, but flee from them the moment they appear, and take shelter in the wounds of Jesus." The same I learned also from the afternoon anthem, which was, "My soul truly waiteth still upon God: for of Him cometh my salvation; He verily is my strength and my salvation, He is my defence, so that I shall not greatly fall. O put your trust in Him always, ye people; pour out your hearts before Him; for God is our hope."

Sat. 27.—Believing one reason of my want of joy was want of time for prayer, I resolved to do no business till I went to church in the morning, but to continue pouring out my heart before Him. And this day my spirit was enlarged; so that though I was now also assaulted by many temptations, I was more than conqueror, gaining more power thereby to trust and to rejoice in God my Saviour.

Sun. 28.—I waked in peace, but not in joy. In the same even, quiet state I was till the evening, when I was roughly attacked in a large company as an enthusiast, a seducer, and a setter-forth of new doctrines. By the blessing of God, I was not moved to anger, but after a calm and short reply went away; though not with so tender a concern as was due to those who were seeking death in the error of their life.

This day I preached in the morning at St George's, Bloomsbury, on, "This is the victory that overcometh the world, even our faith"; and in the afternoon at the chapel in Long Acre, on God's justifying the ungodly; the last time, I understand, I am to preach at either. "Not as I will, but as Thou wilt."

Mon. 29.—I set out for Dummer with Mr Wolf, one of the firstfruits of Peter Böhler's ministry in England. I was much strengthened by the grace of God in him; yet was his state so far above mine, that I was often tempted to doubt whether we had one faith. But without much reasoning about it, I held here: "Though his be strong and mine weak, yet that God hath given some degree of faith even to me, I know by its fruits. For I have constant peace; not one uneasy thought. And I have freedom from sin; not one unholy desire."

Yet on *Wednesday* did I grieve the Spirit of God, not only by not watching unto prayer, but likewise by speaking with sharpness, instead of tender love, of one that was not sound in the faith. Immediately God hid His face, and I was troubled; and in this heaviness I continued till the next morning, June 1; when it pleased God, while I was exhorting another, to give comfort to my soul, and, after I had spent some time in prayer, to direct me to those gracious words, "Having, therefore, boldness to enter into the holiest by the blood of Jesus, let us draw near with a true heart in full assurance of faith. Let us hold fast the profession of our faith without wavering (for He is faithful that promised); and let us consider one another to provoke unto love and to good works."

Sat. June 3.—I was so strongly assaulted by one of my old enemies, that I had scarce strength to open my lips, or even to look up for help. But after I had prayed, faintly, as I could, the temptation vanished away.

Sun. 4.—Was indeed a feast-day. For from the time of my rising till past one in the afternoon, I was praying, reading the Scriptures, singing praise, or calling sinners to repentance. All these days I scarce remember to have opened the Testament, but upon some great and precious promise. And I saw more than ever, that the gospel is in truth but one great promise, from the beginning of it to the end.

Tues. 6.—I had still more comfort, and peace, and joy; on which, I fear, I began to presume; for in the evening I received a letter from Oxford which threw me into much perplexity. It was asserted therein, "that no doubting could consist with the least degree of true faith; that whoever at any time felt any doubt or fear, was not weak in faith, but had no faith at all; and that none hath any faith, till the law of the Spirit of life has made him wholly free from the law of sin and death."

Begging of God to direct me, I opened my Testament on

1 Cor. iii. 1, etc., where St Paul speaks of those whom he terms "babes in Christ," who were "not able to bear strong meat," nay, in a sense, "carnal"; to whom, nevertheless, he says, "Ye are God's building, ye are the temple of God." Surely then these men had some degree of faith; though, it is plain, their faith was but weak.

After some hours spent in the Scripture and prayer, I was much comforted. Yet I felt a kind of soreness in my heart, so that I found my wound was not fully healed. O God, save Thou me, and all that are "weak in the faith," from "doubtful disputations!"

CHAPTER III

A VISIT TO HERNHUTH

FROM JUNE 7, TO AUGUST 14, 1738.

Wednesday, June 7.—I determined, if God should permit, to retire for a short time into Germany.

Thur. 8.—I went to Salisbury to take leave of my mother. The next day I left Sarum, and on *Saturday* came to Stanton-Harcourt. Having preached faith in Christ there on *Sunday*, 11, I went on to Oxford; and thence on *Monday* to London, where I found Mr Ingham just setting out. We went on board the next day, *Tuesday*, 13, and fell down to Gravesend that night. About four in the afternoon on *Wednesday* we lost sight of England. We reached the Maese at eight on *Thursday* morning, and in an hour and a half landed at Rotterdam.

We were eight in all—five English, and three Germans. About seven we came to Goudart, where we were a little surprised at meeting with a treatment which is not heard of in England. Several inns utterly refused to entertain us; so that it was with difficulty we at last found one, where they did us the favour to take our money for some meat and drink, and the use of two or three bad beds. They pressed us much in the morning to see their church, but were displeased at our pulling off our hats when we went in; telling us we must not do so, it was not the custom there. About eight we left Goudart, and in little more than six hours reached Ysselstein.

Here we were at Baron Wattevil's as at home. We found with him a few German brethren and sisters, and seven or eight of our English acquaintance, who had settled here some time before. They lodged just without the town, in three or four little houses, till one should be built that would contain them all. *Saturday*, 17, was their intercession-day. In the morning some of our English brethren desired me to administer the Lord's Supper: the rest of the day we spent with all the brethren and sisters, in hearing the wonderful work which God is beginning to work over all the earth.

At six in the morning we took boat to Amsterdam, whither we came about five in the evening. Here we were entertained with truly Christian hospitality, by Mr Decknatel, a minister of the Mennonists, who suffered us to want nothing while we stayed here, which was till the *Thursday* following.

Mon. 19.—I was at one of the societies, which lasted an hour and a half. About sixty persons were present. The singing was in Low-Dutch (Mr Decknatel having translated into Low-Dutch part of the Hernhuth hymn-book); but the words were so very near the German, that any who understood the original, might understand the translation. The expounding was in High-Dutch.

Thur. 22.—We took boat at eight in the evening, and, landing at four in the morning, walked on to Uutfass, which we left about two, having now another boy added to our number.

Sun. 25.—After spending an hour in singing and prayer, we walked till near noon, before we could meet with any refreshment. We hoped to reach Reinberg in the evening, but could not; being obliged to stop two hours short of it, at a little house where many good Lutherans were concluding the Lord's day, as is usual among them, with fiddling and dancing.

Mon. 26.—We breakfasted at Reinberg. Hence to Colen, the ugliest, dirtiest city I ever yet saw with my eyes.

Wed. 28.—We went to the cathedral, which is mere heaps upon heaps; a huge, misshapen thing, which has no more of symmetry than of neatness belonging to it. I was a little surprised to observe, that neither in this, nor in any other of the Romish churches where I have been, is there, properly speaking, any such thing as joint worship: but one prays at one shrine or altar, and another at another, without any regard to, or communication with, one another.

Walking on the side of the Rhine in the afternoon, I saw, to my great surprise (for I always thought before, no Romanist of any fashion believed anything of the story), a fresh painting, done last year at the public expense, on the outside of the city wall, in "memory of the bringing in the heads of the three Kings," says the Latin inscription, "through the gate adjoining"; which, indeed in reverence, it seems, to them, has been stopped up ever since.

At four we took boat, when I could not but observe the decency of the Papists above us who are called Reformed. As soon as ever we were seated (and so every morning after), they all pulled off their hats, and each used by himself a short prayer for our prosperous journey. And this justice I must do to the very boatmen (who upon the Rhine are generally wicked

even to a proverb) : I never heard one of them take the name
of God in vain, or saw anyone laugh when anything of religion
was mentioned. So that I believe the glory of sporting with
sacred things is peculiar to the English nation !

On *Sunday* evening, July 2, we came to Mentz ; and
Monday, the 3rd, at half an hour past ten, to Frankfort.

After waiting an hour at the gates, we procured a messenger,
whom we sent to Mr Böhler (Peter Böhler's father); who
immediately came, procured us entrance into the city, and
entertained us in the most friendly manner. We set out early
in the morning on *Tuesday*, the 4th, and about one came to
Marienborn. But I was so ill, that, after talking a little with
Count Zinzendorf, I was forced to lie down the rest of the day.

The family at Marienborn consists of about ninety persons,
gathered out of many nations. They live for the present in a
large house hired by the Count, which is capable of receiving a
far greater number ; but are building one, about three English
miles off, on the top of a fruitful hill.

Thur. 6.—The Count carried me with him to the Count of
Solmes, where I observed with pleasure the German frugality.

I lodged with one of the brethren at Eckershausen, an
English mile from Marienborn, where I usually spent the day,
chiefly in conversing with those who could speak either Latin
or English ; not being able, for want of more practice, to speak
German readily. And here I continually met with what I
sought for, viz., living proofs of the power of faith : persons
saved from inward as well as outward sin, by "the love of God
shed abroad in their hearts" ; and from all doubt and fear, by
the abiding witness of "the Holy Ghost given unto them."

Wednesday, 12, was one of the conferences for strangers ;
where one of Frankfort proposing the question, "Can a man
be justified, and not know it?" the Count spoke largely and
scripturally upon it.

We left Jena early on *Tuesday*, reached Weisenfeltz in the
evening, and Merseberg on *Wednesday* morning. Having a
desire to see Halle (two German miles off), we set out after
breakfast, and came thither at two in the afternoon. But we
could not be admitted into the town, when we came. The
King of Prussia's tall men, who kept the gates, sent us backward
and forward, from one gate to another, for near two hours. I
then thought of sending in a note to Professor Francke, the son
of that August Herman Francke whose name is indeed as
precious ointment.

He was not in town. However, we were at length admitted
into the orphan-house ; that amazing proof, that "all things

are" still "possible to him that believeth." There is now a
large yearly revenue for its support, beside what is continually
brought in by the printing-office, the books sold there, and the
apothecary's shop, which is furnished with all sorts of medicines.
The building reaches backward from the front in two wings
for, I believe, a hundred and fifty yards. The lodging-chambers
for the children, their dining-room, their chapel, and all the
adjoining apartments, are so conveniently contrived, and so
exactly clean, as I have never seen any before. Six hundred
and fifty children, we were informed, are wholly maintained
there; and three thousand, if I mistake not, taught. Surely,
such a thing neither we nor our fathers have known, as this
great thing which God has done here!

Tues. Aug. 1.—At three in the afternoon I came to Hernhuth, about thirty English miles from Dresden. It lies in
Upper Lusatia, on the border of Bohemia, and contains about
a hundred houses, built on a rising ground, with evergreen
woods on two sides, gardens and cornfields on the others, and
high hills at a small distance. It has one long street, through
which the great road from Zittau to Lobau goes. Fronting the
middle of this street is the orphan-house; in the lower part
of which is the apothecary's shop; in the upper, the chapel,
capable of containing six or seven hundred people. Another
row of houses runs at a small distance from either end of the
orphan-house, which accordingly divides the rest of the town
(beside the long street) into two squares. At the east end of it
is the Count's house: a small plain building like the rest;
having a large garden behind it, well laid out, not for show, but
for the use of the community.

We had a convenient lodging assigned us in the house
appointed for strangers: and I had now abundant opportunity
of observing whether what I had heard was enlarged by the
relators, or was neither more nor less than the naked truth.

I rejoiced to find Mr Hermsdorf here, whom I had so often
conversed with in Georgia. And there was nothing in his
power which he did not do, to make our stay here useful and
agreeable. About eight we went to the public service, at
which they frequently use other instruments with their organ.
They began, as usual, with singing. Then followed the expounding, closed by a second hymn: prayer followed this;
and then a few verses of a third hymn; which concluded the
service.

Wed. 2.—At four in the afternoon was a love-feast of the
married men, taking their food with gladness and singleness of
heart, and with the voice of praise and thanksgiving.

Thur. 3 (And so every day at eleven), I was at the Bible Conference, wherein Mr Müller (late master of a great school in Zittau, till he left all to follow Christ), and several others, read together, as usual, a portion of Scripture in the original. At five was the conference for strangers, when several questions concerning justification were resolved. This evening Christian David came hither.

On *Friday* and *Saturday*, and so every day in the following week, I had much conversation with the most experienced of the brethren, concerning the great work which God had wrought in their souls, purifying them by faith; and with Martin Döber, and the other teachers and elders of the church, concerning the discipline used therein.

Sun. 6.—We went to church at Bertholdsdorf, a Lutheran village about an English mile from Hernhuth. Two large candles stood lighted upon the altar: the Last Supper was painted behind it; the pulpit was placed over it; and over that, a brass image of Christ on the cross.

After the evening service at Hernhuth was ended, all the unmarried men (as is their custom) walked quite round the town, singing praise with instruments of music; and then on a small hill, at a little distance from it, casting themselves into a ring, joined in prayer. Thence they returned into the great square, and, a little after eleven, commended each other to God.

Tues. 8.—A child was buried. The burying-ground (called by them "Gottes Acker," that is, God's ground) lies a few hundred yards out of the town, under the side of a little wood. There are distinct squares in it for married men and unmarried; for married and unmarried women; for male and female children; and for widows. The corpse was carried from the chapel, the children walking first; next the orphan-father (so they call him who has the chief care of the orphan-house), with the minister of Bertholdsdorf; then four children bearing the corpse; and after them, Martin Döber and the father of the child. Then followed the men; and last of all, the women and girls. They all sung as they went. Being come into the square where the male children are buried, the men stood on two sides of it, the boys on the third, and the women and girls on the fourth. There they sung again: after which the minister used (I think read) a short prayer, and concluded with that blessing, "Unto God's gracious mercy and protection I commit you."

Seeing the father (a plain man, a tailor by trade) looking at the grave, I asked, "How do you find yourself?" He said, "Praised be the Lord, never better. He has taken the soul of my child to Himself. I have seen, according to my desire, his body committed to holy ground. And I know that when it is raised again, both he and I shall be ever with the Lord."

Several evenings this week I was with one or other of the private bands. On *Wednesday* and *Thursday* I had an opportunity of talking with Michael Linner, the eldest of the church, and largely with Christian David, who, under God, was the first planter of it.

Four times also I enjoyed the blessing of hearing him preach, during the few days I spent here; and every time he chose the very subject which I should have desired, had I spoken to him before. Thrice he described the state of those who are "weak in faith," who are justified, but have not yet a new, clean heart; who have received forgiveness through the blood of Christ, but have not received the constant indwelling of the Holy Ghost.

Sat. 12.—Was the Intercession-day, when many strangers were present, some of whom came twenty or thirty miles. I would gladly have spent my life here; but my Master calling me to labour in another part of His vineyard, on *Monday*, 14, I was constrained to take my leave of this happy place; Martin Döber, and a few others of the brethren, walking with us about an hour.

CHAPTER IV

THE UNITED SOCIETIES

FROM SEPTEMBER 17, 1738, TO OCTOBER 31, 1739

Sun. 17.—I began again to declare in my own country the glad tidings of salvation, preaching three times, and afterwards expounding the holy Scripture, to a large company in the Minories. On *Monday* I rejoiced to meet with our little society, which now consisted of thirty-two persons.

The next day I went to the condemned felons, in Newgate, and offered them free salvation. In the evening I went to a society in Bear Yard, and preached repentance and remission of sins. The next evening I spoke the truth in love at a society in Aldersgate Street.

On *Saturday*, 23, I was enabled to speak strong words both at Newgate and at Mr E.'s society; and the next day at St Anne's, and twice at St John's, Clerkenwell; so that I fear they will bear me there no longer.

Sat. 30.—One who had been a zealous opposer of "this way," sent and desired to speak with me immediately. He had all the signs of settled despair, both in his countenance and behaviour. He said, he had been enslaved to sin many years, especially to drunkenness. I desired we might join in prayer. After a short space he rose, and his countenance was no longer sad.

Sun. Oct. 1.—I preached both morning and afternoon at St George's in the East.

Fri. 6.—I preached at St Antholin's once more. In the afternoon I went to the Rev. Mr Bedford, to tell him between me and him alone, of the injury he had done both to God and his brother, by preaching and printing that very weak sermon on assurance, which was an *ignoratio elenchi* from beginning to end; seeing the assurance we preach is of quite another kind from that he writes against. We speak of an assurance of our present pardon; not, as he does, of our final perseverance.

On *Monday*, 9, I set out for Oxford. In walking I read the

truly surprising narrative of the conversions lately wrought in and about the town of Northampton, in New England.

Sun. 15.—I preached twice at the castle, and afterwards expounded at three societies. *Wednesday* evening I came to London again; and on *Friday* met a society (of soldiers chiefly) at Westminster; on *Sunday* [29, I preached] at Islington and at London Wall.

In the evening, being troubled at what some said of "the kingdom of God within us," and doubtful of my own state, I called upon God, and received this answer from His Word: "He Himself also waited for the kingdom of God." "But should not I wait in silence and retirement?" was the thought that immediately struck into my mind. I opened my Testament again, on those words, "Seest thou not, how faith wrought together with his works? And by works was faith made perfect."

Fri. Nov. 3.—I preached at St. Antholin's: *Sunday*, 5, in the morning, at St Botolph's, Bishopsgate; in the afternoon, at Islington; and in the evening, to such a congregation as I never saw before, at St Clement's, in the Strand. As this was the first time of my preaching here, I suppose it is to be the last.

On *Wednesday*, my brother and I went, at their earnest desire, to do the last good office to the condemned malefactors. It was the most glorious instance I ever saw of faith triumphing over sin and death.

My brother took that occasion of declaring the gospel of peace to a large assembly of publicans and sinners.

Friday, 10, I set out, and *Saturday*, 11, spent the evening with a little company at Oxford. I was grieved to find prudence had made them leave off singing psalms. I fear it will not stop here.

Sun. 12.—I preached twice at the castle. In the following week, I began more narrowly to inquire what the doctrine of the Church of England is, concerning the much controverted point of justification by faith; and the sum of what I found in the Homilies, I extracted and printed for the use of others.

Sun. 19.—I only preached in the afternoon, at the castle. On *Monday* night I was greatly troubled in dreams; and about eleven o'clock, waked in an unaccountable consternation, without being able to sleep again. About that time (as I found in the morning), one who had been designed to be my pupil, but was not, came into the porter's lodge (where several persons were sitting), with a pistol in his hand. He presented this, as in sport, first at one, and then at another. He then attempted twice or thrice to shoot himself, but it would not go off. Upon his laying it down, one took it up, and blew out the priming. He was very angry, went and got fresh prime, came in again, sat down, beat the flint with his key, and about twelve, pulling off his hat and wig, said he would die like a gentleman, and shot himself through the head.

Thur. 23.—Returning from preaching at the castle, I met once more with my old companion in affliction, Charles Delamotte; who stayed with me till Monday.

Sun. Dec. 3.—I began reading prayers at Bocardo (the city prison), which had been long discontinued. In the afternoon, I received a letter, earnestly desiring me to publish my account of Georgia; and another, as earnestly dissuading me from it, "because it would bring much trouble upon me." I consulted God in His Word, and received two answers: the first, Ezek. xxxiii. 2-6: the other, "Thou therefore endure hardship, as a good soldier of Jesus Christ."

Tues. 5.—At St Thomas's was a young woman, raving mad, screaming and tormenting herself continually. I had a strong desire to speak to her. The moment I began she was still. The tears ran down her cheeks all the time I was telling her, "Jesus of Nazareth is able and willing to deliver you."

Mon. 11.—Hearing Mr Whitefield was arrived from Georgia, I hastened to London; and on *Tuesday,* 12, God gave us once more to take sweet counsel together.

Mon. Jan. 1, 1739.—Mr Hall, Kinchin, Ingham, Whitefield, Hutchins, and my brother Charles, were present at our love-feast in Fetter Lane, with about sixty of our brethren. About three in the morning, as we were continuing instant in prayer, the power of God came mightily upon us, insomuch that many cried out for exceeding joy, and many fell to the ground. As soon as we were recovered a little from that awe and amazement at the presence of his Majesty, we broke out with one voice, "We praise Thee, O God; we acknowledge Thee to be the Lord."

Sun. 21.—We were surprised in the evening, while I was expounding in the Minories. A well-dressed, middle-aged woman suddenly cried out as in the agonies of death. She continued so to do for some time, with all the signs of the sharpest anguish of spirit. When she was a little recovered, I desired her to call upon me the next day. She then told me, that about three years before, she was under strong convictions of sin, and in such terror of mind, that she had no comfort in anything, nor any rest, day or night: that she sent for the minister of her parish, and told him the distress she was in; upon which he told her husband, she was stark mad, and advised him to send for a physician immediately. A physician was sent for accordingly, who ordered her to be blooded, blistered, and so on. But this did not heal her wounded spirit. So that she continued much as she was before: till the last night, He whose word she at first found to be "sharper than any two-edged sword," gave her a faint hope, that He would undertake her cause, and heal the soul which had sinned against Him.

Sun. 28.—I went (having been long importuned thereto), about five in the evening, with four or five of my friends, to a house where was one of those commonly called French prophets. After a time, she came in. She seemed about four or five and twenty, of an agreeable speech and behaviour. She asked why we came. I said, "To try the spirits, whether they be of God." Presently after she leaned back in her chair, and seemed to have strong workings.

She spoke much, and mostly in Scripture words, of the fulfilling of the prophecies, the coming of Christ now at hand, and the spreading of the gospel over all the earth. Two or three of our company were much affected, and believed she spoke by the Spirit of God. But this was in no wise clear to me. The motion might be either hysterical or artificial. And the same words, any person of a good understanding and well versed in the Scriptures might have spoken. But I let the matter alone; knowing this, that "if it be not of God, it will come to nought."

Sun. Feb. 18.—I was desired to preach at Sir George Wheeler's chapel, in Spitalfields, morning and afternoon. I did so in the morning, but was not suffered to conclude my subject (as I had designed) in the afternoon; a good remembrance, that I should, if possible, declare at every time the whole counsel of God.

Fri. Mar. 2.—It was the advice of all our brethren that I should spend a few days at Oxford; whither I accordingly went on *Saturday*, 3rd.

One of the most surprising instances of His power which I ever remember to have seen, was on the Tuesday following; when I visited one who was above measure enraged at this new way, and zealous in opposing it. Finding argument to be of no other effect, than to inflame her more and more, I broke off the dispute, and desired we might join in prayer; which she so far consented to as to kneel down. In a few minutes she fell into an extreme agony, both of body and soul; and soon after cried out with the utmost earnestness, "Now I know I am forgiven for Christ's sake."

Thurs. 8.—I called upon her and a few of her neighbours, who were met together in the evening ; among whom I found a gentleman of the same spirit she had been of, earnestly labouring to pervert the truth of the gospel. To prevent his going on, as the less evil of the two, I entered directly into the controversy, touching both the cause and the fruits of justification. In the midst of the dispute, one who sat at a small distance felt as it were the piercing of a sword, and before she could be brought to another house, whither I was going, could not avoid crying out aloud, even in the street. But no sooner had we made our request known to God, than He sent her help from His holy place.

Sat. 10.—In the afternoon I came to Dummer ; and on *Sunday* morning had a large and attentive congregation. The next day I returned to Reading, and thence on *Tuesday* to Oxford, where I found many more and more rejoicing in God their Saviour. *Thursday*, 15, I set out early in the morning, and in the afternoon came to London.

During my stay here, I was fully employed ; between our own society in Fetter Lane, and many others, where I was continually desired to expound ; so that I had no thought of leaving London, when I received, after several others, a letter from Mr Whitefield, and another from Mr Stewart, entreating me, in the most pressing manner, to come to Bristol without delay. This I was not at all forward to do ; and perhaps a little the less inclined to it (though I trust I do not count my life dear unto myself, so I may finish my course with joy) because of the remarkable scriptures which offered as often as we inquired, touching the consequence of this removal : probably permitted for the trial of our faith.

Wed. 28.—My journey was proposed to our society in Fetter Lane. But my brother Charles would scarce bear the mention of it ; till appealing to the oracles of God, he received those words as spoken to himself, and answered not again :—" Son of man, behold, I take from thee the desire of thine eyes with a stroke : yet shalt thou not mourn or weep, neither shall thy tears run down." Our other brethren, however, continuing the dispute, without any probability of their coming to one conclusion, we at length all agreed to decide it by lot. And by this it was determined I should go. Several afterwards desiring we might open the Bible, concerning the issue of this, we did so.

Sat. 31.—In the evening I reached Bristol, and met Mr Whitefield there. I could scarce reconcile myself at first to this strange way of preaching in the fields, of which he set me an example on Sunday; having been all my life (till very lately) so tenacious of every point relating to decency and order, that I should have thought the saving of souls almost a sin, if it had not been done in a church.

Sun. April 1.—In the evening (Mr Whitefield being gone) I begun expounding our Lord's Sermon on the Mount (one pretty remarkable precedent of field-preaching, though I suppose there were churches at that time also), to a little society which was accustomed to meet once or twice a week in Nicholas Street.

Mon. 2.—At four in the afternoon, I submitted to be more vile, and proclaimed in the highways the glad tidings of salvation, speaking from a little eminence in a ground adjoining to the city, to about three thousand people. The Scripture on which I spoke was this, "The Spirit of the Lord is upon me, because He hath anointed me to preach the gospel to the poor. He hath sent me to heal the broken-hearted; to preach deliverance to the captives, and recovery of sight to the blind; to set at liberty them that are bruised, to proclaim the acceptable year of the Lord."

At seven I began expounding the Acts of the Apostles, to a society meeting in Baldwin Street; and the next day the Gospel of St John in the chapel at Newgate; where I also daily read the morning service of the Church.

Wed. 4.—At Baptist Mills (a sort of suburb or village about half a mile from Bristol) I offered the grace of God to about fifteen hundred persons from these words, " I will heal their backsliding, I will love them freely."

In the evening three women agreed to meet together weekly, with the same intention as those at London, viz., "to confess their faults one to another, and pray one for another, that they may be healed." At eight, four young men agreed to meet, in pursuance of the same design. How dare any man deny this to be a means of grace, ordained by God? Unless he will affirm that St James's Epistle is an epistle of straw.

Thur. 5.—At five in the evening I began at a society in Castle Street, expounding the Epistle to the Romans; and the next evening at a society in Gloucester Lane, the First Epistle of St John. On Saturday evening, at Weaver's Hall, also, I began expounding t҅҅͟͟ ҅҅͟͟͟ ҅҅͟͟ ҅҅͟͟ ҅͟ the Romans; and declared that Gospel to all which is the " power of God unto salvation to every one that believeth."

Sun. 8.—At seven in the morning I preached to about a thousand persons at Bristol, and afterwards to about fifteen hundred on the top of Hannam Mount in Kingswood. I called to them, in the words of the evangelical Prophet, "Ho! every one that thirsteth, come ye to the waters; come, and buy wine and milk without money and without price." About five thousand were in the afternoon at Rose Green (on the other side of Kingswood); among whom I stood and cried, in the name of the Lord, "If any man thirst, let him come unto Me and drink."

Tues. 10.—I was desired to go to Bath; where I offered to about a thousand souls the free grace of God to "heal their backsliding"; and in the morning to (I believe) more than two thousand. I preached to about the same number at Baptist Mills in the afternoon.

Sat. 14.—I preached at the poor-house. Three or four hundred were within, and more than twice that number without; to whom I explained those comfortable words, "When they had nothing to pay, he frankly forgave them both."

Sun. 15.—I explained at seven, to five or six thousand persons, the story of the Pharisee and the Publican. About three thousand were present at Hannam Mount. I preached at Newgate after dinner to a crowded congregation. Between five and six we went to Rose Green: it rained hard at Bristol, but not a drop fell upon us, while I declared to about five thousand, "Christ, our wisdom, and righteousness, and sanctification, and redemption." I concluded the day by showing at the society in Baldwin Street that "His blood cleanseth us from all sin."

Tues. 17.—At five in the afternoon I was at a little society in the Back Lane. The room in which we were was propped beneath, but the weight of people made the floor give way; so that in the beginning of the expounding, the post which propped it fell down with a great noise. But the floor sunk no farther; so that, after a little surprise at first, they quietly attended to the things that were spoken.

Thence I went to Baldwin Street, and expounded, as it came in course, the fourth chapter of the Acts. We then called upon God to confirm His word. Immediately one that stood by (to our no small surprise) cried out aloud, with the utmost vehemence, even as in the agonies of death. But we continued in prayer, till "a new song was put in her mouth, a thanksgiving unto our God." Soon after, two other persons (well known in this place, as labouring to live in all good conscience towards all men) were seized with strong pain, and constrained to "roar for the disquietness of their heart." But it was not long before they likewise burst forth into praise to God their Saviour. The last who called upon God as out of the belly of hell was I—— E——, a stranger in Bristol. And in a short space he also was overwhelmed with joy and love, knowing that God had healed his backslidings.

Wed. 18.—In the evening L——a S—— (late a Quaker, but baptized the day before), R——a M——, and a few others, were admitted into the society. But R——a M—— was scarcely able either to speak or look up. "The sorrows of death compassed" her "about, the pains of hell got hold upon" her. We poured out our complaints before God, and showed Him of her trouble. And He soon showed, He is a God "that heareth prayer." She felt in herself, that "being justified freely, she had peace with God through Jesus Christ." She "rejoiced in hope of the glory of God," and "the love of God was shed abroad in her heart."

Sat. 21.—At Weaver's Hall a young man was suddenly seized with a violent trembling all over, and in a few minutes, the sorrows of his heart being enlarged, sunk down to the ground. But we ceased not calling upon God, till He raised him up full of "peace, and joy in the Holy Ghost."

Mon. 23.—On a repeated invitation, I went to Pensford, about five miles from Bristol. I sent to the minister, to ask leave to preach in the church; but having waited some time and received no answer, I called on many of the people who were gathered together in an open place, "If any man thirst, let him come unto Me and drink." At four in the afternoon there were above three thousand, in a convenient place near Bristol; to whom I declared, "The hour is coming, and now is, when the dead shall hear the voice of the Son of God, and they that hear shall live."

I preached at Bath to about a thousand on *Tuesday* morning; and at four in the afternoon to the poor colliers, at a place about the middle of Kingswood, called Two-mile-hill. In the evening at Baldwin Street, a young man, after a sharp (though short) agony, both of body and mind, found his soul filled with peace, knowing in whom he had believed.

Thur. 26.—While I was preaching at Newgate, on these words, "He that believeth hath everlasting life," I was insensibly led, without any previous design, to declare strongly and explicitly, that God willeth "all men to be" thus "saved"; and to pray, that, "if this were not the truth of God, He would not suffer the blind to go out of the way; but, if it were, He would bear witness to His word." Immediately one, and another, and another sunk to the earth; they dropped on every side as thunderstruck. One of them cried aloud. We besought God in her behalf, and he turned her heaviness into joy. A second being in the same agony, we called upon God for her also; and He spoke peace unto her soul. In the evening I was again pressed in spirit to declare, that "Christ gave Himself a ransom for all." And almost before we called upon Him to set to His seal, He answered. One was so wounded by the sword of the Spirit, that you would have imagined she could not live a moment. But immediately His abundant kindness was showed, and she loudly sang of His righteousness.

Fri. 27.—All Newgate rang with the cries of those whom the word of God cut to the heart: two of whom were in a moment filled with joy, to the astonishment of those that beheld them.

Sun. 29.—I declared the free grace of God to about four thousand people. At that hour it was, that one who had long continued in sin, from a despair of finding mercy, received a full, clear sense of his pardoning love, and power to sin no more. I then went to Clifton, a mile from Bristol, at the minister's desire, who was dangerously ill; and thence returned to a little plain, near Hannam Mount, where about three thousand were present. After dinner I went to Clifton again. The church was quite full at the prayers and sermon, as was the church-yard at the burial which followed. From Clifton we went to Rose Green, where were, by computation, near seven thousand; and thence to Gloucester Lane society. After which was our first love-feast in Baldwin Street.

Mon. 30.—We understood that many were offended at the cries of those on whom the power of God came: among whom was a physician, who was much afraid there might be fraud or imposture in the case. To-day one whom he had known many years was the first (while I was preaching in Newgate) who broke out "into strong cries and tears." He could hardly believe his own eyes and ears. He went and stood close to her, and observed every symptom, till great drops of sweat ran down her face, and all her bones shook. He then knew not what to think, being clearly convinced, it was not fraud, nor yet any natural disorder. But when both her soul and body were healed in a moment, he acknowledged the finger of God.

Tues. May 1.—Many were offended again, and, indeed, much more than before. For at Baldwin Street my voice could scarce be heard amidst the groanings of some, and the cries of others calling aloud to Him that is "mighty to save."

A Quaker who stood by was not a little displeased at the dissimulation of those creatures, and was biting his lips and knitting his brows, when he dropped down as thunderstruck. The agony he was in was even terrible to behold. We besought

God not to lay folly to his charge. And he soon lifted up his head, and cried aloud, "Now I know thou art a prophet of the Lord."

Wed. 2.—At Newgate another mourner was comforted. I was desired to step thence to a neighbouring house, to see a letter wrote against me, as a "deceiver of the people," by teaching that God "willeth all men to be saved." One who long had asserted the contrary was there, when a young woman came in. Just as we rose from giving thanks, another person reeled four or five steps, and then dropped down. We prayed with her, and left her strongly convinced of sin, and earnestly groaning for deliverance.

I did not mention one J——n H——n, a weaver, who was at Baldwin Street the night before. He was (I understood) a man of a regular life and conversation, one that constantly attended the public prayers and sacrament, and was zealous for the Church, and against Dissenters of every denomination. Being informed that people fell into strange fits at the societies, he came to see and judge for himself. But he was less satisfied than before; insomuch that he went about to his acquaintance, one after another, till one in the morning, and laboured above measure to convince them it was a delusion of the devil. We were going home, when one met us in the street, and informed us, that J——n H——n was fallen raving mad. It seemed he had sat down to dinner, but had a mind first to end a sermon he had borrowed on "Salvation by Faith." In reading the last page, he changed colour, fell off his chair, and began screaming terribly, and beating himself against the ground. The neighbours were alarmed, and flocked together to the house. Between one and two I came in, and found him on the floor, the room being full of people, whom his wife would have kept without; but he cried aloud, "No; let them all come, let all the world see the just judgment of God." Two or three men were holding him as well as they could. He immediately fixed his eyes upon me, and, stretching out his hand, cried, "Ay, this who I said was a deceiver of the people. But God has overtaken me. I said, it was all a delusion; but this is no delusion." He then roared out, "O thou devil! thou cursed devil! yea, thou legion of devils! thou canst not stay. Christ will cast thee out. I know His work is begun. Tear me to pieces, if thou wilt; but thou canst not hurt me." He then beat himself against the ground again; his breast heaving at the same time, as in the pangs of death, and great drops of sweat trickling down his face. We all betook ourselves to prayers. His pangs ceased, and both his body and soul were set at liberty.

Mon. 7.—I was preparing to set out for Pensford, having now had leave to preach in the church, when I received the following note :—

" SIR,—Our minister, having been informed you are beside yourself, does not care you should preach in any of his churches."—I went, however ; and on Priest Down, about half a mile from Pensford, preached Christ our " wisdom, righteousness, sanctification, and redemption."

Wed. 9.—We took possession of a piece of ground, near St James's churchyard, in the Horse Fair, where it was designed to build a room, large enough to contain both the societies of Nicholas and Baldwin Street, and such of their acquaintance as might desire to be present with them, at such times as the Scripture was expounded. And on *Saturday*, 12, the first stone was laid with the voice of praise and thanksgiving.

I had not at first the least apprehension or design of being personally engaged, either in the expense of this work, or in the direction of it ; having appointed eleven feoffees, on whom I supposed these burdens would fall of course. But I quickly found my mistake ; first with regard to the expense : for the whole undertaking must have stood still, had not I immediately taken upon myself the payment of all the workmen ; so that before I knew where I was, I had contracted a debt of more than a hundred and fifty pounds. And this I was to discharge how I could ; the subscriptions of both societies not amounting to one quarter of the sum. And as to the direction of the work, I presently received letters from my friends in London, Mr Whitefield in particular, backed with a message by one just come from thence, that neither he nor they would have anything to do with the building, neither contribute anything towards it, unless I would instantly discharge all feoffees, and do everything in my own name. Many reasons they gave for this ; but one was enough—viz., " that such feoffees always would have it in their power to control me ; and if I preached not as they liked, to turn me out of the room I had built." I accordingly yielded to their advice, and calling all the feoffees together, cancelled (no man opposing) the instrument made before, and took the whole management into my own hands. Money, it is true, I had not, nor any human prospect or probability of procuring it : but I knew " the earth is the Lord's, and the fulness thereof" ; and in His name set out, nothing doubting.

My ordinary employment, in public, was now as follows :— Every morning I read prayers and preached at Newgate. Every evening I expounded a portion of Scripture at one or more of the societies. On Monday, in the afternoon, I preached abroad, near Bristol; on Tuesday, at Bath and Two-mile-hill alternately; on Wednesday, at Baptist Mills; every other Thursday, near Pensford; every other Friday, in another part of Kingswood; on Saturday, in the afternoon, and Sunday morning, in the Bowling Green (which lies near the middle of the city): on Sunday, at eleven, near Hannam Mount; at two, at Clifton; and at five on Rose Green. And hitherto, as my days, so my strength hath been.

Sun. 20.—Seeing many of the rich at Clifton church, my heart was much pained for them, and I was earnestly desirous that some even of them might "enter into the kingdom of heaven." But full as I was, I knew not where to begin in warning them to flee from the wrath to come, till my Testament opened on these words: "I came not to call the righteous, but sinners to repentance"; in applying which, my soul was so enlarged, that methought I could have cried out (in another sense than poor vain Archimedes), "Give me where to stand, and I will shake the earth." God's sending forth lightning with the rain, did not hinder about fifteen hundred from staying at Rose Green. Our Scripture was, "It is the glorious God that maketh the thunder. The voice of the Lord is mighty in operation: the voice of the Lord is a glorious voice." In the evening He spoke to three whose souls were all storm and tempest, and immediately there was a great calm.

To-day, *Monday*, 21, our Lord answered for Himself. For while I was enforcing these words, "Be still, and know that I am God," He began to bare His arm, not in a close room, neither in private, but in the open air, and before more than two thousand witnesses. One, and another, and another was struck to the earth; exceedingly trembling at the presence of His power. Others cried, and with a loud and bitter cry, "What must we do to be saved?" And in less than an hour, seven persons, wholly unknown to me till that time, were rejoicing, and singing, and with all their might giving thanks to the God of their salvation.

In the evening I was interrupted at Nicholas Street, almost as soon as I had begun to speak, by the cries of one who was "pricked at the heart," and strongly groaned for pardon and peace. Yet I went on to declare what God had already done, in proof of that important truth, that He is "not willing any should perish, but that all should come to repentance." Another person dropped down, close to one who was a strong asserter of the contrary doctrine. While he stood astonished at the sight, a little boy near him was seized in the same manner. A young man who stood up behind, fixed his eyes on him, and sunk down himself as one dead ; but soon began to roar out, and beat himself against the ground, so that six men could scarcely hold him. His name was Thomas Maxfield. Except J——n H——n, I never saw one so torn of the evil one. Meanwhile many others began to cry out to the " Saviour of all," that He would come and help them, insomuch that all the house (and indeed all the street for some space) was in an uproar. But we continued in prayer ; and before ten the greater part found rest for their souls.

I was called from supper to one who, feeling in herself such a conviction as she never had known before, had run out of the society in all haste, that she might not expose herself. But the hand of God followed her still ; so that after going a few steps, she was forced to be carried home ; and, when she was there, grew worse and worse. She was in a violent agony when we came. We called upon God, and her soul found rest.

About twelve I was greatly importuned to go and visit one person more. She had only one struggle after I came, and was then filled with peace and joy. I think twenty-nine in all had their heaviness turned into joy this day.

Tues. 22.—I preached to about a thousand at Bath. There were several fine gay things among them, to whom especially I called, "Awake, thou that sleepest, and arise from the dead ; and Christ shall give thee light."

Sat. 26.—One came to us in deep despair ; but, after an hour spent in prayer, went away in peace. The next day, having observed in many a zeal which did not suit with the sweetness and gentleness of love, I preached at Rose Green, on those words (to the largest congregation I ever had there ; I believe upwards of ten thousand souls) : "Ye know not what manner of spirit ye are of. For the Son of man is not come to destroy men's lives, but to save them." At the society in the evening, eleven were deeply convinced of sin, and soon after comforted.

Tues. 29.—I was unknowingly engaged in conversation with a famous infidel, a confirmer of the unfaithful in these parts. He appeared a little surprised, and said he would pray to God to show him the true way of worshipping Him.

On Ascension-day in the morning, some of us went to King's Weston Hill, four or five miles from Bristol. Two gentlemen going by, sent up to us in sport many persons from the neighbouring villages ; to whom, therefore, I took occasion to explain those words : " Thou art ascended up on high, thou hast led captivity captive : thou hast received gifts for men :

J.W.J.—6

yea, for the rebellious also, that the Lord God might dwell among them."

Mon. June 4.—Many came to me, and earnestly advised me not to preach abroad in the afternoon, because there was a combination of several persons, who threatened terrible things. This report being spread abroad, brought many thither of the better sort of people (so called); and added, I believe, more than a thousand to the ordinary congregation. The Scripture to which, not my choice, but the providence of God, directed me, was, " Fear not thou, for I am with thee : be not dismayed, for I am thy God. I will strengthen thee ; yea, I will help thee ; yea, I will uphold thee with the right hand of My righteousness." The power of God came with His word, so that none scoffed, or interrupted, or opened his mouth.

Tues. 5.—There was great expectation at Bath, of what a noted man was to do to me there ; and I was much entreated not to preach, because no one knew what might happen. By this report I also gained a much larger audience, among whom were many of the rich and great. I told them plainly, the Scripture had concluded them all under sin—high and low, rich and poor, one with another. Many of them seemed to be a little surprised, and were sinking apace into seriousness, when their champion appeared, and coming close to me, asked by what authority I did these things. I replied, " By the authority of Jesus Christ, conveyed to me by the (now) Archbishop of Canterbury, when he laid hands upon me, and said, ' Take thou authority to preach the gospel.'" He said, " This is contrary to Act of Parliament : this is a conventicle." I answered, " Sir, the conventicles mentioned in that Act (as the preamble shows) are seditious meetings : but this is not such ; here is no shadow of sedition ; therefore it is not contrary to that Act." He replied, " I say it is : and, beside, your preaching frightens people out of their wits." " Sir, did you ever hear me preach?" " No." " How then can you judge of what you never heard ?" " Sir, by common report." " Common report is not enough. Give me leave, sir, to ask, Is not your name Nash ?" " My name is Nash." " Sir, I dare not judge of you by common report : I think it not enough to judge by." Here he paused awhile, and, having recovered himself, said, " I desire to know what this people comes here for :" on which one replied, " Sir, leave him to me : let an old woman answer him. You, Mr Nash, take care of your body ; we take care of our souls ; and for the food of our souls we come here." He replied not a word, but walked away.

As I returned the street was full of people, hurrying to and fro, and speaking great words. But when any of them asked, "Which is he?" and I replied, "I am he," they were immediately silent. Several ladies following me into Mr Merchant's house, the servant told me there were some wanted to speak to me. I went to them, and said, " I believe, ladies, the maid mistook: you only wanted to look at me." I added, "I do not expect that the rich and great should want either to speak with me, or to hear me ; for I speak the plain truth,—a thing you hear little of, and do not desire to hear." A few more words passed between us, and I retired.

Thur. 7.—I preached at Priest Down. In the midst of the prayer after sermon, two men (hired, as we afterwards understood, for that purpose) began singing a ballad. After a few mild words (for I saw some that were angry), used without effect, we all began singing a psalm, which put them utterly to silence. We then poured out our souls in prayer for them, and they appeared altogether confounded.

Mon. 11.—I received a pressing letter from London (as I had several others before), to come thither as soon as possible ; our brethren in Fetter Lane being in great confusion for want of my presence and advice. I therefore preached in the afternoon on these words : "I take you to record this day, that I am pure from the blood of all men ; for I have not shunned to declare unto you all the counsel of God." After sermon I commended them to the grace of God, in whom they had believed. Surely God hath yet a work to do in this place. I have not found such love, no, not in England ; nor so childlike, artless, teachable a temper as He hath given to this people.

Wed. 13.—In the morning I came to London ; and after receiving the holy communion at Islington, I had once more an opportunity of seeing my mother, whom I had not seen since my return from Germany.

I cannot but mention an odd circumstance here. I had read her a paper in June last year, containing a short account of what had passed in my own soul, till within a few days of that time. She greatly approved it, and said, she heartily blessed God, who had brought me to so just a way of thinking. While I was in Germany, a copy of that paper was sent (without my knowledge) to one of my relations. He sent an account of it to my mother ; whom I now found under strange fears concerning me, being convinced "by an account taken from one of my own papers, that I had greatly erred from the faith." I could not conceive what paper that should be ; but, on inquiry, found it was the same I had read her myself.

At six I warned the women at Fetter Lane (knowing how

they had been lately shaken), " not to believe every spirit, but to try the spirits, whether they were of God." Our brethren met at eight, when it pleased God to remove many misunderstandings and offences that had crept in among them.

Thur. 14.—I went with Mr Whitefield to Blackheath, where were, I believe, twelve or fourteen thousand people. He a little surprised me, by desiring me to preach in his stead; which I did (though nature recoiled) on my favourite subject, "Jesus Christ, who of God is made unto us wisdom, righteousness, sanctification, and redemption."

I was greatly moved with compassion for the rich that were there, to whom I made a particular application. Some of them seemed to attend, while others drove away their coaches from so uncouth a preacher.

Fri. 15.—I had much talk with one who is called a Quaker; but he could not receive my saying. I was too strict for him, and talked of such a perfection as he could not think necessary; being persuaded, there was no harm in costly apparel, provided it was plain and grave; nor in putting scarlet or gold upon our houses, so it were not upon our clothes.

In the evening I went to a society at Wapping, weary in body and faint in spirit. I intended to speak on Rom. iii. 19, but could not tell how how to open my mouth: and all the time we were singing, my mind was full of some place, I knew not where, in the Epistle to the Hebrews. I begged God to direct, and opened the book on Heb. x. 19 : " Having therefore, brethren, boldness to enter into the holiest by the blood of Jesus, by a new and living way." While I was earnestly inviting all sinners to "enter into the holiest" by this "new and living way," many of those that heard began to call upon God with strong cries and tears. Some sunk down, and there remained no strength in them; others exceedingly trembled and quaked; some were torn with a kind of convulsive motion in every part of their bodies, and that so violently that often four or five persons could not hold one of them. I have seen many hysterical and

respects. I immediately prayed, that God would not suffer those who were weak to be offended. But one woman was offended greatly, being sure they might help it if they would,— no one should persuade her to the contrary; and was got three or four yards, when she also dropped down, in as violent an agony as the rest. Twenty-six of those who had been thus affected (most of whom, during the prayers which were made for them, were in a moment filled with peace and joy) promised to call upon me the next day. But only eighteen came; by talking closely with whom, I found reason to believe that some of them had gone home to their house justified. The rest seemed to be waiting patiently for it.

Sat. 16.—We met at Fetter Lane, to humble ourselves before God, and own He had justly withdrawn His Spirit from us for our manifold unfaithfulness. In that hour we found God with us as at the first. Some fell prostrate upon the ground. Others burst out, as with one consent, into loud praise and thanksgiving.

Sun. 17.—I preached, at seven, in Upper Moorfields, to (I believe) six or seven thousand people.

At five I preached on Kennington Common, to about fifteen thousand people, on those words: " Look unto Me, and be ye saved, all ye ends of the earth."

Mon. 18.—I left London early in the morning, and the next evening reached Bristol, and preached to a numerous congregation. Howel Harris called upon me an hour or two after. He said, he had been much dissuaded from either hearing or seeing me, by many who said all manner of evil of me. "But," said he, "as soon as I heard you preach, I quickly found what spirit you was of. And before you had done, I was so overpowered with joy and love, that I had much ado to walk home."

It is scarce credible, what advantage Satan had gained during my absence of only eight days. Disputes had crept into our little society, so that the love of many was already waxed cold. I showed them the state they were in the next day (both at Newgate and at Baptist Mills), from those words: "Simon, Simon, behold, Satan hath desired to have you, that he may sift you as wheat." And when we met in the evening, instead of reviving the dispute, we all betook ourselves to prayer. Our Lord was with us. Our divisions were healed; misunderstandings vanished away; and all our hearts were sweetly drawn together, and united as at the first.

Sun.　—As I was riding to Rose Green, in a smooth, plain part of the road, my horse suddenly pitched upon his head, and rolled over and over. I received no other hurt than a little bruise on one side; which for the present I felt not, but preached without pain to six or seven thousand people on that important direction, "Whether ye eat or drink, or whatever you do, do all to the glory of God." In the evening a girl of thirteen or fourteen, and four or five other persons, some of whom had felt the power of God before, were deeply convinced of sin.

Mon. 25.—About ten in the morning, J——e C——r, as she

was sitting at work, was suddenly seized with grievous terrors of mind, attended with strong trembling. Thus she continued all the afternoon; but at the society in the evening God turned her heaviness into joy. Five or six others were also cut to the heart this day; and soon after found Him whose hands made whole: as did one likewise, who had been mourning many months, without any to comfort her.

Tues. 26.—I preached near the house we had a few days before began to build for a school, in the middle of Kingswood, under a little sycamore tree, during a violent storm of rain, on those words: "As the rain cometh down from heaven, and returneth not thither, but watereth the earth, and maketh it bring forth and bud:—so shall My word be, . . ."

Fri. 29.—The places in Kingswood where I now usually preached, were these: once a fortnight, a little above Connam, a village on the south side of the wood; on Sunday morning, near Hannam Mount; once a fortnight, at the schoolhouse, in the middle of Kingswood; on Sunday, in the evening, at Rose Green; and once a fortnight near the Fishponds, on the north side of the wood.

Tues. July 3.—I preached at Bath, to the most attentive and serious audience I have ever seen there. On *Wednesday* I preached at Newgate, on those words: "Because of the Pharisees, they durst not confess Him.—For they loved the praise of men more than the praise of God." A message was delivered to me when I had done, from the Sheriffs, that I must preach there no more.

Fri. 6.—In the afternoon I was with Mr Whitefield, just come from London, with whom I went to Baptist Mills, where he preached concerning "the Holy Ghost, which all who believe are to receive"; not without a just, though severe, censure of those who preach as if there were no Holy Ghost.

Sat. 7.—I had an opportunity to talk with him of those outward signs which had so often accompanied the inward work of God. I found his objections were chiefly grounded on gross misrepresentations of matter of fact. But the next day he had an opportunity of informing himself better: for no sooner had he begun to invite all sinners to believe in Christ, than four persons sunk down close to him. One of them lay without either sense or motion. A second trembled exceedingly. The third had strong convulsions all over his body, but made no noise, unless by groans. The fourth, equally convulsed, called upon God, with strong cries and tears. From this time, I trust, we shall all suffer God to carry on His own work in the way that pleaseth Him.

On Friday, in the afternoon, I left Bristol with Mr. Whitefield, in the midst of heavy rain. But the clouds soon dispersed, so that we had a fair, calm evening, and a serious congregation at Thornbury.

We had an attentive congregation at Gloucester in the evening. In the morning, Mr Whitefield being gone forward, I preached to about five thousand there. It rained violently at five in the evening; notwithstanding which, two or three thousand people stayed, to whom I expounded that glorious vision of Ezekiel, of the resurrection of the dry bones.

On *Monday*, 16, after preaching to two or three thousand, I returned to Bristol, and preached to about three thousand.

Tues. 17.—I rode to Bradford, five miles from Bath, whither I had been long invited to come. I waited on the minister, and desired leave to preach in his church. He said, it was not usual to preach on the week-days; but if I could come thither on a Sunday, he should be glad of my assistance. Thence I went to a gentleman in the town, who had been present when I preached at Bath, and, with the strongest marks of sincerity and affection, wished me good luck in the name of the Lord. But it was past. I found him now quite cold. He began disputing on several heads; and at last told me plainly, one of our own college had informed him they always took me to be a little crack-brained at Oxford.

However, some persons who were not of his mind, having pitched on a convenient place (called Bearfield, or Buryfield), on the top of the hill under which the town lies ; I there offered Christ to about a thousand people, for " wisdom, righteousness, sanctification, and redemption." Thence I returned to Bath, and preached on, " What must I do to be saved?" to a larger audience than ever before. I was wondering the " god of this world" was so still; when, at my return from the place of preaching, poor R——d Merchant told me, he could not let me preach any more in his ground. I asked him, why ? He said, the people hurt his trees, and stole things out of his ground. " And besides," added he, " I have already, by letting thee be there, merited the displeasure of my neighbours."

Sat. 21.—I began expounding, a second time, our Lord's Sermon on the Mount. In the morning, *Sunday*, 22, as I was explaining, " ———— are the poor in spirit," to about three thousand people, we had a fair opportunity of showing all men, what manner of spirit we were of : for in the middle of the sermon, the press-gang came, and seized on one of the hearers, all the rest standing still and none opening his mouth or lifting up his hand to resist them

Having frequently been invited to Wells, particularly by Mr ——, who begged me to make his house my home, on *Thursday*, August 9th, I went thither, and wrote him word the night before; upon which he presently went to one of his friends, and desired a messenger might be sent to meet me, and beg me to turn back: "otherwise," said he, "we shall lose all our trade." But this consideration did not weigh with him, so that he invited me to his own house; and at eleven I preached in his ground, on, "Christ our wisdom, righteousness, sanctification, and redemption," to about two thousand persons. Some of them mocked at first, whom I reproved before all; and those of them who stayed were more serious. Several spoke to me after, who were for the present much affected.

Fri. 17.—Many of our society met, as we had appointed, at one in the afternoon; and agreed that all the members of our society should obey the Church to which we belong, by observing all Fridays in the year as days of fasting or abstinence. We likewise agreed that as many as had opportunity should then meet to spend an hour together in prayer.

Mon. 27.—For two hours I took up my cross, in arguing with a zealous man, and labouring to convince him that I was not an enemy to the Church of England. He allowed, I taught no other doctrines than those of the Church; but could not forgive my teaching them out of the church walls.

Indeed, the report now current in Bristol was, that I was a Papist, if not a Jesuit. Some added, that I was born and bred at Rome; which many cordially believed.

Tues. 28.—In the evening I met my brother, just come from London. "The Lord hath" indeed "done great things for us" already.

Wed. 29.—I rode with my brother to Wells, and preached on "What must I do to be saved?" In the evening I summed up at the new room, what I had said, at many times, from the beginning, of faith, holiness, and good works, as the root, the tree, and the fruit, which God had joined, and man ought not to put asunder.

Fri. 31.—I left Bristol, and reached London about eight on Sunday morning.

Mon. Sept. 3.—I talked largely with my mother, who told me, that, till a short time since, she had scarce heard such a thing mentioned, as the having forgiveness of sins now, or God's Spirit bearing witness with our spirit: much less did she imagine that this was the common privilege of all true believers. "Therefore," said she, "I never durst ask for it myself. But two or three weeks ago, while my son Hall was **pronouncing** those words, in delivering the cup to me, 'The blood of our Lord Jesus Christ, which was given for thee,' the words struck through my heart, and I knew God for Christ's sake had forgiven me all my sins."

I asked, whether her father (Dr Annesley) had not the same faith; and, whether she had not heard him preach it to others. She answered, he had it himself; and declared, a little before his death, that for more than forty years he had no darkness, no fear, no doubt at all of his being "accepted in the Beloved." But that, nevertheless, she did not remember to have heard him preach, no, not once, explicitly upon it: whence she supposed he also looked upon it as the peculiar blessing of a few; not as promised to all the people of God.

Both at Mr B——'s at six, and at Dowgate Hill at eight, were many more than the houses could contain. Several persons who were then convinced of sin came to me the next morning. One came also, who had been mourning long, and earnestly desired us to pray with her. We had scarce begun, when the enemy began to tear her, so that she screamed out, as in the pangs of death: but his time was short; for within a quarter of an hour she was full of the "peace that passeth all understanding."

Thur. 6.—I was sent for by one who began to feel herself a sinner. But a fine lady unexpectedly coming in, there was scarce room for me to speak. The fourth person in the company was a poor unbred girl; who beginning to tell what God had done for her soul, the others looked one at another, as in amaze, but did not open their mouths. I then exhorted them, not to cease from crying to God till they too could say, as she did, "My Beloved is mine, and I am His: I am as sure of it, as that I am alive. For His Spirit bears witness with my spirit, that I am a child of God."

Sun. 9.—I declared to about ten thousand, in Moorfields, what they must do to be saved. My mother went with us, about five, to Kennington, where were supposed to be twenty thousand people. I again insisted on that foundation of all our hope, "Believe on the Lord Jesus, and thou shalt be saved." From Kennington I went to a society at Lambeth. The house being filled, the rest stood in the garden. The deep attention they showed gave me a good hope, that they will not all be forgetful hearers.

Thence I went to our society at Fetter Lane, and exhorted them to love one another. The want of love was a general complaint. We laid it open before our Lord. We soon found He had sent us an answer of peace. Evil surmisings vanished away. The flame kindled again as at the first, and our hearts were knit together.

Mon. 10.—I accepted a pressing invitation to go to Plaistow. At five in the evening I expounded there, and at eight again.

Wed. 12.—In the evening, at Fetter Lane, I described the life of faith; and many who had fancied themselves strong therein, found they were no more than new-born babes. At eight I exhorted our brethren to keep close to the Church, and to all the ordinances of God; and to aim only at living "a quiet and peaceable life, in all godliness and honesty."

Thur. 13.—A serious clergyman desired to know, in what points we differed from the Church of England. I answered, "To the best of my knowledge, in none. The doctrines we preach are the doctrines of the Church of England; indeed, the fundamental doctrines of the Church, clearly laid down, both in her Prayers, Articles, and Homilies."

He asked, "In what points, then, do you differ from the other clergy of the Church of England?" I answered, "In none from that part of the clergy who adhere to the doctrines of the Church; but from that part of the clergy who dissent from the Church (though they own it not), I differ."

Mon. 24.—I preached once more at Plaistow, and took my leave of the people of that place. In my return, a person galloping swiftly, rode full against me, and overthrew both man and horse; but without any hurt to either. Glory be to Him who saves both man and beast!

Tues. 25.—After dining with one of our brethren who was married this day, I went, as usual, to the society at St James's, weary and weak in body. But God strengthened me for His own work, as He did, at six, at Mr B——'s; and, at eight, in Winchester Yard, where it was believed were present eleven or twelve hundred persons.

Thur. 27.—I went in the afternoon to a society at Deptford, and thence, at six, came to Turner's Hall, which holds (by computation) two thousand persons. The press both within and without was very great. In the beginning of the expounding, there being a large vault beneath, the main beam which supported the floor broke. The floor immediately sunk, which occasioned much noise and confusion among the people. But, two or three days before, a man had filled the vault with hogsheads of tobacco. So that the floor, after sinking a foot or two, rested upon them, and I went on without interruption.

Fri. 28.—I met with a fresh proof, that "whatsoever ye ask, believing, ye shall receive." A middle-aged woman desired me to return thanks for her to God, who, as many witnesses then present testified, was a day or two before really distracted, and as such tied down in her bed. But upon prayer made for her, she was instantly relieved, and restored to a sound mind.

Mon. Oct. 1.—I rode to Oxford ; and found a few who had not yet forsaken the assembling themselves together.

Wed. 3.—I had a little leisure to take a view of the shattered condition of things here. The poor prisoners, both in the castle and in the city prison, had now none that cared for their souls ; none to instruct, advise, comfort, and build them up in the knowledge and love of the Lord Jesus. None was left to visit the workhouses, where, also, we used to meet with the most moving objects of compassion. Our little school, where about twenty poor children at a time had been taught for many years, was on the point of being broke up ; there being none now, either to support or to attend it : and most of those in the town, who were once knit together, and strengthened one another's hands in God, were torn asunder and scattered abroad. "It is time for Thee, Lord, to lay to Thy hand !"

At eleven, a little company of us met to entreat God for "the remnant that" was "left." He immediately gave us a token for good. One who had been long in the gall of bitterness, full of wrath, strife, and envy, particularly against one whom she had once tenderly loved, rose up and showed the change God had wrought in her soul, by falling upon her neck, and, with many tears, kissing her. The same spirit we found reviving in others also. In the evening I reached Gloucester.

Sun. 7.—A few, I trust, out of two or three thousand, were awakened by the explanation of those words : "Ye have not received the spirit of bondage again to fear ; but ye have received the spirit of adoption, whereby we cry, Abba, Father !" About eleven I preached at Runwick, seven miles from Gloucester. The church was much crowded, though a thousand or upwards stayed in the churchyard. In the afternoon I explained further the same words : "What must I do to be saved ?"

Between five and six I called on all who were present (about three thousand) at Stanley, on a little green, near the town, to accept of Christ. I was strengthened to speak as I never did before ; and continued speaking near two hours : the darkness of the night, and a little lightning, not lessening the number, but increasing the seriousness, of the hearers. I concluded the day by expounding part of our Lord's Sermon on the Mount, to a small, serious company at Ebly.

Mon. 8.—About eight I reached Hampton Common, nine or ten miles from Gloucester. There were, it was computed, five or six thousand persons. I could gladly have stayed longer with this loving people; but I was now straitened for time. After sermon, I therefore hastened away, and in the evening came to Bristol.

Tues. 9.—My brother and I rode to Bradford. Finding there had been a general misrepresentation of his last sermon, as if he had asserted reprobation therein, whereby many were greatly offended; he was constrained to explain himself on that head, and to show, in plain and strong words, that God "willeth all men to be saved."

At our return in the evening, not being permitted to meet at Weaver's Hall, we met in a large room on Temple Backs; where, having gone through the Sermon on the Mount, and the Epistles of St John, I began that of St James.

Thur. 11.—We were comforted by the coming in of one who was a notorious drunkard and common swearer. But he is washed, and old things are passed away. In the evening our Lord rose on many who were wounded, "with healing in His wings"; and others who till then were careless and at ease, felt the two-edged sword that cometh out of His mouth.

Fri. 12.—We had fresh occasion to observe the darkness which was fallen on many who lately rejoiced in God. But He did not long hide His face from them. On *Wednesday* the spirit of many revived: on *Thursday* evening many more found Him in whom they had believed, to be "a present help in time of trouble." And never do I remember the power of God to have been more eminently present than this morning; when a cloud of witnesses declared His "breaking the gates of brass, and smiting the bars of iron in sunder."

Yet I could not but be under some concern, with regard to one or two persons, who were tormented in an unaccountable manner; and seemed to be indeed lunatic, as well as "sore vexed." But while I was musing, what would be the issue of these things, the answer I received from the Word of God was, "Glory to God in the highest, and on earth peace, goodwill towards men."

We had a refreshing meeting at one with many of our society; who fail not to observe, as health permits, the weekly fast of our Church, and will do so, by God's help, as long as they call themselves members of it: and would to God, all who contend for the rites and ceremonies of the Church, would first show their own regard for her discipline, in this more important branch of it!

At four I preached near the Fishponds (at the desire of one who had long laboured under the apprehension of it), on the blasphemy against the Holy Ghost ; that is, according to the plain scriptural account, the openly and maliciously asserting, that the miracles of Christ were wrought by the power of the devil.

Sat. 13.—I was with one who, being in deep anguish of spirit, had been the day before to ask a clergyman's advice. He told her, her head was out of order, and she must go and take physic. In the evening we called upon God for medicine, to heal those that were "broken in heart." And five who had long been in the shadow of death, knew they were "passed from death unto life."

The sharp frost in the morning, *Sunday*, 14, did not prevent about fifteen hundred from being at Hannam.

Mon. 15.—Upon a pressing invitation, some time since received, I set out for Wales. About four in the afternoon I preached on a little green, at the foot of the Devauden (a high hill, two or three miles beyond Chepstow), to three or four hundred plain people. After sermon, one who I trust is an old disciple of Christ, willingly received us into his house : whither many following, I showed them their need of a Saviour. In the morning I described more fully the way to salvation ; and then, taking leave of my friendly host, before two came to Abergavenny.

I felt in myself a strong aversion to preaching here. However, I went to Mr W—— (the person in whose ground Mr Whitefield preached), to desire the use of it. He said, with all his heart,—if the minister was not willing to let me have the use of the church : after whose refusal (for I wrote a line to him immediately), he invited me to his house. About a thousand people stood patiently (though the frost was sharp, it being after sunset), while, from Acts xxviii. 22, I simply described the plain, old religion of the Church of England, which is now almost everywhere spoken against, under the new name of Methodism.

Wed. 17.—The frost was sharper than before. However, five or six hundred people stayed, while I explained the nature of that salvation which is through faith, yea, faith alone ; and the nature of that living faith, through which cometh this salvation. About noon I came to Usk, where I preached to a small company of poor people. One grey-headed man wept and trembled exceedingly, and another who was there, I have since heard, as well as two or three who were at the Devauden, are gone quite distracted ; that is, they mourn and refuse to be comforted, till they "have redemption through His blood."

When I came to Pontypool in the afternoon, being unable

to procure any more convenient place, I stood in the street, and cried aloud to five or six hundred attentive hearers, to "believe in the Lord Jesus," that they might "be saved." In the evening I showed His willingness to save all who desire to come unto God through Him. Many were melted into tears.

When we were at the Devauden on Monday, a poor woman, who lived six miles off, came thither in great heaviness. She was deeply convinced of sin, and weary of it; but found no way to escape from it. She walked from thence to Abergavenny on Tuesday, and on Wednesday from Abergavenny to Usk. Thence, in the afternoon, she came to Pontypool; where between twelve and one in the morning, after a sharp contest in her soul, our Lord got unto Himself the victory; and the love of God was shed abroad in her heart, knowing that her sins were forgiven her. She went on her way rejoicing to Cardiff; whither I came in the afternoon. And about five (the minister not being willing I should preach in the church on a week-day), I preached in the Shire Hall. Several were there who laboured much to make a disturbance. But our Lord suffered them not. At seven I explained to a much more numerous audience the blessedness of mourning, and poverty of spirit.

Fri. 19.—I preached in the morning at Newport, to the most insensible, ill-behaved people I have ever seen in Wales. One ancient man, during a great part of the sermon, cursed and swore almost incessantly; and, towards the conclusion, took up a great stone, which he many times attempted to throw. But that he could not do. Such the champions, such the arms against field-preaching!

At four I preached at the Shire Hall of Cardiff again, where many gentry, I found, were present. Such freedom of speech I have seldom had, as was given me in explaining those words: "The kingdom of God is not meat and drink, but righteousness, and peace, and joy in the Holy Ghost." At six almost the whole town (I was informed) came together; to whom I explained the six last Beatitudes: but my heart was so enlarged, I knew not how to give over, so that we continued three hours.

Sat. 20.—I returned to Bristol. I have seen no part of England so pleasant for sixty or seventy miles together, as those parts of Wales I have been in. And most of the inhabitants are indeed ripe for the gospel. I mean (if the expression appear strange) they are earnestly desirous of being instructed in it; and as utterly ignorant of it they are, as any Creek or Cherikee Indians. I do not mean they are ignorant of the name of Christ. Many of them can say both the Lord's Prayer and the Belief; nay, and some, all the Catechism: but take them out of the road of what they have learned by rote, and they know no more (nine in ten of those with whom I conversed) either of gospel salvation, or of that faith whereby alone we can be saved, than Chicali or Tomo Chachi. Now, what spirit is he of, who had rather these poor creatures should perish for lack of knowledge, than that they should be saved, even by the exhortations of Howel Harris, or an itinerant preacher?

Tues. 23.—In riding to Bradford, I read over Mr Law's book on the new birth. Philosophical, speculative, precarious: Behmenish, void, and vain! At eleven I preached at Bearfield to about three thousand, on the spirit of nature, of bondage, and of adoption.

Returning in the evening, I was exceedingly pressed to go back to a young woman in Kingswood. (The fact I nakedly relate, and leave every man to his own judgment of it.) I went. She was nineteen or twenty years old; but, it seems, could not write or read. I found her on the bed, two or three persons holding her. It was a terrible sight. Anguish, horror, and despair, above all description, appeared in her pale face. The thousand distortions of her whole body showed how the dogs of hell were gnawing her heart. The shrieks intermixed were scarce to be endured. But her stony eyes could not weep. She screamed out, as soon as words could find their way, "I am damned, damned; lost for ever! Six days ago you might have helped me. But it is past. I am the devil's now. I have given myself to him. His I am. Him I must serve. With him I must go to hell. I will be his. I will serve him. I will go with him to hell. I cannot be saved. I will not be saved. I must, I will, I will be damned!" She then began praying to the devil. We began—

"Arm of the Lord, awake, awake!"

She immediately sunk down as asleep; but, as soon as we left off, broke out again, with inexpressible vehemence: "Stony hearts, break! I am a warning to you. Break, break, poor stony hearts! Will you not break? What can be done more for stony hearts? I am damned, that you may be saved. Now break, now break, poor stony hearts! You need not be damned, though I must." She then fixed her eyes on the corner of the ceiling, and said, "There he is: ay, there he is! Come, good devil, come! Take me away. You said, you would dash my brains out: come, do it quickly. I am yours. I will be yours.

Come just now. Take me away." We interrupted her by calling again upon God: on which she sunk down as before; and another young woman began to roar out as loud as she had done. My brother now came in, it being about nine o'clock. We continued in prayer till past eleven; when God in a moment spoke peace into the soul, first of the first tormented, and then of the other. And they both joined in singing praise to Him who had "stilled the enemy and the avenger."

Wed. 24.—I preached at Baptist Mills, on those words of St Paul; speaking in the person of one "under the law" (that is, still "carnal, and sold under sin," though groaning for deliverance), "I know that in me dwelleth no good thing." A poor woman told me afterwards, "I does hope as my husband won't hinder me any more. For I minded he did shiver every bone of him, and the tears ran down his cheeks like the rain." I warned our little society in the evening, to beware of levity, slackness in good works, and despising little things; which had caused many to fall again into bondage.

Sat. 27.—I was sent for to Kingswood again, to one of those who had been so ill before. A violent rain began just as I set out, so that I was thoroughly wet in a few minutes. Just at that time, the woman (then three miles off) cried out, "Yonder comes Wesley, galloping as fast as he can." When I was come, I was quite cold and dead, and fitter for sleep than prayer. She burst out into a horrid laughter, and said, "No power, no power; no faith, no faith. She is mine; her soul is mine. I have her, and will not let her go."

We begged of God to increase our faith. Meanwhile her pangs increased more and more; so that one would have imagined, by the violence of the throes, her body must have been shattered to pieces. One who was clearly convinced this was no natural disorder, said, "I think Satan is let loose. I fear he will not stop here." And added, "I command thee, in the name of the Lord Jesus, to tell if thou hast commission to torment any other soul." It was immediately answered, "I have. L——y C——r, and S——h J——s." (Two who lived at some distance, and were then in perfect health.)

We betook ourselves to prayer again; and ceased not, till she began, about six o'clock, with a clear voice, and composed, cheerful look—

"Praise God, from whom all blessings flow.

Sun. 28.—I preached once more at Bradford, at one in the afternoon. The violent rains did not hinder more, I believe, than ten thousand, from earnestly attending to what I spoke on those solemn words, "I take you to record this day, that I am pure from the blood of all men. For I have not shunned to declare unto you all the counsel of God."

Returning in the evening, I called at Mrs. J——'s, in Kingswood. S——h J——s and L——y C——r were there. It was scarce a quarter of an hour, before L——y C——r fell into a strange agony; and presently after, S——h J——s. The violent convulsions all over their bodies were such as words cannot describe. Their cries and groans were too horrid to be borne; till one of them, in a tone not to be expressed, said, "Where is your faith now? Come, go to prayers. I will pray with you. 'Our Father, which art in heaven.'" We took the advice, from whomsoever it came, and poured out our souls before God, till L——y C——r's agonies so increased, that it seemed she was in the pangs of death. But in a moment God spoke: she knew His voice; and both her body and soul were healed.

We continued in prayer till near one, when S—— J——'s voice was also changed, and she began strongly to call upon God. This she did for the greatest part of the night. In the morning we renewed our prayers, while she was crying continually, "I burn! I burn! Oh, what shall I do? I have a fire within me. I cannot bear it. Lord Jesus! Help!"

Amen, Lord Jesus! when Thy time is come.

CHAPTER V

A TIME OF CONFLICT

FROM NOVEMBER 1, 1739, TO SEPTEMBER 1, 1741

Thursday, November 1, 1739.—I left Bristol, and, on Saturday, came to London.

Sun. 4.—Our society met at seven in the morning, and continued silent till eight. One then spoke of looking unto Jesus, and exhorted us all to lie still in His hand.

In the evening I met the women of our society at Fetter Lane; where some of our brethren strongly intimated that none of them had any true faith.

Wed. 7.—At eight our society met at Fetter Lane. We sat an hour without speaking. The rest of the time was spent in dispute.

Fri. 9.—I showed how we are to examine ourselves, whether we be in the faith; and afterwards recommended to all, though especially to them that believed, true stillness, that is, a patient waiting upon God.

All this week I endeavoured also by private conversation to "comfort the feeble-minded," and to bring back "the lame."

Mon. 12.—I left London, and in the evening expounded, at Wycombe, the story of the Pharisee and Publican. The next morning a young gentleman overtook me on the road, and, after a while, asked me if I had seen Whitefield's Journals. I told him I had. "And what do you think of them?" said he. "Don't you think they are d—n'd cant, enthusiasm from end to end? I think so." I asked him, "Why do you think so? Did you ever feel the love of God in your heart? If not, how should you tell what to make of it?"

At four in the afternoon I came to Oxford.

Thur. 15.—My brother and I set out for Tiverton. About eleven I preached at Burford. On *Saturday* evening I explained, at Bristol, the nature and extent of Christian perfection.

Mon. 19.—I earnestly exhorted those who had believed, to beware of two opposite extremes,—the one, the thinking while they were in light and joy, that the work was ended, when it was but just begun; the other, the thinking when they were in heaviness, that it was not begun, because they found it was not ended.

Tues. 20.—We set out, and on *Wednesday,* 21, in the afternoon, came to Tiverton. My poor sister was sorrowing almost as one without hope. Yet we could not but rejoice at hearing, from one who had attended my brother in all his weakness, that, several days before he went hence, God had given him a calm and full assurance of his interest in Christ.

Sat. 24.—We accepted an invitation to Exeter, from one who came thence to comfort my sister in her affliction. And on *Sunday,* 25 (Mr D. having desired the pulpit, which was readily granted both for the morning and afternoon), I preached at St Mary's. Dr W—— told me after the sermon, " Sir, you must not preach in the afternoon. Not," said he, " that you preach any false doctrine. I allow, all that you have said is true. And it is the doctrine of the Church of England. But it is not guarded. It is dangerous. It may lead people into enthusiasm or despair."

Tues. 27.—I writ Mr D. (according to his request) a short account of what had been done in Kingswood :—

" The scene is already changed. Kingswood does not now, as a year ago, resound with cursing and blasphemy. It is no more filled with drunkenness and uncleanness, and the idle diversions that naturally lead thereto. It is no longer full of wars and fightings, of clamour and bitterness, of wrath and envyings. Peace and love are there.

" That their children too might know the things which make for their peace, it was some time since proposed to build a house in Kingswood ; in June last the foundation was laid. The ground made choice of was in the middle of the wood, between the London and Bath roads, not far from that called Two-mile-hill, about three measured miles from Bristol.

" Here a large room was begun for the school, having four small rooms at either end for the schoolmasters (and, perhaps, if it should please God, some poor children) to lodge in. Two persons are ready to teach, so soon as the house is fit to receive them.

" It is true, although the masters require no pay, yet this undertaking is attended with great expense. But let Him that ' feedeth the young ravens' see to that."

Wed. 28.—We left Tiverton, and the next day reached Bristol.

Tues. Dec. 4.—I was violently attacked by some who were exceeding angry at those who cried out so ; " being sure," they said, " it was all a cheat, and that any one might help crying out, if he would." J. B. was one of those who were sure of this. About eight the next morning, while he was alone in his chamber, at private prayer, so horrible a dread overwhelmed him, that he began crying out with all his might. All the family was alarmed. Several of them came running up into his chamber; but he cried out so much the more, till his breath was utterly spent. God then rebuked the adversary; and he is now less wise in his own conceit.

Thur. 6.—I left Bristol, and (after preaching at Malmesbury and Burford in the way) on *Saturday*, 8, came into my old room at Oxford, from which I went to Georgia. Here, musing on the things that were past, and reflecting, how many that came after me were preferred before me, I opened my Testament on those words, "What shall we say then? That the Gentiles, which followed not after righteousness, have attained to righteousness. But Israel, which followed after the law of righteousness, hath not attained to the law of righteousness. Wherefore? Because they sought it not by faith, but as it were by the works of the law."

Tues. 11.—I visited Mrs Platt; one who, having long sought death in the error of her life, was brought back to the great Shepherd of her soul, the first time my brother preached faith in Oxford.

During my short stay here, I received several unpleasing accounts of the state of things in London; a part of which I have subjoined:—

"MANY of our sisters are shaken: J——y C—— says that she never had faith. Betty and Esther H—— are grievously torn by reasonings: the former, I am told, is going to Germany. —On Wednesday night there are but few come to Fetter Lane till near nine o'clock. And then, after the names are called over, they presently depart. It appears plain, our brethren here have neither wisdom enough to guide, nor prudence enough to let it alone."

In another letter which I received a few days after this, were these words:—

"*Dec.* 14, 1739.

"THIS day I was told, by one that does not belong to the bands, that the society would be divided.—I believe brother Hutton, Clark, Edmonds, and Bray are determined to go on, according to Mr Molther's directions, and to raise a church, as they term it; and I suppose above half our brethren are on their side.

"I believe things would be much better if you would come to town."

Wed. 19.—I accordingly came to London, though with a heavy heart. Here I found every day the dreadful effects of our brethren's reasoning and disputing with each other. Scarce one in ten retained his first love; and most of the rest were in the utmost confusion, biting and devouring one another.

Sun. 30.—One came to me, by whom I used to profit much. But her conversation was now too high for me: it was far above, out of my sight. My soul is sick of this sublime divinity. Let me think and speak as a little child! Let my religion be plain, artless, simple! Meekness, temperance, patience, faith, and love, be these my highest gifts: and let the highest words wherein I teach them, be those I learn from the Book of God!

Thur. Jan. 3, 1740.—I left London, and the next evening came to Oxford: where I spent the two following days, in looking over the letters which I had received for the sixteen or eighteen years last past. How few traces of inward religion are here! I found but one among all my correspondents who declared (what I well remember, at that time I knew not how to understand), that God had "shed abroad His love in his heart," and given him the "peace that passeth all understanding." But, who believed his report? Should I conceal a sad truth, or declare it for the profit of others? He was expelled out of his society, as a madman; and, being disowned by his friends, and despised and forsaken of all men, lived obscure and unknown for a few months, and then went to Him whom his soul loved.

Mon. 7.—I left Oxford. On *Wednesday*, 9, I once more described the "exceeding great and precious promises" at Bristol.

Mon. 14.—I began expounding the Scriptures in order, at the new room, at six in the morning; by which means many more attend the College prayers (which immediately follow) than ever before. In the afternoon I preached owning, f miles from Bristol, on, "God hath given unto us eternal an his life is in His Son"; and on *Tuesday*, 15, at Sison, five mil from Bristol, on, "the blood" which "cleanseth us from all si " After preaching I visited a young man, dangerously ill, wh a day or two after cried out aloud, "Lord Jesus, Thou knowest hat I love Thee! and I have Thee, and will never let Thee go ; and died immediately.

Mon. 21.—I preached at Hannam, four miles from Bristol. In the evening I made a collection in our congregation for the relief of the poor, without Lawford's gate; who, having no work (because of the severe frost), and no assistance from the parish wherein they lived, were reduced to the last extremity.

I made another collection on *Thursday*, and a third on *Sunday*; by which we were enabled to feed a hundred, sometimes a hundred and fifty, a day, of those whom we found to need it most.

Sat. 26.—I was strongly convinced, that if we asked of God, He would give light to all those that were in darkness. About noon we had a proof of it: one that was weary and heavy-laden, upon prayer made for her, soon finding rest to her soul. In the afternoon we had a second proof,—another mourner being speedily comforted.

Thur. 31.—I went to one in Kingswood who was dangerously ill; as was supposed, past recovery. But she was strong in the Lord, longing to be dissolved and to be with Christ.

I had now determined, if it should please God, to spend some time in Bristol. But quite contrary to my expectation, I was called away, in a manner I could not resist. A young man, who had no thoughts of religion, had come to Bristol a few months before. One of his acquaintance brought him to me; he approved of what he heard, and for a while behaved well; but soon after, his seriousness wore off; he returned to London, and fell in with his old acquaintance: by some of these he was induced to commit a robbery on the highway; for which he was apprehended, tried, and condemned. He had now a strong desire to speak with me; and some of his words (in a letter to his friend) were "I adjure him, by the living God, that he come and see me before I go hence."

Fri. Feb. 1.—I set out.

Wed. 6.—I went to the poor young man who lay under sentence of death. Of a truth God has begun a good work in his soul

I think it was the next time I was there, that the Ordinary of Newgate came to me, and with much vehemence told me, he was sorry I should turn Dissenter from the Church of England. I told him, if it was so, I did not know it.

Tues. 12.—The young man who was to die the next day, gave me a paper, part of which was as follows:—

"As I am to answer to the God of justice and truth, before whom I am to appear naked to-morrow,

"I came to Bristol, with a design to go abroad, either as a surgeon, or in any other capacity that was suiting. It was there that I unfortunately saw Mr Ramsey. He told me, after one or two interviews, that he was in the service of Mr John Wesley; and that he would introduce me to him, which he did. I cannot but say, I was always fond of the doctrine that I heard from him; however, unhappily, I consented with Mr Ramsey, and I believe between us we might take more than thirty pounds out of the money collected for building the school in Kingswood.

"I acknowledge the justice of God in overtaking me for my sacrilege, in taking that money which was devoted to God. But He, I trust, has forgiven me this and all my sins, washing them away in the blood of the Lamb.

"GWILLAM SNOWDE.

"*Feb.* 12, 1740."

I knew not in the morning whether to rejoice or grieve, when they informed me he was reprieved for six weeks; and afterwards, that he was ordered for transportation.

Mon. Mar. 3.—Rode by Windsor to Reading, where I had left two or three full of peace and love. I now found some from London had been here, grievously troubling these souls also.

After confirming their souls we left Reading, and on *Wednesday*, 5, came to Bristol. It was easy to observe here, in how different a manner God works now, from what He did last spring. He then poured along like a rapid flood, overwhelming all before Him. Whereas now,

> "He deigns His influence to infuse.
> Secret, refreshing as the silent dews."

Wed. 12.—I found a little time to spend with the soldier in Bridewell, who was under sentence of death. This I continued to do once a day; whereby there was also an opportunity of declaring the gospel of peace to several desolate ones that were confined in the same place.

Tues. 18.—In the evening, just after I had explained, as they came in course, those comfortable words of God to St Paul, "Be not afraid; but speak, and hold not thy peace: for I am with thee, and no man shall set on thee to hurt thee; for I have much people in this city,"—a person spoke aloud in the middle of the room, "Sir, I am come to give you notice, that, at the next Quarter Sessions, you will be prosecuted for holding a seditious conventicle."

Tues. 25.—The morning exposition began at five, as I hope it will always for the time to come.

Sat. 29.—I think it was about this time that the soldier was executed. For some time I had visited him every day. But when the love of God was shed abroad in his heart, I told him, "Do not expect to see me any more. He who has now begun a good work in your soul, will, I doubt not, preserve you to the end.

But I believe Satan will separate us for a season." Accordingly, the next day, I was informed that the commanding officer had given strict orders, neither Mr Wesley, nor any of his people, should be admitted; for they were all atheists. But did that man die like an atheist? Let my last end be like his!

Tues. April 1.—While I was expounding the former part of the twenty-third chapter of the Acts (how wonderfully suited to the occasion! though not by my choice), the floods began to lift up their voice. Some or other of the children of Belial had laboured to disturb us several nights before: but now it seemed as if all the host of the aliens were come together with one consent. Not only the court and the alleys, but all the street, upwards and downwards, was filled with people, shouting, cursing and swearing, and ready to swallow the ground with fierceness and rage. The mayor sent order, that they should disperse. But they set him at nought. The chief constable came next in person, who was, till then, sufficiently prejudiced against us. But they insulted him also in so gross a manner, as I believe fully opened his eyes. At length the mayor sent several of his officers, who took the ringleaders into custody, and did not go till all the rest were dispersed. Surely he hath been to us "the minister of God for good."

Wed. 2.—The rioters were brought up to the Court, the Quarter Sessions being held that day. They began to excuse themselves by saying many things of me. But the mayor cut them all short, saying, "What Mr Wesley is, is nothing to you. I will keep the peace: I will have no rioting in this city."

Calling at Newgate in the afternoon, I was informed, that the poor wretches under sentence of death were earnestly desirous to speak with me; but that it could not be; Alderman Beecher having just then sent an express order that they should not. I cite Alderman Beecher to answer for these souls at the judgment-seat of Christ.

Thur. 3.—I went into the room, weak and faint. The Scripture that came in course was, "After the way which they call heresy, so worship I the God of my fathers." I know not whether God hath been so with us from the beginning hitherto: He proclaimed, as it were, a general deliverance to the captives. The chains fell off: they arose and followed Him. The cries of desire, joy, and love were on every side. Fear, sorrow, and doubt fled away.

On Good Friday I was much comforted by Mr. T——'s sermon at All Saint's, which was according to the truth of the gospel; as well as by the affectionate seriousness wherewith he delivered the holy bread to a very large congregation.

Mon. 7.—At the pressing instance of Howel Harris, I again set out for Wales.

Wed. 9.—After reading prayers in Lanhithel church, I preached on those words: "I will heal their backsliding, I will love them freely." In the afternoon Howel Harris told me how earnestly many had laboured to prejudice him against me; especially those who had gleaned up all the idle stories at Bristol, and retailed them in their own country.

Sat. 12.—I came to Bristol, and heard the melancholy news, that ——, one of the chief of those who came to make the disturbance on the 1st instant, had hanged himself. He was cut down, it seems, alive; but died in less than an hour. A second of them had been for some days in strong pain; and had many times sent to desire our prayers. A third came to me himself, and confessed, he was hired that night, and made drunk on purpose; but when he came to the door, he knew not what was the matter, he could not stir, nor open his mouth.

Mon. 14.—I was explaining the "liberty" we have "to enter into the holiest by the blood of Jesus," when one cried out, as in an agony, "Thou art a hypocrite, a devil, an enemy to the Church." I did not perceive that any were hurt thereby; but rather strengthened, by having such an opportunity of confirming their love toward him, and returning good for evil.

Tues. 15.—I received the following note :—

"SIR,—This is to let you understand, that the man which made the noise last night is named John Beon. He now goes by the name of John Darsy. He is a Romish priest. We have people enough here in Bristol that know him."

Sat. 19.—I received a letter from Mr Simpson, and another from Mr William Oxlee, informing me that our poor brethren in Fetter Lane were again in great confusion; and earnestly desiring that, if it were possible, I would come to London without delay.

Mon. 21.—I set out, and the next evening reached London. *Wednesday*, 23, I went to Mr Simpson. He told me, all the confusion was owing to my brother, who would preach up the ordinances: "Whereas believers," said he, "are not subject to ordinances; and unbelievers have nothing to do with them: they ought to be still; otherwise, they will be unbelievers all the days of their life"

After a fruitless dispute of about two hours, I returned home with a heavy heart. Mr Molther was taken ill this day. I believe it was the hand of God that was upon him. In the evening our society met; but cold, weary, heartless, dead. I found nothing of brotherly love among them now; but a harsh, dry, heavy, stupid spirit. For two hours they looked one at another, when they looked up at all, as if one half of them was afraid of the other.

Fri. May 2.—I left London; and lying at Hungerford that night, the next evening came to Bristol.

Fri. 9.—I was a little surprised at some, who were buffeted of Satan in an unusual manner, by such a spirit of laughter as they could in no wise resist, though it was pain and grief unto them. I could scarce have believed the account they gave me, had I not known the same thing ten or eleven years ago. Part of Sunday my brother and I then used to spend in walking in the meadows and singing psalms. But one day, just as we were beginning to sing, he burst out into a loud laughter. I asked him, if he was distracted; and began to be very angry, and presently after to laugh as loud as he. Nor could we possibly refrain, though we were ready to tear ourselves in pieces, but we were forced to go home without singing another line.

Sat. 17.—I found more and more undeniable proofs, that the Christian state is a continual warfare; and that we have need every moment to "watch and pray, lest we enter into temptation." Outward trials indeed were now removed, and peace was in all our borders. But so much the more did inward trials abound; and "if one member suffered, all the members suffered with it." So strange a sympathy did I never observe before.

Wed. 21.—In the evening such a spirit of laughter was among us, that many were much offended. But the attention of all was fixed on poor L——a S——, whom we all knew to be no dissembler. One so violently and variously torn of the evil one did I never see before. At last she faintly called on Christ to help her. And the violence of her pangs ceased.

Most of our brethren and sisters were now fully convinced, that those who were under this strange temptation could not help it. Only E——th B—— and Anne H——n were of another mind: being still sure, any one might help laughing if she would. This they declared to many on *Thursday*; but on *Friday*, 23, God suffered Satan to teach them better. Both of them were suddenly seized in the same manner as the rest, and laughed whether they would or no, almost without ceasing. Thus they continued for two days, a spectacle to all; and were then, upon prayer made for them, delivered in a moment.

Mon. June 2.—I left Bristol, and rode by Avon and Malmsbury (where I preached in the evening) to Oxford. Two or three even here had not yet been persuaded to cast away their confidence : one of whom was still full of her first love, which she had received at the Lord's Table.

Thurs. 5.—I came to London ; where, finding a general temptation prevail, of leaving off good works, in order to an increase of faith, I began on *Friday*, 6, to expound the Epistle of St James, the great antidote against this poison.

Wed. 11.—In the evening I went to Fetter Lane, and plainly told our poor, confused, shattered society, wherein they had erred from the faith It was as I feared : they could not receive my saying. However, I am clear from the blood of these men.

Wed. 18.—My brother set out for Bristol. At six I preached in Marylebone Fields. All were quiet, and the far greater part of the hearers seemed deeply attentive. Thence I went to our own society of Fetter Lane : before whom Mr Ingham (being to leave London on the morrow) bore a noble testimony for the ordinances of God, and the reality of weak faith.

Wed. July 2.—I went to the society; but I found their hearts were quite estranged. *Tuesday*, 15. We had yet another conference at large, but in vain ; for all continued in their own opinions.

One asked, whether they would suffer Mr Wesley to preach at Fetter Lane. After a short debate, it was answered, " No : this place is taken for the Germans."

Fri. 18.—A few of us joined with my mother in the great sacrifice of thanksgiving ; and then consulted how to proceed with regard to our poor brethren of Fetter Lane : we all saw the thing was now come to a crisis, and were therefore unanimously agreed what to do.

Sun. 20.—At Mr Seward's earnest request, I preached once more in Moorfields, on " the work of faith," and the " patience of hope," and " the labour of love."

In the evening I went with Mr Seward to the love-feast in Fetter Lane ; at the conclusion of which, having said nothing till then, I read a paper, the substance whereof was as follows :—

" About nine months ago certain of you began to speak contrary to the doctrine we had till then received. The sum of what you asserted is this—

" 1. That there is no such thing as *weak faith* : that there is no justifying faith where there is ever any doubt or fear, or where there is not, in the full sense, a new, a clean heart.

" 2. That a man ought not to use those ordinances of God

which our Church terms 'means of grace,' before he has such a faith as excludes all doubt and fear, and implies a new, a clean heart.

"You have often affirmed, that to search the Scriptures, to pray, or to communicate, before we have this faith, is to seek salvation by works; and that till these works are laid aside, no man can receive faith.

"I believe these assertions to be flatly contrary to the word of God. I have warned you hereof again and again, and besought you to turn back to the 'law and the testimony.' I have borne with you long, hoping you would turn. But as I find you more and more confirmed in the error of your ways, nothing now remains, but that I should give you up to God. You that are of the same judgment, follow me."

I then, without saying anything more, withdrew, as did eighteen or nineteen of the society.

Wed. 23.—Our little company met at the Foundery, instead of Fetter Lane. About twenty-five of our brethren God hath given us already, all of whom think and speak the same thing; seven or eight and forty likewise, of the fifty women that were in band, desired to cast in their lot with us.

Fri. Aug. 1.—I described that "rest" which "remaineth for the people of God." *Sunday*, 3. At St. Luke's, our parish church, was such a sight as, I believe, was never seen there before: several hundred communicants, from whose very faces one might judge, that they indeed sought Him that was crucified.

Mon. 4.—In the evening many were gathered together at Long Lane, on purpose to make a disturbance; having procured a woman to begin, well known in those parts as neither fearing God nor regarding man. The instant she broke out I turned full upon her, and declared the love our Lord had for her soul. We then prayed that He would confirm the word of His grace. She was struck to the heart; and shame covered her face. From her I turned to the rest, who melted away like water, and were as men that had no strength.

Mon. 11.—Forty or fifty of those who were seeking salvation desired leave to spend the night together, at the society-room, in prayer and giving thanks. Before ten I left them, and lay down. But I could have no quiet rest, being quite uneasy in my sleep, as I found others were too, that were asleep in other parts of the house. Between two and three in the morning I was waked, and desired to come downstairs. I immediately heard such a confused noise, as if a number of men were all putting to the sword. It increased when I came into the room and began to pray. One whom I particularly observed to be roaring aloud for pain was J—— W——, who had been always, till then, very sure that "none cried out but hypocrites": so had Mrs S—ms also. But she too now cried to God with a loud and bitter cry. It was not long before God heard from His holy place. He spake, and all our souls were comforted. He bruised Satan under our feet; and sorrow and sighing fled away.

Tues. 19.—I was desired to go and pray with one who had sent for me several times before, lying in the New Prison, under sentence of death, which was to be executed in a few days. I went; but the gaoler said, Mr Wilson, the curate of the parish, had ordered I should not see him.

Wed. 20.—I offered remission of sins to a small serious congregation near Deptford. Toward the end, a company of persons came in, dressed in habits fit for their work, and laboured greatly either to provoke or divert the attention of the hearers. But no man answering them a word, they were soon weary, and went away.

Sat. 23.—A gentlewoman (one Mrs C——) desired to speak with me, and related a strange story:—On Saturday, the 16th instant (as she informed me), one Mrs G., of Northampton, deeply convinced of sin, and therefore an abomination to her husband, was by him put into Bedlam. On Tuesday she slipped out of the gate with some other company; and after awhile, not knowing whither to go, sat down at Mrs C.'s door. Mrs C., knowing nothing of her, advised her the next day to go to Bedlam again; and went with her, where she was then chained down, and treated in the usual manner.—This is the justice of men! A poor highwayman is hanged; and Mr G. esteemed a very honest man!

Thur. 28.—I desired one who had seen affliction herself, to go and visit Mrs. G. in Bedlam; where it pleased God greatly to knit their hearts together, and with His comforts to refresh their souls.

Disputes being now at an end, and all things quiet and calm, on *Monday*, September 1, I left London, and the next evening found my brother at Bristol, swiftly recovering from his fever.

Thur. 4.—A remarkable cause was tried: some time since, several men made a great disturbance during the evening sermon here, behaving rudely to the women, and striking the men, who spake not to them. A constable standing by, pulled out his staff, and commanded them to keep the peace. Upon this one of them swore he would be revenged; and going immediately to a justice, made oath, that he (the constable) had picked his pocket, who was accordingly bound over to the next sessions. At these not only the same man, but two of his companions, swore the same thing. But there being eighteen or twenty witnesses on the other side, the jury easily saw through the whole proceeding, and without going out at all, or any demur, brought in the prisoner "not guilty."

Sat. 6.—I met the bands in Kingswood, and warned them, with all authority, to beware of being wise above that is written, and to desire to know nothing but Christ crucified.

Mon. 8.—We set out early in the morning, and the next evening came to London. *Wednesday,* 10. I visited one that was in violent pain, and consumed away with pining sickness; but in "everything giving thanks," and greatly "rejoicing in hope of the glory of God." From her we went to another, dangerously ill of the small-pox, but desiring neither life nor ease, but only the holy will of God.

Thur. 11.—I visited a poor woman, who, lying ill between her two sick children, without either physic, or food convenient for her, was mightily praising God her Saviour, and testifying, as often as she could speak, her desire to be dissolved and to be with Christ.

Sun. 14.—As I returned home in the evening, I had no sooner stepped out of the coach, than the mob, who were gathered in great numbers about my door, quite closed me in. I rejoiced and blessed God, knowing this was the time I had long been looking for; and immediately spake to those that were next me, of "righteousness, and judgment to come." At first not many heard, the noise round about us being exceeding great. But the silence spread farther and farther, till I had a quiet, attentive congregation; and when I left them, they all showed much love, and dismissed me with many blessings.

Tues. 16.—Many more, who came in among us as lions, in a short space became as lambs; the tears trickling apace down their cheeks, who at first most loudly contradicted and blasphemed.

Thur. 18.—The prince of the air made another attempt in defence of his tottering kingdom. A great number of men having got into the middle of the Foundery began to speak big, swelling words; so that my voice could hardly be heard, while I was reading the eleventh chapter of the Acts. But immediately after, the hammer of the Word brake the rocks in pieces: all quietly heard the glad tidings of salvation; and some, I trust, not in vain.

Mon. 22.—Wanting a little time for retirement, which it

was almost impossible for me to have in London, I went to Mr Piers's, at Bexley.

Sun. 28.—In the afternoon I described to a numerous congregation at Kennington, the life of God in the soul. One person who stood on the mount made a little noise at the first; but a gentleman, whom I knew not, walked up to him, and, without saying one word, mildly took him by the hand and led him down. From that time he was quiet till he went away.

When I came home, I found an innumerable mob round the door, who opened all their throats the moment they saw me. I desired my friends to go into the house; and then walking into the midst of the people, proclaimed "the name of the Lord, gracious and merciful, and repenting Him of the evil." They stood staring one at another. I told them, they could not flee from the face of this great God: and therefore besought them, that we might all join together in crying to Him for mercy. To this they readily agreed: I then commended them to His grace, and went undisturbed to the little company within.

Tues. 30.—As I was expounding the twelfth of the Acts, a young man, with some others, rushed in, cursing and swearing vehemently; and so disturbed all near him, that, after a time, they put him out. I observed it, and called to let him come in, that our Lord might bid his chains fall off. As soon as the sermon was over, he came and declared before us all that he was a smuggler, then going on that work; as his disguise, and the great bag he had with him, showed. But he said, he must never do this more; for he was now resolved to have the Lord for his God.

Mon. Oct. 20.—I began declaring that "Gospel of Christ" which "is the power of God unto salvation," in the midst of the publicans and sinners, at Short's Gardens, Drury Lane.

Thur. 23.—I was informed of an awful providence. A poor wretch, who was here last week, cursing and blaspheming, and labouring with all his might to hinder the Word of God, had afterwards boasted to many, that he would come again on Sunday, and no man should stop his mouth then. But on Friday, God laid His hand upon him, and on Sunday he was buried.

On *Sunday*, the 26th, while I was enforcing that great question with an eye to the spiritual resurrection, "Why should it be thought a thing incredible with you, that God should raise the dead?" the many-headed beast began to roar again. I again proclaimed deliverance to the captives; and their deep attention showed that the word sent to them did not return empty

Mon. Nov. 3.—We distributed, as every one had need, among the numerous poor of our society, the clothes of several kinds, which many who could spare them had brought for that purpose.

Sun. 9.—I had the comfort of finding all our brethren that are in band, of one heart and of one mind.

Mon. 10.—Early in the morning I set out, and the next evening came to Bristol.

I found my brother (to supply whose absence I came) had been in Wales for some days. The next morning I inquired particularly into the state of the little flock.

Sun. 16.—After communicating at St James's, our parish church, with a numerous congregation, I visited several of the sick. Most of them were ill of the spotted fever; which, they informed me, had been extremely mortal; few persons recovering from it. But God had said, " Hitherto shalt thou come." I believe there was not one with whom we were, but recovered.

Thur. 20.—My brother returned from Wales. So, early on *Friday*, 21, I left Bristol, and on *Saturday*, in the afternoon, came safe to London.

Tues. 25.—After several methods proposed for employing those who were out of business, we determined to make a trial of one which several of our brethren recommended to us. Our aim was, with as little expense as possible, to keep them at once from want and from idleness; in order to which, we took twelve of the poorest, and a teacher, into the society-room, where they were employed for four months, till spring came on, in carding and spinning of cotton. And the design answered: they were employed and maintained with very little more than the produce of their own labour.

Fri. 28.—A gentleman came to me full of goodwill, to exhort me not to leave the Church; or (which was the same thing in his account) to use extemporary prayer; which, said he, " I will prove to a demonstration to be no prayer at all."

Mon. Dec. 1.—Finding many of our brethren and sisters offended at each other, I appointed the several accusers to come and speak face to face with the accused. Some of them came almost every day this week. And most of the offences vanished away.

Fri. 12 —Having received many unpleasing accounts concerning our little society in Kingswood, I left London, and after some difficulty and danger, by reason of much ice on the road, on *Saturday* evening came to my brother at Bristol, who confirmed to me what I did not desire to hear.

Tues. 16.—In the afternoon I preached on, "Let patience

have her perfect work." The next evening Mr Cennick came back from a little journey into Wiltshire. I was greatly surprised when I went to receive him, as usual, with open arms, to observe him quite cold; so that a stranger would have judged he had scarce ever seen me before. However, for the present, I said nothing, but did him honour before the people.

Fri. 19.—I pressed him to explain his behaviour. He told me many stories which he had heard of me: yet it seemed to me, something was still behind; so I desired we might meet again in the morning.

Sat. 20.—A few of us had a long conference together. Mr C—— now told me plainly, he could not agree with me, because I did not preach the truth, in particular with regard to election. We then entered a little into the controversy; but without effect.

At the love-feast which we had in the evening at Bristol, seventy or eighty of our brethren and sisters from Kingswood were present, notwithstanding the heavy snow. We all walked back together, through the most violent storm of sleet and snow which I ever remember; the snow also lying above knee-deep in many places. But our hearts were warmed, so that we went on, rejoicing and praising God for the consolation.

Mon. Jan. 19, 1741.—I found, from several accounts, it was absolutely necessary for me to be at London. I therefore desired the society to meet in the evening, and having settled things in the best manner I could, on *Tuesday* set out, and on *Wednesday* evening met our brethren at the Foundery.

Thur. 22.—I began expounding where my brother had left off, viz., at the fourth chapter of the first Epistle of St John. He had not preached the morning before; nor intended to do it any more. "The Philistines are upon thee, Samson." But the Lord is not "departed from thee." He shall strengthen thee yet again, and thou shalt be "avenged of them for the loss of thy eyes."

Sun. b. 1.—A private letter, wrote to me by Mr Whitefield, hav been printed without either his leave or mine, great numbers (pies were given to our people, both at the door and in the undery itself. Having procured one of them, I related (afte reaching) the naked fact to the congregation, and told them, " will do just what I believe Mr Whitefield would, were he here nself." Upon which I tore it in pieces before them all. Eve y one who had received it, did the same.

Wed. 4.—Being the general fast-day, I preached in the morning on those words: "Shall I not visit for these things, saith the Lord? Shall not My soul be avenged on such a

J.W.J.—8

nation as this?" Coming from the service at St Luke's, I found our house so crowded that the people were ready to tread one upon another. I had not designed to preach; but seeing such a congregation, I could not think it right to send them empty away; and therefore expounded the parable of the barren fig-tree.

From hence I went to Deptford, where many poor wretches were got together, utterly void both of common sense and common decency.

Tues. 10.—(Being Shrove Tuesday.) Before I began to preach, many men of the baser sort, having mixed themselves with the women, behaved so indecently, as occasioned much disturbance. A constable commanded them to keep the peace; in answer to which they knocked him down. Some who were near seized on two of them, and, by shutting the doors, prevented any further contest. Those two were afterwards carried before a magistrate; but on their promise of better behaviour, were discharged.

Thurs. 12.—My brother returned from Oxford, and preached on the true way of waiting for God: thereby dispelling at once the fears of some, and the vain hopes of others; who had confidently affirmed that Mr Charles Wesley was *still* already, and would come to London no more.

Mon. 16.—While I was preaching in Long Lane, the host of the aliens gathered together; and one large stone (many of which they threw) went just over my shoulder, But no one was hurt in any degree; for Thy "kingdom ruleth over all."

All things now being settled according to my wish, on *Tuesday*, 17, I left London. In the afternoon I reached Oxford, and leaving my horse there, set out on foot for Stanton-Harcourt. The night overtook me in about an hour, accompanied with heavy rain. Being wet and weary, and not well knowing my way, I could not help saying in my heart (though ashamed of my want of resignation to God's will), Oh that Thou wouldest "stay the bottles of heaven"; or, at least, give me light, or an honest guide, or some help in the manner Thou knowest! Presently the rain ceased; the moon broke out, and a friendly man overtook me, who set me upon his own horse, and walked by my side, till we came to Mr Gambold's door.

Wed. 18.—I walked on to Burford; on *Thursday* to Malmesbury; and the next day to Bristol.

Tues. 24.—The bands meeting at Bristol, I read over the names of the United Society, being determined that no disorderly walker should remain therein. Accordingly, I took an account of every person: 1. To whom any reasonable objection was made. 2. Who was not known to and recommended by some, on whose veracity I could depend. To those who were sufficiently recommended, tickets were given on the following days. Most of the rest I had face to face with their accusers; and such as either appeared to be innocent, or confessed their faults and promised better behaviour, were then received into the society. The others were put upon trial again, unless they voluntarily expelled themselves. About forty were by this means separated from us; I trust only for a season.

Sun. Mar. 15.—I preached twice at Kingswood, and twice at Bristol, on those words of a troubled soul, "Oh that I had wings like a dove; for then would I flee away, and be at rest."

Sat. 21.—I explained, in the evening, the thirty-third chapter of Ezekiel; in applying which, I was suddenly seized with such a pain in my side, that I could not speak. I knew my remedy, and immediately kneeled down. In a moment the pain was gone; and the voice of the Lord cried aloud to the sinners, "Why will ye die, O house of Israel?"

Finding all things now, both at Kingswood and Bristol, far more settled than I expected, I complied with my brother's request, and setting out on *Wednesday*, 25, the next day came to London.

Sat. 28.—Having heard much of Mr Whitefield's unkind behaviour, since his return from Georgia, I went to him to hear him speak for himself, that I might know how to judge. I much approved of his plainness of speech. He told me, he and I preached two different gospels; and therefore he not only would not join with, or give me the right hand of fellowship, but was resolved publicly to preach against me and my brother, wheresoever he preached at all. Mr Hall (who went with me) put him in mind of the promise he had made but a few days before, that, whatever his private opinion was, he would never publicly preach against us. He said, that promise was only an effect of human weakness, and he was now of another mind.

Mon. 30.—I fixed an hour every day for speaking with each of the bands, that no disorderly walker might remain among them, nor any of a careless or contentious spirit. And the hours from ten to two, on every day but Saturday, I set apart for speaking with any who should desire it.

Mon. April 6.—I had a long conversation with Peter Böhler. I marvel how I refrain from joining these men. I scarce ever see any of them but my heart burns within me. I long to be with them; and yet I am kept from them.

Tues. 7.—I dined with one who had been a professed

atheist for upwards of twenty years. But coming some months since to make sport with the Word of God, it cut him to the heart. And he could have no rest day nor night, till the God whom he had denied spoke peace to his soul.

In the evening, having desired all the bands to meet, I read over the names of the United Society ; and marked those who were of a doubtful character, that full inquiry might be made concerning them. On *Thursday*, at the meeting of that society, I read over the names of these, and desired to speak with each of them the next day, as soon as they had opportunity. Many of them afterwards gave sufficient proof, that they were seeking Christ in sincerity. The rest I determined to keep on trial, till the doubts concerning them were removed.

Fri. May 1.—In the evening I went to a little love-feast which Peter Böhler made for those ten who joined together on this day three years, " to confess our faults one to another." Seven of us were present ; one being sick, and two unwilling to come.

Sun. 3.—I gave the scriptural account of one who is " in Christ a new creature." In the afternoon I explained at Marylebone Fields, to a vast multitude of people, " He hath showed thee, O man, what is good." The devil's children fought valiantly for their master, that his kingdom should not be destroyed. And many stones fell on my right hand and on my left. But when I began to examine them closely, what reward they were to have for their labour, they vanished away like smoke.

Wed. 6, was a day on which we agreed to meet for prayer and humbling our souls before God, if haply He might show us His will concerning our reunion with our brethren of Fetter Lane. And to this intent all the men and women bands met at one in the afternoon. Nor did our Lord cast out our prayer, or leave Himself without witness among us. But it was clear to all, even those who were before the most eagerly desirous of it, that the time was not come.

Thur. 7.—I reminded the United Society, that many of our brethren and sisters had not needful food ; many were destitute of convenient clothing ; many were out of business, and that without their own fault ; and many sick and ready to perish : that I had done what in me lay to feed the hungry, to clothe the naked, to employ the poor, and to visit the sick ; but was not, alone, sufficient for these things ; and therefore desired all whose hearts were as my heart—

1. To bring what clothes each could spare, to be distributed among those that wanted most.

2. To give weekly a penny, or what they could afford, for the relief of the poor and sick.

My design, I told them, is to employ, for the present, all the women who are out of business, and desire it, in knitting.

To these we will first give the common price for what work they do; and then add, according as they need.

Twelve persons are appointed to inspect these, and to visit and provide things needful for the sick.

Each of these is to visit all the sick within their district, every other day; and to meet on Tuesday evening, to give an account of what they have done, and consult what can be done further.

This week the Lord of the harvest began to put in His sickle among us. On Tuesday our brother Price, our sister Bowes on Wednesday, to-day our sister Hawthorn, died. They all went in full and certain hope to Him whom their soul loved.

Fri. 8.—I found myself much out of order. However, I made shift to preach in the evening: but on *Saturday* my bodily strength quite failed, so that for several hours I could scarce lift up my head. *Sunday*, 10. I was obliged to lie down most part of the day, being easy only in that posture. Yet in the evening my weakness was suspended, while I was calling sinners to repentance. But at our love-feast which followed, beside the pain in my back and head, and the fever which still continued upon me, just as I began to pray, I was seized with such a cough that I could hardly speak. At the same time came strongly into my mind, "These signs shall follow them that believe." I called on Jesus aloud, to "increase my faith," and to "confirm the word of His grace." While I was speaking, my pain vanished away, the fever left me; my bodily strength returned; and for many weeks I felt neither weakness nor pain. "Unto Thee, O Lord, do I give thanks."

Mon. 18.—At the pressing instance of my brother, I left London, and the next evening met him at Bristol. I was a little surprised when I came into the room, just after he had ended his sermon. Some wept aloud; some clapped their hands; some shouted: and the rest sang praise, with whom (having soon recovered themselves) the whole congregation joined.

Wed. 20.—I spent most of the morning in speaking with the new members of the society. In the afternoon I saw the sick; but not one in fear, neither repining against God.

Sat. 23.—At a meeting of the stewards of the society (who receive and expend what is contributed weekly), it was found needful to retrench the expenses; the contributions not answering thereto. And it was accordingly agreed to discharge two of the schoolmasters at Bristol, the present fund being barely sufficient to keep two masters and a mistress here, and one master and a mistress at Kingswood.

Mon. June 8.—I set out from Enfield Chace for Leicestershire. In the evening we came to Northampton; and the next afternoon to Mr Ellis's at Markfield, five or six miles beyond Leicester.

For these two days I had made an experiment which I had been so often and earnestly pressed to do;—speaking to none concerning the things of God, unless my heart was free to it. And what was the event? Why, 1. That I spoke to none at all for fourscore miles together; no, not even to him that travelled with me in the chaise, unless a few words at first setting out. 2. That I had no cross either to bear or to take up, and commonly in an hour or two fell fast asleep. 3. That I had much respect shown me wherever I came: every one behaving to me, as to a civil, good-natured gentleman. Oh, how pleasing is all this to flesh and blood! Need ye "compass sea and land" to make "proselytes" to this?

Wed. 10.—In the afternoon we came to J—— C——n's, about ten miles beyond Markfield; a plain, open-hearted man, desirous to know and do the will of God. I was a little surprised at what he said: "A few months since there was a great awakening all round us; but since Mr S—— came, three parts in four are fallen as fast asleep as ever." I spoke to him of drawing people from the Church, and advising them to leave off prayer. He said, there was no Church of England left, and that there was no Scripture for family prayer, nor for praying in private at any other particular times; which a believer need not do. I asked, what our Saviour then meant by saying, "Enter into thy closet and pray." He said, "Oh! that means, Enter into the closet of your heart."

Between five and six we came to Ogbrook, where Mr S——n then was. I asked Mr Greaves what doctrine he taught here. He said, "The sum of all is this: 'If you will believe, be still. Do not pretend to do good (which you cannot do till you believe); and leave off what you call the means of grace, such as prayer, and running to church and sacrament.'"

About eight, Mr Greaves offering me the use of his church, I explained the true gospel stillness; and in the morning, *Thursday*, 11, to a large congregation, "By grace are ye saved through faith."

In the afternoon we went on to Nottingham, where Mr Howe received us gladly. At eight the society met as usual. I could not but observe: 1. That the room was not half full, which used, till very lately, to be crowded within and without. 2. That not one person who came in used any prayer at all; but every one immediately sat down, and began either talking to his neighbour, or looking about to see who was there. 3. That when I began to pray, there appeared a general surprise, none once offering to kneel down, and those who stood, choosing the most easy, indolent posture which they conveniently could. I afterward looked for one of our hymn-books upon the desk (which I knew Mr Howe had brought from London); but both that and the Bible were vanished away; and in the room lay the Moravian hymns and the Count's sermons.

In the evening we came to Markfield again, where the church was quite full.

Sat. 13.—In the morning I preached on those words: "To him that worketh not, but believeth on Him that justifieth the ungodly, his faith is counted to him for righteousness." We then set out for Melbourn, where, finding the house too small to contain those who were come together, I stood under a large tree, and declared Him whom God hath exalted to be a Prince and a Saviour, to give repentance unto Israel, and remission of sins.

Thence I went to Hemmington, where also, the house not being large enough to contain the people, they stood about the door and at both the windows, while I showed "what" we "must do to be saved."

One of our company seemed a little offended when I had done, at "a vile fellow, notorious all over the country for cursing, swearing, and drunkenness; though he was now greyheaded, being near fourscore years of age." He came to me, and catching me hold by the hands, said, "Whether thou art a good or a bad man, I know not; but I know the words thou speakest are good. I never heard the like in all my life. Oh that God would set them home upon my poor soul!" He then burst into tears, so that he could speak no more.

Sun. 14.—I rode to Nottingham again, and at eight preached at the market-place, to an immense multitude of people. I saw only one or two who behaved lightly, whom I immediately spoke to; and they stood reproved. Yet, soon after, a man behind me began aloud to contradict and blaspheme; but upon my turning to him, he stepped behind a pillar, and in a few minutes disappeared.

In the afternoon we returned to Markfield. The church was so excessive hot (being crowded in every corner), that I could not, without difficulty, read the evening service. Being afterwards informed that abundance of people were still without, who could not possibly get into the church, I went out to them, and explained that great promise of our Lord, "I will heal their backslidings: I will love them freely." In the evening I expounded in the church, on her who "loved much, because she had much forgiven."

Mon. 15.—I set out for London, and read over in the way that celebrated book, Martin Luther's *Comment on the Epistle to the Galatians*.

Wed. 17.—I set out, and rode slowly toward Oxford; but before I came to Wycombe, my horse tired. There I hired another, which tired also before I came to Tetsworth. I hired a third here, and reached Oxford in the evening.

Thur. 18.—I inquired concerning the exercises previous to the degree of Bachelor in Divinity, and advised with Mr Gambold concerning the subject of my sermon before the University; but he seemed to think it of no moment: "For," said he, "all here are so prejudiced, that they will mind nothing you say." I know not that. However, I am to deliver my own soul, whether they will hear, or whether they will forbear.

I found a great change among the poor people here. Out of twenty-five or thirty weekly communicants, only two were left. Not one continued to attend the daily prayers of the Church. And those few that were once united together, were now torn asunder, and scattered abroad.

Thur. July 2.—I met Mr Gambold again; who honestly told me, he was ashamed of my company; and therefore must be excused from going to the society with me. This is plain dealing at least!

Thur. 9.—Being in the Bodleian Library, I light on Mr Calvin's account of the case of Michael Servetus; several of whose letters he occasionally inserts; wherein Servetus often declares in terms, "I believe the Father is God, the Son is God, and the Holy Ghost is God." Mr Calvin, however, paints him such a monster as never was,—an Arian, a blasphemer, and what not: besides strewing over him his flowers of "dog, devil, swine," and so on; which are the usual appellations he gives to his opponents. But still he utterly denies his being the cause of Servetus's death. "No," says he, "I *only advised* our magistrates, as having a right to restrain heretics by the sword, to seize upon and try that archheretic. But after he was condemned, *I said not one word about his execution!*"

Fri. 10.—I rode to London, and preached at Short's Gardens, on, "the name of Jesus Christ of Nazareth." *Sunday,* 12. While I was showing, at Charles Square, what it is "to do justly, to love mercy, and to walk humbly with our God," a great shout began. Many of the rabble had brought an ox, which they were vehemently labouring to drive in among the people. But their labour was in vain; for in spite of them all, he ran round and round, one way and the other, and at length broke through the midst of them clear away, leaving us calmly rejoicing and praising God.

Mon. 13.—I returned to Oxford, and on *Wednesday* rode to Bristol. My brother, I found, was already gone to Wales; so that I came just in season; and that, indeed, on another account also; for a spirit of enthusiasm was breaking in upon many, who charged their own imaginations on the will of God, and that not written, but impressed on their hearts. If these impressions be received as the rule of action, instead of the written word, I know nothing so wicked or absurd but we may fall into, and that without remedy.

On *Monday* (my brother being now returned from Wales) I rode back to Oxford.

Sat. 25.—It being my turn (which comes about once in three years), I preached at St Mary's, before the University. The harvest truly is plenteous. So numerous a congregation (from whatever motives they came) I have seldom seen at Oxford. My text was the confession of poor Agrippa, "Almost thou persuadest me to be a Christian." I have "cast my bread upon the waters." Let me "find it again after many days!"

In the afternoon I set out (having no time to spare), and on *Sunday,* 26, preached at the Foundery.

Fri. 31.—Hearing that one of our sisters (Jane Muncy) was ill, I went to see her. She was one of the first women Bands at Fetter Lane; and, when the controversy concerning the means of grace began, stood in the gap, and contended earnestly for the ordinances once delivered to the saints. When, soon after, it was ordered, that the unmarried men and women should have no conversation with each other, she again withstood to the face those who were "teaching for doctrines the commandments of men." Nor could all the sophistry of those who are, without controversy, of all men living, the wisest in their generation, induce her either to deny the faith she had received, or to use less plainness of speech, or to be less zealous in recommending and careful in practising good works. Insomuch that many times, when she had been employed in the labour of love till eight or nine in the evening, she then sat down and wrought with her hands till twelve or one in the morning; not that she wanted anything herself, but that she might have to give to others for necessary uses.

From the time that she was made Leader of one or two bands, she was more eminently a pattern to the flock: in self-denial of every kind, in openness of behaviour, in simplicity and godly sincerity, in steadfast faith, in constant attendance on all the public and all the private ordinances of God. And as she had laboured more than they all, so God now called her forth to suffer.

Fri. Aug. 7.—The body of our sister Muncy being brought to Short's Gardens, I preached on those words, "Write, Blessed are the dead which die in the Lord." In St Giles's churchyard I performed the last office, in the presence of such an innumerable multitude of people as I never saw gathered together before.

Wed. 12.—I visited one whom God is purifying in the fire, in answer to the prayers of his wife, whom he was just going to beat (which he frequently did), when God smote him in a moment, so that his hand dropped, and he fell down upon the ground, having no more strength than a new-born child.

Fri. 14.—Calling on a person near Grosvenor Square, I found there was but too much reason here for crying out of the increase of Popery; many converts to it being continually made by the gentleman who preaches in Swallow Street three days in every week. Now, why do not the champions who are continually crying out, "Popery, Popery," in Moorfields, come hither, that they may not always be fighting "as one that beateth the air"? Plainly, because they have no mind to fight at all, but to show their valour without an opponent. And they well know, they may defy Popery at the Foundery, without any danger of contradiction.

Tues. 25.—I explained, at Chelsea, the nature and necessity of the new birth. One (who, I afterwards heard, was a Dissenting Teacher) asked me when I had done, "*Quid est tibi nomen?*" and on my not answering, turned in triumph to his companions, and said, "Ay, I told you he did not understand Latin!"

Wed. 26.—I was informed of a remarkable conversation, at which one of our sisters was present a day or two before; wherein a gentleman was assuring his friends, that he himself was in Charles Square, when a person told Mr Wesley to his face that he (Mr Wesley) had paid twenty pounds already, on being convicted for selling Geneva; and that he now kept two Popish priests in his house. This gave occasion to another to mention what he had himself heard, at an eminent Dissenting Teacher's, viz., that it was beyond dispute, Mr Wesley had large remittances from Spain, in order to make a party among the poor ; and that as soon as the Spaniards landed, he was to join them with twenty thousand men.

Mon. 31.—I began my course of preaching on the Common Prayer. *Tuesday*, September 1. I read over Mr Whitefield's account of God's dealings with his soul. Great part of this I know to be true.

CHAPTER VI

BUILDING OF THE ORPHAN HOUSE

FROM SEPTEMBER 3, 1741, TO OCTOBER 27, 1743

Sunday, September 6.—Observing some who were beginning to use their liberty as a cloak for licentiousness, I enforced those words of St Paul, "All things are lawful for me; but all things are not expedient."

Mon. 21.—I set out, and the next evening met my brother at Bristol, with Mr Jones, of Fonmon Castle, in Wales; now convinced of the truth as it is in Jesus.

Thur. Oct. 1.—We set out for Wales; but missing our passage over the Severn in the morning, it was sunset before we could get to Newport. We inquired there if we could hire a guide to Cardiff; but there was none to be had. A lad coming in quickly after, who was going (he said) to Lanissan, a little village two miles to the right of Cardiff, we resolved to go thither. At seven we set out: it rained pretty fast, and there being neither moon nor stars, we could neither see any road, nor one another, nor our own horses' heads; but the promise of God did not fail; He gave His angels charge over us; and soon after ten we came safe to Mr Williams's house at Lanissan.

Fri. 2.—We rode to Fonmon Castle. We found Mr Jones's daughter ill of the smallpox; but he could cheerfully leave her and all the rest in the hands of Him in whom he now believed. In the evening I preached at Cardiff, in the Shire Hall, a large and convenient place. There having been a feast in the town that day, I believed it needful to add a few words upon intemperance: and while I was saying, "As for you, drunkard, have no part in this life; you abide in death and hell"; a man cried out vehement ... one; and thither I am going." But I trust Go ... that hour began to show him and others "a mo ... ent way."

... noon we came to Pontypool. A clergyman stopped me in the first street; a few more found me out soon after, whose love I did not find to be cooled at all by the bitter adversaries who had been among them. True, pains had been taken to set them against my brother and me, by men who "know not what manner of spirit" they "are of." But instead of disputing, we betook ourselves to prayer; and all our hearts were knit together as at the first.

In the afternoon we came to Abergavenny. Those who are bitter of spirit have been here also; yet Mrs James (now Mrs Whitefield) received us gladly, as she had done aforetime. But we could not procure even two or three to join with us in the evening beside those of her own household.

Thur. 22.—[Bristol] I called upon Edward W——, who had been ill for several days. I found him in deep despair. Since he had left off prayer, "all the waves and storms were gone over him." We cried unto God, and his soul revived. A little light shone upon him, and, just as we sung—

"Be Thou his strength and righteousness,
His Jesus, and his all,"

his spirit returned to God.

Fri. 23.—I saw several others who were ill of the same distemper. Surely our Lord will do much work by this sickness. I do not find that it comes to any house without leaving a blessing behind it. In the evening I went to Kingswood, and found Ann Steed also praising God in the fires, and testifying that all her weakness and pain wrought together for good.

Sat. 24.—I visited more of the sick, both in Kingswood and Bristol; and it was pleasant work; for I found none of them "sorrowing as men without hope."

Sun. 25.—After the sacrament at All Saints', I took horse for Kingswood; but before I came to Lawrence Hill, my horse fell, and attempting to rise again, fell down upon me. One or two women ran out of a neighbouring house, and when I rose, helped me in. I adore the wisdom of God. In this house were three persons who began to run well, but Satan had hindered them: but they resolved to set out again, and not one of them has looked back since.

Notwithstanding this delay, I got to Kingswood by two. The words God enabled me to speak there, and afterwards at Bristol (so I must express myself still, for I dare not ascribe them to my own wisdom), were as a hammer and a flame; and the same blessing we found at the meeting of the society; but more abundantly at the love-feast which followed. I remember nothing like it for many months. A cry was heard from one end of the congregation to the other; not of grief, but of overflowing joy and love.

The great comfort I found, both in public and private, almost every day of the ensuing week, I apprehend, was to prepare me for what followed : a short account of which I sent to London soon after, in a letter, the copy of which I have subjoined : although I am sensible there are several circumstances therein which some may set down for mere enthusiasm and extravagance.

"DEAR BROTHER,—All last week I found hanging upon me the effects of a violent cold I had contracted in Wales : not, I think (as Mr Turner and Walcam supposed), by lying in a damp bed at St Bride's ; but rather by riding continually in the cold and wet nights, and preaching immediately after. But I believed it would pass off, and so took little notice of it till Friday morning. I then found myself exceeding sick : and as I walked to Baptist Mills (to pray with Susanna Basil, who was ill of a fever), felt the wind pierce me, as it were, through. At my return I found myself something better ; only I could not eat anything at all. Yet I felt no want of strength at the hour of intercession, nor at six in the evening, while I was opening and applying those words, 'Sun, stand thou still in Gibeon ; and thou, moon, in the valley of Ajalon.' I was afterwards refreshed, and slept well : so that I apprehended no further disorder ; but rose in the morning as usual, and declared, with a strong voice and enlarged heart, 'Neither circumcision availeth anything, nor uncircumcision, but faith that worketh by love.' About two in the afternoon, just as I was set down to dinner, a shivering came upon me, and a little pain in my back : but no sickness at all, so that I eat a little ; and then, growing warm, went to see some that were sick. Finding myself worse about four, I would willingly have lain down. But having promised to see Mrs G——, who had been out of order for some days, I went thither first, and thence to Weaver's Hall. A man gave me a token for good as I went along. 'Ay,' said he, 'he will be a martyr too by and by.' Afterwards finding my fever increased, I called on Dr Middleton. By his advice I went home and took my bed : a strange thing to me, who had not kept my bed a day (for five-and-thirty years) ever since I had the smallpox.

"On *Tuesday*, November 3, about noon I was removed to Mr Hooper's.

"*Wed.* 4.—Many of our brethren agreed to seek God to-day by fasting and prayer. I grew better and better till nine ; then I fell asleep, and scarce awaked at all till morning.

"*Thur.* 5.—The noisy joy of the people in the streets did

not agree with me very well; though I am afraid it disordered their poor souls much more than it did my body.

"*Fri.* 6.—Between ten and twelve the main shock began. can give but a faint account of this, not for want of memory, but of words. I felt in my body nothing but storm and tempest, hailstones and coals of fire. But I do not remember that I felt any fear nor any murmuring. The fever came rushing upon me as a lion, ready to break all my bones in pieces. My body grew weaker every moment; but I did not feel my soul put on strength. Then it came into my mind, 'Be still, and see the salvation of the Lord. I will not stir hand or foot: but let Him do with me what is good in His own eyes.' At once my heart was at ease. 'My mouth was filled with laughter, and my tongue with joy.' My eyes overflowed with tears, and I began to sing aloud."

From *Saturday*, 7, to *Sunday*, 15, I found my strength gradually increasing, and was able to read Turretin's *History of the Church* (a dry, heavy, barren treatise), and the Life of that truly good and great man, Mr Philip Henry. On *Monday* and *Tuesday* I read over the *Life of Mr Matthew Henry*,—a man not to be despised, either as a scholar or a Christian, though, I think, not equal to his father. On *Wednesday* I read over once again *Theologia Germanica*. Oh, how was it, that I could ever so admire the affected obscurity of this unscriptural writer? Glory be to God, that now prefer the plain apostles and prophets, before him and all his mystic followers.

Thur. 19.—I read again, with great surprise, part of the *Ecclesiastical History of Eusebius*. But so weak, credulous, thoroughly injudicious a writer have I seldom found. *Friday*, 20, I began Mr Laval's *History of the Reformed Churches in France*; full of the most amazing instances of the wickedness of men, and of the goodness and power of God. About noon, the next day, I went out in a coach as far as the school in Kingswood, where one of the mistresses lay (as was believed) near death, having found no help from all the medicines she had taken. We determined to try one remedy more; so we poured out our souls in prayer to God. From that hour she began to recover strength, and in a few days was out of danger.

Sun. 22.—Being not suffered to go to church as yet, I communicated at home. I was advised to stay at home some time longer; but I could not apprehend it necessary: and therefore, on *Monday*, 23, went to the new room, where we praised God for all His mercies. And I expounded, for about an hour (without any faintness or weariness).

I preached once every day this week, and found no inconvenience by it. *Sunday*, 29. I thought I might go a little further. So I preached both at Kingswood and at Bristol; and afterwards spent near an hour with the society, and about two hours at the love-feast.

Mon. Dec. 7.—I preached on, "Trust ye in the Lord Jehovah; for in the Lord is everlasting strength." I was showing, what cause we had to trust in the Captain of our salvation, when one in the midst of the room cried out, "Who was your captain the other day, when you hanged yourself? I know the man who saw you when you was cut down." This wise story, it seems, had been diligently spread abroad, and cordially believed by many in Bristol. I desired they would make room for the man to come nearer. But the moment he saw the way open, he ran away with all possible speed, not so much as once looking behind him.

Wed. 9.—God humbled us in the evening by the loss of more than thirty of our little company, who I was obliged to exclude, as no longer adorning the gospel of Christ. I believed it best, openly to declare both their names and the reasons why they were excluded. We then all cried unto God, that this might be for their edification, and not for destruction.

Fri. 11.—I went to Bath. I had often reasoned with myself concerning this place, "Hath God left Himself without witnesses?" Did He never raise up such as might be shining lights, even in the midst of this sinful generation? Doubtless He has; but they are either gone "to the desert," or hid under the bushel of prudence. Some of the most serious persons I have known at Bath are either solitary Christians, scarce known to each other, unless by name; or prudent Christians, as careful not to give offence, as if that were the unpardonable sin; and as zealous, to "keep their religion to themselves," as they should be to "let it shine before men."

I returned to Bristol the next day. In the evening one desired to speak with me. I perceived him to be in the utmost confusion, so that for awhile he could not speak. At length, he said, "I am he that interrupted you at the new room, on Monday. I have had no rest since, day or night, nor could have till I had spoken to you. I hope you will forgive me, and that it will be a warning to me all the days of my life."

Tues. 15.—It being a hard frost, I walked over to Bath, and had a conversation of several hours with one who had lived above seventy, and studied divinity above thirty, years; yet remission of sins was quite a new doctrine to him.

In the evening I took down the names of some who desired to strengthen each other's hands in God.

I took coach on *Monday*, 21, and on *Wednesday* came to London.

Sun. 27.—After diligent inquiry made, I removed all those from the congregation of the faithful whose behaviour or spirit was not agreeable to the gospel of Christ; openly declaring the objections I had to each, that others might fear, and cry to God for them.

Thur. 31.—By the unusual overflowing of peace and love to all which I felt, I was inclined to believe some trial was at hand. At three in the afternoon my fever came; but, finding it was not violent, I would not break my word, and therefore went at four and committed to the earth the remains of one who had died in the Lord a few days before; neither could I refrain from exhorting the almost innumerable multitude of people who were gathered together round her grave to cry to God, that they might die the death of the righteous, and their last end be like hers. I then designed to lie down; but Sir John G—— coming, and sending to speak with me, I went to him, and from him into the pulpit, knowing God would renew my strength. I preached, according to her request, who was now with God, on those words with which her soul had been so refreshed a little before she went hence, after a long night of doubts and fears: "Thy sun shall no more go down, neither shall thy moon withdraw itself. For the Lord shall be thine everlasting light, and the days of thy mourning shall be ended."

At the society which followed, many cried after God with a loud and bitter cry. About ten I left them, and committed myself into His hands, to do with me what seemed Him good.

Fri. Jan. 1, 1742.—After a night of quiet sleep, I waked in a strong fever, but without any sickness, or thirst, or pain. I consented, however, to keep my bed; but on condition that every one who desired it, should have liberty to speak with me. I believe fifty or sixty persons did so this day; nor did I find any inconvenience from it. In the evening I sent for all the bands who were in the house, that we might magnify our Lord together. A near relation being with me when they came, I asked her afterwards, if she was not offended. "Offended!" said she; "I wish I could be always among you. I thought I was in heaven."

This night also, by the blessing of God, I slept well, to the utter astonishment of those about me, the apothecary in particular, who said, he had never seen such a fever in his life.

Sun. 3.—Finding myself quite free from pain, I met the Leaders, morning and afternoon; and joined with a little company of them in the great sacrifice of thanksgiving. In the evening, it being the men's love-feast, I desired they would all come up. Those whom the room would not contain stood without; while we all with one mouth sang praise to God.

Mon. 4.—I waked in perfect health. Does not God both kill and make alive? This day, I understand, poor Charles Kinchin died! I preached morning and evening, every day, for the remaining part of the week. On *Saturday*, while I was preaching at Long Lane, a rude rout lift up their voice on high. I fell upon them without delay. Some pulled off their hats, and opened their mouth no more: the rest stole out one after another. All that remained were quiet and attentive.

Mon. 11.—I went twice to Newgate, at the request of poor R—— R——, who lay there under sentence of death; but was refused admittance.

It was above two years before, that, being destitute and in distress, he applied to me at Bristol for relief. I took him in, and employed him for the present, in writing and keeping accounts for me. Not long after I placed him in the little school, which was kept by the United Society. There were many suspicions of him during that time, as well as of his companion, Gwillam Snowde; but no proof appeared, so that after three or four months they quietly returned to London. But they did not deceive God, nor escape His hand. Gwillam Snowde was soon apprehended for a robbery, and, when condemned, sent for me, and said, nothing lay heavier upon him, than his having thus returned evil for good. I believe it was now the desire of poor R—— too, to tell me all that he had done. But the hour was past: I could not now be permitted to see or speak with him.

Fri. 22.—I met the society in Short's Gardens, Drury Lane, for the first time.

Mon. 25.—While I was explaining at Long Lane, "He that committeth sin is of the devil"; his servants were above measure enraged: they not only made all possible noise (although, as I had desired before, no man stirred from his place, or answered them a word); but violently thrust many persons to and fro, struck others, and brake down part of the house. At length they began throwing large stones upon the house, which, forcing their way wherever they came, fell down, together with the tiles, among the people, so that they were in danger of their lives. I then told them, "You must not go on thus; I am ordered by the magistrate, who is, in this respect, to us the minister of God, to inform him of those who break the laws of God and the King: and I must do it, if you persist herein; otherwise I am a partaker of your sin." When I ceased speaking, they were more outrageous than before. Upon this I said, "Let three or four calm men take hold of the foremost, and charge a constable with him, that the law may take its course." They did so, and brought him into the house, cursing and blaspheming in a dreadful manner. I desired five or six to go with him to Justice Copeland, to whom they nakedly related the fact. The justice immediately bound him over to the next sessions at Guildford.

I observed, when the man was brought into the house, that many of his companions were loudly crying out, "Richard Smith, Richard Smith!" who, as it afterward appeared, was one of their stoutest champions. But Richard Smith answered not; he was fallen into the hands of One higher than they. God had struck him to the heart; as also a woman, who was speaking words not fit to be repeated, and throwing whatever came to hand, whom He overtook in the very act. She came into the house with Richard Smith, fell upon her knees before us all, and strongly exhorted him, never to turn back, never to forget the mercy which God had shown to his soul. From this time we had never any considerable interruption or disturbance at Long Lane; although we withdrew our prosecution, upon the offender's submission and promise of better behaviour.

Tues. 26.—I explained, at Chelsea, the faith which worketh by love. I was very weak when I went into the room; but the more "the beasts of the people" increased in madness and rage, the more was I strengthened, both in body and soul; so that I believe few in the house, which was exceeding full, lost one sentence of what I spoke. Indeed they could not see me, nor one another at a few yards' distance, by reason of the exceeding thick smoke, which was occasioned by the wild-fire, and things of that kind, continually thrown into the room. But they who could praise God in the midst of the fires were not to be affrighted by a little smoke.

Fri. Feb. 5.—I set out, and with some difficulty reached Chippenham on Saturday evening.

Mon. 8.—I rode to Bath.

Mon. 15.—Many met together to consult on a proper method for discharging the public debt; and it was at length agreed: 1. That every member of the society, who was able, should contribute a penny a week. 2. That the whole society should be divided into little companies or classes,—about twelve in each class. And, 3. That one person in each class should receive the contribution of the rest, and bring it in to the stewards, weekly.

Fri. Mar. 19.—I rode once more to Pensford, at the earnest request of several serious people. The place where they desired me to preach was a little green spot, near the town. But I had no sooner begun, than a great company of rabble, hired (as we afterwards found) for that purpose, came furiously upon us, bringing a bull, which they had been baiting, and now strove to drive in among the people. But the beast was wiser than his drivers; and continually ran either on one side of us, or the other, while we quietly sang praise to God, and prayed for about an hour. The poor wretches, finding themselves disappointed, at length seized upon the bull, now weak and tired, after having been so long torn and beaten both by dogs and men; and, by main strength, partly dragged, and partly thrust, him in among the people. When they had forced their way to the little table on which I stood, they strove several times to throw it down, by thrusting the helpless beast against it; who, of himself, stirred no more than a log of wood. I once or twice put aside his head with my hand, that the blood might not drop upon my clothes; intending to go on, as soon as the hurry should be a little over. But the table falling down, some of our friends caught me in their arms, and carried me right away on their shoulders; while the rabble wreaked their vengeance on the table, which they tore bit from bit. We went a little way off, where I finished my discourse, without any noise or interruption.

Sun. 21.—In the evening I rode to Marshfield; and on *Tuesday*, in the afternoon, came to London.

Thur. 25.—I appointed several earnest and sensible men to meet me, to whom I showed the great difficulty I had long found of knowing the people who desired to be under my care. After much discourse, they all agreed, there could be no better way to come to a sure, thorough knowledge of each person, than to divide them into classes, like those ristol, under the inspection of those in whom I could m onfide. This was the origin of our classes at London, for   ich I can never sufficiently praise God; the unspeakable sefulness of the institution having ever since been more   d more manifest.

Wed. 31.—My brother set out for O   d.

Sun. April 4.—About two in the   rnoon, being the time my brother was preaching at Oxfor before the University, I desired a few persons to meet wit me, and join in prayer. We continued herein much longe than we at first designed, and believed we had the petition we asked of God.

Fri. 9.—We had the first watchnight in London. We commonly choose for this solemn service the Friday night nearest the full moon, either before or after, that those of the congregation who live at a distance, may have light to their several homes. The service begins at half an hour past eight, and continues till a little after midnight. We have often found a peculiar blessing at these seasons. There is generally a deep awe upon the congregation, perhaps in some measure owing to the silence of the night, particularly in singing the hymn with which we commonly conclude—

> "Hearken to the solemn voice,
> The awful midnight cry!
> Waiting souls, rejoice, rejoice,
> And feel the Bridegroom nigh."

Sun. 25.—At five I preached in Ratcliffe Square, near Stepney, on, "I came not to call the righteous, but sinners to repentance." A multitude of them were gathered together before I came home, and filled the street above and below the Foundery. Some who apprehended we should have but homely treatment, begged me to go in as soon as possible; but I told them, "No: provide you for yourselves; but I have a message to deliver first." I told them, after a few words, "Friends, let every man do as he pleases; but it is my manner, when I speak of the things of God, or when another does, to uncover my head"; which I accordingly did; and many of them did the same. I then exhorted them to repent and believe the gospel. Not a few of them appeared to be deeply affected. Now, Satan, count thy gains

Wed. May 12.—I waited on the Archbishop of Canterbury with Mr Whitefield, and again on Friday, as also on the Bishop of London. I trust if we should be called to appear before princes, we should not be ashamed.

Mon. 17.—I had designed this morning to set out for Bristol; but was unexpectedly prevented. In the afternoon I received a letter from Leicestershire, pressing me to come without delay, and pay the last office of friendship to one whose soul was on the wing for eternity. On *Thursday*, 20, I set out. The next afternoon I stopped a little at Newport-Pagnell, and then rode on till I overtook a serious man, with whom I immediately fell into conversation. He presently gave me to know what his opinions were. therefore I said nothing to contradict them. But that did not content him: he was quite uneasy to know, whether I held the doctrine of the decrees as he did; but I told him over and over, "We had better keep to practical things, lest we should be angry at one another." And so we did for two miles, till he caught me unawares, and dragged me into the dispute before I knew where I was. He then grew warmer and warmer: told me I was rotten at heart, and supposed I was one of John Wesley's followers. I told him, "No, I am John Wesley himself." Upon which,—

*Improvisum aspris veluti qui sentibus anguem
Pressit,——*[1]

he would gladly have run away outright. But being the better mounted of the two, I kept close to his side, and endeavoured to show him his heart, till we came into the street of Northampton. *Saturday*, 22. About five in the afternoon, I reached Donnington Park.

Miss Cowper was just alive. But as soon as we came in, her spirit greatly revived. For three days we rejoiced in the grace of God, whereby she was filled with a hope full of immortality; with meekness, gentleness, patience, and humble love, knowing in whom she had believed.

Tues. 25.—I set out early in the morning with John Taylor (since settled in London); and *Wednesday*, 26, in the evening, reached Birstal, six miles beyond Wakefield.

John Nelson had wrote to me some time before: but at that time I had little thought of seeing him. Hearing he was at home, I sent for him to our inn; whence he immediately carried me to his house, and gave me an account of the strange manner wherein he had been led on, from the time of our parting at London.

He had full business there, and large wages. But from the time of his finding peace with God, it was continually upon his mind, that he must return (though he knew not why) to his native place. He did so, about Christmas, in the year 1740. His relations and acquaintance soon began to inquire, what he thought of this new faith; and whether he believed there was any such thing as a man's knowing that his sins were forgiven: John told them point-blank, that this new faith, as they called it, was the old faith of the gospel; and that he himself was as sure his sins were forgiven, as he could be of the shining of the sun. This was soon noised abroad: more and more came to inquire concerning these strange things: some put him upon the proof of the great truths which such inquiries naturally led him to mention; and thus he was brought unawares to quote, explain, compare, and enforce, several parts of Scripture. This he did at first, sitting in his house, till the

---

[1] As one that has unawares trodden upon a snake.

company increased so that the house could not contain them. Then he stood at the door, which he was commonly obliged to do in the evening, as soon as he came from work. God immediately set His seal to what was spoken ; and several believed, and therefore declared, that God was merciful also to their unrighteousness, and had forgiven all their sins.

Mr Ingham, hearing of this, came to Birstal, inquired into the facts, talked with John himself, and examined him in the closest manner, both touching his knowledge and spiritual experience ; after which he encouraged him to proceed ; and pressed him, as often as he had opportunity, to come to any of the places where himself had been, and speak to the people as God should enable him.

But he soon gave offence, both by his plainness of speech, and by advising people to go to church and sacrament. Mr Ingham reproved him ; but finding him incorrigible, forbade any that were in his societies to hear him. But being persuaded this is the will of God concerning him, he continues to this hour working in the day, that he may be burdensome to no man : and in the evening "testifying the truth as it is in Jesus."

I preached, at noon, on the top of Birstal Hill, to several hundreds of plain people ; and spent the afternoon in talking severally with those who had tasted of the grace of God. All of these, I found, had been vehemently pressed, not to run about to church and sacrament, and to keep their religion to themselves ; to be still ; not to talk about what they had experienced. At eight I preached on the side of Dewsbury Moor, about two miles from Birstal, and earnestly exhorted all who believed, to wait upon God in His own ways, and to let their light shine before men.

Thur. 27.—We left Birstal, and on *Friday*, 28, came to Newcastle-upon-Tyne.

I read, with great expectation, yesterday and to-day, Xenophon's *Memorable Things of Socrates*. I was utterly amazed at his want of judgment. How many of these things would Plato never have mentioned ! But it may be well that we see the shades too of the brightest picture in all heathen antiquity. We came to Newcastle about six ; and, after a short refreshment, walked into the town. I was surprised : so much drunkenness, cursing, and swearing (even from the mouths of little children), do I never remember to have seen and heard before, in so small a compass of time. Surely this place is ripe for Him "who came not to call the righteous, but sinners to repentance."

Sun. 30.—At seven I walked down to Sandgate, the poorest

and most contemptible part of the town ; and, standing at the end of the street with John Taylor, began to sing the hundredth Psalm. Three or four people came out to see what was the matter; who soon increased to four or five hundred. I suppose there might be twelve or fifteen hundred, before I had done preaching ; to whom I applied those solemn words, " He was wounded for our transgressions, He was bruised for our iniquities : the chastisement of our peace was upon Him ; and by His stripes we are healed."

Observing the people, when I had done, to stand gaping and staring upon me, with the most profound astonishment, I told them, " If you desire to know who I am, my name is John Wesley. At five in the evening, with God's help, I design to preach here again."

At five, the hill on which I designed to preach was covered, from the top to the bottom. I never saw so large a number of people together, either in Moorfields, or at Kennington Common. I knew it was not possible for the one half to hear, although my voice was then strong and clear ; and I stood so as to have them all in view, as they were ranged on the side of the hill. The Word of God which I set before them was, " I will heal their backsliding, I will love them freely." After preaching, the poor people were ready to tread me under foot, out of pure love and kindness. It was some time before I could possibly get out of the press. I then went back another way than I came ; but several were got to our inn before me ; by whom I was vehemently importuned to stay with them, at least, a few days ; or, however, one day more. But I could not consent ; having given my word to be at Birstal, with God's leave, on Tuesday night.

Tues. June 1.—As we were riding through Knaresborough, not intending to stop there, a young man stopped me in the street, and earnestly desired me to go to his house. I did so. He told me, our talking with a man, as we went through the town before, had set many in a flame ; and that the sermon we gave him had travelled from one end of the town to the other.

About one we came to Mr More's, at Beeston, near Leeds. His son rode with me, after dinner, to Birstal ; where (a multitude of people being gathered from all parts) I explained to them the spirit of bondage and adoption.

Wed. 2.—I was invited to Mrs Holmes's, near Halifax ; where I preached at noon, on, " Ask, and ye shall receive." Thence I rode to Dr L——'s, the vicar of Halifax ; a candid inquirer after truth.

Sat. 5.—I rode for Epworth.

It being many years since I had been in Epworth before, I went to an inn, in the middle of the town, not knowing whether there were any left in it now who would not be ashamed of my acquaintance. But an old servant of my father's, with two or three poor women, presently found me out. I asked her, "Do you know any in Epworth who are in earnest to be saved?" She answered, "I am, by the grace of God; and I know I am saved through faith." I asked, "Have you then the peace of God? Do you know that He has forgiven your sins?" She replied, "I thank God, I know it well. And many here can say the same thing."

Sun. 6.—A little before the service began, I went to Mr Romley, the curate, and offered to assist him either by preaching or reading prayers. But he did not care to accept of my assistance. The church was exceeding full in the afternoon, a rumour being spread, that I was to preach. But the sermon, on "Quench not the Spirit," was not suitable to the expectation of many of the hearers. Mr Romley told them, one of the most dangerous ways of quenching the Spirit was by enthusiasm; and enlarged on the character of an enthusiast, in a very florid and oratorical manner. After sermon John Taylor stood in the churchyard, and gave notice, as the people were coming out, "Mr Wesley, not being permitted to preach in the church, designs to preach here at six o'clock."

Accordingly at six I came, and found such a congregation as I believe Epworth never saw before. I stood near the east end of the church, upon my father's tombstone, and cried, "The kingdom of heaven is not meat and drink; but righteousness, and peace, and joy in the Holy Ghost."

At eight I went to Edward Smith's, where were many not only of Epworth, but of Burnham, Haxey, Ouston, Belton, and other villages round about, who greatly desired that I would come over to them and help them. I was now in a strait between two; desiring to hasten forward in my journey, and yet not knowing how to leave those poor bruised reeds in the confusion wherein I found them. John Harrison, it seems, and Richard Ridley, had told them in express terms, "All the ordinances are man's inventions; and if you go to church sacrament, you will be damned." Many hereupon wholly forsook the church, and others knew not what to do. At last I determined to spend some days here, that I might have time both to preach in each town, and to speak severally with those, in every place, who had found or waited for salvation.

Mon. 7.—I preached at Burnham, a mile from Epworth, on, "The Son of Man hath power on earth to forgive sins." At eight in the evening I stood again on my father's tomb (as I did every evening this week), and cried aloud to the earnestly-attentive congregation.

Tues. 8.—I walked to Hibbaldstow (about twelve miles from Epworth) to see my brother and sister.

Wed. 9.—I rode over to a neighbouring town, to wait upon a justice of peace, a man of candour and understanding; before whom (I was informed) their angry neighbours had carried a whole waggon-load of these new heretics. But when he asked what they had done, there was a deep silence, for that was a point their conductors had forgot. At length one said, "Why, they pretended to be better than other people; and besides, they prayed from morning to night." Mr S. asked, "But have they done nothing besides?" "Yes, sir," said an old man : "an't please your worship, they have *convarted* my wife. Till she went among them, she had such a tongue ! And now she is as quiet as a lamb." "Carry them back, carry them back," replied the justice, "and let them convert all the scolds in the town."

Sun. 13.—At seven I preached at Haxey, on, "What must I do to be saved?" Thence I went to Wroote, of which (as well as Epworth) my father was rector for several years. Mr Whitelamb offering me the church, I preached in the morning, on, "Ask, and it shall be given you" : in the afternoon, on the difference between the righteousness of the law and the righteousness of faith. But the church could not contain the people, many of whom came from far ; and, I trust, not in vain.

At six I preached for the last time in Epworth churchyard (being to leave the town the next morning), to a vast multitude gathered together from all parts, on the beginning of our Lord's Sermon on the Mount. I continued among them for near three hours ; and yet we scarce knew how to part. Oh, let none think his labour of love is lost because the fruit does not immediately appear ! Near forty years did my father labour here ; but he saw little fruit of all his labour. I took some pains among this people too, and my strength also seemed spent in vain ; but now the fruit appeared. There were scarce any in the town on whom either my father or I had taken any pains formerly, but the seed, sown so long since, now sprung up, bringing forth repentance and remission of sins.

Mon. 14.—Having a great desire to see David Taylor, whom

God had made an instrument of good to many souls, I rode to Sheffield ; but not finding him there, I was minded to go forward immediately : however, the importunity of the people constrained me to stay, and preach both in the evening and in the morning.

Fri. 18.—I left Sheffield, and after preaching at Ripley, by the way, hastened on to Donnington Park : but Miss Cowper, I found, was gone to rest, having finished her course near three weeks before.

I left Donnington Park, and came to Markfield, Coventry, Evesham, Painswick, and Stroud.

Mon. 28.—I rode to Bristol. I soon found disputing had done much mischief here also.

I left Bristol in the evening of *Sunday*, July 18, and on *Tuesday* came to London. I found my mother on the borders of eternity. But she had no doubt or fear ; nor any desire but (as soon as God should call) "to depart and to be with Christ."

Fri. 23.—About three in the afternoon I went to my mother, and found her change was near. I sat down on the bedside. She was in her last conflict ; unable to speak, but I believe quite sensible. Her look was calm and serene, and her eyes fixed upward, while we commended her soul to God. From three to four, the silver cord was loosing, and the wheel breaking at the cistern ; and then without any struggle, or sigh, or groan, the soul was set at liberty. We stood round the bed, and fulfilled her last request, uttered a little before she lost her speech : " Children, as soon as I am released, sing a psalm of praise to God."

Sun. Aug. 1.—Almost an innumerable company of people being gathered together, about five in the afternoon, I committed to the earth the body of my mother to sleep with her fathers. The portion of Scripture from which I afterwards spoke was, " I saw a great white throne, and Him that sat on it, from whose face the earth and the heaven fled away ; and there was found no place for them. And I saw the dead, small and great, stand before God ; and the books were opened : and the dead were judged out of those things which were written in the books, according to their works." It was one of the most solemn assemblies I ever saw, or expect to see this side eternity.

We set up a plain stone at the head of her grave, inscribed with the following words :—

Here lies the Body

OF

MRS SUSANNAH WESLEY

THE YOUNGEST AND
LAST SURVIVING DAUGHTER OF
DR. SAMUEL ANNESLEY.

> In sure and steadfast hope to rise,
> And claim her mansion in the skies,
> A Christian here her flesh laid down
> The cross exchanging for a crown.
>
> True daughter of affliction, she,
> Inured to pain and misery,
> Mourn'd a long night of griefs and fears,
> A legal night of seventy years.
>
> The Father then reveal'd His Son,
> Him in the broken bread made known,
> She knew and felt her sins forgiven,
> And found the earnest of her heaven.
>
> Meet for the fellowship above,
> She heard the call, "Arise, my love!"
> "I come," her dying looks replied,
> And lamb-like, as her Lord, she died.

I cannot but further observe, that even she (as well as her father, and grandfather, her husband, and her three sons) had been, in her measure and degree, a preacher of righteousness. This I learned from a letter, wrote long since to my father, part of which I have here subjoined:—

"*February* 6, 1711-12.

"——As I am a woman, so I am also mistress of a large family. And though the superior charge of the souls contained in it lies upon you, yet, in your absence, I cannot but look upon every soul you leave under my care, as a talent committed to me under a trust, by the great Lord of all the families both of heaven and earth.

"At last it came to my mind, Though I am not a man, nor a minister, yet if my heart were sincerely devoted to God, and I were inspired with a true zeal for His glory, I might do somewhat more than I do. I thought I might pray more for them, and might speak to those with whom I converse with more warmth of affection. I resolved to begin with my own children; in which I observe the following method:—I take such a proportion of time as I can spare every night, to discourse with each child apart. On Monday I talk with Molly; on Tuesday, with Hetty; Wednesday, with Nancy; Thursday, with Jacky; Friday, with Patty; Saturday, with Charles; and with Emily and Suky together on Sunday.

"With those few neighbours that then came to me, I discoursed more freely and affectionately. I chose the best and most awakening sermons we have. And I spent somewhat more time with them in such exercises, without being careful about the success of my undertaking. Since this, our company increased every night; for I dare deny none that ask admittance.

"Last Sunday I believe we had above two hundred. And yet many went away for want of room to stand.

"I cannot conceive why any should reflect upon you, because your wife endeavours to draw people to church, and to restrain them from profaning the Lord's day, by reading to them, and other persuasions. For my part, I value no censure upon this account. I have long since shook hands with the world. And I heartily wish I had never given them more reason to speak against me.

"But there is one thing about which I am much dissatisfied; that is, their being present at family prayers. I do not speak of any concern I am under, barely because so many are present; for those who have the honour of speaking to the Great and Holy God, need not be ashamed to speak before the whole world; but because of my sex. I doubt if it is proper for me to present the prayers of the people to God. Last Sunday I would fain have dismissed them before prayers; but they begged so earnestly to stay, I durst not deny them.

"TO THE REV. MR WESLEY,
"*In St Margaret's Churchyard, Westminster.*'

Sun. 8.—I cried aloud in Ratcliffe Square, "Why will ye die, O house of Israel?" Only one poor man was exceeding noisy and turbulent; but in a moment God touched his heart: he hung down his head: tears covered his face, and his voice was heard no more.

I was constrained this evening to separate from the believers, some who did not show their faith by their works. One of these, Sam. Prig. was deeply displeased, spoke many very bitter words, and went abruptly away. The next morning he called; told me, neither my brother nor I preached the gospel, or knew what it meant. I asked, "What do we preach then?" He said, "Heathen morality: Tully's Offices, and no more. So I wash my hands of you both. We shall see what you will come to in a little time."

Wed. 11.—He sent me a note, demanding the payment of one hundred pounds, which he had lent me about a year before, to pay the workmen at the Foundery. On Friday morning, at eight, he came and said, he wanted his money, and could stay no longer. I told him, I would endeavour to borrow it, and desired him to call in the evening. But he said, he could not stay so long, and must have it at twelve o'clock. Where to get it I knew not. Between nine and ten one came and offered me the use of an hundred pounds for a year: but two others had been with me before, to make the same offer. I accepted the bank-note which one of them brought; and saw that God is over all!

Mon. 16.—I rode to Oxford, and the next day to Evesham. On *Wednesday* and *Thursday*, in riding from Evesham to Bristol, I read over that surprising book, *The Life of Ignatius Loyola*; surely one of the greatest men that ever was engaged in the support of so bad a cause! I wonder any man should judge him to be an enthusiast: no; but he knew the people with whom he had to do: and setting out (like Count Z——) with a full persuasion that he might use guile to promote the glory of God, or (which he thought the same thing) the interest of His Church, he acted, in all things, consistent with his principles.

After having regulated the society here and in Kingswood, I set out again for London.

Sat. Sept. 4.—I was pressed to visit a poor murderer in Newgate, who was much afflicted both in body and soul. I objected; it could not be; for all the turnkeys, as well as the keeper, were so good Christians, they abhorred the name of a Methodist, and had absolutely refused to admit me even to one who earnestly begged it the morning he was to die. However, I went, and found, by a surprising turn, that all the doors were now open to me. I exhorted the sick malefactor to cry unto God with all his might, for grace to repent and believe the gospel. It was not long before the rest of the felons flocked round, to whom I spoke strong words concerning the Friend of sinners, which they received with as great signs of amazement as if it had been a voice from heaven. When I came down into the common hall (I think they called it), one of the prisoners there asking me a question, gave me occasion to speak among them also; more and more still running together, while I declared, God was "not willing any of them should perish, but that all should come to repentance."

Sun. 12.—I was desired to preach in an open place, commonly called the Great Gardens, lying between Whitechapel and Coverlet Fields, where I found a vast multitude gathered together. Many of the beasts of the people laboured much to disturb those who were of a better mind. They endeavoured to drive in a herd of cows among them, but the brutes were wiser than their masters. They then threw whole showers of stones, one of which struck me just between the eyes; but I felt no pain at all; and, when I had wiped away the blood, went on testifying with a loud voice, that God hath given to them that believe, "not the spirit of fear, but of power, and of love, and of a sound mind." And by the spirit which now appeared through the whole congregation, I plainly saw what a blessing it is when it is given us, even in the lowest degree, to suffer for His name's sake.

Tues. 28.—A little before twelve I came to Windsor. I was soon informed, that a large number of the rabble had combined together; and declared, again and again, there should be no preaching there that day. In order to make all sure, they had provided gunpowder enough, and other things, some days before. But Burnham fair coming between, they agreed to go thither first, and have a little diversion there. Accordingly they went, and bestowed a few of their crackers upon their brother-mob at Burnham. But these, not being Methodists, did not take it well, turned upon them and gave them chase. They took shelter in an house. But that would not serve; for those without soon forced a way in, and seized on as many as they could find, who, upon information made, were sent to gaol: the rest ran away, so that when I came, none hindered or interrupted. In the evening I came to London. I proposed spending a fortnight there, and then returning to Bristol.

I spent this time partly in speaking severally to all the members of the society; partly in making a full inquiry into those devices of Satan whereof I had scarce ever heard or read before.

Mon. Oct. 11.—I had designed to leave London; but Mr Richards being taken ill, I put off my journey. He was much better on Tuesday: so I set out the next morning; and before seven in the evening reached the half-way house, four miles short of Hungerford.

I now found it was well I did not set out on Monday, in order to be at Bristol on Tuesday night, as usual. For all the travellers who went that way on Tuesday were robbed. But on Thursday the road was clear; so that I came safe to Kingswood in the afternoon, and in the evening preached at Bristol.

My chief business now was to examine thoroughly the society in Kingswood. This found me full employment for several days. On *Wednesday*, 27, having finished my work, I set out very early, and (though my horse fell lame) on *Thursday* evening came to London.

Sun. 31.—Several of the leaders desired to have an hour's conversation with me. I found they were greatly perplexed about "want of management, ill husbandry, encouraging idleness, improper distribution of money," "being imposed upon by fair pretences," and "men who talked well, but had no grace in their hearts." I asked, who those men were; but that they could not tell. Who encouraged idleness; when and how: what money had been improperly distributed; by whom, and to whom: in what instances I had been imposed on (as I presumed they meant *me*); and what were the particulars of that ill husbandry and mismanagement of which they complained. They stared at one another as men in amaze. I began to be amazed too, not being able to imagine what was the matter, till one dropped a word, by which all came out. They had been talking with Mr Hall, who had started so many objections against all I said or did, that they were in the utmost consternation, till the fire thus broke out, which then at once vanished away.

Wed. Nov. 3.—Two of those who are called *Prophets* desired to speak with me. They told me, they were sent from God with a message to me; which was, that very shortly I should be *born'd* again. One of them added, they would stay in the house till it was done, unless I turned them out. I answered, gravely, "I will not turn you out," and showed them down into the society room. It was tolerably cold; and they had neither meat nor drink: however, there they sat from morning to evening. They then went quietly away, and I have heard nothing from them since.

Mon. 8.—I set out at four, reached Northampton that night, and, on *Saturday*, 13, reached Newcastle.

My brother had been here for some weeks before, and was but just returned to London. At eight I met the wild, staring, loving society.

Sun. 14.—I began preaching about five o'clock (a thing never heard of before in these parts), on, "I came not to call the righteous, but sinners to repentance." And the victorious sweetness of the grace of God was present with His Word. At ten we went to All Saint's, where were such a number of communicants as I have scarce seen but at Bristol or London. At four I preached in the square at the Keelman's Hospital, on,

"By grace are ye saved through faith." It rained and hailed hard, both before and after; but there were only some scattered drops while I preached, which frighted away a few careless hearers. I met the society at six, and exhorted all who had "set their hand to the plough," not to "look back."

Thur. 18.—I could not but observe the different manner wherein God is pleased to work in different places. The grace of God flows here with a wider stream than it did at first either at Bristol or Kingswood. But it does not sink so deep as it did there.

I never saw a work of God, in any other place, so evenly and gradually carried on. Not so much seems to be done at any one time, as hath frequently been at Bristol or London; but something at every time. It is the same with particular souls. I saw none in that triumph of faith, which has been so common in other places. But the believers go on calm and steady.

Sun. 28.—I preached, both at five in the room, and at eight in the hospital. We then walked over to Tanfield Leigh; about seven miles from Newcastle. Here a large company of people were gathered together from all the country round about.

On Thursday morning, between four and five, John Brown, then of Tanfield Leigh, was waked out of sleep by the voice that raiseth the dead; and ever since he has been full of love, and peace, and joy in the Holy Ghost.

Wed. Dec. 1.—We had several places offered, on which to build a room for the society; but none was such as we wanted. And perhaps there was a providence in our not finding any as yet; for, by this means, I was kept at Newcastle, whether I would or no.

Sat. 4.—I was both surprised and grieved at a genuine instance of enthusiasm. J—— B——, of Tanfield Leigh, who had received a sense of the love of God a few days before, came riding through the town, hallooing and shouting, and driving all the people before him: telling them, God had told him he should be a king, and should tread all his enemies under his feet. I sent him home immediately to his work, and advised him to cry day and night to God, that he might be lowly in heart; lest Satan should again get an advantage over him.

To-day a gentleman called and offered me a piece of ground. On Monday an article was drawn, wherein he agreed to put me into possession on Thursday, upon payment of thirty pounds.

Tues. 7.—I was so ill in the morning, that I was obliged to send Mr Williams to the room. He afterwards went to Mr

Stephenson, a merchant in the town, who had a passage through the ground we intended to buy. I was willing to purchase it. Mr Stephenson told him, "Sir, I do not want money; but if Mr Wesley wants ground, he may have a piece of my garden, adjoining to the place you mention. I am at a word. For forty pounds he shall have sixteen yards in breadth, and thirty in length."

Wed. 8.—Mr Stephenson and I signed an article, and I took possession of the ground. But I could not fairly go back from my agreement with Mr Riddel: so I entered on his ground at the same time. The whole is about forty yards in length; in the middle of which we determined to build the house, leaving room for a small court-yard before, and a little garden behind, the building.

Mon. 13.—I removed into a lodging adjoining to the ground where we were preparing to build; but the violent frost obliged us to delay the work. I never felt so intense cold before. In a room where a constant fire was kept, though my desk was fixed within a yard of the chimney, I could not write for a quarter of an hour together, without my hands being quite benumbed.

Mon. 20.—We laid the first stone of the house. Many were gathered, from all parts, to see it; but none scoffed or interrupted, while we praised God and prayed that He would prosper the work of our hands upon us. Three or four times in the evening, I was forced to break off preaching, that we might pray and give thanks to God.

Thur. 23.—It being computed that such a house as was proposed could not be finished under seven hundred pounds, many were positive it would never be finished at all; others, that I should not live to see it covered. I was of another mind; nothing doubting but, as it was begun for God's sake, He would provide what was needful for the finishing it.

Sat. 25.—The physician told me he could do no more; Mr Meyrick could not live over the night. I went up, and found them all crying about him; his legs being cold, and (as it seemed) dead already. We all kneeled down, and called upon God with strong cries and tears. He opened his eyes, and called for me; and, from that hour, he continued to recover his strength, till he was restored to perfect health.—I wait to hear who will either disprove this fact, or philosophically account for it.

Wed. 29.—After preaching (as usual) in the square, I took horse for Tanfield. More than once I was only not blown off my horse. However, at three I reached the Leigh, and explained to a multitude of people the salvation which is through faith. Afterwards I met the society in a large upper room, which rocked to and fro with the violence of the storm. But all was calm within; and we rejoiced together in hope of a kingdom which cannot be moved.

Thur. 30.—I carefully examined those who had lately cried out in the congregation.

At eleven I preached my farewell sermon in the Hospital Square. I could not conclude till one; and then both men, women, and children hung upon me, so that I knew not which way to disengage myself. After some time, I got to the gate, and took horse; but even then "a muckle woman" (as one called her, in great anger) kept her hold, and ran by the horse's side, through thick and thin, down to Sandgate.

Sat. Jan. 1, 1743.—In the evening I reached Epworth. *Sunday*, 2. At five I preached on, "So is every one that is born of the Spirit." About eight I preached from my father's tomb, on Heb. viii. 11. Many from the neighbouring towns asked, if it would not be well, as it was sacrament Sunday, for them to receive it. I told them, "By all means: but it would be more respectful first to ask Mr Romley, the curate's leave." One did so, in the name of the rest; to whom he said, "Pray tell Mr Wesley I shall not give *him* the sacrament; for he is not *fit*."

How wise a God is our God! There could not have been so fit a place under heaven, where this should befall me first, as my father's house, the place of my nativity, and the very place where, "according to the straitest sect of our religion," I had so long "lived a Pharisee!" It was also fit, in the highest degree, that he who repelled me from that very table where I had myself so often distributed the bread of life, should be one who owed his all in this world to the tender love which my father had shown to his, as well as personally to himself.

Mon. 3.—I rode to Birstal, where John Nelson gave a melancholy account of many that *did* run well.

Wed. 5.—I came wet and weary to Sheffield, and on *Friday* to Donnington Park, which I left before eight the next morning, in order to go to Wednesbury, in Staffordshire. About four in the afternoon I came to Wednesbury. At seven I preached in the town-hall.

Sun. 9.—The hall was filled again at five. At eight we met in the place where my brother preached, made, as it were, for the great congregation. It is a large hollow, not half a mile from the town, capable of containing four or five thousand people

Thur. 13.—I rode to Stratford-upon-Avon. I had scarce sat down before I was informed that Mrs K., a middle-aged woman, of Shattery, half a mile from Stratford, had been for many weeks last past in a way which nobody could understand; that she had sent for a minister, but almost as soon as he came began roaring in so strange a manner, that he cried out, "It is the devil, doubtless! It is the devil!" and immediately went away.

I asked, "What good do you think I can do?" One answered, "We cannot tell; but Mrs K. earnestly desired you might come, if you was anywhere near; saying she had seen you in a dream, and should know you immediately: but the devil said, 'I will tear thy throat out before he comes.' But afterwards, she said, his words were, 'if he does come, I will let thee be quiet; and thou shalt be as if nothing ailed thee, till he is gone away.'"

A very odd kind of madness this: I walked over about noon; but when we came to the house, desired all those who came with me to stay below. One showing me the way, I went up straight to her room. As soon as I came to the bedside, she fixed her eyes, and said, "You are Mr Wesley; I am very well now, I thank God: nothing ails me; only I am weak." I called them up, and we began to sing—

> "Jesu, Thou hast bid us pray,
> Pray always and not faint:
> With the word a power convey
> To utter our complaint."

After singing a verse or two we kneeled down to prayer. I had but just begun (my eyes being shut), when I felt as if I had been plunged into cold water; and immediately there was such a roar, that my voice was quite drowned, though I spoke as loud as I usually do to three or four thousand people. However, I prayed on. She was then reared up in the bed, her whole body moving at once, without bending one joint or limb, just as if it were one piece of stone. Immediately after it was writhed into all kinds of postures, the same horrid yell continuing still. But we left her not till all the symptoms ceased, and she was (for the present, at least) rejoicing and praising God.

Mon. 24.—I preached at Bath. Some of the rich and great were present. One of them, my Lord ———, stayed very patiently till I came to the middle of the fourth head. Then, starting up, he said, "'Tis hot! 'Tis very hot," and got downstairs as fast as he could.

Several of the gentry desired to stay at the meeting of the

society; to whom I explained the nature of inward religion, words flowing from me faster than I could speak. One of them (a noted infidel) hung over the next seat in an attitude not to be described ; and when he went, left half a guinea with Mary Naylor, for the use of the poor.

On the following days I spoke with each member of the society in Kingswood. I cannot understand how any minister can hope ever to give up his account with joy, unless (as Ignatius advises) he knows all his flock by name ; not overlooking the men-servants and maid-servants."

Mon. Feb. 14.—I left London, and (riding early and late) the next evening came to Newark.

Fri. 18.—I rode forward for Newcastle. In the evening we came to Boroughbridge, and *Saturday*, 19, to Newcastle.

Sun. 20.—I went on in expounding the Acts of the Apostles, and St Paul's Epistle to the Romans. In the following week I diligently inquired, who they were that did not walk according to the gospel. In consequence of which I was obliged to put away above fifty persons. There remained above eight hundred in the society.

Tues. Mar. 8.—In the afternoon I preached on a smooth part of the fell (or common) near Chowden. I found we were got into the very Kingswood of the north. Twenty or thirty wild children ran round us, as soon as we came, staring as in amaze. They could not properly be said to be either clothed or naked. One of the largest (a girl, about fifteen) had a piece of a ragged, dirty blanket, some way hung about her, and a kind of cap on her head, of the same cloth and colour. My heart was exceedingly enlarged towards them ; and they looked as if they would have swallowed me up.

Sat. 12.—I concluded my second course of visiting, in which I inquired particularly into two things : 1. The case of those who had almost every night the last week cried out aloud, during the preaching. 2. The number of those who were separated from us, and the reason and occasion of it.

Sun. 13.—I went in the morning in order to speak severally with the members of the society at Tanfield. From the terrible instances I met with here (and indeed in all parts of England), I am more and more convinced, that the devil himself desires nothing more than this, that the people of any place should be half-awakened, and then left to themselves to fall asleep again. Therefore I determine, by the grace of God, not to strike one stroke in any place where I cannot follow the blow.

Mon. 14.—I preached again near Chowden ; and this !

continued to do weekly, as well as at all the other places round Newcastle (except Swalwell), where I had preached once.

Thur. 17.—As I was preaching at Pelton, one of the old colliers, not much accustomed to things of this kind, in the middle of the sermon, began shouting amain, for mere satisfaction and joy of heart. But their usual token of approbation (which somewhat surprised me at first) was clapping me on the back.

Fri. 18.—As I was meeting the Leaders, a company of young men, having prepared themselves by strong drink, broke open the door, and came rushing in with the utmost fury. I began praying for them immediately; not one opened his mouth or lifted up a finger against us; and after half an hour, we all went away together in great quietness and love.

Tues. 22.—I went to South Biddick, a village of colliers seven miles south-east of Newcastle. The spot where I stood was just at the bottom of a semicircular hill, on the rising sides of which many hundreds stood; but far more on the plain beneath. Deep attention sat on every face; so that here also I believed it would be well to preach weekly.

Wed. 23.—I met a gentleman in the streets, cursing and swearing in so dreadful a manner, that I could not but stop him. He soon grew calmer; told me he must treat me with a glass of wine; and that he would come and hear me, only he was afraid I should say something against fighting of cocks.

Fri. 25.—At the pressing instance of a cursing, swearing, drunken Papist, who would needs bring me into a state of salvation, I spent some hours in reading an artful book, entitled, *The Grounds of the Old Religion*.

This evening I preached in the shell of the new house.

Sat. 26.—I preached at Burtley, a village four miles south of Newcastle, surrounded by colliers on every side.

Mon. 28.—I was astonished to find it was real fact (what I would not believe before) that three of the Dissenting ministers (Mr A——rs, Mr A——ns, and Mr B——) had agreed together, to exclude all those from the holy communion, who would not refrain from hearing us.

April 1.—(Being *Good Friday*.) I had a great desire to visit a little village called Placey, about ten measured miles north of Newcastle. It is inhabited by colliers only, and such as had been always in the first rank for savage ignorance and wickedness of every kind. Their grand assembly used to be on the Lord's day; on which men, women, and children met together, to dance, fight, curse and swear, and play at chuck, ball, span-farthing, or whatever came next to hand. I felt great compassion for these poor creatures, from the time I heard of them first ; and the more, because all men seemed to despair of them. Between seven and eight I set out with John Heally, my guide. The north wind, being unusually high, drove the sleet in our faces, which froze as it fell, and cased us over presently. When we came to Placey, we could very hardly stand. As soon as we were a little recovered, I went into the square, and declared Him who "was wounded for our transgressions" and "bruised for our iniquities." The poor sinners were quickly gathered together, and gave earnest heed to the things which were spoken. And so they did in the afternoon again, in spite of the wind and snow, when I besought them to receive Him for their King ; to "repent and believe the gospel."

On *Easter Monday* and *Tuesday* I preached there again, the congregation continually increasing. And as most of these had never in their lives pretended to any religion of any kind, they were the more ready to cry to God as mere sinners, for the free redemption which is in Jesus.

Thur. 7.—Having settled all things according to my desire, I cheerfully took leave of all my friends at Newcastle, and rode that day to Sandhutton. At our inn I found a good-natured man sitting and drinking in the chimney-corner; with whom I began a discourse, suspecting nothing less than that he was the minister of the parish. Before we parted I spoke exceeding plain ; and he received it in love, begging he might see me when I came that way again. But before I came, he was gone into eternity.

Fri. 15.—I rode in two days to Wednesbury, but found things surprisingly altered. The inexcusable folly of Mr W——s had so provoked Mr E——n, that his former love was turned into bitter hatred. But he had not yet had time to work up the poor people into the rage and madness which afterwards appeared ; so that they were extremely quiet both this and the following days.

Yet on *Sunday*, 17, the scene began to open : I think I never heard so wicked a sermon, and delivered with such bitterness of voice and manner, as that which Mr E—— preached in the afternoon. I knew what effect this must have in a little time ; and therefore judged it expedient to prepare the poor people for what was to follow ; that, when it came, they might not be offended. Accordingly, on *Tuesday*, 19, I strongly enforced those words of our Lord, " If any man come after Me, and hate not his father and mother,—yea, and his own life, he cannot be My disciple. And whosoever doth not bear his cross, and come after Me, cannot be My disciple."

While I was speaking, a gentleman rode up very drunk; and after many unseemly and bitter words, laboured much to ride over some of the people. I was surprised to hear he was a neighbouring clergyman!

Thur. 21.—I spent an hour with some of my old friends, whom I had not seen for many years. I rejoiced to find them still loving and open of heart, just as they were before I went to Georgia. In the afternoon I called at Barkswell, near Coventry; where I had formerly spent many pleasant hours.— And here likewise I found friendship and openness still: but the master of the house was under heavy affliction.

Fri. 22.—I rode to Painswick; and on *Saturday*, 23, through heavy rain, to Bristol.

I had now a week of rest and peace, which was refreshing both to my soul and body. *Sunday*, May 1, I had an opportunity of receiving the Lord's Supper, at St James's, our parish church.

Tues. 3.—I set out for Wales, in company with one who was my pupil at Oxford. We could get that night no farther than the Bull, five Welsh miles beyond Abergavenny. The next morning we came to Builth, just as the church prayers began. Mr Phillips, the rector of Maesmennys (at whose invitation I came), soon took knowledge of me, and we began a friendship which I trust shall never end. I preached on a tomb at the east end of the church at four, and again at seven. Mr Gwynne and Mr Prothero (Justices of Peace) stood on either hand of me; and all the people before, catching every word, with the most serious and eager attention.

Thur. 5.—I rode over such rugged mountains as I never saw before, to Cardiff. About two I preached at Lantrissent; and at Fonmon Castle in the evening, to a loving and serious congregation.

Sat. 7.—I was desired to preach at Cowbridge. We came into the town about eleven; and many people seemed very desirous to hear for themselves, concerning the way which is everywhere spoken against; but it could not be: the sons of Belial gathered themselves together, headed by one or two wretches called gentlemen; and continued shouting, cursing, blaspheming, and throwing showers of stones, almost without intermission. So that after some time spent in prayer for them, I judged it best to dismiss the congregation.

Mon. 9.—I returned to Bristol.

Tues. 17.—My brother set out for Cornwall; where (according to the accounts we had frequently received) abundance of those who before neither feared God nor regarded man, began to inquire what they must do to be saved: but the same imprudence which had laid the foundation for all the disturbances in Staffordshire had broke out here also, and turned many of our friends into bitter and implacable enemies. Violent persecution was the natural consequence of this; but the power of God triumphed over all.

Sun. 29.—(Being *Trinity-Sunday*.) I began officiating at the chapel in West Street, near the Seven Dials, of which (by a strange chain of providences) we have a lease for several years.

Sat. June 18.—I received a full account of the terrible riots which had been in Staffordshire. I was not surprised at all: neither should I have wondered if, after the advices they had so often received from the pulpit, as well as from the episcopal chair, the zealous High Churchmen had rose, and cut all that were Methodists in pieces.

Mon. 20.—Resolving to assist them as far as I could, I set out early in the morning; and came, *Wednesday*, 22, to Francis Ward's, at Wednesbury.

Although I knew all that had been done here was as contrary to law as it was to justice and mercy, yet I knew not how to advise the poor sufferers, or to procure them any redress. I was then little acquainted with the English course of law, having long had scruples concerning it. But, as many of these were now removed, I thought it best to inquire whether there could be any help from the laws of the land. I therefore rode over to Counsellor Littleton, at Tamworth, who assured us we might have an easy remedy, if we resolutely prosecuted, in the manner the law directed, those rebels against God and the King.

Thur. 23.—I left Wednesbury, and rode on *Wednesday* to Newcastle.

Thur. 30.—I immediately inquired into the state of those whom I left here striving for the mastery.

Monday, July 4, and the following days, I had time to finish the *Instructions for Children*.

Sun. 10.—I preached at eight on Chowden Fell, on, "Why will ye die, O house of Israel?" Ever since I came to Newcastle the first time, my spirit had been moved within me, at the crowds of poor wretches who were every Sunday in the afternoon sauntering to and fro on the Sandhill. I resolved, if possible, to find them a better employ; and as soon as the service at All-Saints was over, walked straight from the church to the Sandhill, and gave out a verse of a psalm. In a few minutes I had company enough; thousands upon thousands crowding together. But the prince of this world fought with all his might, lest his kingdom should be overthrown. Indeed, the very mob of Newcastle, in the height of their rudeness, have commonly some humanity left. I scarce observed that they threw anything at all; neither did I receive the least personal hurt: but they continued thrusting one another to and fro, and making such a noise, that my voice could not be heard: so that, after spending near an hour in singing and prayer, I thought it best to adjourn to our own house.

Thur. 14.—I preached at the Lower Spen, seven or eight (northern) miles from Newcastle. John Brown had been obliged to remove hither from Tanfield Leigh, I believe by the peculiar providence of God. By his rough and strong, though artless, words, many of his neighbours had been much convinced, and began to search the Scriptures as they never had done before; so that they did not seem at all surprised when I declared, "He that believeth hath everlasting life."

Wed. 20.—I preached at Birstal and Hightown. After I had visited all the societies in these parts, and preached at as many of the little towns as I could, on *Monday*, 25, I rode to Barley Hall. Many from Sheffield were there. On *Tuesday* night and *Wednesday* morning I preached at Nottingham; on *Wednesday* evening, at Markfield.

Fri. 28.—We rode to Newport-Pagnell, and *Saturday*, 29, to London.

Sat. Aug. 6.—A convenient chapel was offered me at Snowsfields, on the other side the water. It was built on purpose, it seems, by a poor Arian misbeliever, for the defence and propagation of her bad faith.

Mon. 8.—Upon mention made of my design to preach here, a zealous woman warmly replied, "What! at Snowsfields! Will Mr W. preach at Snowsfields? Surely he will not do it! Why, there is not such another place in all the town. The people there are not men, but devils." However, I resolved to try if God was not stronger than them: so this evening I preached there on that Scripture, "Jesus said, They that be whole, need not a physician; but they that are sick. I came not to call the righteous, but sinners to repentance."

Mon. 22.—After a few of us had joined in prayer, about four I set out, and rode softly to Snow Hill; where, the saddle slipping quite upon my mare's neck, I fell over her head, and she ran back into Smithfield. Some boys caught her, and brought her to me again, cursing and swearing all the way. I spoke plainly to them, and they promised to amend. I was setting forward, when a man cried, "Sir, you have lost your saddle-cloth." Two or three more would needs help me to put it on; but these too swore at nearly every word. I turned to one and another, and spoke in love. They all took it well, and thanked me much. I gave them two or three little books, which they promised to read over carefully.

Before I reached Kensington, I found my mare had lost a shoe. This gave me an opportunity of talking closely, for near half an hour, both to the smith and his servant. I mention these little circumstances, to show how easy it is to redeem every fragment of time (if I may so speak), when we feel any love to those souls for which Christ died.

Tues. 23.—I came to Kingswood in the afternoon, and in the evening preached at Bristol,

Fri. 26.—I set out for Cornwall.

Tues. 30.—In the evening we reached St Ives. At seven I invited all guilty, helpless sinners, who were conscious they "had nothing to pay," to accept of free forgiveness.

Wed. 31.—I spoke severally with those of the society, who were about one hundred and twenty. Near an hundred of these had found peace with God : such is the blessing of being persecuted for righteousness' sake ! As we were going to church at eleven, a large company at the market-place welcomed us with a loud huzza : wit as harmless as the ditty sung under my window (composed, one assured me, by a gentlewoman of their *own* town)—

"Charles Wesley has come to town,
To try if he can pull the churches down."

In the evening I explained "the promise of the Father." After preaching, many began to be turbulent; but John Nelson went into the midst of them, spoke a little to the loudest, who answered not again, but went quietly away.

Thur. Sept. 1.—We had a day of peace. *Friday,* 2. I preached at Morva, about nine miles west of St Ives, on the north sea. My text was, "The land of Zabulon, and the land of Nephthalim, by the way of the sea ;—the people which sat in darkness saw a great light; and to them which sat in the region and shadow of death light is sprung up."

Sat. 3.—I rode to the Three-cornered Down (so called), nine or ten miles east of St Ives, where we found two or three hundred tinners, who had been some time waiting for us. They all appeared quite pleased and unconcerned : and many of them ran after us to Gwennap (two miles east), where their number was quickly increased to four or five hundred. One who lived near invited us to lodge at his house, and conducted us back to the Green in the morning. We came thither just as the day dawned

At six I preached at Sennan, near the Land's End ; and

appointed the little congregation (consisting chiefly of old, grey-headed men) to meet me again at five in the morning. But on *Sunday*, 11, great part of them were got together between three and four o'clock: so between four and five we began praising God.

We went afterwards down, as far as we could go safely, toward the point of the rocks at the Land's End. It was an awful sight! But how will these melt away, when God ariseth to judgment!

Between eight and nine I preached at St Just, on the green plain near the town, to the largest congregation (I was informed) that ever had been seen in these parts.

Soon after one, we had such another congregation, on the north side of Morva church.

At Zennor I preached about five, and then hastened to St Ives, where we concluded the day in praising God with joyful lips.

Mon. 12.—I preached at one on Trezuthan Downs, and in the evening at St Ives. The dread of God fell upon us while I was speaking, so that I could hardly utter a word; but most of all in prayer.

I had had for some time a great desire to go and publish the love of God our Saviour, if it were but for one day, in the Isles of Scilly; and I had occasionally mentioned it to several. This evening three of our brethren came and offered to carry me thither, if I could procure the mayor's boat, which, they said, was the best sailer of any in the town. I sent, and he lent it me immediately. So the next morning, *Tuesday*, 13, John Nelson, Mr Shepherd, and I, with three men and a pilot, sailed from St Ives. It seemed strange to me to attempt going in a fisher-boat, fifteen leagues upon the main ocean, especially when the waves began to swell, and hang over our heads. But I called to my companions, and we all joined together in singing lustily and with a good courage—

> "When passing through the watery deep,
>   I ask in faith His promised aid;
> The waves an awful distance keep,
>   And shrink from my devoted head;
> Fearless their violence I dare:
> They cannot harm,—for God is there."

About half an hour after one, we landed on St Mary's, the chief of the inhabited islands.

We immediately waited upon the Governor, with the usual present, viz. a newspaper. I desired him, likewise, to accept of an *Earnest Appeal*. The minister not being willing I should preach in the church, I preached, at six, in the street, to almost all the town, and many soldiers, sailors, and workmen, on "Why will ye die, O house of Israel?" It was a blessed time, so that I scarce knew how to conclude. After sermon I gave them some little books and hymns, which they were so eager to receive, that they were ready to tear both them and me to pieces.

At five in the morning I preached again. And between nine and ten, having talked with many in private, and distributed both to them and others between two and three hundred hymns and little books, we left this barren, dreary place, and set sail for St Ives, though the wind was strong, and blew directly in our teeth. Our pilot said we should have good luck if we reached the land; but he knew not Him whom the winds and seas obey. Soon after three we were even with the Land's End, and about nine we reached St Ives.

Fri. 16.—In the evening, as I was preaching at St Ives, Satan began to fight for his kingdom. The mob of the town burst into the room, and created much disturbance; roaring and striking those that stood in their way, as though Legion himself possessed them. I would fain have persuaded our people to stand still; but the zeal of some, and the fear of others, had no ears: so that, finding the uproar increase, I went into the midst, and brought the head of the mob up with me to the desk. I received but one blow on the side of the head; after which we reasoned the case, till he grew milder and milder, and at length undertook to quiet his companions.

Mon. 19.—We were informed, the rabble had designed to make their general assault in the evening. But one of the aldermen came, at the request of the mayor, and stayed with us the whole time of the service. So that no man opened his mouth, while I explained, "None is like unto the God of Jeshurun, who rideth upon the heavens unto thy help, and in His excellency upon the sky."

Tues. 20.—I concluded my preaching here. We reached Gwennap a little before six, and found the plain covered from end to end. It was supposed there were ten thousand people. I could not conclude till it was so dark we could scarce see one another. And there was on all sides the deepest attention; none speaking, stirring, or scarce looking aside.

One of those who were present was Mr P——, once a violent adversary. Before sermon began, he whispered one of his acquaintance, "Captain, stand by me; don't stir from me." He soon burst out into a flood of tears, and quickly after sunk down. His friend caught him, and prevented his falling to the ground.

Wed. 21.—I was waked, between three and four, by a large company of tinners, who, fearing they should be too late, had gathered round the house, and were singing and praising God. At five I preached once more.

We rode to Launceston that day. *Thursday*, 22. As we were riding through a village called Sticklepath, one stopped me in the street, and asked abruptly, "Is not thy name John Wesley?" Immediately two or three more came up, and told me I must stop there. I did so; and before we had spoke many words, our souls took acquaintance with each other. I found they were called Quakers: but that hurt not me, seeing the love of God was in their hearts.

Sun. Oct. 2.—Fearing my strength would not suffice for preaching more than four times in the day, I only spent half an hour in prayer with the society in the morning.

Mon. 3.—I returned to Bristol, and employed several days in examining and purging the society, which still consisted (after many were put away) of more than seven hundred persons. The next week I examined the society in Kingswood, in which I found but a few things to reprove.

Sat. 15.—The Leaders brought in what had been contributed, in their several classes, toward the public debt; and we found it was sufficient to discharge it; which was therefore done without delay.

Thur. 20.—I rode to Wednesbury. At twelve I preached in a ground near the middle of the town, to a far larger congregation than was expected. I believe every one present felt the power of God: and no creature offered to molest us, either going or coming; but the Lord fought for us, and we held our peace.

I was writing at Francis Ward's, in the afternoon, when the cry arose that the mob had beset the house. We prayed that God would disperse them; and it was so: one went this way, and another that; so that, in half an hour, not a man was left. I told our brethren, "Now is the time for us to go"; but they pressed me exceedingly to stay. So that I might not offend them, I sat down, though I foresaw what would follow. Before five the mob surrounded the house again in greater numbers than ever. The cry of one and all was, "Bring out the minister; we will have the minister." I desired one to take their captain by the hand, and bring him into the house. After a few sentences interchanged between us, the lion was become a lamb. I desired him to go and bring one or two more of the most angry of his companions. He brought in two, who were ready to swallow the ground with rage; but in two minutes they were as calm as he. I then bade them make way, that I might go out among the people. As soon as I was in the midst of them, I called for a chair; and standing up, asked, "What do any of you want with me?" Some said, "We want you to go with us to the justice." I replied, "That I will, with all my heart." I then spoke a few words, which God applied; so that they cried out, with might and main, "The gentleman is an honest gentleman, and we will spill our blood in his defence." I asked, "Shall we go to the justice to-night, or in the morning?" Most of them cried "To-night, to-night"; on which I went before, and two or three hundred followed; the rest returning whence they came.

The night came on before we had walked a mile, together with heavy rain. However, on we went to Bentley Hall, two miles from Wednesbury. One or two ran before, to tell Mr Lane they had brought Mr Wesley before his Worship. Mr Lane replied, "What have I to do with Mr Wesley? Go and carry him back again." By this time the main body came up, and began knocking at the door. A servant told them Mr Lane was in bed. His son followed, and asked what was the matter. One replied, "Why, an't please you, they sing psalms all day; nay, and make folks rise at five in the morning. And what would your Worship advise us to do?" "To go home," said Mr Lane, "and be quiet."

Here they were at a full stop, till one advised, to go to Justice Persehouse, at Walsal. All agreed to this; so we hastened on, and about seven came to his house. But Mr P—— likewise sent word that he was in bed. Now they were at a stand again; but at last they all thought it the wisest course to make the best of their way home. About fifty of them undertook to convoy me. But we had not gone a hundred yards, when the mob of Walsal came, pouring in like a flood, and bore down all before them. The Darlaston mob made what defence they could; but they were weary, as well as outnumbered: so that in a short time, many being knocked down, the rest ran away, and left me in their hands.

To attempt speaking was vain; for the noise on every side was like the roaring of the sea. So they dragged me along till we came to the town; where, seeing the door of a large house open, I attempted to go in; but a man, catching me by the hair, pulled me back into the middle of the mob. They made no more stop till they had carried me through the main street, from one end of the town to the other. I continued speaking all the time to those within hearing, feeling no pain or weariness. At the west end of the town, seeing a door half open, I made toward it, and would have gone in; but a gentleman in the shop would not suffer me, saying, they would pull the house down to the ground. However, I stood at the door, and asked, "Are you willing to hear me speak?" Many cried out, "No, no! knock his brains out; down with him; kill him at once." Others said, "Nay, but we will hear him first." I began asking, "What evil have I done? Which of you all have I wronged in word or deed?" And continued speaking for above a quarter of an hour, till my voice suddenly failed; then the floods began to lift up their voice again; many crying out, "Bring him away! bring him away!"

In the meantime my strength and my voice returned, and I broke out aloud into prayer. And now the man who just before headed the mob, turned, and said, "Sir, I will spend my life for you: follow me, and not one soul here shall touch a hair of your head." Two or three of his fellows confirmed his words, and got close to me immediately. At the same time, the gentleman in the shop cried out, "For shame, for shame! Let him go." An honest butcher, who was a little farther off, said it was a shame they should do thus; and pulled back four or five, one after another, who were running on the most fiercely. The people then, as if it had been by common consent, fell back to the right and left; while those three or four men took me between them, and carried me through them all. But on the bridge the mob rallied again; we therefore went on one side, over the mill dam, and thence through the meadows; till, a little before ten, God brought me safe to Wednesbury; having lost only one flap of my waistcoat, and a little skin from one of my hands.

I never saw such a chain of providences before; so many convincing proofs, that the hand of God is on every person and thing, overruling all as it seemeth Him good.

The poor woman of Darlaston, who had headed that mob, and sworn, that none should touch me, when she saw her followers give way, ran into the thickest of the throng, and knocked down three or four men, one after another. But many assaulting her at once, she was soon overpowered, and had probably been killed in a few minutes (three men keeping her down and beating her with all their might), had not a man called to one of them, "Hold, Tom, hold!" "Who is there?" said Tom: "what, honest Munchin! Nay, then, let her go." So they held their hand, and let her get up and crawl home as well as she could.

From the beginning to the end, I found the same presence of mind, as if I had been sitting in my own study. But I took no thought for one moment before another; only once it came into my mind, that if they should throw me into the river, it would spoil the papers that were in my pocket. For myself, I did not doubt but I should swim across, having but a thin coat, and a light pair of boots.

The circumstances that follow, I thought, were particularly remarkable. 1. That many endeavoured to throw me down while we were going downhill on a slippery path to the town; as well judging, that if I was once on the ground, I should hardly rise any more. But I made no stumble at all, nor the least slip till I was entirely out of their hands. 2. That although many strove to lay hold on my collar or clothes, to pull me down, they could not fasten at all: only one got fast hold of the flap of my waistcoat, which was soon left in his hand; the other flap, in the pocket of which was a bank-note, was torn but half off. 3. That a lusty man just behind struck at me several times with a large oaken stick; with which if he had struck me once on the back part of my head, it would have saved him all further trouble. But every time the blow was turned aside, I know not how; for I could not move to the right hand or left. 4. That another came rushing through the press, and raising his arm to strike, on a sudden let it drop, and only stroked my head, saying, "What soft hair he has!" 5. That I stopped exactly at the mayor's door, as if I had known it (which the mob doubtless thought I did), and found him standing in the shop, which gave the first check to the madness of the people. 6. That the very first men whose hearts were turned were the heroes of the town, the captains of the rabble on all occasions, one of them having been a prize-fighter at the bear-garden. 7. That, from first to last, I heard none give a reviling word, or call me by any opprobrious name whatever; but the cry of one and all was "The preacher! The preacher! The parson! The minister!" 8. That no creature, at least within my hearing, laid anything to my charge, either true or false; having in the hurry quite forgot to provide themselves with an accusation of any kind. And, lastly, that they were as utterly at a loss what they should do with me; none proposing any determinate thing; only, "Away with him! Kill him at once!"

By how gentle degrees does God prepare us for His will! Two years ago a piece of brick grazed my shoulders. It was a year after that the stone struck me between the eyes. Last month I received one blow, and this evening two; one before we came into the town, and one after we were gone out; but both were as nothing: for though one man struck me on the breast with all his might, and the other on the mouth with such a force that the blood gushed out immediately, I felt no more pain from either of the blows, than if they had touched me with a straw.

It ought not to be forgotten, that when the rest of the society made all haste to escape for their lives, four only would not stir, William Sitch, Edward Slater, John Griffiths, and Joan Parks: these kept with me, resolving to live or die together; and none of them received one blow, but William Sitch, who held me by the arm, from one end of the town to the other. He was then dragged away and knocked down; but he soon rose and got to me again. I afterwards asked him, what he expected when the mob came upon us. He said, "To die for Him who had died for us": and he felt no hurry or fear; but calmly waited till God should require his soul of him.

I asked J. Parks, if she was not afraid, when they tore her from me. She said, "No; no more than I am now. I could trust God for you, as well as for myself. From the beginning I had a full persuasion that God would deliver you. I knew not how; but I left that to Him, and was as sure as if it were already done." I asked, if the report was true, that she had fought for me. She said, "No; I knew God would fight for His children." And shall these souls perish at the last?

When I came back to Francis Ward's I found many of our brethren waiting upon God. Many also whom I never had seen before came to rejoice with us. And the next morning, as I rode through the town on my way to Nottingham, every one I met expressed such a cordial affection, that I could scarce believe what I saw and heard.

I cannot close this head without inserting as great a curiosity in its kind as, I believe, was ever yet seen in England; which had its birth within a very few days of this remarkable occurrence at Walsal.

"STAFFORDSHIRE.

"To all High-Constables, Petty-Constables, and other of His Majesty's Peace Officers, within the said County, and particularly to the Constable of Tipton" (near Walsal):

"WHEREAS, we, His Majesty's Justices of the Peace for the said County of Stafford, having received information that several disorderly persons, styling themselves Methodist Preachers, go about raising routs and riots, to the great damage of His Majesty's liege people, and against the peace of our Sovereign Lord the King:

"These are, in His Majesty's name, to command you and every one of you, within your respective districts, to make diligent search after the said Methodist Preachers, and to bring him or them before some of us His said Majesty's Justices of the Peace, to be examined concerning their unlawful doings.

"Given under our hands and seals, this   day of October, 1743.

"J. LANE.
"W. PERSEHOUSE."

(*N.B.*—The very justices to whose houses I was carried, and who severally refused to see me!)

Sat. 22.—I rode from Nottingham to Epworth, and on Monday set out for Grimsby: but at Ferry we were at a full stop, the boatmen telling us we could not pass the Trent; it was as much as our lives were worth to put from shore before the storm abated. We waited an hour; but, being afraid it would do much hurt, if I should disappoint the congregation at Grimsby, I asked the men if they did not think it possible to get to the other shore: they said, they could not tell; but if we would venture our lives, they would venture theirs. So we put off, having six men, two women, and three horses, in the boat. Many stood looking after us on the riverside, in the middle of which we were, when, in an instant, the side of the boat was under water, and the horses and men rolling one over another. We expected the boat to sink every moment; but I did not doubt of being able to swim ashore. The boatmen were amazed as well as the rest; but they quickly recovered and rowed for life. And soon after, our horses leaping overboard, lightened the boat, and we all came unhurt to land.

They wondered what was the matter I did not rise (for I lay along in the bottom of the boat), and I wondered too, till, upon examination, I found that a large iron crow, which the boatmen sometimes used, was (none knew how) run through the string of my boot, which pinned me down that I could not stir; so that if the boat had sunk, I should have been safe enough from swimming any further.

The same day, and, as near as we could judge, the same hour, the boat in which my brother was crossing the Severn, at the New Passage, was carried away by the wind, and in the utmost danger of splitting upon the rocks. But the same God, when all human hope was past, delivered them as well as us.

In the evening, the house at Grimsby not being able to contain one-fourth of the congregation, I stood in the street, and exhorted every prodigal to "arise and go to" his "father." One or two endeavoured to interrupt; but they were soon stilled by their own companions. The next day, *Tuesday*, 25, one in the town promised us the use of a large room; but he was prevailed upon to retract his promise before the hour of preaching came. I then designed going to the Cross, but the rain prevented; so that we were a little at a loss, till we were offered a very convenient place, by a "woman which was a sinner." I there declared "Him" (about one o'clock) whom "God hath exalted, to give repentance and remission of sins." And God so confirmed the word of His grace, that I marvelled anyone could withstand Him.

However, the prodigal held out till the evening, when I enlarged upon her sins and faith, who "washed our Lord's feet with tears, and wiped them with the hairs of her head." She was then utterly broken in pieces (as, indeed, was well-nigh the whole congregation), and came after me to my lodging, crying out, "Oh, sir! what must I do to be saved?" Being now informed of her case, I said, "Escape for your life. Return instantly to your husband." She said, "But how can it be? Which way can I go? He is above an hundred miles off. I have just received a letter from him, and he is at Newcastle-upon-Tyne." I told her, "I am going for Newcastle in the morning: you may go with me. William Blow shall take you behind him." And so he did. Glory be to the Friend of sinners! He hath plucked one more brand out of the fire.— Thou poor sinner, thou hast "received a Prophet in the name of a Prophet"; and thou art found of Him that sent him

William Blow, Mrs S., and I set out at six. During our whole journey to Newcastle, I scarce observed her to laugh or even smile once. Nor did she ever complain of anything, or appear moved in the least with those trying circumstances which many times occurred in our way. A steady seriousness, or sadness rather, appeared in her whole behaviour and conversation, as became one that felt the burden of sin and was groaning after salvation. In the same spirit, by all I could observe or learn, she continued during her stay at Newcastle. Not long after, her husband removed from thence, and wrote to her to follow him. She set out in a ship bound for Hull. A storm met them by the way; the ship sprung a leak; but though it was near the shore, on which many people flocked together, yet the sea ran so exceeding high, that it was impossible to make any help. Mrs S. was seen standing on the deck, as the ship gradually sunk, and afterwards hanging by her hands on the ropes, till the masts likewise disappeared. Even then, for some moments, they could observe her floating upon the waves, till her clothes, which buoyed her up, being thoroughly wet, she sunk,—I trust, into the ocean of God's mercy.

CHAPTER VII

PERILS AND PERSECUTIONS

FROM OCTOBER 28, 1743, TO NOVEMBER 17, 1746

Friday, October 28, 1743.—We rode with William Holmes, "an Israelite indeed," from Epworth to Sykehouse. Here I preached at ten, and hastened on to Leeds; from whence, setting out early in the morning, I had hopes of reaching Wensley Dale before it was dark; but it could not be: so in the dusk of the evening, understanding we had five or six miles still to ride, I thought it best to procure a guide. In less than an hour, it being extremely dark, I perceived we were got out of all road. We were in a large meadow, near a river, and (it seemed to me) almost surrounded with water. I asked our guide, "Do you know where you are?" and he honestly answered, "No." So we rode on as we could, till about eight we came to a little house, whence we were directed into a lane which led to Wensley.

Sun. 30.—Mr Clayton read prayers, and I preached, on, "What must I do to be saved?" As I went back through the churchyard, many of the parish were in high debate what religion this preacher was of. Some said, "He must be a Quaker"; others, "an Anabaptist": but, at length, one deeper learned than the rest, brought them all clearly over to his opinion, that he was a *Presbyterian Papist*.

Mon. 31.—We set out early in the morning, and in the evening came to Newcastle.

Wed. Nov. 2.—The following advertisement was published:—

FOR THE BENEFIT OF MR ESTE.

By the Edinburgh Company of Comedians, on *Friday, November* 4, will be acted a Comedy, called,

THE CONSCIOUS LOVERS;

To which will be added, a Farce, called,

TRICK UPON TRICK, OR METHODISM DISPLAYED.

On *Friday*, a vast multitude of spectators were assembled in the Moot Hall to see this. It was believed there could not be less than fifteen hundred people, some hundreds of whom sat on rows of seats built upon the stage. Soon after the comedians had begun the first act of the play, on a sudden all those seats fell down at once, the supporters of them breaking like a rotten stick. The people were thrown one upon another, about five foot forward, but not one of them hurt. After a short time, the rest of the spectators were quiet, and the actors went on. In the middle of the second act, all the shilling seats gave a crack, and sunk several inches down. A great noise and shrieking followed, and as many as could readily get to the door went out, and returned no more. Notwithstanding this, when the noise was over, the actors went on with the play. In the beginning of the third act the entire stage suddenly sunk about six inches: the players retired with great precipitation; yet in a while they began again. At the latter end of the third act, all the sixpenny seats, without any kind of notice, fell to the ground. There was now a cry on every side; it being supposed that many were crushed in pieces: but, upon inquiry, not a single person (such was the mercy of God!) was either killed or dangerously hurt. Two or three hundred remaining still in the hall, Mr Este (who was to act the Methodist) came upon the stage and told them, for all this he was resolved the farce should be acted. While he was speaking, the stage sunk six inches more; on which he ran back in the utmost confusion, and the people as fast as they could out of the door, none staying to look behind him.

Which most is surprising—that those players acted this farce the next week, or that some hundreds of people came again to see it?

Thur. 17.—I preached at the Spen, on, Christ Jesus, our "wisdom, righteousness, sanctification, and redemption." I have seldom seen an audience so greatly moved, since the time of my first preaching at Bristol. Men, women, and children wept and groaned, and trembled exceedingly; many could not contain themselves in these bounds, but cried with a loud and bitter cry.

Wed. 23.—I rode to Leeds: *Sat*. 26, to Nottingham: *Mon*. 28, to Breson. and spent an hour or two in conversation with Mr Simpson: the oddest, honestest enthusiast, surely, that ever was upon earth. Before we parted he told me, "One thing I don't like; your taking away my flock at Nottingham. Just now that text is brought to my mind; it is the very case;

pray read it out." I did so, as follows: "And Abraham reproved Abimelech, because of the well which Abimelech's servants had violently taken away." I desired him to read my answer in the next verse: "And Abimelech said unto Abraham, I wot not who hath done this thing; neither heard I anything thereof from thee, save this day."

In the afternoon I rode to Markfield, and on *Thursday*, Dec. 1, to London.

I had full employment here for some weeks following, in speaking severally to the members of the society. Many of these I was obliged to set aside; there remained about two-and-twenty hundred persons.

Sun. Jan. 8, 1744.—In the evening I rode to Brentford, on *Monday* to Marlborough, and the next day to Bristol.

Wed. 11.—I began examining the society; and not before it was wanted: for the plague was begun. I found many crying out, "Faith, faith! Believe, believe!" but making little account of the fruits of faith, either of holiness or good works. In a few days they came to themselves, and had a more thorough understanding of the truth as it is in Jesus.

Wed. Feb. 1.—About this time the soldiers abroad began to meet together, as we learned from the following letter:—

"GHENT, *February* 2, 1744.

"SIR,—I make bold to send you these lines. February 18, 1743, we began our march for Germany. I was then much cast down, and my heart was ready to break. But the day we marched to Maestricht, I found the love of God shed abroad in my heart, that I thought my very soul was dissolved into tears. But this lasted not above three weeks, and then I was in heaviness again; till, on April 24, as I was walking in the fields, God broke my hard heart in pieces. And yet I was not delivered from the fear of death. I went to my quarters very sick and weak, in great pain of soul and body. By the morning I was so weak I could scarce go: but this proved a sweet night to my soul; for now I knew there was no condemnation for me, believing in Christ Jesus.

"June 16.—The day we engaged the French at Dettingen, as the battle began, I said, 'Lord, in Thee have I trusted; let me never be confounded.' Joy overflowed my soul, and I told my comrades, 'If I fall this day, I shall rest in the everlasting arms of Christ.' Now I felt I could be content to be cast into the sea, for the sake of my dear brethren, so their eyes might be opened, and they might see, before it was too late, the things that belong unto their peace.

"When we came to winter quarters, there were but three of us joined together. But now, by the blessing of God, we are increased to twelve: and we have reason to believe the hand of the Lord is with us. I desire, for the sake of Him whom we follow after, that you would send us some instructions, how to proceed in our little society. God is become a mouth to me, and has blessed even my word to some of their souls. All praise, and glory, and honour, be unto Him and to the Lamb for ever and ever.—From your affectionate brother,

"J. H."

Wed. 15.—We were informed of the invasion intended by the French, who were expected to land every hour. I therefore exhorted the congregation, in the words of our Lord, Luke xxi. 36, "Watch ye therefore, and pray always, that ye may be accounted worthy to escape all these things that shall come to pass, and to stand before the Son of Man."

We observed *Friday*, 17, as a day of solemn fasting and prayer. In the afternoon, many being met together, I exhorted them, now, while they had opportunity, to make to themselves "friends of the mammon of unrighteousness"; to deal their bread to the hungry, to clothe the naked, and not to hide themselves from their own flesh. And God opened their hearts, so that they contributed near fifty pounds, which I began laying out the very next hour, in linen, woollen, and shoes for them whom I knew to be diligent and yet in want.

Sat. 18. I received an account, from James Jones, of another kind of invasion in Staffordshire. The substance of it was as follows:—

"On Monday, January 23, a great mob gathered together at Darlaston, a mile from Wednesbury. They fell upon a few people who were going to Wednesbury, and, among the rest, on Joshua Constable's wife, of Darlaston. Some of them threw her down, and five or six held her down, that another might force her. But she continued to resist, till they changed their purpose, beat her much, and went away.

"Mon. 30.—The mob gathered again, broke into Joshua Co........................ of it down, broke some of his goods .. ...., and carried the rest away; particularly all his shop-goods, to a considerable value. But not satisfied with this, they sought for him and his wife, swearing they would knock their brains out. Their little children meantime, as well as themselves, wandered up and down, no one daring to relieve or take them in, lest they should hazard their own lives.

"Tues. 31.—About a hundred of the mob met together, on the

Church Hill at Wednesbury. But hearing some of Wednesbury were resolved to defend themselves, they dispersed for that time.

"Wed. February 1.—Mr Charles Wesley came to Birmingham, and the next day preached at Wednesbury. The whole congregation was quiet and attentive, nor had we any noise or interruption.

"Mon. 6.—I accompanied him part of his way, and in the afternoon came back to Wednesbury. I found the society met together, and commending themselves to God in prayer, having been informed that many, both at Darlaston and other places, had bound themselves by an oath, to come on Shrove-Tuesday (the next day), and plunder all the Methodists in Wednesbury.

"We continued in prayer till the evening. I desired, as many as could, to meet me again at eight in the morning. But I had scarce begun to speak, when one came running with all speed, and told us, a large mob was coming into the town, and had broke into some houses already. I immediately retired to my father's house; but he did not dare to receive me. Nor did anyone else; till at length Henry Parks took me in; whence, early in the morning, I went to Birmingham.

"The mob had been gathering all Monday night, and on Tuesday morning they began their work. They assaulted, one after another, all the houses of those who were called Methodists. They first broke all their windows, suffering neither glass, lead, nor frames to remain therein. Then they made their way in; and all the tables, chairs, chests of drawers, with whatever was not easily removable, they dashed in pieces, particularly shop-goods, and furniture of every kind. What they could not well break, as feather-beds, they cut in pieces, and strewed about the room. William Sitch's wife was lying-in: but that was all one; they pulled away her bed too, and cut it in pieces." (Had the French come in that place, would they have done more?) "All this time none offered to resist them. Indeed, most part, both men and women, fled for their lives; only the children stayed, not knowing whither to go. Wearing apparel, and things which were of value, or easily saleable, they carried away; every man loading himself with as much as he could well carry, of whatever he liked best.

"Some of the gentlemen who had set the mob to work, or threatened to turn away collier or miner out of their service, that did not come and do his part, now drew up a paper for those of the society to sign, importing, that they would never invite or receive any Methodist preacher more. On this condition, they told them they would stop the mob at once: otherwise they must take what followed.

"This they offered to several; but they declared, one and all, 'We have already lost all our goods; and nothing more can follow, but the loss of our lives, which we will lose too, rather than wrong our consciences.'

"On Wednesday the mob divided into two or three companies, one of which went to Aldridge, four miles from Wednesbury, and plundered many houses there, as they had done in several other villages. Here also they loaded themselves with clothes and goods of all sorts, as much as they could stand under. They came back through Walsal with their spoils; but the gentlemen of Walsal being apprised of their coming, raised a body of men, who met them, took what they had away, and laid it up in the town-hall. Notice was then sent to Aldridge, that every man who had been plundered, might come and take his own goods.

"Mr Wood, of Wednesbury, likewise told several, they should have what could be found of their goods, on condition they would promise not to receive or hear those preachers any more.

"On Friday, in the afternoon, I went from Birmingham, designing to go to Tipton Green: but finding the mob were still raging up and down, I returned to Birmingham, and soon after (having as yet no more place in these parts), set out for London."

Any who desire to see a fuller and more particular account of these surprising transactions, may read a small tract, entitled "Modern Christianity exemplified at Wednesbury."

Before I leave this subject, it may be proper to insert an advertisement, which was not long after inserted in the public papers.

In the *Whitehall and London Evening Post*, Saturday, February 18, was a paragraph with some mistakes, which it may not be amiss to rectify. "By a private letter from Staffordshire, we have advice of an insurrection *of* the people called Methodists,"—the insurrection was not *of* the people called Methodists, but *against* them,—"who upon some *pretended* insults of the Church party,"—they *pretended* no insults from the Church party; being themselves no other than *true* members of the Church of England; but were *more* than insulted by a mixed multitude of church-goers (who seldom, if ever, go near a church), Dissenters, and Papists,—"have assembled themselves in a riotous manner."—Here is another small *error personæ*. Many hundreds of the mob did assemble themselves in a riotous manner, having given public notice several days before (particularly by a paper set up in Walsal

market-place), that on Shrove-Tuesday they intended to come and destroy the Methodists, and inviting all the country to come and join them. "And having committed several outrages,"—without ever committing any, they have suffered all manner of outrages for several months past,—" they proceeded at last to burn the house of one of their adversaries."
—Without burning any house or making any resistance, some hundreds of them, on Shrove-Tuesday last, had their own houses broken up, their windows, window-cases, beds, tools, goods of all sorts, broke all to pieces, or taken away by open violence ; their live goods driven off, themselves forced to fly for their lives, and most of them stripped of all they had in the world.

Ever since the 20th of last June the mob of Walsal, Darlaston, and Wednesbury, hired for that purpose by their betters, have broke open their poor neighbours' houses at their pleasure, by night and by day ; extorted money from the few that had it ; took away or destroyed their victuals and goods ; beat and wounded their bodies ; threatened their lives ; abused their women (some in a manner too horrible to name), and openly declared they would destroy every Methodist in the country : the Christian country, where His Majesty's innocent and loyal subjects have been so treated for eight months ; and are now, by their wanton persecutors, publicly branded for rioters and incendiaries !

Sat. 25.—In returning at night from Snowsfields, at the corner of Joyner Street, the coach, wherein five of us were, was overturned ; but without anyone's being hurt ; although the shock was so great as not only to dash out the forewindows in pieces, but to break the axle-tree in two.

Mon. 27.—Was the day I had appointed to go out of town ; but understanding a Proclamation was just published, requiring all Papists to go out of London before the Friday following, I was determined to stay another week, that I might cut off all occasion of reproach. I was the more willing to stay, that I might procure more raiment for the poor before I left London.

For this purpose I made a second collection, which amounted to about thirty pounds. But perceiving that the whole money received would not answer one-third of the expense, I determined to go round the classes, and beg for the rest, till I had gone through the whole society.

Tuesday, Mar. 20.—Having received a summons from the justices of Surrey, to appear at their court at St ~aret's Hill, I did so; and asked, " Has anyone anything to l..

my charge?" None made any reply. At length, one of the justices said, "Sir, are you willing to take the oaths to His Majesty, and to sign the declaration against Popery?" I said, "I am", which I accordingly did, and returned home.

Thur. 22.—I gave the society an account of what had been done with regard to the poor. By the contributions and collections I had received about one hundred and seventy pounds; with which above three hundred and thirty poor had been provided with needful clothing. Thirty or forty remaining still in want, and there being some debts for the clothes already distributed, the next day, being *Good-Friday*, I made one collection more, of about six-and-twenty pounds. This treasure, at least, "neither rust nor moth" shall "corrupt," "nor thieves break through and steal."

Mon. April 2.—I preached at five, and rode on toward Launceston. The hills were covered with snow, as in the depth of winter, About two we came to Trewint, wet and weary enough, having been battered by the rain and hail for some hours. I preached in the evening to many more than the house would contain, on the happiness of him whose sins are forgiven. In the morning Degory Ishel undertook to pilot us over the great moor, all the paths being covered with snow; which, in many places, was driven together, too deep for horse or man to pass. The hail followed us for the first seven miles; we had then a fair, though exceeding sharp day. I preached at Gwennap in the evening, to a plain, simple-hearted people; and God comforted us by each other.

Wed. 4.—About eleven we reached St Ives. I was a little surprised at entering John Nance's house; being received by many, who were waiting for me there, with a loud (though not bitter) cry. But they soon recovered; and we poured out our souls together in praises and thanksgiving.

As soon as we went out, we were saluted, as usual, with a huzza, and a few stones, or pieces of dirt. But in the evening none opened his mouth, while I proclaimed, "I will love Thee, O Lord, my strength.—I will call upon the Lord, who is worthy to be praised; so shall I be saved from my enemies."

Thur. 5.—I took a view of the ruins of the house which the mob had pulled down a little before, for joy that Admiral Matthews had beat the Spaniards. Such is the Cornish method of thanksgiving. I suppose, if Admiral Lestock had fought too, they would have knocked all the Methodists on the head.

Sat. 7.—I took down part of the account of the late riot which (to show the deep regard of the actors herein for His

Majesty) was on the self-same day on which His Majesty's Proclamation against rioters was read. Yet I see much good has been brought out of it already ; particularly the great peace we now enjoy.

About eleven John Nance and I set out for Morva. Having both the wind and rain full in our faces, we were thoroughly wet before we came to Rosemargay, where some of our brethren met us. I found there had been a shaking among them, occasioned by the confident assertions of some, that they had seen Mr Wesley, a week or two ago, with the Pretender in France ; and others, that he was in prison at London. Yet the main body still stood firm together, and were not removed from the hope of the gospel.

The wind and rain beat hard upon us again, as we walked from Morva to St Just, which also frighted many from coming. However, some hundreds were there, to whom I declared, " If ye have nothing to pay, God will frankly forgive you all." It is remarkable, that those of St Just were the chief of the whole country for hurling, fighting, drinking, and all manner of wickedness ; but many of the lions are become lambs, are continually praising God, and calling their old companions in sin to come and magnify the Lord together.

Tues. 10.—I was inquiring, how Dr B——e, a person of unquestioned sense and learning, could speak evil of "this way," after he had seen such a change in the most abandoned of his parishioners : but I was satisfied, when Jonathan Reeves informed me, that on the Doctor's asking him who had been the better for this preaching, and his replying, " The man before you (John Daniel) for one, who never before knew any work of God upon his soul," the Doctor answered, " Get along : you are a parcel of mad, cr⸺headed fellows " ; and, taking him by the shoulder, fairly⸺ust him to the door.

Wed. 11.—Being the P⸺ıc Fast, the church at St Ives was well filled. After read⸺ ⸺hose strong words, " If they have called the master ⸺ ⸺ house Beelzebub, how much more them of his housel⸺. !" Mr H. fulfilled them, by vehemently declaiming agains⸺ *the new sect*, as enemies of the Church, Jacobites, Papists and what not ! After church, we met, and spent an hour in prayer, not forgetting the poor sinner against his own soul.

In the evening I preached at Gwennap. I stood on the wall, in the calm, still evening, with the setting sun behind me, and almost an innumerable multitude before, behind, and on either hand. Many, likewise, sat on the little hills, at some distance from the bulk of the congregation. But they could all hear distinctly, while I read, "The disciple is not above his Master," and the rest of those comfortable words, which are day by day fulfilled in our ears.

Thur. 12.—About eleven I preached at Crowan. In the afternoon we heard of the success of Mr H.'s sermon. James Wheatley was walking through the town in the evening, when the mob gathered, and began to throw stones from all quarters. He stepped into an house; but the master of it followed him, like a lion, to drag him out. Yet, after a few words, his mind was changed, and he swore nobody should hurt him. Meantime one went for a Justice of Peace, who came and promised to see him safe home. The mob followed, hallooing and shouting amain. Near John Paynter's house the justice left him: they quickly beset the house. But a messenger came from the mayor, forbidding any to touch Mr Wheatley, at his peril. He then went home. But between seven and eight the mob came and beset John Nance's house. John Nance and John Paynter went out, and stood before the door; though they were quickly covered with dirt. The cry was, "Bring out the preacher! Pull down the house!" And they began to pull down the boards which were nailed against the windows. But the mayor, hearing it, came without delay, and read the Proclamation against riots: upon which, after many oaths and imprecations, they thought proper to disperse.

About six I reached Morva, wet through and through; the rain having continued with scarce any intermission. However, a little company were gathered together, to whom I preached, on, "Ask, and it shall be given you." The next day I had time to dry my clothes at Mr John's, near Penzance. At noon I preached on the Downs, not far from his house; about three at Gulval, and at St Ives in the evening.

Sat. 14.—I took my leave of St Ives.

At five I preached at Gwennap, on a little hill, near the usual place. It rained from the time I began till I concluded. I felt no pain while I spoke; but the instant I had done, and all the time I was with the society, my teeth and head ached so violently, that I had hardly any senses. I lay down as soon as I could, and fell asleep. In the morning (blessed be God) I ailed nothing.

Degory Ishel informed me of an accusation against me, current in those parts. It was really one which I did not expect; no more than that other, vehemently asserted at St Ives, of my bringing the Pretender with me last autumn, under the name of John Downes. It was, that I called myself John Wesley; whereas everybody knew Mr Wesley was dead.

Thur. 19.—Having a sloop ready, which came on purpose, we ran over the Channel in about four hours. Some of our friends were waiting for us on the shore. About one we came to Fonmon Castle. I found a natural wish, "Oh for ease and a resting-place!" Not yet. But eternity is at hand!

On *Saturday*, 28, I returned to Bristol.

After resting here for eight days (though not unemployed), on *Monday*, May 7, I set out for the north.

Fri. 11.—I preached at Sheffield; on *Saturday*, 12, about ten, at Barley Hall. In the afternoon I rode to Epworth, and immediately went to Mr Maw's, to return him thanks for his good offices to Mr Downes; and his honest and open testimony for the truth, before the worshipful Bench at Kirton. It was not his fault, that those honourable men regarded not the laws either of God or the King. But a soldier they were resolved he should be, right or wrong,—because he was a preacher. So, to make all sure, they sent him away,—a prisoner to Lincoln gaol!

My first design was, to have gone the shortest way from Sheffield to Newcastle. But it was well I did not, considering the inexpressible panic which had spread itself in all places. So that I came just in time to remind all the poor frighted sheep, that "even the hairs of" our "head are all numbered."

I preached thrice at Epworth on *Sunday*; and on *Monday*, 14, at Ferry. The constable who took Mr Downes for a soldier, with one of the churchwardens, were of my audience. I was informed, they had threatened great things before I came: but their threatenings vanished into air.

At two, many of our brethren at Epworth met, whom I cheerfully commended to the grace of God. We were riding gently toward Fishlake, when two or three persons met us, and begged we would not go that way; for the town, they said, was all up in arms, and abundance were waiting for us in the way, many of whom had made themselves very drunk, and so were ripe for any manner of mischief. We accordingly rode to Sykehouse another way. Some came in all haste hither also, to tell us, all the men in the congregation would be pressed. Others affirmed, the mob was just a-coming; and that they would certainly fire the house, or pull it down to the ground. I told them, then our only way was, to make the best use of it while it was standing: so I began expounding the tenth chapter of St Matthew. But no man opened his lips against us.

Tues. 15.—After comforting the little flock at Norton, I rode the shortest way to Birstal. Here I found our brethren partly mourning, and partly rejoicing, on account of John Nelson. On Friday, the 4th instant (they informed me) the constables took him, just as he had ended his sermon at Adwalton; and the next day carried him before the commissioners at Halifax; the most active of whom was Mr Coleby, vicar of Birstal. Many were ready to testify, that he was in no respect such a person as the Act of Parliament specified. But they were not heard. He was a preacher: that was enough. So he was sent for a soldier at once.[1]

At seven I preached on the hill; no man interrupting me. Afterwards I inquired into the state of the society; and found great cause to bless God, whose grace, even in those trying times, was sufficient for them.

Mon. June 11.—I left Newcastle, and in the afternoon met John Nelson, at Durham, with Thomas Beard; another quiet and peaceable man, who had lately been torn from his trade, and wife and children, and sent away as a soldier; that is, banished from all that was near and dear to him, and constrained to dwell among lions, for no other crime, either committed or pretended, than that of calling sinners to repentance. But his soul was in nothing terrified by his adversaries. Yet the body, after a while, sunk under its burden. He was then lodged in the hospital, at Newcastle, where he still praised God continually. His fever increasing, he was let blood. His arm festered, mortified, and was cut off: two or three days after which, God signed his discharge, and called him up to His eternal home.

> "Servant of God, well done! Well hast thou fought
> The better fight; who single hast maintain'd,
> Against revolted multitudes, the cause
> Of God; in word, mightier than they in arms."

Thur. 14.—I accompanied John Bennet into Lancashire.
Wed. 20.—Met my brother in London.

Monday, 25, and the five following days, we spent in conference with many of our brethren (come from several parts), who desire nothing but to save their own souls, and those that hear them.

The next week we endeavoured to purge the society of all that did not walk according to the gospel. By this means we reduced the number of members to less than nineteen hundred. But number is an inconsiderable circumstance. May God increase them in faith and love!

Tues. Aug. 14.—Mr Piers rode over with me to Shoreham, and introduced me to Mr Perronet. I hope to have cause of blessing God for ever for the acquaintance begun this day.

[1] All the particulars of this memorable transaction are set down in "The Case of John Nelson, written by himself."

Tues. 21.—I set out with a few friends for Oxford. On *Wednesday*, my brother met us from Bristol. *Friday*, 24 (St Bartholomew's day), I preached, I suppose the last time, at St Mary's. Be it so. I am now clear of the blood of these men. I have fully delivered my own soul.

The beadle came to me afterwards, and told me the Vice-Chancellor had sent him for my notes. I sent them without delay, not without admiring the wise providence of God. Perhaps few men of note would have given a sermon of mine the reading, if I had put it into their hands; but by this means it came to be read, probably more than once, by every man of eminence in the University.

All this summer, our brethren in the west had as hot service as those in the north of England: the war against the Methodists, so called, being everywhere carried on with far more vigour than that against the Spaniards. I had accounts of this from all parts.

Sun. Dec. 2.—I was with two persons who believe they are saved from all sin. Be it so, or not, why should we not rejoice in the work of God, so far as it is unquestionably wrought in them? For instance, I ask John C., "Do you pray always? Do you rejoice in God every moment? Do you in everything give thanks? In loss? In pain? In sickness, weariness, disappointments? Do you desire nothing? Do you fear nothing? Do you feel the love of God continually in your heart? Have you a witness in whatever you speak or do, that it is pleasing to God?" If he can solemnly and deliberately answer in the affirmative, why do I not rejoice and praise God on his behalf? Perhaps, because I have an exceeding complex idea of sanctification, or a sanctified man. And so, for fear he should not have attained all I include in that idea, I cannot rejoice in what he has attained.

Thur. 27.—I called on the solicitor whom I had employed in the suit lately commenced against me in Chancery; and here I first saw that foul monster, a Chancery bill! A scroll it was of forty-two pages, in large folio, to tell a story which needed not to have taken up forty lines! and stuffed with such stupid, senseless, improbable lies (many of them, too, quite foreign to the question) as, I believe, would have cost the compiler his life in any heathen court either of Greece or Rome. And this is equity in a Christian country! This is the English method of redressing other grievances!

Sat. Jan. 5, 1745.—Desiring to see once more our old acquaintance Mr Gambold, my brother and I called at James Hutton's.

I had often wondered at myself (and sometimes mentioned it to others), that ten thousand cares, of various kinds, were no more weight or burden to my mind, than ten thousand hairs were to my head. Perhaps I began to ascribe something of this to my own strength. And thence it might be, that on *Sunday*, 13, that strength was withheld, and I felt what it was to be troubled about many things. One, and another, hurrying me continually, it seized upon my spirit more and more, till I found it absolutely necessary to fly for my life; and that without delay. So the next day, *Monday*, 14, I took horse, and rode away for Bristol.

As soon as we came to the house at Bristol, my soul was lightened of her load, of that insufferable weight which had lain upon my mind, more or less, for several days. On *Sunday*, several of our friends from Wales, and other parts, joined with us in the great sacrifice of thanksgiving.

I found peculiar reason to praise God for the state of the society, both in Bristol and Kingswood. They seemed at last clearly delivered from all vain jangling, from idle controversies and strife of words, and "determined not to know anything, save Jesus Christ, and Him crucified."

Wed. 30.—All our family were at St James's, our parish church. At twelve we met together, to pour out our souls before God, and to provoke each other to love and to good works. The afternoon I set apart for visiting the sick.

Mon. Feb. 18.—I set out with Richard Moss for Newcastle.

Fri. 22.—There was so much snow about Boroughbridge, that we could go on but very slowly; insomuch, that the night overtook us when we wanted six or seven miles to the place where we designed to lodge. But we pushed on, at a venture, across the moor, and, about eight, came safe to Sandhutton.

Sat. 23.—We found the roads abundantly worse than they had been the day before; not only because the snows were deeper, which made the causeways in many places unpassable (and turnpike-roads were not known in these parts of England till some years after), but likewise because the hard frost, succeeding the thaw, had made all the ground like glass. We were often obliged to walk, it being impossible to ride, and our horses several times fell down while we were leading them, but not once while we were riding them, during the whole journey. It was past eight before we got to Gateshead Fell, which appeared a great pathless waste of white. The snow filling up and covering all the roads, we were at a loss how to proceed; when an honest man of Newcastle overtook and guided us safe into the town.

Many a rough journey have I had before, but one like this
I never had; between wind, and hail, and rain, and ice, and
snow, and driving sleet, and piercing cold.

On *Monday* and *Tuesday* I diligently inquired who were
offended at each other; this being the sin which, of all others,
most easily besets the people of Newcastle. And as many of
them as had leisure to meet, I heard face to face.

February 27.—(Being *Ash-Wednesday*). After the public
prayers, the little church in our house met together. Misunderstandings were cleared up, and we all agreed to set
out anew.

Sun. Mar. 3.—As I was walking up Pilgrim Street, hearing
a man call after me, I stood still. He came up, and used
much abusive language, intermixed with many oaths and
curses. Several people came out to see what was the matter;
on which he pushed me twice or thrice, and went away.

Upon inquiry, I found this man had signalised himself of
a long season, by abusing and throwing stones at any of our
family who went that way. Therefore I would not lose the
opportunity, but on *Monday*, 4, sent him the following note:—

"ROBERT YOUNG,—I expect to see you, between this and
Friday, and to hear from you, that you are sensible of your
fault; otherwise, in pity to your soul, I shall be obliged to
inform the magistrates of your assaulting me yesterday in the
street.—I am, your real friend,

"JOHN WESLEY."

Within two or three hours, Robert Young came and promised
a quite different behaviour.

Sat. 16.—I visited part of the sick. The following week
I visited the societies in the country. On *Thursday*, 28, a
gentleman called at our house, who informed me his name was
Adams; that he lived about forty miles from Newcastle, at
Osmotherly, in Yorkshire; and had heard so many strange
accounts of the Methodists, that he could not rest till he came
to inquire for himself. I told him he was welcome to stay as
long as he pleased, if he could live on our lenten fare. He
made no difficulty of this, and willingly stayed till the Monday
se'nnight following; when he returned home, fully satisfied
with his journey.

Sat. April 6.—Mr Stephenson, of whom I bought the ground
on which our house is built, came at length, after delaying it
more than two years, and executed the writings. So I am
freed from one more care. May I in everything make known
my request to God!

Mon. 15.—We met at half-hour past four, and the room was filled from end to end. Many of the rich and honourable were there; so that I found it was time for me to fly away. At Darlington (it being the fair-day) we could scarce find a place to hide our head. At length we got into a little inn, but were obliged to be in a room where there was another set of company, some of whom were cursing and swearing much. Before we went away, I stepped to them, and asked, "Do you think yourselves that this kind of talking is right?" One of them warmly replied, "Sir, we have said nothing which we have need to be ashamed of." I said, "Have you not need to be ashamed of disobliging your best friend? And is not God the best friend you have?" They stared first at me, and then at one another; but no man answered a word.

In the evening I preached at the inn, in Northallerton, where Mr Adams and some of his neighbours met me. On his saying, he wished I could have time to preach in his house, at Osmotherly, I told him, I would have time, if he desired it; and ordered our horses to be brought out immediately. We came thither between nine and ten. It was about an hour before the people were gathered together. It was after twelve before I lay down; yet (through the blessing of God) I felt no weariness at all.

Tues. 16.—I preached at five, on Rom. iii. 22, to a large congregation, part of whom had sat up all night, for fear they should not wake in the morning. Many of them, I found, either were, or had been, Papists. Oh how wise are the ways of God! How am I brought, without any care or thought of mine, into the centre of the Papists in Yorkshire! Oh that God would arise and maintain His own cause; and all the idols let Him utterly abolish!

After sermon an elderly woman asked me abruptly, "Dost thou think water baptism an ordinance of Christ?" I said, "What saith Peter? 'Who can forbid water, that these should not be baptized, who have received the Holy Ghost even as we?'" I spoke but little more, before she cried out, "'Tis right! 'tis right! I will be baptized." And so she was, the same hour.

Wed. 17.—I rode by Epworth to Grimsby. I began preaching before eight; but to a congregation stupidly rude and noisy, encouraged thereto by their fore-speaker, a drunken alehouse-keeper. I singled him out, and fastened upon him, till he chose to withdraw. The rest were soon calmed, and behaved very quietly till the service was ended.

Fri. 19.—William Fenwick rode with me to L——d; the

minister of which had told him again and again, "Be sure to bring Mr Wesley with you, when he comes. It is for my soul; for the good of my poor soul." When we were alone, he told me, "Sir, I have read your writings; but I could not believe them till very lately. Now I know your doctrine is true. God Himself has shown it to me."

I rode to Epworth. *Sunday*, 21. I preached in the house at five, on, "Quench not the Spirit"; about eight, at the Cross; and again in the evening, to most of the adults in the town. Poor Mr R.'s sermon, from beginning to end, was another "railing accusation." Father, forgive him: for he knoweth not what he doeth!

Friday and *Saturday*, at John Bennet's request, I preached at several places in Lancashire and Cheshire.

Sun. 28.—I preached at five (as I had done overnight), about a mile from Altringham.

At nine I preached near Stockport, to a large congregation: thence we rode to Bongs, in Derbyshire, a lone house, on the side of a high, steep mountain, whither abundance of people were got before us. I preached on God's justifying the ungodly; and His word was as dew upon the tender herb. At five I preached at Mill Town, near Chapel-en-le-Frith. The poor miller, near whose pond we stood, endeavoured to drown my voice, by letting out the water, which fell with a great noise. But it was labour lost; for my strength was so increased, that I was heard to the very skirts of the congregation.

Fri. May 3.—In the evening we came to Wednesbury. A while ago "the waves" here were "mighty, and raged terribly. But the Lord that dwelleth on high is mightier," as stilled the madness of the people. I preached at s..., without any noise or hindrance at all. All was equally quiet on *Saturday*.

Sun. 5.—The number of people even at five obliged me to preach abroad. About one I preached at Tipton Green, and about four at Wednesbury. A few persons at first threw some clods; but they were quickly glad to retreat: so that there was no interruption at all while I applied those gracious words of our Lord, "Come unto Me, all ye that labour and are heavy-laden, and I will give you rest."

I made haste from hence to Goston's Green, near Birmingham, where I had appointed to preach at six. But it was dangerous for any who stood to hear; for the stones and dirt were flying from every side, almost without intermission, for near an hour. However, very few persons went away. I afterwards met the society, and exhorted them, in spite of men and devils, to continue in the grace of God.

Sat. 11.—I came to London. The sower of tares, I found, had not been idle, but shaken many, and moved some from their steadfastness, who once seemed to be pillars.

Thur. 23.—We had one more conversation with one that had often strengthened our hands; but now earnestly exhorted us (what is man!) to return to the Church, to renounce all our lay-assistants, to dissolve our societies, to leave off field-preaching, and to accept of honourable preferment.

Wed. 29.—I talked at large with Howel Harris, not yet carried away by the torrent of Antinomianism.

I would wish all to observe, that the points in question between us and either the German or English Antinomians are not points of opinion, but of practice. We break with no man for his opinion. We think, and let think.

We left Bristol early on *Friday*, June 14, and on *Sunday* morning reached St Gennis. The church was moderately filled with serious hearers, but few of them appeared to feel what they heard.

Tues. 18.—Being invited by the rector of St Mary Week (about seven miles from St Gennis) to preach in his church, we went thither in the afternoon. Thence we rode to Laneast, where Mr Bennet read prayers, and I preached on "the redemption that is in Jesus Christ."

Wed. 19.—Tresmere church was filled within and without, while I preached on Rom. iv. 7. In the evening Mr Thompson and Shepherd rode with me to St Eath, and the next day to Redruth.

Being informed here of what had befallen Mr Maxfield, we turned aside toward Crowan Church Town. But in the way we received information, that he had been removed from thence the night before. It seems, the valiant constables who guarded him, having received timely notice, that a body of five hundred Methodists were coming to take him away by force, had, with great precipitation, carried him two miles farther, to the house of one Henry Tomkins.

Here we found him, nothing terrified by his adversaries. I desired Henry Tomkins to show me the warrant. It was directed by Dr Borlase, and his father, and Mr Eustick, to the constables and overseers of several parishes, requiring them to "apprehend all such able-bodied men as had no lawful calling or sufficient maintenance"; and to bring them before the aforesaid gentlemen at Marazion, on Friday, 21, to be examined, whether they were proper persons to serve His Majesty in the land-service.

It was indorsed, by the steward of Sir John St Aubyn, with the names of seven or eight persons, most of whom were well known to have lawful callings, and a sufficient maintenance thereby. But that was all one: they were called "Methodists"; therefore, soldiers they must be. Underneath was added, "A person, his name unknown, who disturbs the peace of the parish."

A word to the wise. The good men easily understood, this could be none but the Methodist preacher; for who "disturbs the peace of the parish" like one who tells all drunkards, whoremongers, and common swearers, "You are in the high road to hell"?

When we came out of the house, forty or fifty myrmidons stood ready to receive us. But I turned full upon them, and their courage failed: nor did they recover till we were at some distance. Then they began blustering again, and throwing stones; one of which struck Mr Thompson's servant.

Fri. 21.—We rode to Marazion (vulgarly called Market Jew). Finding the justices were not met, we walked up St Michael's Mount. The house at the top is surprisingly large and pleasant. Sir John St Aubyn had taken much pains, and been at considerable expense, in repairing and beautifying the apartments; and when the seat was finished, the owner died!

About two, Mr Thompson and I went into the room where the justices and commissioners were. After a few minutes, Dr Borlase stood up and asked, whether we had any business. I told him, "We have." We desired to be heard concerning one who was lately apprehended at Crowan. He said, "Gentlemen, the business of Crowan does not come on yet. You shall be sent for when it does." So we retired, and waited in another room, till after nine o'clock. They delayed the affair of Mr Maxfield (as we imagined they would) to the very last. About nine he was called. I would have gone in then; but Mr Thompson advised to wait a little longer. The next information we received was, that they had sentenced him to go for a soldier. Hearing this, we went straight to the Commission Chamber. But the honourable gentlemen were gone.

They had ordered Mr Maxfield to be immediately put on board a boat, and carried for Penzance. We were informed, they had first offered him to a captain of a man-of-war, that was just come into the harbour. But he answered, "I have no authority to take such men as these, unless you would have me give him so much a week, to preach and pray to my people."

Sat. 22.—We reached St Ives about two in the morning. At five I preached on, "Love your enemies"; and at Gwennap, in the evening, on, "All that will live godly in Christ Jesus shall suffer persecution."

We heard to-day, that as soon as Mr Maxfield came to Penzance, they put him down into the dungeon; and that the mayor being inclined to let him go, Dr Borlase had gone thither on purpose, and had himself read the Articles of War in the Court, and delivered him to one who was to act as an officer.

Sun. 23.—I preached in Gwennap at five, and about eight at Stithians, to a large and quiet congregation. Thence we went to Wendron church. At two I preached a mile and a half from the church, under a large shady tree, on part of the Epistle for the day, "Marvel not, if the world hate you." At five I began at Crowan, the headquarters of the people that delight in war. While I was expounding part of the second morning lesson, Captain R—ds came with a party of men, ready for battle. But their master riding away in two or three minutes, their countenances quickly fell. One and another stole off his hat, till they were all uncovered; nor did they either move or speak, till I had finished my discourse.

We rode hence to St Ives; where, *Monday*, 24, I preached at five on, "Watch and pray, that ye enter not into temptation." As we returned from church at noon, a famous man of the town attacked us, for the entertainment of his masters. I turned back and spoke to him, and he was ashamed. In the afternoon, as I was walking over the market-place, he just put out his head; but after one scream, ran back into the house with great precipitation. We expected a visit in the evening from some of the devil's drunken champions, who swarm here on a holyday, so called; but none appeared: so, after a comfortable hour, we praised God, and parted in peace.

Tues. 25.—We rode to St Just. I preached at seven to the largest congregation I have seen since my coming. At the meeting of the earnest, loving society, all our hearts were in a flame; and again at five in the morning, while I explained, "There is no condemnation to them which are in Christ Jesus."

When the preaching was ended, the constable apprehended Edward Greenfield (by a warrant from Dr Borlase), a tinner, in the forty-sixth year of his age, having a wife and seven children. Three years ago he was eminent for cursing, swearing, drunkenness, and all manner of wickedness; but those old things had been for some time passed away, and he was then remarkable for a quite contrary behaviour.

I asked a little gentleman at St Just, what objection there was to Edward Greenfield: he said, "Why, the man is well enough in other things; but his impudence the gentlemen cannot bear. Why, sir, he says, he knows his sins are forgiven!"—And for this cause he is adjudged to banishment or death!

Saturday, 29, I preached at St Just again, and at Morva and Zennor on *Sunday*, 30. About six in the evening, I began preaching at St Ives, in the street, near John Nance's door. A multitude of people were quickly assembled, both high and low, rich and poor; and I observed not any creature to laugh or smile, or hardly move hand or foot. I expounded the gospel for the day, beginning with, "Then drew near all the publicans and sinners for to hear Him." A little before seven came Mr Edwards from the mayor, and ordered one to read the proclamation against riots. I concluded quickly after; but the body of the people appeared utterly unsatisfied, not knowing how to go away. Forty or fifty of them begged they might be present at the meeting of the society; and we rejoiced together for an hour in such a manner as I had never known before in Cornwall.

Tues. July 2.—I preached in the evening at St Just. I observed not only several gentlemen there, who I suppose never came before, but a large body of tinners, who stood at a distance from the rest; and a great multitude of men, women, and children, beside, who seemed not well to know why they came. Almost as soon as we had done singing, a kind of gentlewoman began. I have seldom seen a poor creature take so much pains. She scolded, and screamed, and spit and stamped, and wrung her hands, and distorted her face and body all manner of ways. I took no notice of her at all, good or bad; nor did almost anyone else. Afterwards I heard she was one that had been bred a Papist; and when she heard we were so, rejoiced greatly. No wonder she should be proportionably angry, when she was disappointed of her hope.

Mr Eustick, a neighbouring gentleman, came, just as I was concluding my sermon. The people opening to the right and left, he came up to me, and said, "Sir, I have a warrant from Dr Borlase, and you must go with me." Then turning round, he said, "Sir, are you Mr Shepherd? If so, you are mentioned in the warrant too. Be pleased, sir, to come with me." We walked with him to a public-house, near the end of the town. Here he asked me, if I was willing to go with him to the Doctor. I told him, just then, if he pleased. "Sir," said he, "I must wait upon you to your inn; and in the morning, if you will be so good as to go with me, I will show you the way." So he handed me back to my inn, and retired.

Wed. 3.—I waited till nine; but no Mr Eustick came. I then desired Mr Shepherd to go and inquire for him at the to serve His Majesty." He replied, "I seize you! And violently carry you away! No, sir, no. Nothing like it. I asked you to go with me to my house, and you said you was willing; and if so, you are welcome; and if not, you are welcome to go where you please." I answered, "Sir, I know not if it would be safe for me to go back through this rabble." "Sir," said he, "I will go with you myself." He then called for his horse, and another for me, and rode back with me to the place from whence he took me.

Thur. 4.—I rode to Falmouth. About three in the afternoon I went to see a gentlewoman who had been long indisposed. Almost as soon as I was set down, the house was beset on all sides by an innumerable multitude of people. A louder or more confused noise could hardly be at the taking of a city by storm. At first Mrs B. and her daughter endeavoured to quiet them. But it was labour lost. They might as well have attempted to still the raging of the sea. They were soon glad to shift for themselves, and leave K. E. and me to do as well as we could. The rabble roared with all their throats, "Bring out the Canorum! Where is the Canorum?" (an unmeaning word which the Cornish generally use instead of Methodist). No answer being given, they quickly forced open the outer door, and filled the passage. Only a wainscot-partition was between us, which was not likely to stand long. I immediately took down a large looking-glass which hung against it, supposing the whole side would fall in at once. When they began their work with abundance of bitter imprecations, poor Kitty was utterly astonished, and cried out, "Oh, sir, what must we do?" I said, "We must pray." Indeed at that time, to all appearance, our lives were not worth an hour's purchase. She asked, "But, sir, is it not better for you to hide yourself? to get into the closet?" I answered, "No. It is best for me to stand just where I am." Among those without, were the crews of some privateers, which were lately come into the harbour. Some of these, being angry at the slowness of the rest, thrust them away, and, coming up all together, set their shoulders to the inner door, and cried out, "Avast, lads, avast!" Away went all the hinges at once, and the door fell back into the room. I stepped forward at once into the midst of them, and said, "Here I am. Which of you has anything to say to me? To which of you have I done any wrong? To you? or you? or you?" I continued speaking till I came, bare-headed as I was (for I purposely left my hat that they might all see my face), into the middle of the street, and then raising my voice, said, "Neighbours, countrymen! Do you desire to hear me speak?" They cried vehemently, "Yes, yes. He shall speak. He shall. Nobody shall hinder him." But having nothing to stand on, and no advantage of ground, I could be heard by few only. However, I spoke without intermission, and, as far as the sound reached, the people were still; till one or two of their captains turned about and swore, not a man should touch him. Mr Thomas, a clergyman, then came up, and asked, "Are you not ashamed to use a stranger thus?" He was soon seconded by two or three gentlemen of the town, and one of the aldermen; with whom I walked down the town, speaking all the time, till I came to Mrs Maddern's house. The gentlemen proposed sending for my horse to the door, and desired me to step in and rest the meantime. But on second thoughts, they judged it not advisable to let me go out among the people again: so they chose to send my horse before me to Penrhyn, and to send me thither by water; the sea running close by the back-door of the house in which we were.

I never saw before, no, not at Walsal itself, the hand of God so plainly shown as here. There I had many companions who were willing to die with me: here, not a friend, but one simple girl, who likewise was hurried away from me in an instant, as soon as ever she came out of Mrs B.'s door. There I received some blows, lost part of my clothes, and was covered over with dirt: here, although the hands of perhaps some hundreds of people were lifted up to strike or throw, yet they were one and all stopped in the midway; so that not a man touched me with one of his fingers; neither was anything thrown from first to last; so that I had not even a speck of dirt on my clothes. Who can deny that God heareth the prayer, or that He hath all power in heaven and earth?

I took boat at about half an hour past five. Many of the mob waited at the end of the town, who, seeing me escaped out of their hands, could only revenge themselves with their tongues. But a few of the fiercest ran along the shore, to receive me at my landing. I walked up the steep narrow passage from the sea, at the top of which the foremost man stood. I looked him in the face, and said, "I wish you a good night." He spake not, nor moved hand or foot till I was on horseback. Then he said, "I wish you was in hell," and turned back to his companions.

As soon as I came within sight of Tolcarn (in Wendron parish), where I was to preach in the evening, I was met by many, running as it were for their lives, and begging me to go no farther. I asked, "Why not?" They said, "The church-

wardens and constables, and all the heads of the parish, are
waiting for you at the top of the hill, and are resolved to have
you: they have a special warrant from the justices met at
Helstone, who will stay there till you are brought." I rode
directly up the hill, and observing four or five horsemen, well
dressed, went straight to them, and said, "Gentlemen, has
any of you anything to say to me?—I am John Wesley." One
of them appeared extremely angry at this, that I should presume
to say I was "Mr John Wesley." And I know not how I might
have fared for advancing so bold an assertion, but that Mr
Collins, the minister of Redruth (accidentally, as he said) came
by. Upon his accosting me, and saying he knew me at Oxford,
my first antagonist was silent, and a dispute of another kind
began: whether this preaching had done any good. I appealed
to matter of fact. He allowed (after many words), "People
are the better for the present"; but added, "To be sure, by
and by they will be as bad, if not worse than ever."

When he rode away, one of the gentlemen said, "Sir, I
would speak with you a little: let us ride to the gate." We
did so, and he said, "Sir, I will tell you the ground of this. All
the gentlemen of these parts say, that you have been a long
time in France and Spain, and are now sent hither by the
Pretender; and that these societies are to join him." Nay,
surely "all the gentlemen in these parts" will not lie against
their own conscience!

I rode hence to a friend's house, some miles off, and found
the sleep of a labouring man is sweet. I was informed there
were many here also who had an earnest desire to hear "this
preaching," but they did not dare; Sir —— V——n having
solemnly declared, nay, and that in the face of the whole
congregation, as they were coming out of church, "If any man
of this parish dares hear these fellows, he shall not—come to
my Christmas feast!"

Fri. 5.—As we were going to Trezilla (in Gulval parish),
several met us in a great consternation, and told us, the
constables and churchwardens were come, and waited for us.
I went straight on, and found a serious congregation; but
neither churchwarden nor constable, nor any creature to molest
us, either at the preaching, or at the meeting of the society.
After so many storms we now enjoyed the calm, and praised
God from the ground of the heart.

Sat. 6.—I rode with Mr Shepherd to Gwennap. Here also
we found the people in the utmost consternation. Word was
brought, that a great company of tinners, made drunk on
purpose, were coming to do terrible things. I laboured much

to compose their minds: but fear had no ears; so that abundance of people went away. I preached to the rest, on "Love your enemies." The event showed this also was a false alarm, an artifice of the devil, to hinder men from hearing the Word of God.

Sun. 7.—I preached, at five, to a quiet congregation, and about eight, at Stithians. Between six and seven in the evening we came to Tolcarn. Hearing the mob was rising again, I began preaching immediately. I had not spoke a quarter of an hour before they came in view. One Mr Trounce rode up first, and began speaking to me, wherein he was roughly interrupted by his companions. Yet, as I stood on a high wall, and kept my eyes upon them, many were softened, and grew calmer and calmer; which some of their champions observing, went round and suddenly pushed me down. I light on my feet, without any hurt; and finding myself close to the warmest of the horsemen, I took hold of his hand and held it fast, while I expostulated the case. As for being convinced, he was quite above it: however, both he and his fellows grew much milder, and we parted very civilly.

Mon. 8.—I preached at five, on, "Watch and pray," to a quiet and earnest congregation. We then rode on to St Ives, the most still and honourable post (so are the times changed) which we have in Cornwall.

Tues. 9.—I had just begun preaching at St Just, when Mr E. came once more, took me by the hand, and said, I must go with him. To avoid making a tumult, I went. He said, I had promised, last week, not to come again to St Just for a month. I absolutely denied the having made any such promise. After about half an hour, he handed me back to my inn.

Wed. 10.—In the evening I began to expound (at Trevonan, in Morva), "Ho! every one that thirsteth, come ye to the waters." In less than a quarter of an hour, the constable and his companions came, and read the proclamation against riots. When he had done, I told him, "We will do as you require: we will disperse within an hour"; and went on with my sermon. After preaching, I had designed to meet the society alone. But many others also followed with such earnestness, that I could not turn them back: so I exhorted them all, to love their enemies, as Christ hath loved us. They felt what was spoken. Cries and tears were on every side.

Sun. 14.—At eight I preached at Stithians, and earnestly exhorted the society, not to think of pleasing men, but to count all things loss, so that they might win Christ. Before I had done, the constables and churchwardens came, and pressed one of the hearers for a soldier.

Mon. 15.—Mr Bennet met us at Trewint, and told us, Francis Walker had been driven thence, and had since been an instrument of great good, wherever he had been. Indeed I never remember so great an awakening in Cornwall, wrought in so short a time, among young and old, rich and poor, from Trewint quite to the seaside.

Wed. 17.—I rode to Mr Thompson's, near Barnstaple ; and the next evening, to Minehead. Early on *Friday*, 19, we went on board, and, in about four hours, crossed the Channel and reached Fonmon.

We were here, as it were, in a new world, in peace, and honour, and abundance. How soon should I melt away in this sunshine ! But the goodness of God suffered it not.

Thursday, August 1, and the following days, we had our second Conference, with as many of our brethren that labour in the Word as could be present.

Mon. Sept. 9.—I left London, and the next morning called on Dr Doddridge, at Northampton. It was about the hour when he was accustomed to expound a portion of Scripture to the young gentlemen under his care. He desired me to take his place. It may be the seed was not altogether sown in vain.

In the evening, the church at Markfield was full.

Wed. 11.—I preached at Sheffield. I had designed to go round by Epworth ; but hearing of more and more commotions in the north, I judged it best to go straight on to Newcastle.

Wed. 18.—About five we came to Newcastle, in an acceptable time. We found the generality of the inhabitants in the utmost consternation ; news being just arrived, that, the morning before, at two o'clock, the Pretender had entered Edinburgh. A great concourse of people were with us in the evening, to whom I expounded the third chapter of Jonah ; insisting particularly on that verse, "Who can tell, if God will return, and repent, and turn away from His fierce anger, that we perish not ?"

Thur. 19.—The mayor (Mr Ridley) summoned all the householders of the town to meet him at the town-hall; and desired as many of them as were willing, to set their hands to a paper, importing that they would, at the hazard of their goods and lives, defend the town against the common enemy. Fear and darkness were now on every side ; but not on those who had seen the light of God's countenance.

Fri. 20.—The mayor ordered the townsmen to be under

arms, and to mount guard in their turns, over and above the guard of soldiers, a few companies of whom had been drawn into the town on the first alarm. Now, also, Pilgrim Street gate was ordered to be walled up. Many began to be much concerned for us, because our house stood without the walls. Nay, but the Lord is a wall of fire unto all that trust in Him.

I had desired all our brethren to join with us this day in seeking God by fasting and prayer. About one we met, and poured out our souls before Him; and we believed He would send an answer of peace.

Sat. 21.—The same day the action was, came the news of General Cope's defeat. Orders were now given for the doubling of the guard, and for walling up Pandon and Sally-port gates. In the afternoon I wrote the following letter:—

"*To the Worshipful the Mayor of Newcastle.*

"SIR,—My not waiting upon you at the town-hall was not owing to any want of respect. I reverence you for your office' sake; and much more for your zeal in the execution of it. I would to God every magistrate in the land would copy after such an example! Much less was it owing to any disaffection to His Majesty King George. But I knew not how far it might be either necessary or proper for me to appear on such an occasion. I have no fortune at Newcastle: I have only the bread I eat, and the use of a little room for a few weeks in the year.

"All I can do for His Majesty, whom I honour and love,—I think not less than I did my own father—is this, I cry unto God, day by day, in public and in private, to put all his enemies to confusion: and I exhort all that hear me to do the same; and, in their several stations, to exert themselves as loyal subjects; who, so long as they fear God, cannot but honour the King.

"Permit me, sir, to add a few words more, out of the fulness of my heart. I am persuaded you fear God, and have a deep sense that His kingdom ruleth over all. Unto whom, then (I may ask you), should we flee for succour, but unto Him whom, by our sins, we have justly displeased? Oh, sir, is it not possible to give any check to these overflowings of ungodliness? to the open, flagrant wickedness, the drunkenness and profaneness, which so abound, even in our streets? I just take leave to suggest this. May the God whom you serve direct you in this, and all things! This is the daily prayer of, sir,—Your obedient servant, for Christ's sake,

"J. W."

Sun. 22.—The walls were mounted with cannon, and all things prepared for sustaining an assault. Meantime our poor neighbours, on either hand, were busy in removing their goods. And most of the best houses in our street were left without either furniture or inhabitants. Those within the walls were almost equally busy in carrying away their money and goods; and more and more of the gentry every hour rode southward as fast as they could. At eight I preached at Gateshead, in a broad part of the street, near the Popish chapel, on the wisdom of God in governing the world. How do all things tend to the furtherance of the gospel!

I never saw before so well-behaved a congregation in any church at Newcastle, as was that at St Andrew's this morning. The place appeared as indeed the house of God; and the sermon Mr Ellison preached was strong and weighty, which he could scarce conclude for tears.

All this week the alarms from the north continued, and the storm seemed nearer every day. Many wondered we would still stay without the walls: others told us we must remove quickly; for if the cannon began to play from the top of the gates, they would beat all the house about our ears. This made me look how the cannons on the gates were planted; and I could not but adore the providence of God, for it was obvious: 1. They were all planted in such a manner, that no shot could touch our house. 2. The cannon on New-gate so secured us on one side, and those upon Pilgrim Street gate on the other, that none could come near our house, either way, without being torn in pieces.

On *Friday* and *Saturday* many messengers of lies terrified the poor people of the town, as if the rebels were just coming to swallow them up. Upon this the guards were increased, and abundance of country gentlemen came in, with their servants, horses, and arms. Among those who came from the north was one whom the mayor ordered to be apprehended, on suspicion of his being a spy. As soon as he was left alone he cut his own throat; but a surgeon coming quickly, sewed up the wound, so that he lived to discover those designs of the rebels, which were thereby effectually prevented.

Sun. 29.—Advice came that they were in full march southward, so that it was supposed they would reach Newcastle by Monday evening At eight I called on a multitude of sinners in Gateshead, to seek the Lord while He might be found. Mr Ellison preached another earnest sermon, and all the people seemed to bend before the Lord. In the afternoon I expounded part of the lesson for the day,—Jacob wrestling with the angel.

The congregation was so moved, that I began again and again, and knew not how to conclude. And we cried mightily to God to send His Majesty King George help from His holy place, and to spare a sinful land yet a little longer, if haply they might know the day of their visitation.

On *Monday* and *Tuesday* I visited some of the societies in the country; and, on *Wednesday*, October 2, returned to Newcastle, where they were just informed that the rebels had left Edinburgh on Monday, and were swiftly marching toward them. But it appeared soon that this also was a false alarm; it being only a party which had moved southward, the main body still remaining in their camp, a mile or two from Edinburgh.

On *Thursday* and *Friday* I visited the rest of the country societies. On *Saturday* a party of the rebels (about a thousand men) came within seventeen miles of Newcastle. This occasioned a fresh alarm in the town; and orders were given by the General that the soldiers should march against them on Monday morning. But these orders were countermanded.

Mr Nixon (the gentleman who had some days since, upon being apprehended, cut his own throat) being still unable to speak, wrote as well as he could, that the design of the Prince (as they called him) was to seize on Tynemouth Castle, which he knew was well provided both with cannon and ammunition; and thence to march to the hill on the east side of Newcastle, which entirely commands the town. And if this had been done, he would have carried his point, and gained the town without a blow. The mayor immediately sent to Tynemouth Castle, and lodged the cannon and ammunition in a safer place.

Tues. 8.—I wrote to General Husk as follows:—

"A surly man came to me this evening, as he said, from you. He would not deign to come upstairs to me, nor so much as into the house; but stood in the yard till I came, and then obliged me to go with him into the street, where he said, 'You must pull down the battlements of your house, or to-morrow the General will pull them down for you.'

"Sir, to me this is nothing. But I humbly conceive it would not be proper for this man, whoever he is, to behave in such a manner to any other of His Majesty's subjects, at so critical a time as this.

"I am ready, if it may be for His Majesty's service, to pull not only the battlements, but the house down; or to give up any part of it, or the whole, into your Excellency's hands."

Wed. 9.—It being supposed that the danger was over for

the present, I preached at four in Gateshead (at John Lyddel's), on, "Stand fast in the faith, quit you like men, be strong"; and then, taking horse with Mr Shepherd, in the evening reached Sandhutton.

Thur. 10.—We dined at Ferrybridge, where we were conducted to General Wentworth, who did us the honour to read over all the letters we had about us. We lay at Doncaster, nothing pleased with the drunken, cursing, swearing soldiers, who surrounded us on every side.

Fri. 11.—I rode to Epworth, and preached in the evening on the third of Jonah. I read to-day part of the *Meditations of Marcus Antoninus*. What a strange Emperor! And what a strange heathen! Giving thanks to God for all the good things he enjoyed! in particular for his good inspiration, and for twice revealing to him in dreams things whereby he was cured of (otherwise) incurable distempers. I make no doubt, but this is one of those "many" who "shall come from the east and the west, and sit down with Abraham, Isaac, and Jacob," while "the children of the kingdom," nominal Christians, are "shut out."

Sun 13.—I had the satisfaction of hearing Mr Romley preach an earnest, affectionate sermon, exhorting all men to prevent the judgments of God, by sincere, inward, universal repentance.

Tues. 15.—I wrote "A Word in Season: or, Advice to an Englishman."

Tues. 22.—I came to Newcastle in the evening, just as Mr Trembath was giving out the hymn; and as soon as it was ended began preaching, without feeling any want of strength.

Wed. 23.—I found all things calm and quiet; the consternation of the people was over. But the seriousness which it had occasioned in many continued and increased.

Tues. 29.—A young gentleman called upon me, whose father is an eminent minister in Scotland, and was in union with Mr Glass, till Mr Glass renounced him, because they did not agree as to the eating of blood. (Although I wonder any should disagree about this, who have read the fifteenth chapter of the Acts, and considered, that no Christian in the universe did eat it till the Pope repealed the law which had remained at least ever since Noah's flood.)

Thur. 31.—At ten I preached on the Town Moor, at a small distance from the English camp (the Germans lying by themselves). None attempted to make the least disturbance, from the beginning to the end. Yet I could not reach their hearts. The words of a scholar did not affect them, like those of a dragoon or a grenadier.

Sun. Nov. 3.—Between one and two in the afternoon, I went to the camp once more. Abundance of people now flocked together, horse and foot, rich and poor, to whom I declared, "There is no difference; for all have sinned, and come short of the glory of God." I observed many Germans standing disconsolate at the skirts of the congregation: to these I was constrained (though I had discontinued it so long) to speak a few words in their own language. Immediately they gathered up close together, and drank in every word.

Having now delivered my own soul, on *Monday*, 4, I left Newcastle. Before nine we met several expresses, sent to countermand the march of the army into Scotland; and to inform them, that the rebels had passed the Tweed, and were marching southward. *Tuesday*, 5. In the evening I came to Leeds, and found the town full of bonfires, and people shouting, firing of guns, cursing and swearing, as the English manner of keeping holidays is. I immediately sent word to some of the magistrates, of what I had heard on the road. This ran through the town, as it were, in an instant: and I hope it was a token for good. The hurry in the streets was quashed at once;—some of the bonfires indeed remained; but scarce anyone was to be seen about them, but a few children warming their hands.

Fri. 8.—Understanding that a neighbouring gentleman, Dr C., had affirmed to many, that Mr Wesley was now with the Pretender, near Edinburgh, I wrote him a few lines. It may be, he will have a little more regard to truth, or shame, for the time to come.

Wednesday, 13, I reached London.

Fri. 22.—The alarm daily increasing, concerning the rebels on one hand, and the French on the other, we perceived the wisdom and goodness of Him who hath His way in the whirlwind. The generality of people were a little inclined to think; and many began to own the hand of God.

Mon. 25.—I retired to Newington, in order to finish the "Farther Appeal"; the state of the public affairs loudly demanding, that whatever was done should be done quickly.

Thur. 21.—I wrote "A Word to a Drunkard."

Mon. Dec. 2.—The alarms still increased in London, on account of the nearer approach of the rebels. About this time I received some further accounts from the army.

Wed. 18.—Being the day of the national fast, we met at four in the morning. Abundance of people were at West

Street chapel, and at the Foundery, both morning and evening; as also (we understood) at every place of public worship throughout London and Westminster. We had given away some thousands of little tracts among the common people. And it pleased God hereby to provoke others to jealousy. Insomuch that the Lord Mayor had ordered a large quantity of papers, dissuading from cursing and swearing, to be printed, and distributed to the train-bands. And this day " An Earnest Exhortation to Serious Repentance " was given at every church-door, in or near London, to every person who came out ; and one left at the house of every householder who was absent from church. I doubt not but God gave a blessing therewith.

It was on this very day that the Duke's army was so remarkably preserved in the midst of the ambuscades at Clifton Moor. The rebels fired many volleys upon the King's troops, from the hedges and walls, behind which they lay. And yet, from first to last, only ten or twelve men fell, the shot flying over their heads.

Mon. Jan. 20, 1746.—I set out for Bristol. On the road I read over Lord King's *Account of the Primitive Church.* In spite of the vehement prejudice of my education, I was ready to believe that this was a fair and impartial draught ; but if so, it would follow that bishops and presbyters are (essentially) of one order ; and that originally every Christian congregation was a Church independent on all others.

Tues. 21.—I read Bishop Butler's *Discourse on Analogy*, a strong and well-wrote treatise ; but, I am afraid, far too deep for their understanding to whom it is primarily addressed.

Sun. Feb. 16.—I took my leave of Bristol and Kingswood ; and *Monday*, 17, set out for Newcastle.

Friday, 21. We breakfasted at Bradbury Green, whence we rode on to Marsden ; and the next day, *Saturday*, 22, to Leeds. I preached at five. As we went home a great mob followed, and threw whatever came to hand. I was struck several times, once or twice in the face, but not hurt at all. I walked on to the Recorder's, and told him the case. He promised to prevent the like for the time to come.

Wednesday, 26.—I came to Newcastle. *Sat.* Mar. 1.—I visited the sick, who increased daily in every quarter of the town. It is supposed that two thousand of the soldiers only, have died since their encampment : the fever or flux sweeping them away by troops, in spite of all the physicians could do.

I preached on *Wednesday*, 12, at Sunderland, where I endeavoured to bring the little society into some kind of order. In the afternoon, being at Mrs Fenwick's, and seeing a child there of ten or twelve years old, I asked, "Does your daughter know Christ, or know she has need of Him?" She replied, with much concern, "I fear not : nothing has ever affected her at all." Immediately that word came into my mind, " Before they call, I will answer." I was going to say, "Come, let us call upon God to show her she has need of a Saviour " ; but, before the words were pronounced, the child turned away her face, and began crying as if she would break her heart. I could get no word from her but, " My sins, my sins ! " We then besought God to carry on His own work.

Mon. 17.—I took my leave of Newcastle, and set out with Mr Downes and Mr Shepherd. But when we came to Smeton, Mr Downes was so ill, that he could go no farther. When Mr Shepherd and I left Smeton, my horse was so exceeding lame that I was afraid I must have lain by too. We could not discern what it was that was amiss ; and yet he would scarce set his foot to the ground. By riding thus seven miles, I was thoroughly tired, and my head ached more than it had done for some months. I then thought, " Cannot God heal either man or beast, by any means, or without any? " Immediately my weariness and headache ceased, and my horse's lameness in the same instant. Nor did he halt any more either that day or the next. A very odd accident this also !

Tues. 18.—I rode to Pontefract ; on *Wednesday*, to Epworth ; and on *Thursday*, by Barley Hall, to Sheffield. I was glad of having an opportunity here of talking with a child I had heard of.

Fri. 21.—I came to Nottingham. I had long doubted what it was which hindered the work of God here. But upon inquiry the case was plain. So many of the society were either triflers or disorderly walkers, that the blessing of God could not rest upon them ; so I made short work, cutting off all such at a stroke, and leaving only that little handful who (as far as could be judged) were really in earnest to save their souls.

Sat. 22.—I came to Wednesbury. The Antinomian teachers had laboured hard to destroy this poor people. *Sunday*, 23.—I talked an hour with the chief of them, Stephen Timmins. I was in doubt whether pride had not made him mad.

In the evening I preached at Birmingham. Here another o their pillars, J—— W——d, came to me. I will set down the conversation, dreadful as it was, in the very manner wherein it passed ; that every serious person may see the true picture of Antinomianism full grown, and may know what these men mean by their favourite phrase, of being " perfect in Christ, not in themselves."

house wherein he had lodged; *si forte edormisset hoc villi:*[1] he met him coming, as he thought, to our inn. But after waiting some time, we inquired again, and learned he had turned aside to another house in the town. I went thither, and asked, "Is Mr. Eustick here?" After some pause, one said, "Yes"; and showed me into the parlour. When he came down, he said, "Oh, sir, will you be so good as to go with me to the Doctor's?" I answered, "Sir, I came for that purpose." "Are you ready, sir?" I answered, "Yes." "Sir, I am not quite ready. In a little time, sir, in a quarter of an hour, I will wait upon you. I will come to William Chenhall's." In about three-quarters of an hour he came, and finding there was no remedy, he called for his horse, and put forward towards Dr Borlase's house; but he was in no haste: so that we were an hour and a quarter riding three or four measured miles. As soon as we came into the yard, he asked a servant, "Is the Doctor at home?" upon whose answering, "No, sir, he is gone to church"; he presently said, "Well, sir, I have executed my commission. I have done, sir, I have no more to say."

About noon Mr Shepherd and I reached St Ives. After a few hours' rest, we rode to Gwennap. Finding the house would not contain one-fourth of the people, I stood before the door. I was reading my text, when a man came, raging as if just broken out of the tombs; and, riding into the thickest of the people, seized three or four, one after another, none lifting up a hand against him. A second (gentleman, so called) soon came after, if possible, more furious than he; and ordered his men to seize on some others, Mr Shepherd in particular. Most of the people, however, stood still as they were before, and began singing an hymn. Upon this Mr B. lost all patience, and cried out with all his might, "Seize him, seize him. I say, seize the preacher for His Majesty's service. But no one stirring, he rode up and struck several of his attendants, cursing them bitterly for not doing as they were bid. Perceiving still that they would not move, he leaped off his horse, swore he would do it himself, and caught hold of my cassock, crying, "I take you to serve His Majesty." A servant taking his horse, he took me by the arm, and we walked arm in arm for about three-quarters of a mile. He entertained me all the time with the "wickedness of the fellows belonging to the society." When he was taking breath, I said, "Sir, be they what they will, I apprehend it will not justify you, in seizing me in this manner and violently carrying me away, as you said,

[1] If perchance, during sleep, the fumes of his wine had evaporated.—ED.

"Do you believe you have nothing to do with the law of God?" "I have not: I am not under the law: I live by faith." "Have you, as living by faith, a right to everything in the world?" "I have: all is mine, since Christ is mine." "May you, then, take anything you will anywhere? suppose, out of a shop, without the consent or knowledge of the owner?" "I may, if I want it; for it is mine: only I will not give offence." "Have you also a right to all the women in the world?" "Yes, if they consent." "And is not that a sin?" "Yes, to him who thinks it is a sin; but not to those whose hearts are free." The same thing that wretch, Roger Ball, affirmed in Dublin. Surely these are the firstborn children of Satan!

Mon. April 7.—I preached at Kingswood, and laid the first stone of the new house there. In the evening I rode (with Mr Shepherd) to Bath; and *Tuesday*, the 8th, to Newbury. Here we met with several of the little society in Blewbury; some of whom were truly alive to God. What a proof is this, that God sends by whom He will send! Who hath begotten us these? David Jeffries!

Wed. 9.—In the evening I preached at Brentford. Many were got together there who threatened great things. I went and took one or two of their chiefs by the hand, and desired them to come in. They did so, and were calm and silent. The next morning we rode to London.

In the afternoon I buried the body of Ann Clowney, a poor woman, whom many could never think to be a believer, because she was a fool. (One of exceeding weak understanding, though not directly a natural.) But in the time of sickness and pain, none could deny the work of God. Neither did she die as a fool dieth.

Tues. 22.—I rode with Mr Piers to see one who called himself a prophet. We were with him about an hour. But I could not at all think that he was sent of God: 1. Because he appeared to be full of himself, vain, heady, and opinionated. 2. Because he spoke with extreme bitterness, both of the King, and of all the bishops, and all the clergy. 3. Because he aimed at talking Latin, but could not; plainly showing that he understood not his own calling.

Fri. May 23.—I made over the houses in Bristol and Kingswood, and the next week, that at Newcastle, to seven trustees, reserving only to my brother and myself the liberty of preaching and lodging there.

Sun. July 6.—After talking largely with both the men and women leaders, we agreed it would prevent great expense, as well of health as of time and money, if the poorer people of our society could be persuaded to leave off drinking of tea. We resolved ourselves to begin and set the example. I expected some difficulty in breaking off a custom of six-and-twenty years' standing. And, accordingly, the three first days, my head ached, more or less, all day long, and I was half-asleep from morning to night. The third day, on *Wednesday*, in the afternoon, my memory failed, almost entirely. In the evening I sought my remedy in prayer. On *Thursday* morning my headache was gone. My memory was as strong as ever. And I have found no inconvenience, but a sensible benefit in several respects, from that very day to this.

Thur. 17.—I finished the little collection which I had made among my friends for a lending-stock: it did not amount to thirty pounds; which a few persons afterwards made up to fifty. And by this inconsiderable sum, about two hundred and fifty persons were relieved in one year.

Mon. Aug. 4.—I received a letter from Yorkshire, part of which was in these words:—

"On Wednesday, July 16, I called on good old Mr Clayton. He was exceeding weak, and seemed like one that had not long to continue here. I called again on Monday, 21, and found him very ill. He told me, no one else should have been admitted; that he had much to say to me to tell you; and desired me to send his kind respects to you, and wished you prosperity in your pious undertakings. Finding he was not able to talk much, I took my leave, not thinking it would be the last time. But when I returned into these parts on Saturday last, I found he died that morning between two and three. On Monday last I went to his burial, and I was unexpectedly made mourner for my good old friend. I followed his corpse to the ground, where I saw it solemnly interred. Many of his parishioners dropped tears, he having been a father to the poor. He died very poor, though he had an estate of forty pounds a year, and a living of near three hundred, of which he has been rector three-and-forty years."

I altered my design; and going to Lanzufried, the next day rode to Leominster.

At six in the evening, I began preaching on a tombstone, close to the south side of the church. The multitude roared on every side; but my voice soon prevailed, and more and more of the people were melted down, till they began ringing the bells; but neither thus did they gain their point, for my voice prevailed still. Then the organs began to play amain. Mr C., the curate, went into the church, and endeavoured to stop them; but in

Perils and Persecutions

vain. So I thought it best to remove to the corn-market. The whole congregation followed, to whom many more were joined, who would not have come to the churchyard. Here we had a quiet time; and I showed what that sect is, which is "everywhere spoken against." I walked with a large train to our inn; but none, that I heard, gave us one ill word. A Quaker followed me in, and told me, "I was much displeased with thee, because of thy last 'Appeal'; but my displeasure is gone: I heard thee speak, and my heart clave to thee."

Fri. 15.—I preached at five to a large company of willing hearers. We breakfasted with a lovely old woman, worn out with sickness and pain, but full of faith and love, and breathing nothing but prayer and thanksgiving.

About ten we came to Kington, three hours' ride (which they call eight miles) from Leominster. I preached at one end of the town. The congregation divided itself into two parts. One half stood near, the other part remained a little way off, and loured defiance: but the bridle from above was in their mouth; so they made no disturbance at all.

Mon. 18.—I rode with Mr Hodges to Neath. Here I found twelve young men, whom I could almost envy. They lived together in one house, and continually gave away whatever they earned above the necessaries of life. Most of them (they told me) were Predestinarians, but so little bigoted to their opinion, that they would not suffer a Predestinarian to preach among them, unless he would lay all controversy aside. And on these terms they gladly received those of the opposite opinion.

Wed. Sept. 3.—About one we came to Plymouth. After dinner I walked down to Herbert Jenkins, and with him to the dock. Herbert preached a plain, honest sermon; but the congregation was greatly displeased; and many went away as soon as he began, having come on purpose to hear me.

Thur. 4.—We dined at Looe (a town near half as large as Islington, which sends only four burgesses to the Parliament), called at Grampound in the afternoon, and just at seven reached Gwennap. The congregation waiting, I began without delay, and found no faintness or weariness.

Fri. 5.—I inquired concerning John Trembath's late illness. It was a second relapse into the spotted fever; in the height of which they gave him sack, cold milk, and apples, plums, as much as he could swallow. I can see no way to account for his recovery, but that he had not then finished his work. In the evening I preached at St Ives.

Sat. 13.—I took my leave of our brethren of St Ives, and between one and two in the afternoon began preaching before

Mr Probis's house, at Bray. Many were there who had been vehement opposers; but from this time they opposed no more.

At six I preached at Sithney. Before I had done, the night came on; but the moon shone bright upon us. I intended, after preaching, to meet the society; but it was hardly practicable; the poor people so eagerly crowding in upon us: so I met them all together, and exhorted them not to leave their first love.

Sun. 14.—For the sake of those who came from far, I delayed preaching till eight o'clock. Many of Helstone were there, and most of those who in time past had signalised themselves by making riots. But the fear of God was upon them; they all stood uncovered, and calmly attended from the beginning to the end.

About one I began preaching near Porkellis; and, about half an hour after four, at Gwennap, to an immense multitude of people, on, "To me to live is Christ, and to die is gain." I was at first afraid my voice would not reach them all; but without cause, for it was so strengthened, that I believe thousands more might have heard every word. In the close of my sermon, I read them the account of Thomas Hitchin's death; and the hearts of many burned within them. At six we took horse; and about nine (having bright moonshine) reached St Columb.

Mon. 15.—A guide, meeting us at Camelford, conducted us to St Mary Week. Mr Bennet overtook us on the road, and Mr Thompson came in soon after; having lost his way, and so picked up Mr Meyrick and Butts, who were wandering they knew not where. It was the time of the yearly revel, which obliged me to speak very plain. Thence we rode to Laneast, where was a much larger congregation, and of quite another spirit.

Thur. 18.—About one I preached at Beercrocomb. About five we reached Bridgewater. We expected much tumult here, the great vulgar stirring up the small. But we were disappointed. The very week before our coming, the Grand Jury had found the bill against the rioters, who had so often assaulted Mary Lockyer's house. This, and the awe of God, which fell upon them, kept the whole congregation quiet and serious.

Tues. 23.—I went on to Rood, where the mob threatened aloud. I determined, however, to look them in the face; and at twelve I cried, to the largest congregation by far which I had ever seen in these parts, "Seek ye the Lord while He may be found; call ye upon Him while He is near." The despisers stood as men astonished, and neither spoke nor stirred till I had concluded my sermon.

Fri. 26.—Mr B. went to the mayor of Wycombe, and said, " Sir, I come to inform against a common swearer. I believe he swore an hundred oaths last night ; but I marked down only twenty." " Sir," said the mayor, " you do very right in bringing him to justice. What is his name?" He replied, " R—— D——." " R—— D——!" answered the mayor ; " why, that is my son !" " Yes, sir," said Mr B., " so I understand." " Nay, sir," said he, " I have nothing to say in his defence. If he breaks the law, he must take what follows."

Sat. Oct. 4.—We took horse at nine, and soon after one came to Sevenoaks. After refreshing ourselves a little, we went to an open place near the free-school, where I declared, to a large, wild company, " There is no difference ; for all have sinned, and come short of the glory of God." They grew calmer and calmer till I had done, and then went quietly away. As we returned, a poor Shimei came to meet us, bitterly cursing and blaspheming. But we walked straight on, and even his companions, the mob, neither laughed nor opened their mouth.

Thur. 9.—The day of public thanksgiving for the victory of Culloden was to us a day of solemn joy.

Wed. Nov. 12.—In the evening, at the chapel, my teeth pained me much. In coming home, Mr Spear gave me an account of the rupture he had had for some years, which, after the most eminent physicians had declared it incurable, was perfectly cured in a moment. I prayed with submission to the will of God. My pain ceased, and returned no more.

I received from several of our brethren abroad, an account of the deliverance God had lately wrought for them :—

" BUSH OF BRABANT.

" REV. SIR,—I have long had a desire to write, but had not an opportunity till we came to our winter quarters. When we came over we thought we should have had brother Haime with us, as formerly ; but we were disappointed. We were about three weeks upon our march, and endured a great deal through the heat of the weather, and for want of water. At Villear camp, we lay so near the enemy, and were forced to mount so many guards, that we had hardly any time to ourselves, nor had John Haime time to meet with us. We left this camp in twelve or fourteen days' time, and wherever we marched, we had the French always in our view ; only a few days, when we were marching through woods, and over high mountains. Coming back to Maestricht, at some camps we have lain so near the enemy, that their sentries and ours have taken snuff with one another; having then no orders to fire at or hurt each other. But the day we came off, we found it otherwise; for at eleven o'clock the night before, orders came for us to be ready to turn out an hour before day, which was the 30th of September. At daybreak, orders came to our regiment, and Colonel Graham's, to advance about a mile and a half toward the French. We were placed in a little park, and Graham's regiment in another, to the right of us. We lay open to the French; only we cut down the hedge breast-high, and filled it up with loose earth. Thus we waited for the enemy several hours, who came first with their right wing upon the Dutch, that were upon our left. They engaged in our sight, and fired briskly upon each other, cannon and small shot, for two hours. Then the Dutch, being overpowered, gave way, and the French advanced upon us, and marched a party over the ditch, on the left of Graham's, and fell in upon them, notwithstanding our continual firing, both with our small arms and four pieces of cannon. So when the French had got past us, our regiment retreated, or we should have been surrounded. In our retreat, we faced about twice, and fired on the enemy, and so came off with little loss; though they fired after us with large cannon-shot, I believe four-and-twenty pounders.

"We lost one brother of Graham's regiment, and two of ours, —Andrew Paxton, shot dead in our retreat, and Mark Bend, who was wounded, and left on the field. The Lord gave us all on that day an extraordinary courage, and a word to speak to our comrades, as we advanced toward the enemy, to tell them how happy they were that had made their peace with God. We likewise spoke to one another while the cannon were firing, and we could all rely on God, and resign ourselves to His will.

"A few of us meet here twice a day; and, thanks be to God, His grace is still sufficient for us. We desire all our brethren to praise God on our behalf. And we desire all your prayers, that the Lord may give us to be steadfast, unmovable, always abounding in the work of the Lord.—I remain, your loving brother, S. S.

October 17."

CHAPTER VIII

TRIUMPHANT PROGRESS

FROM DECEMBER 4, 1746, TO APRIL 8, 1749

Thursday, Dec. 4, 1746.—I mentioned to the society my design of giving physic to the poor. About thirty came the next day, and in three weeks about three hundred. This we continued for several years, till the number of patients still increasing, the expense was greater than we could bear: meantime, through the blessing of God, many who had been ill for months or years, were restored to perfect health.

Mon. 15.—Most of this week I spent at Lewisham in writing *Lessons for Children*.

Sun. Jan. 11, 1747.—In the evening I rode to Brentford; the next day to Newbury; and, *Tuesday*, 13, to the Devizes. The town was in an uproar from end to end, as if the French were just entering; and abundance of swelling words we heard, oaths, curses, and threatenings.

Wed. 14.—I rode on to Bristol, and spent a week in great peace. *Thursday*, 22. About half-hour after twelve I took horse for Wick, where I had appointed to preach at three. I was riding by the wall through St Nicholas Gate (my horse having been brought to the house where I dined) just as a cart turned short from St Nicholas Street, and came swiftly down the hill. There was just room to pass between the wheel of it and the wall, but that space was taken up by the carman. I called to him to go back, or I must ride over him; but the man, as if deaf, walked straight forward. This obliged me to hold back my horse. In the meantime, the shaft of the cart came full against his shoulder with such a shock as beat him to the ground. He shot me forward over his head, as an arrow out of a bow, where I lay, with my arms and legs, I know not how, stretched out in a line close to the wall. The wheel ran by, close to my side, but only dirtied my clothes. I found no flutter of spirit, but the same composure as if I had been sitting in my study. When the cart was gone, I rose.

Abundance of people gathered round, till a gentleman desired me to step into his shop. After cleaning myself a little, I took horse again, and was at Wick by the time appointed.

I returned to Bristol (where the report of my being killed had spread far and wide) time enough to praise God in the great congregation, and to preach on, "Thou, Lord, shall save both man and beast."

Tues. Feb. 10.—My brother returned from the north, and I prepared to supply his place there. *Monday*, 16, I rose soon after three, lively and strong, and found all my complaints were fled away like a dream.

I was wondering the day before, at the mildness of the weather; such as seldom attends me in my journeys. But my wonder now ceased: the wind was turned full north, and blew so exceeding hard and keen, that when we came to Hatfield, neither my companions nor I had much use of our hands or feet. After resting an hour, we bore up again through the wind and snow, which drove full in our faces. But this was only a squall. In Baldock Field the storm began in earnest. The large hail drove so vehemently in our faces, that we could not see, nor hardly breathe. However, before two o'clock we reached Baldock, where one met and conducted us safe to Potten.

About six I preached to a serious congregation. *Tuesday*, 17. We set out as soon as it was well light; but it was really hard work to get forward; for the frost would not well bear or break; and the untracked snow covering all the roads, we had much ado to keep our horses on their feet. Meantime the wind rose higher and higher, till it was ready to overturn both man and beast. However, after a short bait at Bugden, we pushed on, and were met in the middle of an open field with so violent a storm of rain and hail as we had not had before. It drove through our coats, great and small, boots, and everything, and yet froze as it fell, even upon our eyebrows; so that we had scarce either strength or motion left when we came into our inn at Stilton.

We now gave up our hopes of reaching Grantham, the snow falling faster and faster. However, we took the advantage of a fair blast to set out, and made the best of our way to Stamford Heath. But here a new difficulty arose, from the snow lying in large drifts. Sometimes horse and man were well-nigh swallowed up. Yet in less than an hour we were brought safe to Stamford. Being willing to get as far as we could, we made but a short stop here: and about sunset came, cold and weary, yet well, to a little town called Brig Casterton.

Wed. 18.—Our servant came up and said, " Sir, there is no travelling to-day. Such a quantity of snow has fallen in the night, that the roads are quite filled up." I told him, " At least we can walk twenty miles a day, with our horses in our hands." So in the name of God we set out. The north-east wind was piercing as a sword, and had driven the snow into such uneven heaps, that the main road was unpassable. However, we kept on, afoot or on horseback, till we came to the White Lion at Grantham.

On the road we overtook a clergyman and his servant ; but the toothache quite shut my mouth. We reached Newark about five.

Thur. 19.—The frost was not so sharp, so that we had little difficulty till we came to Haxey Car ; but here the ice which covered the dikes, and great part of the common, would not bear nor readily break ; nor did we know (there being no track of man or beast) what parts of the dikes were fordable. However, we committed ourselves to God, and went on. We hit all our fords exactly ; and, without any fall or considerable hindrance, came to Epworth in two hours, full as well as when we left London.

Sun. 22.—I preached at five and at eight in the room ; after evening prayers, at the Cross. I suppose most of the grown people in the town were present. A poor drunkard made a noise for some time, till Mr Maw (the chief gentleman of the town) took him in hand and quieted him at once.

Mon. 23.—Leaving Mr Meyrick here, I set out with Mr Larwood and a friend from Grimsby. At two I preached at Laseby in the way, to a quiet and serious congregation. We reached Grimsby by five, and spoke to as many of the society as could conveniently come at that time. About seven I would have preached to a very large audience, but a young gentleman, with his companions, quite drowned my voice, till a poor woman took up the cause, and, by reciting a few passages of his life, wittily and keenly enough, turned the laugh of all his companions full upon him. He could not stand it, but hastened away. When he was gone, I went on with little interruption.

Tues. 24.—I wrote a few lines to Mr C., giving him an account of his kinsman's behaviour. He obliged him to come straight to me and ask my pardon. Since that time we have had no disturbance at Grimsby.

At noon I examined the little society at Tetney. I have not seen such another in England. In the class-paper (which gives an account of the contribution for the poor) I observed one gave eightpence, often tenpence, a week ; another, thirteen, fifteen, or eighteen pence; another, sometimes one, sometimes two shillings. I asked Micah Elmoor, the Leader (an Israelite indeed, who now rests from his labour), "How is this? Are you the richest society in all England?" He answered, "I suppose not; but all of us who are single persons have agreed together, to give both ourselves and all we have to God: and we do it gladly; whereby we are able, from time to time, to entertain all the strangers that come to Tetney; who often have no food to eat, nor any friend to give them a lodging."

Sat. 28.—I called at Shipton, on Mr C., the minister of Acomb, who had desired to see me; and, after half an hour both agreeably and usefully spent, rode on to Thirsk.

Here I rejoiced with T. Brooke and his wife, lights shining in a dark place. God has lately added to them a third; one formerly famous for all manner of wickedness, who was cut to the heart while Mr Brooke was talking to him, and went down to his house justified. This had struck the whole town; so that when I went down, about five, to preach in a vacant house, it was quickly filled within and without, the justice being one of the congregation. In the morning, about six, I preached again to a congregation more numerous than before; nor did any man open his mouth, either at the time of preaching, or while I walked through the town; unless it were to bid me God-speed, or to inquire when I would come again.

Sun. Mar. 1.—I came to Osmotherly about ten o'clock, just as the minister (who lives some miles off) came into town. I sent my service to him, and told him, if he pleased, I would assist him either by reading prayers or preaching. On receiving the message, he came to me immediately; and said, he would willingly accept of my assistance. As we walked to church he said, "Perhaps it would fatigue you too much, to read prayers and preach too." I told him, No; I would choose it, if he pleased; which I did accordingly. After service was ended, Mr D. said, "Sir, I am sorry I have not an house here to entertain you. Pray let me know whenever you come this way." Several asking, where I would preach in the afternoon, one went to Mr D. again, and asked, if he was willing I should preach in the church. He said, "Yes. .. never Mr Wesley pleases." We had a large congregation at three o'clo. Those who in time past had been the most bitter gainsayers, seemed now to be melted into love. All were convinced we are no Papists. How wisely does God order all things in their season!

Mon. 2.—I rode to Newcastle. The next day, I met the

stewards, men who have approved themselves in all things. They are of one heart and of one mind. I found all in the house of the same spirit; pouring out their souls to God many times in a day together, and breathing nothing but love and brotherly kindness.

Wed. 4.—(Being *Ash-Wednesday.*) I spent some hours in reading *The Exhortations of Ephrem Syrus*. Surely never did any man, since David, give us such a picture of a broken and contrite heart.

This week I read over with some young men, a compendium of Rhetoric, and a system of Ethics. I see not, why a man of tolerable understanding may not learn in six months' time more of solid philosophy than is commonly learned at Oxford in four (perhaps seven) years.

On *Monday, Tuesday,* and *Thursday* I examined the classes. I had been often told, it was impossible for me to distinguish the precious from the vile, without the miraculous discernment of spirits. But I now saw, more clearly than ever, that this might be done, and without much difficulty, supposing only two things: first, courage and steadiness in the examiner; secondly, common sense and common honesty in the Leader of each class. I visit, for instance, the class in the Close, of which Robert Peacock is Leader. I ask, "Does this and this person in your class live in drunkenness or any outward sin? Does he go to church, and use the other means of grace? Does he meet you as often as he has opportunity?" Now, if Robert Peacock has common sense, he can answer these questions truly; and if he has common honesty, he will. And if not, some other in the class has both, and can and will answer for him. Where is the difficulty, then, of finding out if there be any disorderly walker in this class, and, consequently, in any other? The question is not concerning the heart, but the life. And the general tenor of this, I do not say cannot be known, but cannot be hid without a miracle.

The society, which the first year consisted of above eight hundred members, is now reduced to four hundred. But, according to the old proverb, the half is more than the whole. We shall not be ashamed of any of these, when we speak with our enemies in the gate.

In some of the following days I snatched a few hours to read *The History of the Puritans*. I stand in amaze: first, at the execrable spirit of persecution which drove those venerable men out of the Church, and with which Queen Elizabeth's clergy were as deeply tinctured as ever Queen Mary's were; secondly, at the weakness of those holy confessors, many of whom spent so much of their time and strength in disputing about surplices and hoods, or kneeling at the Lord's Supper.

Thur. 19.—I considered, "What would I do now, if I was sure I had but two days to live?" All outward things are settled to my wish; the houses at Bristol, Kingswood, and Newcastle are safe; the deeds whereby they are conveyed to the trustees took place on the 5th instant: my will is made; what have I more to do, but to commend my soul to my merciful and faithful Creator?

Some days I spent in every week in examining the societies round Newcastle. And great cause I found to rejoice over them.

Tues. 24.—I rode to Blanchland, about twenty miles from Newcastle. The rough mountains round about were still white with snow. In the midst of them is a small winding valley, through which the Derwent runs. On the edge of this the little town stands, which is indeed little more than a heap of ruins. There seems to have been a large cathedral church, by the vast walls which still remain. I stood in the churchyard under one side of the building, upon a large tombstone, round which, while I was at prayers, all the congregation kneeled down on the grass. They were gathered out of the lead-mines from all parts; many from Allandale, six miles off. A row of little children sat under the opposite wall, all quiet and still. The whole congregation drank in every word with such earnestness in their looks, I could not but hope that God will make this wilderness sing for joy.

In the evening I came back to Newlands, where also John Brown has gathered a society. Oh, what may not a man of small natural talents do, if he be full of faith and love!

Sun. April 5.—We set out early, and about eight went out into the market-place at Hexham. A multitude of people soon ran together, the greater part mad as colts untamed. Many had promised to do mighty things. But the bridle was in their teeth. I cried aloud, "Let the wicked forsake his way, and the unrighteous man his thoughts." They felt the sharpness of the two-edged sword, and sunk into seriousness on every side: insomuch that I heard not one unkind or uncivil word, till we left them standing, and staring one at another. At one I preached at Horsley, and about five in the evening at Newcastle.

April 19.—(Being *Easter-Day*.) I preached in Gateshead for the last time; afterwards at Swalwell, and at Newcastle in the evening. I could gladly have spent six weeks more in these parts; but my time being now expired, I preached my farewell sermon at five. On *Monday*, 20, a great part of the congregation (which filled the room) were some of the finest people I had ever seen there. Surely God is working a new thing in the earth. Even to the rich is the gospel preached!

About nine I preached to a large congregation at Renton, and before six reached Osmotherly. Finding Mr D. (as I expected) had been vehemently attacked by the neighbouring clergy and gentry, that he might be exposed to no further difficulty on my account, I did not claim his promise, but preached on a tombstone near the church, on, "The Lord is risen indeed."

Here John Nelson met me. On Thursday, Friday, and Saturday he had preached at Acomb, and the neighbouring places: on Good-Friday, in particular, on Heworth Moor, to a large and quiet congregation. On Easter-Sunday, at eight, he preached there again, to a large number of serious hearers. Towards the close of his discourse, a mob came from York, hired and headed by some (miscalled) gentlemen. They stood still, till an eminent Papist cried out, "Why do not you knock the dog's brains out?" On which they immediately began throwing all that came to hand, so that the congregation was quickly dispersed. John spoke a few words, and walked towards York. They followed with showers of bricks and stones; one of which struck him on the shoulder, one on the back, and, a little before he came to the city, part of a brick hit him on the back part of the head, and felled him to the ground. When he came to himself, two of Acomb lifted him up, and led him forward between them. The gentlemen followed, throwing as before, till he came to the city gate, near which lived an honest tradesman, who took him by the arm, and pulled him into his house. Some of the rioters swore they would break all his windows if he did not turn him out. But he told them resolutely, "I will not; and let any of you touch my house at your peril; I shall make you remember it as long as you live." On this they thought good to retire.

After a surgeon had dressed the wound in his head, John went softly on to Acomb. About five he went out, in order to preach, and began singing an hymn. Before it was ended the same gentlemen came in a coach from York, with a numerous attendance. They threw clods and stones so fast on every side, that the congregation soon dispersed. John walked down into a little ground, not far from Thomas Slaton's house. Two men quickly followed, one of whom swore desperately he would have his life. And he seemed to be in good earnest. He struck him several times, with all his force, on the head and breast; and at length threw him down, and stamped upon him, till he left him for dead. But, by the mercy of God, being carried into an house, he soon came to himself; and after a night's rest, was so recovered, that he was able to ride to Osmotherly.

Tues. 21.—I called at Thirsk; but, finding the town full of holiday folks, drinking, cursing, swearing, and cock-fighting, I did not stop at all, but rode on to Boroughbridge, and in the afternoon to Leeds.

Tues. May 5.—I preached at Roughlee at five; about eleven at Hinden, and about three at Widdap, a little village in the midst of huge, barren mountains, where also there was a society. But Mr B. had effectually dispersed them, so that I found but three members left.

We rode thence about five miles to Stonesey Gate, which lies in a far more fruitful country. Here was a larger congregation at six o'clock than I had seen since my leaving Birstal. They filled both the yard and the road to a considerable distance, and many were seated on a long wall adjoining, which, being built of loose stones, in the middle of the sermon, all fell down at once. I never saw, heard, nor read of such a thing before. The whole wall, and the persons sitting upon it, sunk down together, none of them screaming out, and very few altering their posture: and not one was hurt at all; but they appeared sitting at the bottom just as they sat at the top. Nor was there any interruption either of my speaking, or of the attention of the hearers.

Wed. 6.—I rode to Shore, four miles south from Stonesey, lying about half-way down an huge steep mountain. Here I preached at twelve to a loving, simple-hearted people. We then climbed up to Todmorden Edge, the brow of a long chain of mountains, where I called a serious people to "repent and believe the gospel."

Thur. 7.—We left the mountains, and came down to the fruitful valley of Rosendale. Here I preached to a large congregation of wild men; but it pleased God to hold them in chains. So that even when I had done, none offered any rudeness, but all went quietly away.

We came to Manchester between one and two. I had no thought of preaching here, till I was informed, John Nelson had given public notice that I would preach at one o'clock. I was now in a great strait. Their house would not contain a tenth part of the people; and how the unbroken spirits of so large a town would endure preaching in the street, I knew not. Besides that, having rode a swift trot for several hours, and in so sultry a day, I was both faint and weary. But after considering that I was not going a warfare at my own cost, I walked straight to Salford Cross. A numberless crowd of people partly ran before, partly followed after me. I thought it best not to sing, but, looking round, asked abruptly, "Why do you look as if you had never seen me before? Many of you have seen me in the neighbouring church, both preaching and administering the sacrament." I then began, "Seek ye the Lord while He may be found; call upon Him while He is near." None interrupted at all, or made any disturbance, till, as I was drawing to a conclusion, a big man thrust in, with three or four more, and bade them bring out the engine. Our friends desired me to remove into a yard just by, which I did, and concluded in peace.

Thur. June 4.—I reduced the sixteen stewards to seven; to whom were given the following instructions:—

"1. You are to be men full of the Holy Ghost and wisdom, that you may do all things in a manner acceptable to God.

". . . . .

"10. In all debates you are to watch over your spirits; avoiding, as fire, all clamour and contention; being 'swift to hear, slow to speak'; in honour, every man preferring another before himself.

"11. If you cannot relieve, do not grieve the poor; give them soft words, if nothing else: abstain from either sour looks or harsh words. Let them be glad to come, even though they should go empty away. Put yourself in the place of every poor man; and deal with him as you would God should deal with you."

Sat. 6.—I appointed to speak with those who had applied to us on a physical account. I found there had been about six hundred in about six months. More than three hundred of these came twice or thrice, and we saw no more of them. About twenty of those who had constantly attended, did not seem to be either better or worse. Above two hundred were sensibly better; and fifty-one thoroughly cured. The entire expense, from the beginning till this time, was about thirty pounds.

Mon. 15.—Our Conference began, and ended on *Saturday,* 20. The minutes of all that passed therein were some time after transcribed and published.

Tues. 23.—We took horse at three, breakfasted at Chippenham, and dined at Kingswood; whence I walked to Bristol.

Within two miles of Plymouth, one overtook and informed us that, the night before, all the dock was in an uproar; and a constable, endeavouring to keep the peace, was beaten and much hurt. As we were entering the dock, one met us, and desired we would go the back-way: "For," said he, "there are thousands of people waiting about Mr Hide's door." We rode up straight into the midst of them. They saluted us with three huzzas; after which I alighted, took several of them by the hand, and began to talk with them. I would gladly have passed an hour among them; and believe, if I had, there had been an end of the riot. But the day being far spent (for it was past nine o'clock), I was persuaded to go in. The mob then recovered their spirits, and fought valiantly with the doors and windows: but about ten they were weary, and went every man to his own home.

Sat. 27.—I preached at four, and then spoke severally to part of the society. As yet I have found only one person among them who knew the love of God, before my brother came. No wonder the devil was so still; for his goods were in peace.

About six in the evening, I went to the place where I preached the last year. A little before we had ended the hymn, came the lieutenant, a famous man, with his retinue of soldiers, drummers, and mob. When the drums ceased, a gentleman barber began to speak: but his voice was quickly drowned in the shouts of the multitude, who grew fiercer and fiercer, as their numbers increased. After waiting about a quarter of an hour, perceiving the violence of the rabble still increasing, I walked down into the thickest of them, and took the captain of the mob by the hand. He immediately said, "Sir, I will see you safe home. Sir, no man shall touch you. Gentlemen, stand off: give back. I will knock the first man down that touches him." We walked on in great peace; my conductor every now and then stretching out his neck (he was a very tall man) and looking round to see if any behaved rudely, till we came to Mr Hide's door. We then parted in much love. I stayed in the street near half an hour after he was gone, talking with the people, who had now forgot their anger, and went away in high good humour.

Tues. 30.—We came to St Ives before morning prayers, and walked to church without so much as one huzza. How strangely has one year changed the scene in Cornwall! This is now a peaceable, nay, honourable station. They give us good words almost in every place. What have we done, that the world should be so civil to us?

Wed. July 1.—I spoke severally to all those who had votes in the ensuing election. I found them such as I desired. Not one would even eat or drink at the expense of him for whom he voted. Five guineas had been given to W. C., but he returned them immediately. T. M. positively refused to accept anything. And when he heard that his mother had received money privately, he could not rest till she gave him the three guineas, which he instantly sent back.

Thursday, 2, was the day of election for Parliament-men. It was begun and ended without any hurry at all. I had a large congregation in the evening, among whom two or three roared for the disquietness of their heart: as did many at the meeting which followed; particularly those who had lost their first love.

Sun. 5.—We rode to St Agnes. At two I preached to a large multitude of quiet hearers, many of whom seemed deeply affected. Yet soon after I had done, some began to divert themselves with throwing dirt and clods. Mr Shepherd's horse was frighted at this; and as one of them stooped down, leaped clear over him. The man screamed amain; but finding himself not hurt, he and his comrades poured a shower of stones after him. Knowing nothing of the matter, I rode soon after through the midst of them, and none lifted up a hand or opened his mouth.

About half-hour after five I began at Gwennap. I was afraid my voice would not suffice for such an immense multitude. But my fear was groundless; as the evening was quite calm, and the people all attention.

It was more difficult to be heard in meeting the society, amid the cries of those, on the one hand, who were pierced through as with a sword, and of those, on the other, who were filled with joy unspeakable.

Mon. 6.—I preached, about twelve, at Bray, but neither the house nor the yard would contain the congregation; and all were serious; the scoffers are vanished away. I scarce saw one in the county.

I preached in the evening at Camborne to an equally serious congregation. I looked about for John Rogers, the champion, who had so often sworn I should never more preach in that parish. But it seems, he had given up the cause, saying, "One may as well blow against the wind."

Tues. 7.—I preached at St Ives; *Wednesday*, 8, at Sithney. On *Thursday* the stewards of all the societies met. I now diligently inquired what exhorters there were in each society; whether they had gifts meet for the work; whether their lives were eminently holy; and whether there appeared any fruit of their labour. I found, upon the whole: 1. That there were no less than eighteen exhorters in the county. 2. That three of these had no gifts at all for the work, neither natural nor supernatural. 3. That a fourth had neither gifts nor grace, but was a dull, empty, self-conceited man. 4. That a fifth had considerable gifts, but had evidently made shipwreck of the grace of God. These, therefore, I determined immediately to set aside, and advise our societies not to hear them. 5. That J. B., A. L., and J. W. had gifts and grace, and had been much blessed in the work. Lastly, That the rest might be helpful when there was no preacher in their own or the neighbouring societies, provided they would take no step without the advice of those who had more experience than themselves.

Sun. 12.—At five I preached at St Just; at twelve, to the largest congregation I ever saw at Morva. I then went to church at Zennor; and when the service was ended, preached under the churchyard wall.

Hence I rode to Newlyn, a little town on the south sea, about a mile from Penzance. At five I walked to a rising ground, near the seashore, where was a smooth white sand to stand on. An immense multitude of people was gathered together, but their voice was as the roaring of the sea. I began to speak, and the noise died away; but before I had ended my prayer some poor wretches of Penzance began cursing and swearing, and thrusting the people off the bank. In two minutes I was thrown into the midst of them; when one of Newlyn, a bitter opposer till then, turned about, and swore, "None shall meddle with the man: I will lose my life first." Many others were of his mind: so I walked an hundred yards forward and finished my sermon without any interruption.

Mon. 13.—I preached at Terdinny, in Buryan parish, where was a large and earnest congregation, notwithstanding the wonderful stories which they have frequently heard related in the pulpit for certain truths. In the morning I wrote as follows:—

"TERDINNY, *July* 14, 1747.

"REV. SIR,—I was exceedingly surprised when I was informed yesterday, of your affirming publicly in the church, in the face of a whole congregation, 'Now Wesley has sent down for an hundred pounds; and it must be raised directly. Nay, it is true.' Oh, sir, is this possible? Can it be, that you should be so totally void (I will not say of conscience, of religion, but) of good nature, as to credit such a tale? and of good manners and common sense, as thus to repeat it?

"I must beg that you would either justify or retract this (for it is a point of no small concern); and that I may know what you propose to do, before I set out for London.—I am, reverend sir, your brother and servant, for Christ's sake."

But he never favoured me with an answer.

Fri. 31.—About noon I preached at Taunton. Much opposition was expected; and several young gentlemen came, as it seemed, with that design; but they did not put it in execution. From hence we rode to Bridgewater; and even at this dry, barren place God largely watered us with the dew of heaven.

Sun. Aug. 2.—I preached in Kingswood at eight; in the afternoon at Connam; and at five in the Old Orchard, to the largest congregation which I ever remember to have seen at Bristol. What hath God wrought in this city! And yet perhaps the hundredth part of His work does not now appear.

Tues. 4.—I set out for Ireland.

Wed. 5.—Taking horse early in the morning, we rode over the rough mountains of Radnorshire and Montgomeryshire into Merionethshire. In the evening I was surprised with one of the finest prospects, in its kind, that ever I saw in my life. We rode in a green vale, shaded with rows of trees, which made an arbour for several miles. The river laboured along on our left hand, through broken rocks of every size, shape, and colour. On the other side of the river, the mountain rose to an immense height, almost perpendicular: and yet the tall straight oaks stood, rank above rank, from the bottom to the very top; only here and there, where the mountain was not so steep, were interposed pastures or fields of corn. At a distance, as far as the eye could reach, as it were by way of contrast,

> "A mountain huge uprear'd
> Its broad bare back,"

with vast, rugged rocks hanging over its brow, that seemed to nod portending ruin.

Thur. 6.—Between three and four in the afternoon we, with some difficulty, reached Carnarvon. This has the face of a fortified town, having walls (such as they are), and a castle as considerable as that of Cardiff. Here we parted with our guide and interpreter, Mr Philips. Mr Tucker and I set out for Holyhead.

Fri. 7.—We made a little stop at Llangevenye, seven miles from the ferry. We should have hired a guide to have steered over the sands, but it was quite out of my mind till we came to them; so we went straight across, and came to Holyhead without any stop or hindrance at all.

Sat. 8.—Finding one of the packet-boats ready, we went on board about eight o'clock in the morning. It was a dead calm when we rowed out of the harbour: but about two in the afternoon the wind sprung up, and continued till near four on Sunday morning, when we were within sight of the Irish shore.

I could not but observe: 1. That while we were sailing with a fresh gale, there was no wind at all a mile off: but a ship which lay abreast of us was quite becalmed, till we left her out of sight. 2. That a French privateer, which for several days had taken every ship which sailed on that coast, was taken and brought into Dublin Bay, the very morning we arrived there.

Before ten we came to St George's Quay. Soon after we landed, hearing the bells ringing for church, I went thither directly. Mr Lunell came to the quay just after I was gone, and left word at the house where our things were, he would call again at one. He did so; and took us to his house. About three I wrote a line to the curate of St Mary's, who sent me word, he should be glad of my assistance: so I preached there (another gentleman reading prayers), to as gay and senseless a congregation as ever I saw.

Mon. 10.—Between eight and nine I went to Mr R., the curate of St Mary's. He professed abundance of goodwill, commended my sermon in strong terms, and begged he might see me again the next morning. But, at the same time, he expressed the most rooted prejudice against lay-preachers, or preaching out of a church; and said, the Archbishop of Dublin was resolved to suffer no such irregularities in his diocese.

I went to our brethren, that we might pour out our souls before God. I then went straight to wait on the archbishop myself; but he was gone out of town.

If my brother or I could have been here for a few months, I question if there might not have been a larger society here, than even in London itself.

Tues. 11.—I waited on the archbishop at Newbridge, ten miles from Dublin. I had the favour of conversing with him two or three hours; in which I answered abundance of objections.

Thur. 13.—We walked in the afternoon to see two persons that were sick near Phœnix Park. That part of it which joins to the city is sprinkled up and down with trees, not unlike Hyde Park. But about a mile from the town is a thick grove of old, tall oaks; and in the centre of this, a round, open green (from which are vistas all four ways), with a handsome stone pillar in the midst, having a Phœnix on the top.

I continued preaching, morning and evening, to many more than the house would contain, and had more and more reason to hope they would not all be unfruitful hearers.

Fri. 14.—I procured a genuine account of the great Irish massacre in 1641. Surely never was there such a transaction before, from the beginning of the world! More than two hundred thousand men, women, and children, butchered within a few months, in cool blood, and with such circumstances of cruelty as makes one's blood run cold! It is well if God has not a controversy with the nation, on this very account, to this day.

Sat. 15.—I stayed at home, and spoke to all that came. But I found scarce any Irish among them. At least ninety-nine in an hundred of the native Irish remain in the religion of their forefathers. The Protestants, whether in Dublin or elsewhere, are almost all transplanted lately from England. Nor is it any wonder that those who are born Papists generally live and die such, when the Protestants can find no better ways to convert them than Penal Laws and Acts of Parliament.

Sun. 16.—We went to St James's church in the morning (there being no service at St Patrick's), and in the afternoon, to Christ Church. When I came out of the choir, I could not but observe wellnigh the whole congregation drawn up in rows in the body of the church, from the one end to the other. I walked through the midst of them; and they stared their fill: but scarce one spoke either good or bad.

In the evening I had a large number of them in Marlborough Street, both within doors and without.

Mon. 17. I began examining the society, which I finished the next day. It contained about two hundred and fourscore members, many of whom appeared to be strong in faith.

Wed. 26.—About two in the afternoon we landed at Holyhead.

Tues. Sept. 29.—I retired to Mrs. Sparrow's, at Lewisham, where also I preached every evening. *Saturday*, October 3, I returned to London.

The former part of the next week, and of some others, I spent at Newington and Lewisham in writing.

Fri. ... I went with two or three friends to see what are call.. the electrical experiments. How must these also confound those poor half-thinkers, who will believe nothing but what they can comprehend! Who can comprehend, how fire lives in water, and passes through it more freely than through air? How flame issues out of my finger, real flame, such as sets fire to spirits of wine? How these, and many more as strange phenomena, arise from the turning round a glass globe? It is all mystery: if haply by any means God may hide pride from man!

Mon. Nov. 2.—I preached at Windsor at noon, and in the afternoon rode to Reading. Mr J. R. had just sent his brother word, that he had hired a mob to pull down his preaching-house that night. In the evening Mr S. Richards overtook a large company of bargemen walking towards it, whom he immediately accosted, and asked, if they would go with him and hear a good sermon; telling them, "I will make room for you, if you were as many more." They said, they would go with all their hearts. "But, neighbours," said he, "would it not be as well to leave those clubs behind you? Perhaps some of the women may be frighted at them." They threw them all away, and walked quietly with him to the house, where he set them in a pew.

In the conclusion of my sermon, one of them who used to be their captain, being the head taller than his fellows, rose up, and looking round the congregation, said, "The gentleman says nothing but what is good: I say so; and there is not a man here that shall dare to say otherwise."

Sun. 22.—I spent an hour with Mary Cheesebrook, a strange monument of the mercy of God. About six years ago, she was without God in the world, being a kept mistress. An acquaintance brought her one evening to the chapel in West Street, where God gave her a new heart. She shed abundance of tears, she plucked out the right eye and cast it from her; and from that time procured for herself by hard labour what was needful for life and godliness. She missed no opportunity of coming to the preaching; often after a hard day's work, at May Fair, she came to the Foundery in the evening, running the greater part of the way. Every Saturday, after paying her little debts, she gave away all the money that remained; leaving the morrow to take thought for the things of itself.

Two years ago she catched a violent cold, which she neglected, till it settled upon her lungs. I knew nothing of her illness till it was past cure, she being then worn to a skeleton. Upon my mentioning her case to Mrs ——, she sent her half-a-guinea. Molly immediately sent for a poor man, a baker, of whom she had lately taken her bread. She owed him about ten shillings: but an earnest dispute arose between them; for the man would not take the money, saying, she wanted it more than he. But at length she prevailed, saying, she could not die in peace, if she owed any man anything.

But I found something still lay upon her mind. Upon my pressing her to speak freely, she told me, it was concern for her child, a girl about eight years old, who, after she was gone, would have no friend to take care either of her soul or body.

I replied, "Be at rest in this thing also ; I will take care of the child." From that time she lay (two or three weeks) quietly waiting for the salvation of God.

Mon. Dec. 21.—I went to Newington. Here, in the intervals of writing, I read the deaths of some of the Order *de la Trappe*. I am amazed at the allowance which God makes for invincible ignorance. Notwithstanding the mixture of superstition which appears in every one of these, yet what a strong vein of piety runs through all ! What deep experience of the inward work of God ; of righteousness, peace, and joy in the Holy Ghost !

Fri. Jan. 1, 1748.—We began the year at four in the morning, with joy and thanksgiving.

Sat. 16.—Upon reviewing the account of the sick, we found great reason to praise God. Within the year, about three hundred persons have received medicines occasionally. About one hundred had regularly taken them, and submitted to a proper regimen : more than ninety of these were entirely cured of diseases they had long laboured under. And the expense of medicines for the entire year amounted to some shillings above forty pounds.

Sun. 17.—I made a public collection towards a lending-stock for the poor. Our rule is, to lend only twenty shillings at once, which is repaid weekly within three months. I began this about a year and a half ago : thirty pounds sixteen shillings were then collected ; and out of this, no less than two hundred and fifty-five persons have been relieved in eighteen months. Dr W., hearing of this design, sent a guinea toward it ; as did an eminent Deist the next morning.

Thur. 28.—I set out for Deverel Long Bridge. About ten o'clock we were met by a loaded waggon, in a deep, hollow way. There was a narrow path between the road and the bank : I stepped into this, and John Trembath followed me. When the waggon came near, my horse began to rear, and to attempt climbing up the bank. This frightened the horse which was close behind, and made him prance and throw his head to and fro, till the bit of the bridle catched hold of the cape of my greatcoat, and pulled me backward off my horse. I fell as exact on the path, between the waggon and the bank, as if one had taken me in his arms and laid me down there. Both our horses stood stock still, one just behind me, the other before ; so, by the blessing of God, I rose unhurt, mounted again, and rode on.

Tues. Feb. 9.—I met about sixty of the society in Bristol, to consult about enlarging the room ; and indeed securing it, for there was no small danger of its falling upon our heads. In two or three days, two hundred and thirty pounds were subscribed. We immediately procured experienced builders to make an estimate of the expense; and I appointed five stewards (beside those of the society) to superintend the work.

Fri. 12.—After preaching at Oakhill about noon, I rode to Shipton, and found them all under a strange consternation. A mob, they said, was hired, prepared, and made sufficiently drunk, in order to do all manner of mischief. I began preaching between four and five: none hindered or interrupted at all. We had a blessed opportunity, and the hearts of many were exceedingly comforted. I wondered what had become of the mob. But we were quickly informed, they mistook the place, imagining I should alight (as I used to do) at William Stone's house, and had summoned, by drum, all their forces together, to meet me at my coming: but Mr Swindells innocently carrying me to the other end of the town, they did not find their mistake till I had done preaching; so that the hindering this, which was one of their designs, was utterly disappointed.

However, they attended us from the preaching-house to William Stone's, throwing dirt, stones, and clods, in abundance: but they could not hurt us; only Mr Swindells had a little dirt on his coat, and I a few specks on my hat.

After we were gone into the house, they began throwing great stones, in order to break the door. But perceiving this would require some time, they dropped that design for the present. They first broke all the tiles on the pent-house over the door, and then poured in a shower of stones at the windows. One of their captains, in his great zeal, had followed us into the house, and was now shut in with us. He did not like this, and would fain have got out; but it was not possible; so he kept as close to me as he could, thinking himself safe when he was near me: but, staying a little behind,—when I went up two pair of stairs, and stood close on one side, where we were a little sheltered,—a large stone struck him on the forehead, and the blood spouted out like a stream. He cried out, "Oh, sir, are we to die to-night? What must I do? What must I do?" I said, "Pray to God. He is able to deliver you from all danger." He took my advice, and began praying in such a manner as he had scarce done ever since he was born.

Mr Swindells and I then went to prayer; after which I told him, "We must not stay here; we must go down immediately." He said, "Sir, we cannot stir; you see how the stones fly about." I walked straight through the room, and down the stairs; and not a stone came in, till we were at the bottom.

The mob had just broke open the door when we came into the lower room ; and exactly while they burst in at the one door, we walked out at the other. Nor did one man take any notice of us, though we were within five yards of each other.

They filled the house at once, and proposed setting it on fire. But one of them, happening to remember that his own house was next, with much ado persuaded them not to do it. Hearing one of them cry out, "They are gone over the grounds," I thought the advice was good ; so we went over the grounds, to the farther end of the town, where Abraham Jenkins waited, and undertook to guide us to Oakhill.

I was riding on in Shipton Lane, it being now quite dark, when he cried out, " Come down : come down from the bank." I did as I was bid ; but the bank being high, and the side very near perpendicular, I came down all at once, my horse and I tumbling over one another. But we both rose unhurt. In less than an hour we came to Oakhill, and the next morning to Bristol.

Mon. 15.—I set out for Ireland.

Sun. 21.—I preached in the morning in Lanzunfried church. The service at Builth was not over till past two ; I then began in the churchyard, notwithstanding the north-east wind, to call sinners to repentance. More than all the town were gathered together in that pleasant vale, and made the woods and mountains echo while they sung—

> "Ye mountains and vales, in praises abound ;
> Ye hills and ye dales, continue the sound ;
> Break forth into singing, ye trees of the wood ;
> For Jesus is bringing lost sinners to God."

In the evening I preached again at Garth, and on *Monday*, 22, at five in the morning. A little before sunrise we took horse, it being a clear, sharp frost. We had waited four days in hopes the snow would melt, fearing the drifts of it would lie deep upon the mountains, particularly as we journeyed northward ; but quite contrary to our expectation, the farther northward we went, the less snow we found, so that it scarce hindered us after the first day. About eleven we came to Llanidloes. At the earnest request of one who lived there, I preached at noon in the market-place, to such a congregation as no one could expect at an hour's warning.

It was as much as we could do to reach Machynlleth that night. It snowed again from about midnight till morning ; so that no path was to be seen for several miles. However, we found our way to Tannabull, and passed the sands in the afternoon, being determined to reach Carnarvon, if possible. And so we did, notwithstanding my horse's losing a shoe; but not till between nine and ten at night.

Wed. 24.—We hastened on to Holyhead.

Wed. Mar. 16.—I inquired into the state of the society. Most pompous accounts had been sent me, from time to time, of the great numbers that were added to it; so that I confidently expected to find therein six or seven hundred members. And how is the real fact? I left three hundred and ninety-four members; and I doubt if there are now three hundred and ninety-six.

Let this be a warning to us all, how we give in to that hateful custom of painting things beyond the life. Let us make a conscience of magnifying or exaggerating anything. Let us rather speak under, than above, the truth. We, of all men, should be punctual in all we say; that none of our words may fall to the ground.

Wed. 23.—I talked with a warm man, who was always very zealous for the Church, when he was very drunk, and just able to stammer out the Irish proverb, "No gown, no crown." He was quickly convinced, that, whatever we were, he was himself a child of the devil. We left him full of good resolutions, which held several days.

Thur. 31.—One would have dissuaded me from preaching at five, being sure none would rise so soon. But I kept my hour, and had a large and serious congregation.

Sun. April 3.—I preached at five to, at least, three hundred hearers. I walked from thence to see a poor woman that was sick, about a mile from the town. About an hundred and fifty people ran after me. After I had prayed with the sick person, being unwilling so many people should go empty away, I chose a smooth, grassy place, near the road, where we all kneeled down to prayer; after which we sung a psalm, and I gave them a short exhortation. At eleven we went to church, and heard a plain, useful sermon. At two I preached on the Connaught side of the bridge, where there are only (they informed me) five or six families of Protestants. Such a company of people (many said) had never before been seen at Athlone; many coming from all the country round, and (for the present) receiving the Word with joy. I preached again, at six, in the same place, and to nearly the same (only a little larger) congregation; the greater part whereof (notwithstanding the prohibition of their priests) I afterwards found were Papists.

Mon. 4.—I preached once more at five, and a great part of the congregation was in tears. Indeed almost all the town appeared to be moved, full of goodwill and desires of salvation. But the waters spread too wide to be deep. I found not one under any strong conviction; much less had anyone attained the knowledge of salvation, in hearing above thirty sermons. So that, as yet, no judgment could be formed of the future work of God in this place.

I took horse at ten, and about twelve preached at Moat. I could not but observe the zeal of these young disciples. They were vehemently angry at a man's throwing a cabbage-stalk. Let them keep their courage till they see such a sight as that at Walsal or Shepton.

Wed. 6.—I baptized seven persons educated among the Quakers. In the afternoon we rode to Philipstown.

As soon as I mounted my horse, he began to snort and run backward, without any visible cause. One whipped him behind, and I before; but it profited nothing. He leaped to and fro, from side to side, till he came over against a gateway, into which he ran backward, and tumbled head over heels. I rose unhurt. He then went on quietly.

Sat. 9.—I preached in Connaught, a few miles from Athlone. Many heard; but I doubt, felt nothing.

The Shannon comes within a mile of the house where I preached. I think there is not such another river in Europe: it is here ten or twelve miles over, though scarce thirty miles from its fountain-head. There are many islands in it, once well inhabited, but now mostly desolate. In almost every one is the ruins of a church: in one, the remains of no less than seven. I fear, God hath still a controversy with this land, because it is defiled with blood.

April 10.—(*Easter-Day.*) Never was such a congregation seen before at the sacrament in Athlone. I preached at three. Abundance of Papists flocked to hear; so that the priest, seeing his command did not avail, came in person at six, and drove them away before him like a flock of sheep.

Tues. 12.—I rode to Clara, where I was quickly informed, that there was to begin in an hour's time a famous cockfight, to which almost all the country was coming from every side. Hoping to engage some part of them in a better employ, I began preaching in the street, as soon as possible. One or two hundred stopped, and listened a while, and pulled off their hats, and forgot their diversion.

Thur. 14.—The house was full at five. In the evening many of the neighbouring gentlemen were present, but none mocked. That is not the custom here; all attend to what is spoken in the name of God; they do not understand the making sport with sacred things; so that whether they approve or no, they behave with seriousness.

Sat. 23.—I read, some hours, an extremely dull book, Sir James Ware's *Antiquities of Ireland*. By the vast number of ruins which are seen in all parts, I had always suspected what he shows at large, namely, that in ancient times it was more populous, tenfold, than it is now; many that were large cities, being now ruinous heaps; many shrunk into inconsiderable villages.

I visited one in the afternoon who was ill of a fever, and lay in a very close room. While I was near him, I found myself not well. After my return home, I felt my stomach out of order. But I imagined it was not worth any notice, and would pass off before the morning.

Sun. 24.—I preached at Skinner's Alley at five; and on Oxmantown Green at eight. I was weak in body, but was greatly revived by the seriousness and earnestness of the congregation. Resolving to improve the opportunity, I gave notice of preaching there again in the afternoon; which I did to a congregation much more numerous, and equally attentive. As I came home I was glad to lie down, having a quinsy, attended with a fever. However, when the society met, I made a shift to creep in among them. Immediately my voice was restored. I spoke without pain, for near an hour together. And great was our rejoicing over each other; knowing that God would order all things well.

Mon. 25.—Finding my fever greatly increased, I judged it would be best to keep my bed, and to live awhile on apples and apple-tea. On *Tuesday* I was quite well, and should have preached, but that Dr Rutty (who had been with me twice) insisted on my resting for a time.

I read to-day what is accounted the most correct history of St Patrick that is extant; and, on the maturest consideration, I was much inclined to believe, that St Patrick and St George were of one family. The whole story smells strong of romance. To touch only on a few particulars:—I object to his first setting out: the Bishop of Rome had no such power in the beginning of the fifth century as this account supposes; nor would his uncle, the Bishop of Tours, have sent him in that age to Rome for a commission to convert Ireland, having himself as much authority over that land as any Italian bishop whatever. Again: if God had sent him thither, he would not so long have buried his talent in the earth. I never heard before of an apostle sleeping thirty-five years, and beginning to preach at threescore. But his success staggers me the most of all: no blood of the martyrs is here; no reproach, no scandal of the cross; no persecution to those that will live godly. Nothing is to be heard of, from the beginning to the end, but kings, nobles, warriors, bowing down before him. Thousands are converted, without any opposition at all; twelve thousand at one sermon. If these things were so, either there was then no devil in the world, or St Patrick did not preach the gospel of Christ.

Thursday, 28, was the day fixed for my going into the country: but all about me began to cry out, "Sure, you will not go to-day? See how the rain pours down!" I told them, "I must keep my word, if possible." But before five, the man of whom I had bespoke an horse sent word, his horse should not go out in such a day. I sent one who brought him to a better mind. So about six I took horse. About nine I called at Killcock: the old landlord was ill of the gout, and his wife of a complication of distempers; but when I told her, "The Lord loveth whom He chasteneth, and all these are tokens of His love," she burst out, "O Lord, I offer Thee all my sufferings, my pain, my sickness! If Thou lovest me, it is enough. Here I am: take me, and do with me what Thou wilt."

Fri. 29.—I rode to Temple-Macqueteer, and thence toward Athlone. We came at least an hour before we were expected. Nevertheless we were met by many of our brethren. The first I saw, about two miles from the town, were a dozen little boys running with all their might, some bareheaded, some barefooted and barelegged; so they had their desire of speaking to me first, the others being still behind.

Sat. 30.—I found the roaring lion began to shake himself here also. Some Papists, and two or three good Protestant families, were cordially joined together, to oppose the work of God; but they durst not yet do it openly, the stream running so strong against them.

Wed. May 4.—I rode to Clara, and preached to a small company, who were not afraid of a stormy day. I spent half an hour after sermon with a few serious people, and then rode to Tullamore.

One who looks on the common Irish cabins, might imagine Saturn still reigned here—

Cum frigida parvas
Præberet spelunca domos; ignemque laremque,
Et pecus et dominos, communi clauderet umbrâ.[1]

Communi umbrâ indeed: for no light can come into the earth

[1] "The narrow cave a cold retreat affords,
And beasts and men screens with one common shade."

or straw built cavern, on the master and his cattle, but at one hole; which is both window, chimney, and door.

Sun. 8. I preached at five, though I could not well stand. I then set out for Aghrim, in the county of Galway, thirteen Connaught (that is Yorkshire) miles from Athlone. The morning prayers (so called) began about twelve; after which we had a warm sermon against enthusiasts. I could not have come at a better time: for I began immediately; and all that were in the church, high and low, rich and poor, stopped to hear me. In explaining the inward kingdom of God, I had a fair occasion to consider what we had just heard; and God renewed my strength, and, I trust, applied His Word to the hearts of most of the hearers.

Mr S., a neighbouring Justice of Peace, as soon as I had done, desired me to dine with him. After dinner I hastened back to Athlone, and began preaching about six: five clergymen were of the audience, and abundance of Romanists. Such an opportunity I never had before in these parts.

Mon. 9.—Having not had an hour's sound sleep, from the time I lay down till I rose, I was in doubt whether I could preach or not: however, I went to the market-place as usual, and found no want of strength, till I had fully declared "the redemption that is in Jesus Christ." I had designed, afterwards, to settle the society thoroughly; but I was not able to sit up so long.

Many advised me not to go out at night, the wind being extremely cold and blustering. But I could in no wise consent to spare myself, at such a time as this. I preached on, "Come unto Me, all ye that labour and are heavy-laden." And I found myself at least as well when I had done, as I was before I begun.

Tues. 10.—With much difficulty I broke away from this immeasurably-loving people: and not so soon as I imagined neither; for when we drew near to the turnpike, about a mile from the town, a multitude waited for us at the top of the hill. They fell back on each side, to make us way, and then joined and closed us in. After singing two or three verses, I put forward, when, on a sudden, I was a little surprised by such a cry of men, women, and children as I never heard before. Yet a little while, and we shall meet, to part no more; and sorrow and sighing shall flee away for ever.

Instead of going straight to Tullamore, I could not be easy without going round by Coolylough: I knew not why; for I did not know then that Mr Handy's wife, who had been brought to bed a few days, had an earnest desire to see me once more before I left the kingdom. She could not avoid praying for it, though her sister checked her again and again, telling her, it could not be. Before the debate was concluded, I came in: so they wondered, and praised God.

I took the straight road from hence to Dublin. Here likewise I observed abundance of ruined buildings: but I observed also, that some of them were never finished; and some had been pulled down by those who built them. Such is the amazing fickleness of this people. Almost every one who has his fortune in his own hands, *diruit, ædificat, mutat quadrata rotundis*;[1] and leaves those monuments of his folly to all succeeding generations.

I reached Dublin in the evening, faint and weary; but the two next days I rested.

Wed. 18.—We took ship. The wind was small in the afternoon, but exceeding high towards night. About eight I laid me down on the quarter-deck. I was soon wet from head to foot, but I took no cold at all. About four in the morning we landed at Holyhead, and in the evening reached Carnarvon.

Mon. June 13.—I spent an hour or two with Dr Pepusch. He asserted, that the art of music is lost; that the ancients only understood it in its perfection; that it was revived a little in the reign of King Henry VIII., by Tallys and his cotemporaries; as also in the reign of Queen Elizabeth, who was a judge and patroness of it; that after her reign it sunk for sixty or seventy years, till Purcell made some attempts to restore it; but that ever since, the true, ancient art, depending on nature and mathematical principles, had gained no ground; the present masters having no fixed principles at all.

Wed. 15.—I preached once more at St Bartholomew's. How strangely is the scene changed? What laughter and tumult was there among the best of the parish, when we preached in a London church ten years ago! And now all are calm and quietly attentive, from the least even to the greatest.

Friday, 24, the day we had appointed for opening the school at Kingswood, I preached there, on, "Train up a child in the way that he should go; and when he is old, he will not depart from it." My brother and I administered the Lord's Supper to many who came from far. We then agreed on the general rules of the school, which we published presently after.

Wed. 29.—We took horse at four, and, calling at Studley, found a woman of a broken heart, mourning continually after

[1] "Pulls down, builds up, and changes square things into round."—ED.

God, and scarce able to speak without tears. About one I began preaching in the open air at Birmingham.

At half an hour after six I preached at Wednesbury, to an exceeding large congregation; and every man, woman, and child behaved in a manner becoming the gospel.

Sat. July 2.—I rode to Epworth, and preached to a large congregation, many of them stablished in the grace of God.

Sun. 3.—I was quite surprised when I heard Mr R. preach. That soft, smooth, tuneful voice, which he so often employed to blaspheme the work of God, was lost, without hope of recovery: all means had been tried, but none took place. He now spoke in a manner shocking to hear, and impossible to be heard distinctly by one quarter of the congregation.

Mr Hay, the rector, reading prayers, I had once more the comfort of receiving the Lord's Supper at Epworth. After the evening service, I preached at the Cross again, to almost the whole town. I see plainly, we have often judged amiss, when we have measured the increase of the work of God, in this and other places, by the increase of the society only. The society here is not large; but God has wrought upon the whole place. Sabbath-breaking and drunkenness are no more seen in these streets; cursing and swearing are rarely heard. Wickedness hides its head already. Who knows but, by and by, God may utterly take it away?

I was peculiarly pleased with the deep seriousness of the congregation at church, both morning and evening: and all the way as we walked down the Church-Lane, after the sermon was ended, I scarce saw one person look on either side, or speak one word to another.

Tues. 5.—We rode to Coningsby, on the edge of the Fens. Mr B., a Baptist minister, had wrote to me at London, begging me to lodge with him, whenever I came to Coningsby: but he was gone out of town that very morning. However, one rode after him, and brought him back in the afternoon. I was scarce set down in his house, before he . " upon the point of baptism. I waived the dispute for some time; but finding there was no remedy, I came close to the question, and we kept to it for about an hour and half. From that time we let the matter rest, and confirmed our love towards each other.

Sat. 9.—Setting out from Boroughbridge between two and three, we reached Newcastle about three in the afternoon.

Mon. 18.—I began my journey northward, having appointed to preach in Morpeth at noon. As soon as I had sung a few verses at the Cross, a young man appeared at the head of his troop, and told me very plainly and roughly, "You shall not preach there." I went on ; upon which he gave the signal to his companions, who prepared to force me into better manners ; but they quickly fell out among themselves. Meantime I began my sermon, and went on without any considerable interruption ; the congregation softening more and more, till, toward the close, the far greater part appeared exceeding serious and attentive.

In the afternoon we rode to Widdrington, which belonged to the Lord Widdrington, till the rebellion in 1716. The people flocked in from all parts, so that the congregation here was larger than at Morpeth. It was a delightful evening, and a delightful place, under the shade of tall trees ; and every man hung upon the word ; none stirred his head or hand, or looked to the right or left, while I declared, in strong terms, "the grace of our Lord Iesus Christ."

Tues. 19.—We rode to Alemouth, a small seaport town, famous for all kinds of wickedness. The people here are sinners convict ; they have nothing to pay, but plead guilty before God. Therefore, I preached to them without delay Jesus Christ, for "wisdom, righteousness, sanctification, and redemption."

After dinner we rode to Alnwick, one of the largest inland towns in the county of Northumberland.

Wed. 20.—We took horse between eight and nine, and a little before two came to Berwick. I sent to the commander of the garrison to desire the use of a green place near his house, which he readily granted. I preached at seven to (it was judged) two thousand people. I found the generality of them just such as I expected ; serious and decent, but not easy to be convinced of anything. For who can tell them what they did not know before ?

Thur. 21.—After preaching we walked round the walls, which they were repairing and rebuilding. I could not but observe to-day, how different the face of things was, from what it appeared yesterday ; especially after I had preached at noon. Yesterday we were hallooed all along the streets : to-day none opened his mouth as we went along ; the very children were all silent. The grown people pulled off their hats on every side ; so that we might even have fancied ourselves at Newcastle.

At seven I preached to a far larger congregation than before. And now the Word of God was as a fire and an hammer. I began again and again, after I thought I had done ; and the latter words were still stronger than the former ; so that I was not surprised at the number which attended in the morning, when we had another joyful, solemn hour.

Fri. 22.—I preached about noon at Tuggle, a village about three miles from Barnborough; and then went on to Alnwick, where, at seven, was such a congregation as one would not have thought the whole town could afford.

Sun. 24.—I preached at five in the Newcastle house; at half-hour past eight in the Castle Garth, and at four in the afternoon. I was weary and faint when I began to speak; but my strength was quickly renewed. Thence we went to the society. I had designed to read the rules; but I could not get forward. As we began so we went on till eight o'clock, singing, and rejoicing, and praising God.

Sun. 31.—At eight I preached in the street, at Sunderland, and at one in the afternoon. I rode thence straight to the Castle Garth, and found abundance of people gathered together. Many were in tears all round, while those comfortable words were opened and applied, "He healeth them that are broken in heart, and giveth medicine to heal their sickness."

Mon. Aug. 1.—One of my old companions returned—my headache; which I never had while I abstained from animal food. But I regarded it not, supposing it would go off in a day or two of itself.

Wed. 3.—I found it absolutely necessary to publish the following advertisement:—

"WHEREAS one Thomas Moor, *alias* Smith, has lately appeared in Cumberland and other parts of England, preaching (as he calls it) in a clergyman's habit, and then collecting money of his hearers: this is to certify, whom it may concern, that the said Moor is no clergyman, but a cheat and impostor; and that no preacher in connection with me, either directly or indirectly, asks money of anyone.   JOHN WESLEY."

Thur. 4.—I preached in the evening at Spen. *Friday*, 5. About noon, at Horsley. As I rode home I found my headache increase much. But as many people were come from all parts (it being the monthly watch-night), I could not be content to send them empty away. I almost forgot my pain while I was speaking; but was obliged to go to bed as soon as I had done.

Sat. 6.—The pain was much worse than before. I then applied cloths dipped in cold water: immediately my head was easy, but I was exceeding sick. When I laid down, the pain returned, and the sickness ceased: when I sat up, the pain ceased, and the sickness returned. In the evening I took ten grains of ipecacuanha: it wrought for about ten minutes. The moment it had done I was in perfect health, and felt no more either of pain or sickness.

Sun. 7—I preached as usual at five, and at half-hour after eight. In the afternoon all the street was full of people, come from all parts to see the judges. But a good part of them followed me into the Castle Garth, and found something else to do. This put a zealous man that came by quite out of patience, so that I had hardly named my text, when he began to scold and scream, and curse and swear, to the utmost extent of his throat. But there was not one of the whole multitude, rich or poor, that regarded him at all.

Fri. 12.—In riding to Newcastle, I finished the tenth *Iliad* of Homer. What an amazing genius had this man! To write with such strength of thought, and beauty of expression, when he had none to go before him! And what a vein of piety runs through his whole work, in spite of his pagan prejudices! Yet one cannot but observe such improprieties intermixed, as are shocking to the last degree.

What excuse can any man of common sense make for

"His scolding heroes, and his wounded gods"?

Nay, does he not introduce even his "father of gods and men," one while shaking heaven with his nod, and soon after using his sister and wife, the empress of heaven, with such language as a carman might be ashamed of? And what can be said for a king, full of days and wisdom, telling Achilles how often he had given him wine, when he was a child and sat in his lap, till he had vomited it up on his clothes? Are these some of those "divine boldnesses which naturally provoke short-sightedness and ignorance to show themselves"?

Sat. 20.—At the earnest desire of the little society, I went to Wakefield. I knew the madness of the people there: but I knew also they were in God's hand. At eight I would have preached in Francis Scot's yard: but the landlord would not suffer it; saying the mob would do more hurt to his houses than ever we should do him good; so I went, perforce, into the main street, and proclaimed pardon for sinners. None interrupted, or made the least disturbance, from the beginning to the end.

About one I preached at Oulton, where likewise all is now calm, after a violent storm of several weeks, wherein many were beaten, and wounded, and outraged various ways; but none moved from their steadfastness. In the evening I preached at Armley to many who want a storm, being quite unnerved by constant sunshine.

Mon. 22.—After preaching at Heaton, I rode to Skircoat Green. Our brethren here were much divided in their judgment. Many thought I ought to preach at Halifax Cross: others judged it to be impracticable; the very mention of it as a possible thing having set all the town in an uproar. However, to the Cross I went. There was an immense number of people, roaring like the waves of the sea. But the far greater part of them were still as soon as I began to speak. They seemed more and more attentive and composed; till a gentleman got some of the rabble together, and began to throw money among them, which occasioned much hurry and confusion. Finding my voice could not be heard, I made signs to the people, that I would remove to another place. I believe nine in ten followed me to a meadow, about half a mile from the town, where we spent so solemn an hour as I have seldom known, rejoicing and praising God.

Tues. 23.—The congregation was larger at five in the morning than it was in the evening when I preached here before. About one I preached at Baildon, and in the evening at Bradford; where none behaved indecently but the curate of the parish.

Wed. 24.—At eight I preached at Eccleshill, and about one at Keighley. At five Mr Grimshaw read prayers and I preached at Haworth, to more than the church could contain. We began the service in the morning at five, and even then the church was nearly filled.

Thur. 25.—I rode with Mr Grimshaw to Roughlee, where T. Colbeck, of Keighley, was to meet us. We were stopped again and again, and begged not to go on; for a large mob from Colne was gone before us. Coming a little farther, we understood they had not yet reached Roughlee. So we hastened on, that we might be there before them. All was quiet when we came. I was a little afraid for Mr Grimshaw: but it needed not: he was ready to go to prison or death for Christ's sake.

At half-hour after twelve I began to preach. I had about half finished my discourse, when the mob came pouring down the hill like a torrent. After exchanging a few words with their captain, to prevent any contest, I went with him as he required. When we came to Barrowford, two miles off, the whole army drew up in battle-array before the house into which I was carried, with two or three of my friends. After I had been detained above an hour, their captain went out, and I followed him, and desired him to conduct me whence I came. He said, he would; but the mob followed after; at which he was so enraged, that he must needs turn back to fight them, and so left me alone.

A further account is contained in the following letter, which I wrote the next morning:—

"WIDDOP, *Aug.* 26, 1748.

"SIR,—Yesterday, between twelve and one o'clock, while I was speaking to some quiet people, without any noise or tumult, a drunken rabble came, with clubs and staves, in a tumultuous and riotous manner, the captain of whom, Richard B. by name, said he was a deputy-constable, and that he was come to bring me to you. I went with him; but I had scarce gone ten yards, when a man of his company struck me with his fist in the face with all his might; quickly after, another threw his stick at my head: I then made a little stand; but another of your champions, cursing and swearing in the most shocking manner, and flourishing his club over his head, cried out, 'Bring him away!'

"With such a convoy I walked to Barrowford, where they informed me you was; their drummer going before, to draw all the rabble together from all quarters.

"When your deputy had brought me into the house, he permitted Mr Grimshaw, the minister of Haworth, Mr Colbeck, of Keighley, and one more, to be with me, promising that none should hurt them. Soon after, you and your friends came in, and required me to promise, I would come to Roughlee no more. I told you, I would sooner cut off my hand than make any such promise: neither would I promise that none of my friends should come. After abundance of rambling discourse (for I could keep none of you long to any one point), from about one o'clock till between three and four (in which one of you frankly said, 'No; we will not be like Gamaliel, we will proceed like the Jews'), you seemed a little satisfied with my saying, 'I will not preach at Roughlee at this time.' You then undertook to quiet the mob, to whom you went and spoke a few words, and their noise immediately ceased. I then walked out with you at the back door.

"I should have mentioned that I had several times before desired you to let me go, but in vain; and that when I attempted to go with Richard B., the mob immediately followed, with oaths, curses, and stones; that one of them beat me down to the ground; and when I rose again, the whole body came about me like lions, and forced me back into the house.

"While you and I went out at one door, Mr Grimshaw and Mr Colbeck went out at the other. The mob imediately closed them in, tossed them to and fro with the utmost violence, threw Mr Grimshaw down, and loaded them both with dirt and mire of every kind; not one of your friends offering to call off your bloodhounds from the pursuit.

"The other quiet, harmless people, who followed me at a

distance, to see what the end would be, they treated still worse, not only by the connivance, but by the express order, of your deputy. They made them run for their lives, amidst showers of dirt and stones, without any regard to age or sex. Some of them they trampled in the mire, and dragged by the hair, particularly Mr Mackford, who came with me from Newcastle. Many they beat with their clubs without mercy. One they forced to leap down (or they would have thrown him headlong) from a rock, ten or twelve feet high, into the river. And when he crawled out, wet and bruised, they swore they would throw him in again, which they were hardly persuaded not to do. All this time you sat well-pleased close to the place, not attempting in the least to hinder them.

"And all this time you were talking of justice and law! Alas, sir, suppose we were Dissenters (which I deny), suppose we were Jews or Turks, are we not to have the benefit of the laws of our country? Proceed against us by the law, if you can or dare; but not by lawless violence; not by making a drunken, cursing, swearing, riotous mob, both judge, jury, and executioner. This is flat rebellion against God and the King, as you may possibly find to your cost."

Between four and five we set out from Roughlee. But observing several parties of men upon the hills, and suspecting their design, we put on and passed the lane they were making for before they came. One of our brothers, not riding so fast, was intercepted by them. They immediately knocked him down, and how it was that he got from amongst them he knew not.

Before seven we reached Widdop. The news of what had passed at Barrowford made us all friends. The person in whose house Mr B. preached, sent and begged I would preach there; which I did at eight, to such a congregation as none could have expected on so short a warning. He invited us also to lodge at his house, and all jealousies vanished away.

Fri. 26.—I preached at five to much the same congregation. At twelve we came to Heptonstall Bank. The house stands on the side of a steep mountain, and commands all the vale below. The place in which I preached was an oval spot of ground, surrounded with spreading trees, scooped out, as it were, in the side of the hill, which rose round like a theatre. The congregation was equal to that at Leeds; but such serious and earnest attention! It lifted up my hands, so that I preached as I scarce ever did in my life.

About four I preached again to nearly the same congregation, and God again caused the power of His love to be known. Thence we rode to Midgley. Many flocked from all parts, to whom I preached till near an hour after sunset. The calmness of the evening agreed well with the seriousness of the people; every one of whom seemed to drink in the Word of God, as a thirsty land the refreshing showers.

Sat. 27.—I preached once more at seven to the earnest people at the Bank, and then rode to Todmorden Edge. Here several prisoners were set at liberty, as was Mr Mackford the day before. At five I preached at Mellar Barn, in Rosendale. There were a few rude people; but they kept at a distance; and it was well they did, or the unawakened hearers would have been apt to handle them roughly. I observed here what I had not then seen, but at one single place in England :—When I had finished my discourse, and even pronounced the blessing, not one person offered to go away; but every man, woman, and child stayed just where they were, till I myself went away first.

Sun. 28.—I was invited by Mr U., the minister of Goodshaw, to preach in his church. I began reading prayers at seven; but perceiving the church would scarce contain half of the congregation, after prayers I went out, and standing on the churchyard wall, in a place shaded from the sun, explained and enforced those words in the second lesson, "Almost thou persuadest me to be a Christian."

I wonder at those who still talk so loud of the indecency of field-preaching. The highest indecency is in St Paul's church, when a considerable part of the congregation are asleep, or talking, or looking about, not minding a word the preacher says. On the other hand, there is the highest decency in a churchyard or field, when the whole congregation behave and look as if they saw the Judge of all, and heard Him speaking from heaven.

At one I went to the Cross in Bolton. There was a vast number of people, but many of them utterly wild. As soon as I began speaking, they began thrusting to and fro; endeavouring to throw me down from the steps on which I stood. They did so once or twice; but I went up again, and continued my discourse. They then began to throw stones; at the same time some got upon the Cross behind me to push me down; on which I could not but observe, how God overrules even the minutest circumstances. One man was bawling just at my ear, when a stone struck him on the cheek, and he was still. A second was forcing his way down to me, till another stone hit him on the forehead: it bounded back, the blood ran down, and he came no farther. The third, being got close to me, stretched out his hand, and in the instant a sharp stone came upon the joints of his fingers. He shook his hand, and was very quiet till I concluded my discourse and went away.

In the evening I preached at Booth Bank. *Tuesday*, 30. I preached about one at Oldfield Brow. We rode in the afternoon to Woodley. We saw by the way many marks of the late flood; of which John Bennet, who was then upon the place, gave us the following account—

"On Saturday, the 23rd of July last, there fell for about three hours, in and about Hayfield, in Derbyshire, a very heavy rain, which caused such a flood as had not been seen by any now living in those parts.

"The rocks were loosened from the mountains: one field was covered with huge stones from side to side.

"Several water-mills were clean swept away, without leaving any remains.

"The trees were torn up by the roots, and whirled away like stubble.

"Two women of a loose character were swept away from their own door and drowned. One of them was found near the place; the other was carried seven or eight miles.

"Hayfield churchyard was all torn up, and the dead bodies swept out of their graves. When the flood abated, they were found in several places. Some were hanging on trees; others left in meadows or grounds; some partly eaten by dogs, or wanting one or more of their members."

Wed. 31.—John Bennet showed me a gentleman's house, who was, a few years since, utterly without God in the world. But two or three years ago, God laid His hand both upon his body and soul. His sins dropped off. He lived holy and unblamable in all things. And not being able to go about doing good, he resolved to do what good he could at home. To this end he invited his neighbours to his house, every Sunday morning and evening (not being near any church), to whom he read the prayers of the Church and a sermon. Sometimes he had an hundred and fifty or two hundred of them at once. At Bongs I received an invitation from him; so John Bennet and I rode down together, and found him rejoicing under the hand of God, and praising Him for all his pain and weakness.

Sat. Oct. 1.—I rode quietly on to Bristol.

I examined the society the following week, leaving out every careless person, and every one who wilfully and obstinately refused to meet his brethren weekly. By this means their number was reduced from nine hundred to about seven hundred and thirty.

Sun. 9.—I began examining the classes in Kingswood ; and was never before so fully convinced of the device of Satan, which has often made our hands hang down, and our minds evil affected to our brethren. Now, as ten times before, a cry was gone forth, " What a scandal do these people bring upon the gospel ! What a society is this ! with all these drunkards and tale-bearers and evil-speakers in it ! " I expected, therefore, that I should find an heavy task upon my hands ; and that none of *these scandalous people* might be concealed, I first met all the Leaders, and inquired particularly of each person in every class. I repeated this inquiry when the classes themselves met. And what was the ground of all this outcry? Why, *two* persons had relapsed into drunkenness within three months' time : and *one* woman was proved to have made, or at least related, an idle story concerning another. I should rather have expected *two-and-twenty* instances of the former, and *one hundred* of the latter kind.

Fri. 14.—I preached at Reading ; and on *Saturday,* 15, rode to London.

Sat. 22.—I spent an hour in observing the various works of God in the Physic Garden at Chelsea. It would be a noble improvement of the design, if some able and industrious person were to make a full and accurate inquiry into the use and virtues of all these plants: without this, what end does the heaping them thus together answer, but the gratifying an idle curiosity ?

Tues. Nov. 1.—Being All-Saints' day, we had a solemn assembly at the chapel ; as I cannot but observe, we have had on this very day, for several years. Surely, " right dear in the sight of the Lord is the death of His saints ! "

Sun. 13.—Sarah Peters, a lover of souls, a mother in Israel, went to rest. During a close observation of several years, I never saw her, upon the most trying occasions, in any degree ruffled or discomposed, but she was always loving, always happy. It was her peculiar gift, and her continual care, to seek and save that which was lost ; to support the weak, to comfort the feeble-minded, to bring back what had been turned out of the way. And in doing this, God endued her, above her fellows, with the love that " believeth, hopeth, endureth all things."

" For these four years last past," says one who was intimately acquainted with her, " we used once or twice a week to unbosom ourselves to each other. I never knew her to have one doubt concerning her own salvation. I was sometimes jealous that she carried her charity too far, not allowing herself what was needful. But she would answer, 'I can live upon one meal a day, so that I may have to give to them that have none.'"

On Sunday, October 9, she went, with one more, to see the condemned malefactors in Newgate. They inquired for John Lancaster, in particular, who had sent to desire their coming. He asked them to go into his cell, which they willingly did; although some dissuaded them from it, because the gaol distemper (a kind of pestilential fever) raged much among the prisoners. They desired he would call together as many of the prisoners as were willing to come. Six or seven of those who were under sentence of death came. They sung a hymn, read a portion of Scripture, and prayed. Their little audience were all in tears. Most of them appeared deeply convinced of their lost estate. From this time her labours were unwearied among them; praying with them and for them night and day.

Some being of opinion it would not be difficult to procure a pardon for John Lancaster, S. Peters, though she never mentioned this to him, resolved to leave no means unattempted. She procured several petitions to be drawn, and went herself to Westminster, to Kensington, and to every part of the town where anyone lived who might possibly assist therein. In the meantime, she went constantly to Newgate, sometimes alone, sometimes with one or two others, visited all that were condemned in their cells, exhorted them, prayed with them, and had the comfort of finding them, every time, more athirst for God than before.

It was the earnest desire of them all, that they whom God had made so helpful to them might spend the last night with them. Accordingly she came to Newgate at ten o'clock, but could not be admitted on any terms. However, six of them were suffered to be in one cell. They spent the night, wrestling with God in prayer. She was admitted about six in the morning.

S. Peters, having finished her work, felt the body sink apace. On Wednesday, November 3, she took to her bed, having the symptoms of a malignant fever. She praised God in the fires for ten days; continually witnessing the good confession, "I have fought the good fight; I have kept the faith; I am going to receive the crown": and a little after midnight, on Sunday, the 13th, her spirit also returned to God.

Mon. 21.—I set out for Leigh, in Essex. It had rained hard in the former part of the night, which was succeeded by a sharp frost; so that most of the road was like glass; and the northeast wind set just in our face. However, we reached Leigh by four in the afternoon. Here was once a deep open harbour;

but the sands have long since blocked it up, and reduced a once flourishing town to a small ruinous village. I preached to most of the inhabitants of the place in the evening ; to many in the morning, and then rode back to London.

Tues. Feb. 14, 1749.—I rode with my brother to Oxford, and preached to a small company in the evening.

Thur. 16.—We rode to Ross, and on *Friday* to Garth.

Sun. 19.—My brother preached at Maesmennys in the morning. I preached at Builth in the afternoon, and at Garth in the evening. *Tuesday*, 21. I rode to Ragland, and the next day to Kingswood.

Thur. 23.—My design was to have as many of our preachers here, during the Lent, as could possibly be spared ; and to read lectures to them every day, as I did to my pupils in Oxford. I had seventeen of them in all. These I divided into two classes ; and read to one, Bishop Pearson on the *Creed* ; to the other, Aldrich's *Logic* ; and to both, *Rules for Action and Utterance*.

Fri. Mar. 3.—I corrected the extract of John Arndt, designed for part of the "Christian Library."

Tues. 14.—Having set apart an hour weekly for that purpose, I met the children of our four schools together : namely, the boys boarded in the new house, the girls boarded in the old ; the day-scholars (boys) taught by James Harding, and the girls taught by Sarah Dimmock. We soon found the effect of it in the children, some of whom were deeply and lastingly affected.

Mon. April 3.—We waited more than four hours at the Passage ; by which delay, I was forced to disappoint a large congregation at Newport.

In the evening, and the next morning (*Tues.* 4), I preached at Cardiff. Oh what a fair prospect was here some years ago ! Surely this whole town would have known God, from the least even to the greatest, had it not been for men leaning to their own understanding, instead of " the law and the testimony."

About noon we came to Aberdare, just as the bell was ringing for a burial. This had brought a great number together, to whom, after the burial, I preached in the church. We had almost continued rain from Aberdare to the great rough mountain that hangs over the vale of Brecknock ; but as soon as we gained the top of this, we left the clouds behind us. We had a mild, fair, sunshiny evening the remainder of our journey.

Fri. 7.—We reached Garth. *Saturday*, 8. I married my brother and Sarah Gwynne. It was a solemn day, such as became the dignity of a Christian marriage.

CHAPTER IX

CALM AFTER STORM

FROM AUGUST 1, 1749, TO OCTOBER 26, 1754

Tues. Aug. 1, 1749.—I spent a solemn hour with our children at Kingswood. After having settled all things there and at Bristol, I returned to London, where I received a remarkable account from Cork. On August 19, twenty-eight depositions were laid before the Grand Jury there, but they threw them all out ; and at the same time made that memorable presentment, which is worthy to be preserved in the annals of Ireland, to all succeeding generations :—

"We find and present Charles Wesley to be a person of ill fame, a vagabond, and a common disturber of His Majesty's peace ; and we pray he may be transported.

"We find and present Daniel Sullivan to be a person of ill fame, a vagabond, and a common disturber of His Majesty's peace ; and we pray he may be transported."

Daniel Sullivan was an honest baker, who had lived in Cork many years, I suppose in as good fame as any of his trade in the city ; but he had entertained my brother, and several other Methodists ; nay, and suffered them to preach in his house. The other names (only most of them miserably mangled and murdered) were designed for the names of eight preachers who had been there.

Mon. 28.—I left London, and in the evening came to Great Potton.

Wed. Sept. 6.—I reached Newcastle ; and after resting a day, and preaching two evenings and two mornings, with such a blessing as we have not often found, on *Friday* set out to visit the northern societies.

Thur. 21.—Moved by the pressing instances of Mr. Cownley, and convinced the providence of God called me thither, I left all my company, but Mr. Perronet, at Hinely Hill, and set out for Whitehaven. The next day I preached there in the market-place, to a multitude of people, on, "Ye know the grace of our Lord Jesus Christ." I saw they were moved, and resolved to improve the opportunity. So, after preaching, I desired those who determined to serve God, to meet me apart from the great congregation. To these I explained the design, nature, and use of Christian societies. Abundance were present again at five in the morning, though we had no room but the market-place. At three in the afternoon I preached at Hensingham, a large colliery, about a mile from the town. The eagerness of the people put me in mind of the early days at Kingswood. Oh, why should we not be always what we were once? Why should any leave their first love? At six I preached again in Whitehaven, on, "Come unto Me, all ye that labour and are heavy-laden"; and at eight endeavoured to mould as many as desired it into a regular society.

Sun. 24.—I began examining them one by one. At eight I preached at the Gins, another village, full of colliers, about half a mile from the town. The congregation was very large, and deeply attentive. Between one and two I preached again at Hensingham, to as many as my voice could command, on "Repent ye, and believe the gospel." Thence I hastened to church; and in the midst of the service I felt a sudden stroke. Immediately a shivering ran through me, and in a few minutes I was in a fever. I thought of taking a vomit immediately, and going to bed. But when I came from church, hearing there was a vast congregation in the market-place, I could not send them empty away. And while I was speaking to them, God remembered me, and strengthened me both in soul and body.

Tues. 26.—Having appointed, before I left Hinely Hill, to preach there again on *Wednesday* evening, I set out about two in the afternoon, though extremely weak, having had a flux for some days. But God renewed my strength, so that I felt less pain and weariness every hour. I had a solemn and delightful ride to Keswick, having my mind stayed on God.

Wed. 27.—I took horse at half an hour past three. There was no moon, or stars, but a thick mist; so that I could see neither road, nor anything else; but I went as right as if it had been noonday. When I drew nigh Penruddock Moor, the mist vanished, the stars appeared, and the morning dawned; so I imagined all the danger was past; but when I was on the middle of the moor, the mist fell again on every side, and I quickly lost my way. I lifted up my heart. Immediately it cleared up, and I soon recovered the high road. On Alstone Moor I missed my way again; and what, I believe, no stranger has done lately, rode through all the bogs without any stop, till I came to the vale, and thence to Hinely Hill.

A large congregation met in the evening. I expounded

part of the twentieth chapter of the Revelation. But oh, what a time was this! It was as though we were already standing before the "great white throne." God was no less present with us in prayer; when one just by me cried with a loud and bitter cry. I besought God to give us a token that all things should work together for good. He did so: He wrote pardon upon her heart; and we all rejoiced unto Him with reverence.

Thursday, 28, we set apart for fasting and prayer: John Brown and Mr Hopper were with me. It was a day that ought not to be forgotten. We had all free access to the throne of grace; and a firm, undoubting confidence, that He in whom we believed would do all things well.

Fri. 29.—I set out again for Whitehaven. The storm was exceeding high, and drove full in my face, so that it was not without difficulty I could sit my horse; particularly as I rode over the broad, bare backs of those enormous mountains which lay in my way. However, I kept on as I could, till I came to the brow of Hatside. So thick a fog then fell, that I was quickly out of all road, and knew not which way to turn. But I knew where help was to be found, in either great difficulties or small. The fog vanished in a moment, and I saw Gamblesby at a distance (the town to which I was going). I set out early on *Saturday*, the 30th, and in the afternoon reached Whitehaven.

About this time I was refreshed with a friendly letter from an excellent man, whom I had not heard from for several years.

What a truly Christian piety and simplicity breathe in these lines! And yet this very man, when I was at Savannah, did I refuse to admit to the Lord's Table, because he was not baptized; that is, not baptized by a minister who had been episcopally ordained.

Can anyone carry High Church zeal higher than this? And how well I have been since beaten with mine own staff!

Sun. Oct. 1.—I preached at the Gins about eight, to the usual congregation; and surely God was in the midst of them, breaking the hearts of stone. I was greatly comforted at church, not only from the Lessons, both morning and afternoon, and in the Lord's Supper, but even in the Psalms which were sung both at morning and evening service.

Mon. 2.—Just before I began preaching, I received a letter from Mr Whitefield, desiring me to meet him at Leeds, on Wednesday evening; the very time at which I before purposed to be there. So we set out early on *Tuesday*, 3; one of our brethren, who was a Yorkshireman, undertaking to put us into the way.

Thur. 5.—Mr Whitefield preached at five in the morning.

About five in the evening he preached at Birstal; and God gave him both strong and persuasive words; such as, I trust, sunk deep into many hearts.

Fri. 6.—I preached at five, and then returned to my brother, whom I had left at Leeds. At noon we spent an hour with several of our preachers, in exhortation and prayer. About one I preached to a crowded audience of high and low, rich and poor; but their number was abundantly enlarged at five; as was my strength both of soul and body. I cried aloud to them all, to look unto Jesus; and scarce knew when to leave off.

I then waited upon Mr M., for an hour. Oh how could I delight in such an acquaintance! But the will of God be done! Let me "acquaint" myself "with Him," and it is enough.

Wed. 18.—I rode, at the desire of John Bennet, to Rochdale, in Lancashire. As soon as ever we entered the town, we found the streets lined on both sides with multitudes of people, shouting, cursing, blaspheming, and gnashing upon us with their teeth. Perceiving it would not be practicable to preach abroad, I went into a large room, open to the street, and called aloud, "Let the wicked forsake his way, and the unrighteous man his thoughts." The Word of God prevailed over the fierceness of man. None opposed or interrupted; and there was a very remarkable change in the behaviour of the people, as we afterwards went through the town.

We came to Bolton about five in the evening. We had no sooner entered the main street, than we perceived the lions at Rochdale were lambs in comparison of those at Bolton. Such rage and bitterness I scarce ever saw before, in any creatures that bore the form of men. They followed us in full cry to the house where we went; and as soon as we were gone in, took possession of all the avenues to it, and filled the street from one end to the other. After some time the waves did not roar quite so loud. Mr P—— thought he might then venture out. They immediately closed in, threw him down, and rolled him in the mire; so that when he scrambled from them, and got into the house again, one could scarce tell what or who he was. When the first stone came among us through the window, I expected a shower to follow; and the rather, because they had now procured a bell to call their whole forces together. But they did not design to carry on the attack at a distance: presently one ran up and told us, the mob had burst into the house: he added, that they had got J—— B—— in the midst of them. They had; and he laid hold of the opportunity to tell them of "the terrors of the Lord." Meantime D—— T—— engaged another part of them with smoother and softer words. Believing the time was now come, I walked down into the thickest of them. They had now filled all the rooms below. I called for a chair. The winds were hushed, and all was calm and still. My heart was filled with love, my eyes with tears, and my mouth with arguments. They were amazed, they were ashamed, they were melted down, they devoured every word. What a turn was this! Oh how did God change the counsel of the old Ahithophel into foolishness; and bring all the drunkards, swearers, Sabbath-breakers, and mere sinners in the place, to hear of His plenteous redemption!

Thur. 19.—Abundantly more than the house could contain were present at five in the morning, to whom I was constrained to speak a good deal longer than I am accustomed to do. Perceiving they still wanted to hear, I promised to preach again at nine, in a meadow near the town. Thither they flocked from every side; and I cried aloud, "All things are ready; come unto the marriage." Oh how a few hours changed the scene! We could now walk through every street of the town, and none molested or opened his mouth, unless to thank or bless us.

At one I preached at Shackerley, four miles from Bolton, and thence rode on to Davy-Hulme. Here I received a letter from Richard Cawley, of Alpraham, with an invitation from the minister of Acton. After preaching in the morning at Davy-Hulme, and about ten at Boothbank, in the afternoon, *Friday*, 20, I rode on, and, between four and five, came to Alpraham. A large congregation was waiting for me, whom I immediately called to seek God "while He may be found." Many came again at five in the morning, and seemed just ready not only to "repent," but also "believe the gospel."

On *Tuesday*, 24, about noon, we came to Dudley. At one I went to the market-place, and proclaimed the name of the Lord to a huge, unwieldy, noisy multitude; the greater part of whom seemed in no wise to know "wherefore they were come together." I continued speaking about half an hour, and many grew serious and attentive, till some of Satan's servants pressed in, raging and blaspheming, and throwing whatever came to hand. I then retired to the house from which I came. The multitude poured after, and covered over with dirt many that were near me; but I had only a few specks. I preached in Wednesbury at four, to a nobler people, and was greatly comforted among them: so I was likewise in the morning, *Wednesday*, 25. How does a praying congregation strengthen the preacher!

After preaching again at one, I rode to Birmingham. This had been long a dry uncomfortable place ; so I expected little good here : but I was happily disappointed. Such a congregation I never saw there before : not a scoffer, nor a trifler, not an inattentive person (so far as I could discern) among them ; and seldom have I known so deep, solemn a sense of the power, and presence, and love of God. The same blessing we had at the meeting of the society; and again at the morning preaching. Will then God at length cause even this barren wilderness to blossom and bud as the rose?

Mon. 30.—I retired to Kingswood, to write part of the volume of Sermons which I had promised to publish this winter.

Wed. Nov. 8.—I preached in Bath, and on *Friday* in London.

Sun. 12.—Many complaints were made to me of a general deadness among the people of London, at the very time that those in most other parts of England were so remarkably alive to God. It was chiefly owing to a few persons who were continually labouring to spread offences among them. But it was not long before the plague was stayed : some of these incendiaries separating from us ; others being convinced that they had been doing the work of the devil, in the name of the Lord.

Mon. 20.—I rode to Mr Perronet's, at Shoreham, that I might be at leisure to write.

Mon. Dec. 4.—I retired to Lewisham.

Mon. 11.—I retired to Newington once more, and on *Saturday*, 16, finished my Sermons.

Mon. Jan. 1, 1750.—A large congregation met at four o'clock, and began the year of jubilee in a better manner than they at Rome are accustomed to do. On several days this week I called upon many who had left their "first love"; but they none of them justified themselves : one and all pleaded " guilty before God." Therefore there is reason to hope that He will return, and will abundantly pardon.

Thur. 11.—I read, to my no small amazement, the account given by Monsieur Montgeron, both of his own conversion, and of the other miracles wrought at the tomb of Abbé Paris. I had always looked upon the whole affair as a mere legend, as I suppose most Protestants do ; but I see no possible way to deny these facts, without invalidating all human testimony. I may full as reasonably deny there is such a person as Mr Montgeron, or such a city as Paris, in the world. Indeed, in many of these instances I see great superstition as well as strong faith. But "the times of ignorance God" does "wink at" still; and bless the faith, notwithstanding the superstition.

If it be said, "But will not the admitting these miracles establish Popery?" Just the reverse. Abbé Paris lived and died in open opposition to the grossest errors of Popery; and in particular to that diabolical Bull Unigenitus, which destroys the very foundations of Christianity.

Sun. 14.—I read prayers and preached at Snowsfields, to a crowded congregation, at seven in the morning. I then hastened to the chapel in West Street; and, after the service there, to Knightsbridge, where I had promised to preach in the afternoon, for the benefit of the poor children. The little church was quite full before I came. Knowing it to be the greatest charity to awaken those that sleep in sin, I preached on, "What is a man profited, if he shall gain the whole world, and lose his own soul?"

Fri. 19.—In the evening I read prayers at the chapel in West Street, and Mr Whitefield preached a plain, affectionate discourse. *Sunday*, 21. He read prayers, and I preached: so, by the blessing of God, one more stumbling-block is removed.

Mon. 22.—I prayed in the morning at the Foundery, and Howell Harris preached: a powerful orator, both by nature and grace; but he owes nothing to art or education.

Wed. 24.—I was desired to call on one that was sick, though I had small hopes of doing him any good; he had been so harmless a man for ninety years: yet he was not out of God's reach. He was quickly convinced that his own righteousness could not recommend him to God. I could then pray for him in confidence of being heard. A few days after he died in peace.

Sun. 28.—I read prayers, and Mr Whitefield preached. How wise is God in giving different talents to different preachers! Even the little improprieties both of his language and manner were a means of profiting many, who would not have been touched by a more correct discourse, or a more calm and regular manner of speaking.

Mon. 29.—I rode to Canterbury. The congregation in the evening was deeply serious, and most of them present again at five in the morning. I hope God will again have much people in this place, who will worship Him with more knowledge, and as much earnestness as their forefathers did the Virgin Mary, or even St Thomas à Becket.

Sun. Feb. 4.—I preached at Hayes. What a change is here within a year or two! Instead of the parishioners going out of church, the people come now from many miles round. The church was filled in the afternoon likewise ; and all behaved well but the singers, whom I therefore reproved before the congregation, and some of them were ashamed.

Mon. 5.—I rode to Mrs C——, at St Ann's, near Chertsey. It was her design that I should preach in the evening in her summer-house, a large eight-square room, which was supported by a frame of wood. This was quickly filled : but as it was not intended to bear such a weight, the main beam beneath split in sunder. This I did not then know ; but finding the room too small, I went out, and stood in the gallery before it. The people then came out too, went down and stood below, without any hurry or confusion.

Thur. 8.—It was about a quarter after twelve, that the earthquake began at the skirts of the town. It began in the south-east, went through Southwark, under the river, and then from one end of London to the other. It was observed at Westminster and Grosvenor Square a quarter before one. (Perhaps, if we allow for the difference of the clocks, about a quarter of an hour after it began in Southwark.) There were three distinct shakes, or wavings to and fro, attended with an hoarse, rumbling noise, like thunder. How gently does God deal with this nation ! Oh that our repentance may prevent heavier marks of His displeasure !

Fri. 9.—We had a comfortable watch-night at the chapel. About eleven o'clock it came into my mind, that this was the very day and hour in which, forty years ago, I was taken out of the flames. I stopped, and gave a short account of that wonderful providence. The voice of praise and thanksgiving went up on high, and great was our rejoicing before the Lord.

On *Monday*, 12, I had designed to set out for Bristol : but I could not go yet, there was such a flame kindled in London. However, I rode to Brentford, and preached as I had appointed ; and then went on to Chertsey. Word had been industriously spread about the town, that I would not come that night. However, many came to see whether I would or no ; to whom I offered " the grace of our Lord Jesus Christ."

Wed. 14.—The watch-night at the Foundery seemed the shortest I had ever known. Indeed, we knew not how the hours stole away, while prayer was lost in praise and thanksgiving.

Fri. 16.—We had a solemn fast-day, meeting, as before, at five, seven, ten, and one. Many of the rich were at the chapel in the evening. "Who hath warned you to flee from the wrath to come ?"

Wed. 21.—I preached in the old French church, in Grey Eagle Street, Spitalfields.

Thur. 22.—Having been sent for several times, I went to see a young woman in Bedlam But I had not talked with her long, before one gave me to know, that none of these preachers were to come there. So we are forbid to go to Newgate, for fear of making them wicked; and to Bedlam, for fear of driving them mad !

Tues. 27.—I at length forced myself from London. We dined a little beyond Colnbrook, spoke plain to all in the house, and left them full of thankfulness, and of good resolutions.

Sun. Mar. 4.—I desired John W—— to preach at five ; and I no longer wondered at the deadness of his hearers.

Tues. 6.—I began writing a short French Grammar. We observed *Wednesday*, 7, as a day of fasting and prayer.

Thur. 8.—I desired all the preachers that were in Bristol to meet me at four in the afternoon ; and so every day while I was in town. In the evening God rent the rocks again.

To-day God gave the people of London a second warning ; of which my brother wrote as follows :—

"This morning, a quarter after five, we had another shock of an earthquake, far more violent than that of February 8. I was just repeating my text, when it shook the Foundery so violently, that we all expected it to fall upon our heads. A great cry followed from the women and the children. I immediately cried out, 'Therefore will we not fear, though the earth be moved, and the hills be carried into the midst of the sea : for the Lord of hosts is with us ; the God of Jacob is our refuge.' He filled my heart with faith, and my mouth with words, shaking their souls as well as their bodies."

The earth moved westward, then east, then westward again, through all London and Westminster. It was a strong and jarring motion, attended with a rumbling noise, like that of distant thunder. Many houses were much shaken, and some chimneys thrown down, but without any further hurt.

Sat. 10.—I talked at large with the masters of Kingswood School, concerning the children and the management. They all agreed, that one of the boys studiously laboured to corrupt the rest. I would not suffer him to stay any longer under the roof, but sent him home that very hour.

Sun. 11.—I began visiting the society at Kingswood strangely continuing without either increase or decrease. On the following days I visited that at Bristol. What cause have we to be humbled over this people ! Last year more than an hundred members were added: this year near an hundred are lost. Such a decay has not been in this society before, ever since it began to meet together.

I should willingly have spent more time in Bristol; finding more and more proofs that God was reviving His work; but that the accounts I received from Ireland made me think it my duty to be there as soon as possible; so, on *Monday,* 19, I set out with Christopher Hopper for the New Passage.

Tues. 20.—Expecting to preach at Aberdare, sixteen Welsh miles from Cardiff, I rode thither over the mountains. But we found no notice had been given: so, after resting an hour, we set out for Brecknock. The rain did not intermit at all, till we came within sight of it. Twice my horse fell down, and threw me over his head; but without any hurt, either to man or beast.

Fri. 23.—Before we looked out, we heard the roaring of the wind, and the beating of the rain. We took horse at five. It rained incessantly all the way we rode. And when we came on the great mountain, four miles from the town (by which time I was wet from my neck to my waist), it was with great difficulty I could avoid being borne over my mare's head, the wind being ready to carry us all away: nevertheless, about ten we came safe to Dannabull, praising Him who saves both man and beast.

Our horses being well tired, and ourselves thoroughly wet, we rested the remainder of the day; the rather, because several of the family understood English,—an uncommon thing in these parts. We spoke closely to these, and they appeared much affected, particularly when we all joined in prayer.

Sat. 24.—We set out at five, and at six came to the sands. But the tide was in, so that we could not pass: so I sat down in a little cottage for three or four hours, and translated Aldrich's *Logic*. About ten we passed, and before five came to Baldon Ferry, and found the boat ready for us: but the boatmen desired us to stay a while, saying, the wind was too high, and the tide too strong. The secret was, they stayed for more passengers; and it was well they did: for while we were walking to and fro, Mr Jenkin Morgan came; at whose house, near half-way between the Ferry and Holyhead, I had lodged three years before. The night soon came on; but our guide, knowing all the country, brought us safe to his own door.

Sun. 25.—I preached at Howell Thomas's, in Trefollwin parish, to a small, earnest congregation. As many did not understand, one of the brethren repeated the substance of the sermon in Welsh. In the afternoon I went to William Pritchard's, though much against my will, as there was none there to interpret, and I was afraid very few of my hearers could understand English. But I was mistaken: the congregation was larger than I had ever seen in Anglesey. A considerable number of them understood English tolerably well; and the looks, sighs, and gestures of those that did not, showed that God was speaking to their hearts. It was a glorious opportunity: the whole congregation seemed to be melted down; so little do we know the extent of God's power. If He will work, what shall hinder Him?

The wind being contrary, I accepted of the invitation of an honest exciseman (Mr Holloway), to stay at his house till it should change. Here I was in a little, quiet, solitary spot (*maximè animo exoptatum meo!*[1]), where no human voice was heard but those of the family. On *Tuesday* I desired Mr Hopper to ride over to Holyhead, and inquire concerning our passage. He brought word, that we might probably pass in a day or two: so on *Wednesday* we both went thither. Here we overtook John Jane, who had set out on foot from Bristol with three shillings in his pocket. Six nights out of the seven since he set out, he had been entertained by utter strangers. He went by us we could not tell how, and reached Holyhead on *Sunday*, with one penny left.

By him we sent back our horses to Mr Morgan's. I had a large congregation in the evening. It almost grieved me, I could give them but one sermon, now they were at length willing to hear. About eleven we were called to go on board, the wind being quite fair: and so it continued till we were just out of the harbour. It then turned west, and blew a storm. There was neither moon nor stars, but rain and wind enough; so that I was soon tired of staying on deck. But we met another storm below: for who should be there, but the famous Mr G——, of Carnarvonshire,—a clumsy, overgrown, hard-faced man; whose countenance I could only compare to that (which I saw in Drury Lane thirty years ago) of one of the ruffians in *Macbeth*. I was going to lie down, when he tumbled in, and poured out such a volley of ribaldry, obscenity, and blasphemy, every second or third word being an oath, as was scarce ever heard at Billingsgate. Finding there was no room for me to speak, I retired into my cabin, and left him to Mr Hopper. Soon after, one or two of his own company interposed, and carried him back to his cabin.

Thur. 29.—We wrought our way four or five leagues toward Ireland; but were driven back in the afternoon to the very mouth of the harbour: nevertheless, the wind shifting one or

[1] Retreat, most heartily desired by me.—ED.

two points, we ventured out again ; and by midnight we were got about half seas over ; but the wind then turning full against us, and blowing hard, we were driven back again, and were glad, about nine, to get into the bay once more.

In the evening I was surprised to see, instead of some poor, plain people, a room full of men, daubed with gold and silver. That I might not go out of their depth, I began expounding the story of Dives and Lazarus. It was more applicable than I was aware ; several of them (as I afterwards learned) being eminently wicked men. I delivered my own soul, but they could in no wise bear it. One and another walked away, murmuring sorely. Four stayed till I drew to a close : they then put on their hats, and began talking to one another. I mildly reproved them ; on which they rose up and went away, railing and blaspheming. I had then a comfortable hour with a company of plain, honest Welshmen.

In the night there was a vehement storm. Blessed be God that we were safe on shore ! *Saturday*, 31. I determined to wait one week longer, and, if we could not sail then, to go and wait for a ship at Bristol. At seven in the evening, just as I was going down to preach, I heard a huge noise, and took knowledge of the rabble of gentlemen. They had now strengthened themselves with drink and numbers, and placed Captain Gr—— (as they called him) at their head. He soon burst open both the outward and inner door, struck old Robert Griffith, our landlord, several times, kicked his wife, and, with twenty full-mouthed oaths and curses, demanded, " Where is the parson ? " Robert Griffith came up, and desired me to go into another room, where he locked me in. The captain followed him quickly, broke open one or two doors, and got on a chair, to look on the top of a bed : but his foot slipping (as he was not a man made for climbing), he fell down backward all his length. He rose leisurely, turned about, and, with his troop, walked away.

I then went down to a small company of the poor people, and spent half an hour with them in prayer. About nine, as we were preparing to go to bed, the house was beset again. The captain burst in first. Robert Griffith's daughter was standing in the passage with a pail of water, with which (whether with design or in her fright, I know not) she covered him from head to foot. He cried as well as he could, " M—urder ! murder ! " and stood very still for some moments. In the meantime Robert Griffith stepped by him and locked the door. Finding himself alone, he began to change his voice, and cry, " Let me out ! Let me out ! " Upon his giving his word and honour, that none of the rest should come in, they opened the door, and all went away together.

Sun. April 1.—We set out, having one of Holyhead for our guide, reached a church six or seven miles off, about eleven (where we stopped till the service was ended), and went on to William Pritchard's, near Llanerellymadd.

Many who were come from the town earnestly pressed me to go and preach there, assuring me it was the general desire of the inhabitants. I felt a strong aversion to it, but would not refuse, not knowing what God might have to do. So I went: but we were scarce set down, when the "sons of Belial," from all parts, gathered together, and compassed the house. I could just understand their oaths and curses, which were broad English, and sounded on every side. The rest of their language was lost upon me, as mine was upon them. Our friends would have had me stay within; but I judged it best to look them in the face, while it was open day. So I bade them open the door, and Mr Hopper and I walked straight through the midst of them. Having procured a guide, we then went on without hindrance, to our retreat at Mr Holloway's. Surely this journey will be for good: for hitherto we have had continual storms, both by sea and land.

Tues. 3.—Mr William Jones, of Trefollwin, called and told us an exhorter was preaching a little way off. We went and found him on the Common, standing on a little rock, in the midst of an attentive congregation. After he had done, I preached, and then returned to my study at Llangefnye.

Fri. 6.—I preached near Llanerellymadd at noon, and at Trefollwin in the evening. Observing at night the wind was changed, I rode to Holyhead early in the morning. A ship was just ready to sail; so we went on board, and in the evening landed at Dublin.

Sun. 8.—I preached morning, afternoon, and evening, and then exhorted the society to stand fast in the good old Bible-way; and not move from it, to the right hand or to the left.

I found Mr Lunell in so violent a fever, that there was little hope of his life. But he revived the moment he saw me, and fell into a breathing sweat. He began to recover from that time. Perhaps for this also was I sent.

Mon. 9.—I found, upon inquiry, many things had been represented to me worse than they really were. But it is well: if they had not been so represented, I should scarce have come over this year.

Thur. 12.—I breakfasted with one of the society, and found she had a lodger I little thought of. It was the famous Mrs

Pilkington, who soon made an excuse for following me upstairs. I talked with her seriously about an hour: we then sung, "Happy Magdalene." She appeared to be exceedingly struck: how long the impression may last, God knows.

We dined at Mr P——'s. A young married woman was there, who was lately a zealous Papist, and had converted several Protestant heretics to the Romish faith: but setting on some of the Methodists, they converted her; at least, convinced her of the great truths of the gospel. Immediately her relations, her husband in particular, renounced her. But she was moved by none of these things; desiring nothing on earth, but to experience the faith which once she persecuted.

In the evening I was sent for by one who had reasoned himself out of all his Christianity; and was now in doubt, whether the soul would survive the body. Surely even speculative faith is the gift of God! nor, without Him, can we hold even this fast.

Wed. 25.—I dined at Mr K——'s, who had lived utterly without God for about seventy years; but God had now made both him and most of his household " partakers of like precious faith." When I first came into the house, he was in an agony of pain, from an hurt of about forty-five years standing. I advised to apply hot nettles. The pain presently ceased, and he arose and praised God.

Thur. 26.—I examined the class of children, many of whom are rejoicing in God. I then sought after some of the sheep that were lost, and left all I spoke with determined to return. About noon I read the letters, and in the afternoon rode cheerfully to Mount Melick. I found the society here much increased in grace, and yet lessened in number: a case which I scarce remember to have met with before, in all England and Ireland.

About one I administered the Lord's Supper to a sick person, with a few of our brethren and sisters. Being straitened for time, I used no extemporary prayer at all; yet the power of God was so unusually present, during the whole time, that several knew not how to contain themselves, being quite overwhelmed with joy and love.

Fri. May 4.—I preached about noon at Cooly Lough, and about six in the market-house at Athlone.

Sun. 6.—In the evening I preached on the Connaught side of the river. In the midst of the sermon a man, with a fine curvetting horse, drew off a large part of the audience. I paused a little, and then raising my voice, said, " If there are any more of you who think it is of more concern to see a dancing horse, than to hear the gospel of Christ, pray go after them." They took the reproof: the greater part came back directly, and gave double attention.

Mon. 7.—When I met the society in the evening, one who had been always afraid of exposing herself, was struck so that she could not help crying out aloud, being in strong agonies both of soul and body. Indeed her case was quite peculiar. She felt no fear of hell, but an inexpressible sense of the sufferings of Christ, accompanied with sharp bodily pain, as if she had literally suffered with Him. We continued in prayer till twelve o'clock, and left her patiently waiting for salvation.

Fri. 18.—I dined at Killmallock, once a flourishing city, now a vast heap of ruins. In the afternoon we called at Killdorrery. A clergyman was there a little before us, who would talk with me, whether I would or no. After an hour's conversation, we parted in love. *Saturday*, 19. I preached about eleven; and in the afternoon rode on to Cork. About nine in the evening I came to Alderman Pembrock's.

Sun. 20.—Understanding the usual place of preaching would by no means contain those who desired to hear, about eight I went to Hammond's Marsh. The congregation was large and deeply attentive. A few of the rabble gathered at a distance; but by little and little they drew near, and mixed with the congregation, so that I have seldom seen a more quiet and orderly assembly at any church in England or Ireland.

In the afternoon, a report being spread abroad that the mayor designed to hinder my preaching on the Marsh in the evening, I desired Mr Skelton and Mr Jones to wait upon him, and inquire concerning it. Mr Skelton asked, if my preaching there would be disagreeable to him; adding, "Sir, if it would, Mr Wesley will not do it." He replied warmly, "Sir, I'll have no mobbing." Mr Skelton replied, "Sir, there was none this morning." He answered, "There was. Are there not churches and meeting-houses enough? I will have no more mobs and riots." Mr Skelton replied, "Sir, neither Mr Wesley nor they that heard him made either mobs or riots." He answered plain, "I will have no more preaching; and if Mr Wesley attempts to preach, I am prepared for him."

I began preaching in our own house soon after five. Mr Mayor meantime was walking in the 'Change, and giving orders to the town-drummers and to his serjeants,—doubtless to go down and keep the peace! They accordingly came down to the house, with an innumerable mob attending them. They continued drumming, and I continued preaching, till I finished my discourse. When I came out, the mob immediately closed me in. Observing one of the serjeants standing by, I desired him to keep the King's peace; but he replied, "Sir, I have no orders to do that." As soon as I came into the street, the rabble threw whatever came to hand; but all went by me, or flew over my head; nor do I remember that one thing touched me. I walked on straight through the midst of the rabble, looking every man before me in the face; and they opened on the right and left, till I came near Dant's Bridge. A large party had taken possession of this, one of whom was bawling out, "Now, hey for the Romans!" When I came up, they likewise shrunk back, and I walked through them to Mr Jenkins's house; but a Papist stood just within the door, and endeavoured to hinder my going in; till one of the mob (I suppose aiming at me, but missing) knocked her down flat. I then went in, and God restrained the wild beasts, so that not one attempted to follow me.

But many of the congregation were more roughly handled, particularly Mr Jones, who was covered with dirt, and escaped with his life almost by miracle. The main body of the mob then went to the house, brought out all the seats and benches, tore up the floor, the door, the frames of the windows, and whatever of woodwork remained; part of which they carried off for their own use, and the rest they burnt in the open street.

Finding there was no probability of their dispersing, I sent to Alderman Pembrock, who immediately desired Mr Alderman Windthrop, his nephew, to go down to Mr Jenkins, with whom I walked up the street, none giving me an unkind or disrespectful word.

Mon. 21.—I rode on to Bandon. From three in the afternoon till past seven, the mob of Cork marched in grand procession, and then burnt me in effigy near Dant's Bridge.

While they were so busily employed, Mr Haughton took the opportunity of going down to Hammond's Marsh. He called at a friend's house there, where the good woman, in great care, locked him in; but observing many people were met, he threw up the sash, and preached to them out of the window. Many seemed deeply affected, even of those who had been persecutors before; and they all quietly retired to their several homes before the mob was at leisure to attend them.

Tues. 22.—The mob and drummers were moving again, between three and four in the morning. The same evening they came down to the Marsh, but stood at a distance from Mr Stockdale's house, till the drums beat, and the mayor's serjeant beckoned to them, on which they drew up and began the attack. The mayor being sent for, came with a party of soldiers, and said to the mob, "Lads, once, twice, thrice, I bid you go home : now I have done." He then went back, taking the soldiers with him; on which the mob, pursuant to their instructions, went on, and broke all the glass and most of the window-frames in pieces.

Wed. 23.—The mob was still patrolling the streets, abusing all that were called Methodists, and threatening to murder them and pull down their houses, if they did not leave this way.

Thur. 24.—They again assaulted Mr Stockdale's house, broke down the boards he had nailed up against the windows, destroyed what little remained of the window-frames and shutters, and damaged a considerable part of his goods.

Fri. 25.—One Roger O'Ferrall fixed up an advertisement at the public Exchange, that he was ready to head any mob, in order to pull down any house that should dare to harbour a swaddler. (A name given to Mr Cennick first, by a Popish priest, who heard him speak of a child wrapped in swaddling clothes; and probably did not know the expression was in the Bible, a book he was not much acquainted with.)

All this time God gave us great peace at Bandon, notwithstanding the unwearied labours, both public and private, of good Dr B——, to stir up the people. But, *Saturday*, 26, many were under great apprehensions of what was to be done in the evening. I began preaching in the main street at the usual hour, but to more than twice the usual congregation. After I had spoke about a quarter of an hour, a clergyman who had planted himself near me, with a very large stick in his hand, according to agreement, opened the scene. (Indeed his friends assured me he was in drink, or he would not have done it.) But before he had uttered many words, two or three resolute women, by main strength, pulled him into a house; and, after expostulating a little, sent him away through the garden. But here he fell violently on her that conducted him, not in anger, but love (such as it was); so that she was constrained to repel force by force, and cuff him soundly before he would let her go.

The next champion that appeared was one Mr M——, a young gentleman of the town. He was attended by two others, with pistols in their hands. But his triumph, too, was but short; some of the people quickly bore him away, though with much gentleness and civility.

The third came on with greater fury; but he was encountered by a butcher of the town (not one of the Methodists), who used him as he would an ox, bestowing one or two hearty blows upon his head. This cooled his courage, especially as none took his part. So I quietly finished my discourse.

Thurs. 31.—I rode to Rathcormuck. There being a great burying in the afternoon, to which people came from all parts, Mr Lloyd read part of the burial service in the church; after which I preached on, "The end of all things is at hand." I was exceedingly shocked at (what I had only heard of before) the Irish howl which followed. It was not a song, as I supposed, but a dismal, inarticulate yell, set up at the grave by four shrill-voiced women, who (we understood) were hired for that purpose. But I saw not one that shed a tear; for that, it seems, was not in their bargain.

Tues. June 5.—I returned to Limerick. In examining the society here, I could not but take particular notice of about sixty of the Highland regiment of soldiers,—men fit to appear before princes. Their zeal, "according to knowledge," has stirred up many; and they still speak for God, and are not ashamed.

Sat. July 14.—I returned to Dublin, and on *Sunday*, 15, preached on Oxmantown Green, to such a congregation as I never saw in Dublin, nor often in Ireland before. Abundance of soldiers were of the number.

Thur. 19.—I met the class of soldiers: nineteen are resolved to "fight the good fight of faith"; eleven or twelve of whom already rejoice in God through Christ, by whom they have received the atonement.

Sun. Sept. 2.—We rode to Shaftesbury, where I preached, between six and seven, to a serious and quiet congregation. We had another happy opportunity at five in the morning, when abundance of people were present. I preached, at noon, in the most riotous part of the town, just where four ways met; but none made any noise, or spoke one word, while I called "the wicked to forsake his way." Soon after I was sat down, a constable came, and said, "Sir, the Mayor discharges you from preaching in this borough any more." I replied, "While King George gives me leave to preach, I shall not ask leave of the Mayor of Shaftesbury."

Sat. 8.—I came to London.

Here I had the following account from one of our preachers:—

"John Jane was never well after walking from Epworth to Hainton, on an exceeding hot day, which threw him into a fever. But he was in great peace and love, even to those who greatly wanted love to him. He was some time at Alice Shadforth's house, with whom he daily talked of the things of God. He was never without the love of God, spent much time in private prayer, and joined likewise with her in prayer several times in a day. On Friday, August 24, growing, as she thought, stronger in body, he sat in the evening by the fireside : about six he fetched a deep sigh, and never spoke more. He was alive till the same hour on Saturday ; at which, without any struggle, or any sign of pain, with a smile on his face, he passed away. His last words were, 'I find the love of God in Christ Jesus.'

"All his clothes, linen and woollen, stockings, hat, and wig, are not thought sufficient to answer his funeral expenses, which amount to one pound seventeen shillings and threepence. All the money he had was one shilling and fourpence." Enough for any unmarried preacher of the gospel to leave to his executors.

Mon. 17.—My brother set out for the north; but returned the next day, much out of order. How little do we know the counsels of God ! But we know they are all wise and gracious.

Wed. 19.—When I came home in the evening, I found my brother abundantly worse. He had had no sleep for several nights ; and expected none, unless from opiates. I went down to our brethren below, and we made our request known to God. When I went up again he was in a sound sleep, which continued till the morning.

Fri. 21.—We had a watch-night at Spitalfields. I often wonder at the peculiar providence of God on these occasions. I do not know that in so many years one person has ever been hurt, either in London, Bristol, or Dublin, in going so late in the night to and from all parts of the town.

Mon. 24.—I reached Kingswood in the evening; and the next day selected passages of Milton for the eldest children to transcribe and repeat weekly.

Thur. 27.—I went into the school, and heard half the children their lessons, and then selected passages of the *Moral and Sacred Poems. Friday,* 28. I heard the other half of the children. *Saturday,* 29. I was with them from four to five in the morning. I spent most of the day in revising Kennet's *Antiquities,* and marking what was worth reading in the school.

Wed. Oct. 3.—I revised, for the use of the children, Archbishop Potter's *Grecian Antiquities* ; a dry, dull, heavy book. *Thursday,* 4. I revised Mr Lewis's *Hebrew Antiquities* ; something more entertaining than the other, and abundantly more instructive.

Sat. 6.—I nearly finished the abridgement of Dr Cave's *Primitive Christianity* ; a book wrote with as much learning, and as little judgment, as any I remember to have read in my whole life ; serving the ancient Christians just as Xenophon did Socrates ; relating every weak thing they ever said or did.

Thur. 11.—I prepared a short *History of England,* for the use of the children; and on *Friday* and *Saturday* a short *Roman History,* as an introduction to the Latin historians.

Mon. 15.—I read over Mr Holmes's *Latin Grammar*; and extracted from it what was needful to perfect our own.

Wed. Jan. 30, 1751.—Having received a pressing letter from Dr Isham, then the Rector of our College, to give my vote at the election for a Member of Parliament, which was to be the next day, I set out early, in a severe frost, with the north-west wind full in my face. The roads were so slippery, that it was scarce possible for our horses to keep their feet: indeed one of them could not; but fell upon his head, and cut it terribly. Nevertheless, about seven in the evening, God brought us safe to Oxford. A congregation was waiting for me at Mr Evans's, whom I immediately addressed in those awful words, "What is a man profited, if he shall gain the whole world, and lose his own soul?"

Thur. 31.—I went to the schools, where the convocation was met: but I did not find the decency and order which I expected. The gentleman for whom I came to vote was not elected: yet I did not repent of my coming; I owe much more than this to that generous, friendly man, who now rests from his labours.

I was much surprised wherever I went, at the civility of the people,—gentlemen as well as others. There was no pointing, no calling of names, as once; no, nor even laughter. What can this mean? Am I become a servant of men? Or is the scandal of the cross ceased?

Sat. Feb. 2.—Having received a full answer from Mr P——, I was clearly convinced that I ought to marry. For many years I remained single because I believed I could be more useful in a single, than in a married state. And I praise God, who enabled me so to do. I now as fully believed, that in my present circumstances, I might be more useful in a married state; into which, upon this clear conviction, and by the advice of my friends, I entered a few days after.

Wed. 6.—I met the single men, and showed them on how many accounts it was good for those who had received that gift from God, to remain "single for the kingdom of heaven's sake"; unless where a particular case might be an exception to the general rule.

Sun. 10.—After preaching at five, I was hastening to take my leave of the congregation at Snowsfields, purposing to set out in the morning for the north; when, on the middle of London Bridge, both my feet slipped on the ice, and I fell with great force, the bone of my ankle lighting on the top of a stone. However, I got on, with some help, to the chapel, being resolved not to disappoint the people. After preaching, I had my leg bound up by a surgeon, and made a shift to walk to the Seven Dials. It was with much difficulty that I got up into the pulpit ; but God then comforted many of our hearts.

I went back in a coach to Mr B——'s, and from thence in a chair to the Foundery ; but I was not able to preach, my sprain growing worse. I removed to Threadneedle Street ; where I spent the remainder of the week, partly in prayer, reading, and conversation, partly in writing an *Hebrew Grammar*, and *Lessons for Children*.

Sun. 17.—I was carried to the Foundery, and preached, kneeling (as I could not stand), on part of the twenty-third Psalm ; my heart being enlarged, and my mouth opened to declare the wonders of God's love.

Mon. Mar. 4.—Being tolerably able to ride, though not to walk, I set out for Bristol. I came thither on *Wednesday*, thoroughly tired ; though, in other respects, better than when I set out.

I came to London on *Thursday*, and, having settled all affairs, left it again on *Wednesday*, 27. I cannot understand, how a Methodist preacher can answer it to God, to preach one sermon, or travel one day less, in a married than in a single state. In this respect surely, "it remaineth, that they who have wives be as though they had none."

Thur. April 11.—The barber who shaved me said, "Sir, I praise God on your behalf. When you was at Bolton last, I was one of the most eminent drunkards in the town ; but I came to listen at the window, and God struck me to the heart. I then earnestly prayed for power against drinking ; and God gave me more than I asked : He took away the very desire of it. Yet I felt myself worse and worse, till, on the 5th of April last, I could hold out no longer. I knew I must drop into hell that moment, unless God appeared to save me ; and He did appear. I knew He loved me ; and felt sweet peace. Yet I did not dare to say I had faith, till, yesterday was twelvemonth, God gave me faith ; and His love has ever since filled my heart."

Sat. May 11.—We returned to Epworth, to a poor, senseless people : at which I did not wonder, when I was informed : 1. That some of our preachers there had diligently gleaned up and retailed all the evil they could hear of me ; 2. That some of them had quite laid aside our hymns, as well as the doctrine they formerly preached ; 3. That one of them had frequently spoke against our rules, and the others quite neglected them. Nothing, therefore, but the mighty power of God could have kept the people so well as they were.

Mon. 13.—I learned the particulars of Mr R——'s case, of which I had heard but a confused account before. "In November last he was desired to baptize a child of John Varley's. It was observed, his voice, which had been lost several years, was entirely restored. He read the Office with great emotion and many tears, so as to astonish the whole congregation. But going home from church, he behaved in so strange a manner, that it was thought necessary to confine him. During the first week of his confinement, he was for constraining every one that came near him to kneel down and pray; and frequently cried out, 'You will be lost, you will be damned, unless you know your sins are forgiven.' Upon this, Mr —— roundly averred that the Methodists had turned his head. After seven or eight days he grew much worse, though still with intervals of reason; and in about a fortnight, by a judgment mixed with mercy, God took him to Himself."

Thur. March 26,1752.—We rode through wind and snow, and reached Manchester at night. I was grieved to hear in all places, from my coming into Cheshire till now, that John Bennet was still speaking all manner of evil; averring, wherever he came, that Mr W. preached nothing but Popery, denying justification by faith, and making nothing of Christ. Lord, lay not this sin to his charge!

Mar. 27.—(Being *Good Friday*). I went to the old church, where Mr Clayton read prayers; I think the most distinctly, solemnly, and gracefully, of any man I have ever heard; and the behaviour of the whole congregation was serious and solemn in every part of the service. But I was surprised to see such a change in the greater part of them, as soon as ever the sacrament was over. They were then bowing, courtesying, and talking to each other, just as if they were going from a play.

Wed. April 8.—We rode to Heptonstal, a little town on the round top of a very high mountain, with a steep descent on every side. I preached in a vacant place, on the brow of the hill. A captain who came from the minister's house, laboured much to divert the attention of the people; but none regarded him at all. When we went away, he followed us down the hill. One took him by the hand and spoke a few words; on which he shook like a leaf, and said, he hoped this would be an happy day for him, and that he should think more than he had done in time past.

Fri. 10.—I preached at Dewsbury, where the case of the

vicar and his curate will not soon be forgotten. After a conversation I had with the vicar, above three years ago, he was deeply serious, till he conversed again with rich and honourable men, who soon cured him of that distraction. Yet in a while ne relapsed, and was more serious than ever, till he was taken ill. The physician made light of his illness, and said, he would do well enough, if they did but keep those Methodists from him. They did so: however, in a few days he died, and, according to his own express order, was carried to the grave, at seven in the morning, by eight poor men (whom he had named), and buried on the north side of the church. The curate who buried him, sickening the same week, insisted that the Methodists should not be kept from him. About ten days after, he died; and, according to his desire, was, about the same hour, carried also by eight poor men, and laid in a grave close to that of Mr Robson.

Sat. 11.—I preached at R——, once a place of furious riot and persecution; but quiet and calm, since the bitter rector is gone to give an account of himself to God.

Mon. 13.—In the evening I preached at Sheffield, in the shell of the new house. All is peace here now, since the trial at York, at which the magistrates were sentenced to rebuild the house which the mob had pulled down. Surely the magistrate has been the minister of God to us for good!

Fri. 17.—I called on the gentleman who told me he was "sinner enough," when I preached first at Epworth on my father's tomb; and was agreeably surprised, to find him strong in faith, though exceeding weak in body. For some years, he told me, he had been rejoicing in God, without either doubt or fear: and was now waiting for the welcome hour when he should "depart and be with Christ."

Mon. 20.—I rode by Hainton to Coningsby. The next day I preached at Wrangle, where we expected some disturbance, but found none. The light punishment inflicted on the late rioters (though their expense was not great, as they submitted before the trial) has secured peace ever since. Such a mercy it is, to execute the penalty of the law on those who will not regard its precepts! So many inconveniences to the innocent does it prevent, and so much sin in the guilty.

Fri. 24.—When I landed at the quay in Hull, it was covered with people, inquiring, "Which is he? Which is he?" But they only stared and laughed; and we walked unmolested to Mr A——'s house.

I went to prayers at three in the old church,—a grand and venerable structure. Between five and six the coach called, and took me to Mighton Car, about half a mile from the town. An huge multitude, rich and poor, horse and foot, with several coaches, were soon gathered together; to whom I cried with a loud voice and a composed spirit, "What shall it profit a man, if he shall gain the whole world, and lose his own soul?" Some thousands of the people seriously attended; but many behaved as if possessed by Moloch. Clods and stones flew about on every side; but they neither touched nor disturbed me. When I had finished my discourse, I went to take coach; but the coachman had driven clear away. We were at a loss, till a gentlewoman invited my wife and me to come into her coach. She brought some inconveniences on herself thereby; not only as there were nine of us in the coach, three on each side, and three in the middle; but also as the mob closely attended us, throwing in at the windows (which we did not think it prudent to shut) whatever came next to hand. But a large gentlewoman who sat in my lap, screened me, so that nothing came near me.

The mob, who were increased to several thousands, when I stepped out of the coach into Mr A——'s house, perceiving I was escaped out of their hands, revenged themselves on the windows with many showers of stones, which they poured in, even into the rooms four stories high. Mr A—— walked through them to the mayor's house, who gave him fair words, but no assistance; probably not knowing that himself (the mayor) might be compelled to make good all the damage which should be done. He then went in quest of constables, and brought two with him about nine o'clock. With their help he so thoroughly dispersed the mob, that no two of them were left together. But they rallied about twelve, and gave one charge more, with oaths, and curses, and bricks, and stones. After this, all was calm, and I slept sound till near four in the morning.

Thur. May 14.—[Berwick.] At five the soldiers made a considerable part of the congregation. At noon they came again in troops. One of them, T—— W——, came last year from the Highlands, and went through Westmoreland to beat up for recruits. He had been earnestly warned, before he left Scotland, on no account to go near the Methodists. But in Kendal he lighted on two or three; from which time they were not one day asunder. It was not long before God clearly assured him of His pardoning love. A fortnight after, he was ordered to follow the regiment to Berwick; where he is continually exhorting his comrades to be "good soldiers of Jesus Christ"; and many already have listed under His banner.

Tues. 19.—I preached at Wickham, before Mrs Armstrong's door. I was a little surprised at the account she gave of God's late dealings with her. When her ancient husband, with whom she had lived from her youth, was, on account of a debt contracted by his son, hurried away, and thrown into Durham Gaol,—which soon put an end to his life; when she was likely to lose all she had, and to be turned out of doors at fourscore years of age; still the oracles of God, which she had loved from a child, were her delight and her counsellors. But one day, when she put on her spectacles to read, she could not see a word. She was startled at first; but soon said, "It is the Lord; let Him do what seemeth Him good." She laid her spectacles down, and casting her eye on the corner of the Bible, thought she could discern some letters. Taking up the book, she read as well as her daughter could; and, from that hour, she could not only read without spectacles; but sew, or thread the finest needle, with the same ease as when she was thirty years of age.

Mon. 25.—We rode to Durham, and thence, through very rough roads, and as rough weather, to Barnard Castle. I was exceeding faint when we came in: however, the time being come, I went into the street, and would have preached; but the mob was so numerous and so loud, that it was not possible for many to hear. Nevertheless, I spoke on, and those who were near listened with huge attention. To prevent this, some of the rabble fetched the engine, and threw a good deal of water on the congregation; but not a drop fell on me. After about three-quarters of an hour, I returned into the house.

Mon. June 8.—We rode to Rough Lee; and found a large, serious, and quiet congregation. There have been no tumults since Mr White was removed. He was for some years a Popish priest. Then he called himself a Protestant, and had the living of Colne. It was his manner first to hire, and then to head the mob, when they and he were tolerably drunk. But he drank himself first into a gaol, and then into his grave.

In the evening I preached at Heptonstall. An attorney, who happened to be in the town, endeavoured to interrupt; relating some low, threadbare stories, with a very audible voice. But some of the people cut him short in the midst by carrying him quietly away.

Tues. 9.—I preached at six to abundance of people near Ewood; and with an uncommon blessing. Hence we rode to Todmorden. The minister was slowly recovering from a violent fit of a palsy, with which he was struck immediately after he had been preaching a virulent sermon against the Methodists.

My lodging was not such as I should have chosen; but what Providence chooses is always good. My bed was considerably underground, the room serving both for a bedchamber and a cellar. The closeness was more troublesome at first than the coolness: but I let in a little fresh air, by breaking a pane of paper (put by way of glass) in the window; and then slept sound till the morning.

Mon. 15.—I had many little trials in this journey, of a kind I had not known before. I had borrowed a young, strong mare, when I set out from Manchester. But she fell lame before I got to Grimsby. I procured another, but was dismounted again between Newcastle and Berwick. At my return to Manchester, I took my own: but she had lamed herself in the pasture. I thought, nevertheless, to ride her four or five miles to-day; but she was gone out of the ground, and we could hear nothing of her. However, I comforted myself, that I had another at Manchester, which I had lately bought. But when I came thither, I found one had borrowed her too, and rode her away to Chester.

Mon. 22.—I preached at six in the evening, in the Square [Chester], to a vast multitude, rich and poor. The far greater part, the gentry in particular, were seriously and deeply attentive; though a few of the rabble, most of them drunk, laboured much to make a disturbance. One might already perceive a great increase of earnestness in the generality of the hearers. So is God able to cut short His work, to wound or heal, in whatever time it pleaseth Him.

Fri. July 3.—I was saying in the morning to Mr Parker, "Considering the good which has been done there already, I wonder the people of Chester are so quiet." He answered, "You must not expect they will be so always." Accordingly, one of the first things I heard after I came into the town was, that for two nights before the mob had been employed in pulling down the house where I had preached. I asked, "Were there no magistrates in the city?" Several answered me, "We went to the mayor after the first riot, and desired a warrant to bring the rioters before him; but he positively refused to grant any, or to take any informations about it." So, being undisturbed, they assembled again the next night, and finished their work.

Sun. 5.—I stood, at seven in the morning, near the ruins of the house, and explained the principles and practice of that sect which is "everywhere spoken against." I went afterwards to

St Martin's church, which stands close to the place. The gentleman who officiated seemed to be extremely moved at several passages of the second lesson, Luke xvii.; particularly, "It is impossible but that offences will come; but woe unto him through whom they come."

Sat. Aug. 8.—I called on a lively man, who is just married, in the ninety-second year of his age. He served as an officer both in King William's and Queen Anne's wars; and a year or two ago began to serve the Prince of Peace. He has all his faculties of body and mind entire, works in his garden some hours every day, and praises God who has prolonged his life to so good a purpose. [Ireland].

Tues. 25.—I preached in the market-place at Kinsale. The next morning, at eight, I walked to the Fort. On the hill above it we found a large, deep hollow, capable of containing two or three thousand people. On one side of this, the soldiers soon cut a place with their swords for me to stand, where I was screened both from the wind and sun, while the congregation sat on the grass before me. Many eminent sinners were present, particularly of the army; and I believe God gave them a loud call to repentance.

Thur. Sept. 14.—(So we must call it now, seeing the new style now takes place.) I rode to the bog of Boiree, where a great and effectual door is opened. On *Friday* evening we rode on to Goree, and the next day to Dublin.

Sat. 23.—We reached Cork. *Sunday*, 24. In the evening I proposed to the society the building a preaching-house. The next day ten persons subscribed an hundred pounds; another hundred was subscribed in three or four days, and a piece of ground taken. I saw a double providence now in our not sailing last week. If we had, probably this house had never been built; and it is most likely we should have been cast away. Above thirty ships, we were informed, have been lost on these coasts in the late storm.

Fri. Oct. 13.—I read over Pascal's *Thoughts*. What could possibly induce such a creature as Voltaire to give such an author as this a good word; unless it was, that he once wrote a satire? And so his being a satirist might atone even for his being a Christian.

Sun. Dec. 29, was an useful day to my soul. I found more than once trouble and heaviness; but I called upon the name of the Lord; and He gave me a clear, full approbation of His way, and a calm, thankful acquiescence in His will.

I cannot but stand amazed at the goodness of God. Otners are most assaulted on the weak side of their soul; but with me it is quite otherwise: if I have any strength at all (and I have none but what I have received), it is in forgiving injuries: and on this very side am I assaulted, more frequently than on any other. Yet leave me not here one hour to myself, or I shall betray myself and Thee!

In the remaining part of this, and in the following month, I prepared the rest of the books for the "Christian Library"; a work by which I have lost above two hundred pounds. Perhaps the next generation may know the value of it.

Sat. Feb. 3, 1753.—I visited one in the Marshalsea Prison; a nursery of all manner of wickedness. Oh, shame to man, that there should be such a place, such a picture of hell, upon earth! And shame to those who bear the name of Christ, that there should need any prison at all in Christendom!

Thur. 8.—A proposal was made for devolving all temporal business, books and all, entirely on the stewards; so that I might have no care upon me (in London at least) but that of the souls committed to my charge. Oh when shall it once be! From this day? *In me mora non erit ulla.*[1]

In the afternoon I visited many of the sick; but such scenes, who could see unmoved? There are none such to be found in a pagan country. If any of the Indians in Georgia were sick (which indeed exceeding rarely happened, till they learned gluttony and drunkenness from the Christians), those that were near him gave him whatever he wanted. Oh who will convert the English into honest heathens!

On *Friday* and *Saturday* I visited as many more as I could. I found some in their cells underground; others in their garrets, half starved both with cold and hunger, added to weakness and pain. But I found not one of them unemployed, who was able to crawl about the room. So wickedly, devilishly false is that common objection, "They are poor, only because they are idle." If you saw these things with your own eyes, could you lay out money in ornaments or superfluities?

Sat. 17.—From Dr Franklin's *Letters* I learned: 1. That electrical fire (or ether) is a species of fire, infinitely finer than any other yet known. 2. That it is diffused, and in nearly equal proportions, through almost all substances. 3. That as long as it is thus diffused, it has no discernible effect. 4. That if any quantity of it be collected together, whether by art or nature, it then becomes visible in the form of fire, and inexpressibly powerful. 5. That it is essentially different from the light of the sun; for it pervades a thousand bodies which light cannot penetrate, and yet cannot penetrate glass,

[1] "In me shall no delay occur."—ED.

which light pervades so freely. 6. That lightning is no other than electrical fire, collected by one or more clouds. 7. That all the effects of lightning may be performed by the artificial electric fire. 8. That anything pointed, as a spire or tree, attracts the lightning, just as a needle does the electrical fire. 9. That the electrical fire, discharged on a rat or a fowl, will kill it instantly; but discharge on one dipped in water, will slide off, and do it no hurt at all. In like manner the lightning which will kill a man in a moment, will not hurt him, if he be thoroughly wet. What an amazing scene is here opened for after-ages to improve upon!

Wed. 21.—I visited more of the poor sick. The industry of many of them surprised me. Several who were ill able to walk, were nevertheless at work; some without any fire (bitterly cold as it was), and some, I doubt, without any food; yet not without that "meat which endureth to everlasting life."

Tues. March 27.—We rode to Chester, where we found the scene quite changed since I was here before. There is no talk of pulling down houses. The present mayor, being a man of courage as well as honesty, will suffer no riot of any kind; so that there is peace through all the city.

Wed. 28.—The house was full of serious hearers at five. In the evening some gay young men made a little disturbance, and a large mob was gathered about the door; but in a short time they dispersed of themselves. However, we thought it best to acquaint the mayor with what had passed; on which he ordered the city crier to go down the next evening, and proclaim, that all riots should be severely punished; and promised, if need were, to come down himself, and read the Act of Parliament. But it needed not: after his mind was known, none was so hardy as to make a disturbance.

I did not expect the mob at Nantwich (whither I was now much pressed to go) would be so quiet as that at Chester. We were saluted with curses and hard names, as soon as we entered the town. But from the time I alighted from my horse, I heard no one give us an ill word; and I had as quiet and attentive an audience as we used to have at Bristol, while I exhorted the "wicked to forsake his way, and the unrighteous man his thoughts."

Sat. 31.—I preached at Boothbank, where I met Mr C——, late gardener to the Earl of W——. Surely it cannot be! Is it possible the Earl should turn off an honest, diligent, well-tried servant, who had been in the family above fifty years, for no other fault than hearing the Methodists?

In the evening I preached at Manchester, and on *Monday*, April 2, at Davy-Hulme. Here I found (what I had never heard of in England) a whole clan of infidel peasants. A neighbouring alehouse-keeper drinks, and laughs, and argues into Deism all the ploughmen and dairymen he can light on. But no mob rises against him : and reason good : Satan is not divided against himself.

Wed. 4.—I made an end of examining the society at Manchester ; among whom were seventeen of the dragoons. It is remarkable, that these were in the same regiment with John Haime, in Flanders ; but they utterly despised both him and his Master, till they removed to Manchester : here it was that one and another dropped in, he scarce knew why, to hear the preaching. And they now are a pattern of seriousness, zeal, and all holy conversation.

Wed. 18.—I walked over the city [Glasgow], which I take to be as large as Newcastle-upon-Tyne. The University (like that of Dublin) is only one College, consisting of two small squares ; I think not larger, nor at all handsomer, than those of Lincoln College, in Oxford. The habit of the students gave me surprise. They wear scarlet gowns, reaching only to their knees. Most I saw were very dirty, some very ragged, and all of very coarse cloth. The high church is a fine building. The outside is equal to that of most cathedrals in England ; but it is miserably defaced within ; having no form, beauty, or symmetry left.

Fri. 20.—Mr G. desired me to preach in his church ; where I began between seven and eight. Surely with God nothing is impossible ! Who would have believed, five-and-twenty years ago, either that the minister would have desired it, or that I should have consented to preach in a Scotch kirk ?

We had a far larger congregation, at four in the afternoon, than the church could have contained. At seven Mr G. preached another plain, homely, affectionate sermon. Has not God still a favour for this city ? It was long eminent for serious religion ; and He is able to repair what is now decayed, and to build up the waste places.

Sat. 21.—I had designed to ride to Edinburgh ; but at the desire of many, I deferred my journey till Monday. Here was now an open and effectual door, and not many adversaries. I could hear of none but a poor Seceder ; who went up and down, and took much pains. But he did not see much fruit of his labour : the people *would* come and hear for themselves, both in the morning, when I explained (without touching the controversy), " Who shall lay anything to the charge of God's elect?" and in the afternoon, when I enforced, "Seek ye the Lord while He may be found."

Wed. 25.—We came to Alnwick on the day whereon those who have gone through their apprenticeship are made free of the corporation. Sixteen or seventeen, we were informed, were to receive their freedom this day, and, in order thereto (such is the unparalleled wisdom of the present corporation, as well as of their forefathers), to walk through a great bog (purposely preserved for the occasion; otherwise it might have been drained long ago), which takes up some of them to the neck, and many of them to the breast.

Fri. May 4.—We had the first general quarterly meeting of all the stewards round Newcastle, in order thoroughly to understand both the spiritual and temporal state of every society.

Tues. 8.—I rode to Robin Hood's Bay, near Whitby. The town is very remarkably situated: it stands close to the sea, and is in great part built on craggy and steep rocks, some of which rise perpendicular from the water. And yet the land, both on the north, south, and west, is fruitful and well cultivated. I stood on a little rising near the quay, in a warm, still evening, and exhorted a multitude of people, from all parts, to "seek the Lord while He may be found." They were all attention; and most of them met me again at half an hour after four in the morning. I could gladly have spent some days here; but my stages were fixed: so, on *Wednesday*, 9, I rode on to York.

Sun. 27.—I was afraid many of the congregation at Birstal would not be able to hear. But my fear was needless; for my voice was so strengthened, that even those who sat in John Nelson's window, an hundred yards off, could (as they afterwards told me) distinctly hear every word.

Wed. 30.—I rode to Haworth, where Mr Grimshaw read prayers, and I preached to a crowded congregation. But having preached ten or eleven times in three days, besides meeting the societies, my voice began to fail. Not that I was hoarse at all; but I had not strength to speak. However, it was restored at Heptonstall in the afternoon, so that the whole congregation could hear. When shall we learn to take thought only for the present hour? Is it not enough, that God gives help when we want it?

Sun. June 24.—Mr Walsh preached at Short's Gardens in Irish. Abundance of his countrymen flocked to hear, and some were cut to the heart. How many means does God use, to bring poor wanderers back to Himself!

Sun. July 1.—He preached in Irish in Moorfields. The

congregation was exceeding large, and behaved seriously;
though probably many of them came purely to hear what
manner of language it was. For the sake of these he preached
afterwards in English, if by any means he might gain some.

On *Wednesday*, 25, the stewards met at St Ives, from the
western part of Cornwall. The next day I began examining
the society; but I was soon obliged to stop short. I found an
accursed thing among them: well-nigh one and all bought or sold
uncustomed goods. I therefore delayed speaking to any more
till I had met them all together. This I did in the evening,
and told them plain, either they must put this abomination away,
or they would see my face no more. *Friday*, 27. They
severally promised so to do. So I trust this plague is stayed.

Tues. Aug. 14.—I willingly accepted the offer of preaching
in the house lately built for Mr Whitefield, at Plymouth Dock.
Thus it behoveth us to trample on bigotry and party zeal.
Ought not all who love God to love one another?

Fri. 24.—I endeavoured once more to bring Kingswood
school into order. Surely the importance of this design is
apparent, even from the difficulties that attend it. I have spent
more money, and time, and care, on this, than almost any
design I ever had: and still it exercises all the patience I have.
But it is worth all the labour.

Mon. Sept. 10.—I called on Stephen Plummer, once of our
society, but now a zealous Quaker. He was much pleased
with my calling, and came to hear me preach. Being straitened
for time, I concluded sooner than usual; but as soon as I
had done, Stephen began. After I had listened half an hour,
finding he was no nearer the end, I rose up to go away. His
sister then begged him to leave off; on which he flew into a
violent rage, and roared louder and louder, till an honest man
took him in his arms, and gently carried him away.

What a wise providence was it, that this poor young man
turned Quaker some years before he ran mad! So the honour
of turning his brain now rests upon them, which otherwise
must have fallen upon the Methodists.

Fri. Oct. 19.—I returned to London. *Saturday*, 20. I
found myself out of order, but believed it would go off. On
Sunday, 21, I was considerably worse, but could not think of
sparing myself on that day.

Thur. Nov. 8.—In the night my disorder returned more
violent than it had been since I left Cornwall.

Mon. 12.—I set out in a chaise for Leigh, having delayed
my journey as long as I could. I preached at seven, but was
extremely cold all the time, the wind coming strong from a

door behind, and another on one side ; so that my feet felt just as if I had stood in cold water.

Mon. 26.—Dr F—— told me plain, I must not stay in town a day longer ; adding, "If anything does thee good, it must be the country air, with rest, asses' milk, and riding daily." So (not being able to sit an horse) about noon I took coach for Lewisham.

In the evening (not knowing how it might please God to dispose of me), to prevent vile panegyric, I wrote as follows :—

Here lieth the Body

OF

JOHN WESLEY,

A BRAND PLUCKED OUT OF THE BURNING:
WHO DIED OF A CONSUMPTION IN THE
FIFTY-FIRST YEAR OF HIS AGE,
NOT LEAVING, AFTER HIS DEBTS ARE
PAID, TEN POUNDS BEHIND HIM:
PRAYING,
GOD BE MERCIFUL TO ME, AN
UNPROFITABLE SERVANT!

He ordered, that this, if any inscription, should be placed on his tombstone.

On *Wed.* Jan. 2, 1754, I set out in a machine, and the next afternoon came to Chippenham. Here I took a post-chaise, in which I reached Bristol about eight in the evening.

Fri. 4.—I began drinking the water at the Hot-well, having a lodging at a small distance from it ; and on *Sunday*, 6, I began writing Notes on the New Testament ; a work which I should scarce ever have attempted, had I not been so ill as not to be able to travel or preach, and yet so well as to be able to read and write.

Mon. 7.—I went on now in a regular method, rising at my hour, and writing from five to nine at night ; except the time of riding, half an hour for each meal, and the hour between five and six n the evening.

Wed. Feb. 27.—My brother came down from London, and and we spent several days together, in comparing the translation of the evangelists with the original, and reading Dr Heylyn's *Lectures*, and Dr Doddridge's *Family Expositor*.

Sun. Mar. 10.—I took my leave of the Hot-well, and removed to Bristol.

Tues. 19.—Having finished the rough draught, I began transcribing the Notes on the Gospels.

Tues. 26.—I preached for the first time, after an intermission of four months.

Wed. May 22.—Our Conference began; and the spirit of peace and love was in the midst of us. Before we parted, we all willingly signed an agreement, not to act independently of each other : so that the breach lately made has only united us more closely together than ever.

Mon. Sept. 9.—I preached at Charlton, a village six miles from Taunton, to a large congregation gathered from the towns and country for many miles round. All the farmers here had some time before entered into a joint engagement to turn all out of their service, and give no work to any, who went to hear a Methodist preacher. But there is no counsel against the Lord. One of the chief of them, Mr G——, was not long after convinced of the truth, and desired those very men to preach at his house. Many of the other confederates came to hear, whom their servants and labourers gladly followed. So the whole device of Satan fell to the ground ; and the Word of God grew and prevailed.

Tues. 17.—I rode to Trowbridge, where one who found peace with God while he was a soldier in Flanders, and has been much prospered in business since his discharge, has built a preaching-house at his own expense. He had a great desire that I should be the first who preached in it ; but before I had finished the hymn, it was so crowded, and consequently so hot, that I was obliged to go out and stand at the door : there was a multitude of hearers, rich and poor.

Wed. Oct. 2.—I walked to Old Sarum, which, in spite of common sense, without house or inhabitants, still sends two members to the Parliament. It is a large, round hill, encompassed with a broad ditch, which, it seems, has been of a considerable depth. At the top of it is a corn-field ; in the midst of which is another round hill, about two hundred yards in diameter, encompassed with a wall, and a deep ditch. Probably before the invention of cannon, this city was impregnable. Troy was ; but now it is vanished away, and nothing left but " the stones of emptiness."

Thur. 3.—I rode to Reading, and preached In the evening. Observing a warm man near the door (which was once of the society), I purposely bowed to him ; but he made no return. During the first prayer he stood, but sat while we sung. In the sermon his countenance changed, and in a little while he turned his face to the wall. He stood at the second hymn, and then kneeled down. As I came out he catched me by the hand, and dismissed me with a hearty blessing.

Fri. 4.—I came to London. On *Monday*, 7, I retired to a little place near Hackney, formerly a seat of Bishop Bonner's (how are the times changed !), and still bearing his name. Here I was as in a college.

Sat. 26.—Mr. Gilbert Tennent, of New England, called upon me, and informed me of his design, now ready to be executed, of founding an American College for Protestants of every denomination : an admirable design, if it will bring Protestants of every denomination to bear with one another.

CHAPTER X.

THE PREACHER

FROM APRIL 14, 1755, TO MAY 1, 1760.

Mon. April 14, 1755.—I rode by Manchester (where I preached about twelve) to Warrington, At six in the morning, *Tuesday*, 15, I preached to a large and serious congregation ; and then went on to Liverpool, one of the neatest, best-built towns I have seen in England : I think it is full twice as large as Chester ; most of the streets are quite straight. Two-thirds of the town, we were informed, have been added within these forty years. If it continue to increase in the same proportion, in forty years more it will nearly equal Bristol. The people in general are the most mild and courteous I ever saw in a seaport town ; as indeed appears by their friendly behaviour, not only to the Jews and Papists who live among them, but even to the Methodists (so called). The preaching-house is a little larger than that at Newcastle.

Fri. 25.—About ten I preached near Todmorden. The people stood, row above row, on the side of the mountain. They were rough enough in outward appearance ; but their hearts were as melting wax.

One can hardly conceive anything more delightful than the vale through which we rode from hence.

Mon. 28.—I preached at Keighley ; on *Tuesday* at Bradford, which is now as quiet as Birstal. Such a change has God wrought in the hearts of the people since John Nelson was in the dungeon here. My brother met me at Birstal in the afternoon.

Wed. 30.—We began reading together, "A Gentleman's Reasons for his Dissent from the Church of England." It is an elaborate and lively tract, and contains the strength of the cause ; but it did not yield us one proof that it is lawful for us (much less our duty) to separate from it.

Thur. May 1.—I finished the "Gentleman's Reasons" (who is a Dissenting minister at Exeter). In how different a spirit does this man write from honest Richard Baxter ! The one dipping, as it were, his pen in tears, the other in vinegar and gall. Surely one page of that loving, serious Christian, weighs more than volumes of this bitter, sarcastic jester.

Tues. 6.—Our Conference began at Leeds. The point on which we desired all the preachers to speak their minds at large was, " Whether we ought to separate from the Church ? " Whatever was advanced on one side or the other was seriously and calmly considered ; and on the third day we were all fully agreed in that general conclusion,—that (whether it was lawful or not) it was no ways expedient.

Mon. 12.—We rode (my wife and I) to Northallerton.

Tues. 13.—I rode on to Newcastle. I did not find things here in the order I expected. Many were on the point of leaving the Church, which some had done already ; and, as they supposed, on my authority !

In the following week I spake to the members of the society severally, and found far fewer than I expected prejudiced against the Church : I think not above forty in all. And I trust the plague is now stayed.

Sat. June 7.—[York.] One of the residentiaries sent for Mr Williamson, who had invited me to preach in his church, and told him, " Sir, I abhor persecution : but if you let Mr Wesley preach, it will be the worse for you." He desired it nevertheless ; but I declined. Perhaps there is a providence in this also. God will not suffer my little remaining strength to be spent on those who will not hear me but in an honourable way.

Sun. 8.—We were at the minster in the morning, and at our parish church in the afternoon. The same gentleman preached at both ; but though I saw him at the church, I did not know I had ever seen him before. In the morning he was all life and motion ; in the afternoon he was as quiet as a post. At five in the evening, the rain constrained me to preach in the oven again.

Mon. 9.—I took my leave of the richest society, number for number, which we have in England. I hope this place will not prove (as Cork has for some time done) the Capua of our preachers.

Tues. July 22.—To oblige a friendly gentlewoman, I was a witness to her will, wherein she bequeathed part of her estate to charitable uses ; and part, during his natural life, to her dog Toby. I suppose, though she should die within the year, her legacy to Toby may stand good ; but that to the poor is null and void, by the statute of Mortmain !

Wed. Aug. 6.—I mentioned to the congregation another

means of increasing serious religion, which had been frequently practised by our forefathers, and attended with eminent blessing ; namely, the joining in a covenant to serve God with all our heart and with all our soul. I explained this for several mornings following ; and on *Friday* many of us kept a fast unto the Lord, beseeching Him to give us wisdom and strength, to promise unto the Lord our God and keep it.

Mon. 11.—I explained once more the nature of such an engagement, and the manner of doing it acceptably to God. At six in the evening we met for that purpose, at the French church in Spitalfields. After I had recited the tenor of the covenant proposed, in the words of that blessed man, Richard Alleine, all the people stood up, in testimony of assent, to the number of about eighteen hundred persons. Such a night I scarce ever saw before. Surely the fruit of it shall remain for ever.

Sat. 30.—As I was riding through Truro, one stopped my horse, and insisted on my alighting. Presently two or three more of Mr Walker's society came in ; and we seemed to have been acquainted with each other many years : but I was constrained to break from them. About five I found the congregation waiting in a broad, convenient part of the street, in Redruth. I was extremely weary ; and our friends were so glad to see me, that none once thought of asking me to eat or drink : but my weariness vanished when I began to speak. Surely God is in this place also.

Sun. 31.—At five I preached in Gwennap, to several thousands ; but not one of them light or inattentive. After I had done, the storm arose, and the rain poured down, till about four in the morning : then the sky cleared, and many of them that feared God gladly assembled before Him.

Tues. Sept. 2.—We went to Falmouth. The town is not now what it was ten years since : all is quiet from one end to the other.

After preaching again, to a congregation who now appeared ready to devour every word, I walked up to Pendennis Castle ; finely situated on the high point of land which runs out between the bay and the harbour, and commanding both. It might easily be made exceeding strong ; but our wooden castles are sufficient.

In the afternoon we rode to Helstone, once turbulent enough, but now quiet as Penryn. I preached at six, on a rising ground, about a musket-shot from the town. Two drunken men strove to interrupt ; but one soon walked away : the other leaned on his horse's neck, and fell fast asleep.

What has done much good here is, the example of W—— T——. He was utterly without God in the world, when his father died, and left him a little estate, encumbered with huge debt. Seven or eight years ago he found peace with God. He afterwards sold his estate, paid all his debts, and, with what he had left, furnished a little shop. Herein God has blessed him in an uncommon manner. Meantime, all his behaviour is of a piece ; so that more and more of his neighbours say, " Well, this is a work of God ! "

About noon, *Friday*, 5, I called on W. Row, in Breage, in my way to Newlyn.

I had given no notice of preaching here ; but seeing the poor people flock from every side, I could not send them empty away. So I preached at a small distance from the house ; and none opened his mouth ; for the lions of Breage too are now changed into lambs. That they were so fierce ten years ago is no wonder ; since their wretched minister told them, from the pulpit (seven years before I resigned my fellowship), that " John Wesley was expelled the College for a base child, and had been quite mazed ever since : that all the Methodists, at their private societies, put out the lights," etc. ; with abundance more of the same kind. But a year or two since, it was observed, he grew thoughtful and melancholy ; and, about nine months ago, he went into his own necessary house, and hanged himself.

Sat. 13.—I preached once more at St Just, on the first stone of their new society-house. In the evening, as we rode to Camborne, John Pearce, of Redruth, was mentioning a remarkable incident :—While he lived at Helstone, as their class was meeting one evening, one of them cried, with an uncommon tone, " We will not stay here : we will go to " such an house, which was in a quite different part of the town. They all rose immediately, and went ; though neither they nor she knew why. Presently after they were gone, a spark fell into a barrel of gunpowder, which was in the next room, and blew up the house. So did God preserve those who trusted in Him, and prevent the blasphemy of the multitude.

Sun. 14.—I rode on to Cubert.

Mon. 15.—We walked an hour near the seashore, among those amazing caverns, which are full as surprising as Pool's Hole, or any other in the Peak of Derbyshire. Some part of the rock in these natural vaults glitters as bright and ruddy as gold : part is a fine sky-blue ; part green ; part enamelled, exactly like mother-of-pearl ; and a great part, especially near the Holy Well (which bubbles up, on the top of a rock, and is famous for curing either scorbutic or scrofulous disorders), is crusted over, wherever the water runs, with an hard, white coat like alabaster.

Wed. Nov. 5.—Mr Whitefield called upon me ;—disputings are now no more : we love one another, and join hand in hand to promote the cause of our common Master.

Tues. Dec. 23.—I was in the robe-chamber, adjoining to the House of Lords, when the King put on his robes. His brow was much furrowed with age, and quite clouded with care. And is this all the world can give even to a king, all the grandeur it can afford? A blanket of ermine round his shoulders, so heavy and cumbersome he can scarce move under it ! An huge heap of borrowed hair, with a few plates of gold and glittering stones upon his head ! Alas, what a bauble is human greatness !

Wed. Feb. 25, 1756.—I dined with Colonel ——, who said, "No men fight like those who fear God: I had rather command five hundred such, than any regiment in His Majesty's army."

Wed. Mar. 3.—I found Bristol all in a flame: voters and non-voters being ready to tear each other in pieces. I had not recovered my voice, so as either to preach, or speak to the whole society : but I desired those members who were freemen to meet me by themselves ; whom I mildly and lovingly informed how they ought to act in this hour of temptation : and I believe the far greater part of them received and profited by the advice.

Thur. 11.—I rode to Pill, and preached to a large and attentive congregation. A great part of them were sea-faring men. In the middle of my discourse, a press-gang landed from a man-of-war, and came up to the place : but after they had listened a while, they went quickly by, and molested nobody.

Fri. Aug. 13.—Having hired horses for Chester, we set out about seven.

September 8 and 9, *Wednesday* and *Thursday*, I settled my temporal business. It is now about eighteen years since I began writing and printing books ; and how much in that time have I gained by printing? Why, on summing up my accounts, I found that on March 1, 1756 (the day I left London last), I had gained by printing and preaching together, a debt of twelve hundred and thirty-six pounds.

Sun. Oct. 10.—I preached to an huge multitude in Moorfields, on, "Why will ye die, O house of Israel ? " It is fieldpreaching which does the execution still: For usefulness there is none comparable to it.

Mon. 11.—I went to Leigh.

Monday, Nov. 1, was a day of triumphant joy, as All-Saints' Day generally is. How superstitious are they who scruple giving God solemn thanks for the lives and deaths of His saints?

Tues. 9.—Having procured an apparatus on purpose, I ordered several persons to be electrified, who were ill of various disorders; some of whom found an immediate, some a gradual, cure. From this time I appointed, first some hours in every week, and afterwards an hour in every day, wherein any that desired it, might try the virtue of this surprising medicine. Two or three years after, our patients were so numerous that we were obliged to divide them : so part were electrified in Southwark, part at the Foundery, others near St Paul's, and the rest near the Seven Dials : the same method we have taken ever since; and to this day, while hundreds, perhaps thousands, have received unspeakable good, I have not known one man, woman, or child, who has received any hurt thereby : so that when I hear any talk of the danger of being electrified (especially if they are medical men who talk so), I cannot but impute it to great want either of sense or honesty.

Thur. Feb. 10, 1757.—About this time the following note was given into my hand at Wapping :—

"JOHN WHITE, master-at-arms, aboard His Majesty's ship *Tartar*, now at Plymouth, desires to return Almighty God thanks, for himself and all the ship's company, for their preservation in four different engagements they have had with four privateers which they have taken; particularly the last, wherein the enemy first boarded them. They cleared the deck, boarded, in their turn, and took the ship, thirty of the enemy being killed, and fifty more wounded. Only two of our crew were wounded, who, it is hoped, will recover."

Sun. 27.—I had been long desired to see the little flock at Norwich; but this I could not decently do, till I was able to rebuild part of the Foundery there, to which I was engaged by my lease. A sum sufficient for that end was now unexpectedly given me, by one of whom I had no personal knowledge. So I set out on *Monday*, 28, and preached in Norwich on *Tuesday* evening, March 1. Mr Walsh had been there twelve or fourteen days, and not without a blessing. After preaching I entered into contract with a builder, and gave him part of the money in hand.

Sun. March 6.—I had no help, and I wanted none : for God

renewed my strength: but on *Sunday*, 13, finding myself weak at Snowsfields, I prayed (if He saw good) that God would send me help at the chapel; and I had it. A clergyman, whom I never saw before, came and offered me his assistance; and as soon as I had done preaching, Mr Fletcher came, who had just then been ordained priest, and hastened to the chapel on purpose to assist, as he supposed me to be alone.

Mon. 14.—I went with T. Walsh to Canterbury, where I preached in the evening with great enlargement of spirit; but with greater in the morning, being much refreshed at the sight of so large a number of soldiers. And is not God able to kindle the same fire in the fleet which He has already begun to kindle in the army?

Sun. 20.—Mr Fletcher helped me again. How wonderful are the ways of God! When my bodily strength failed, and none in England were able and willing to assist me, He sent me help from the mountains of Switzerland; and an helpmeet for me in every respect: where could I have found such another?

Tues. April 12.—I set out at five for Bedford. Mr Parker, now mayor, received us gladly. He hath not borne the sword in vain. There is no cursing or swearing heard in these streets; no work done on the Lord's day. Indeed, there is no open wickedness of any kind now to be seen in Bedford. Oh, what may not one magistrate do who has a single eye, and a confidence in God!

Thur. 14.—We rode to Leicester, where John Brandon has gathered a small society.

Thur. 28.—I talked with one who by the advice of his pastor, had, very calmly and deliberately, beat his wife with a large stick, till she was black and blue, almost from head to foot. And he insisted, it was his duty so to do, because she was surly and ill-natured; and that he was full of faith all the time he was doing it, and had been so ever since.

Mon. May 23.—We reached Ambleside in the evening.

Fri. June 10.—At six William Coward and I went to the market-house at Kelso. We stayed some time, and neither man, woman, nor child came near us. At length I began singing a Scotch psalm, and fifteen or twenty people came within hearing; but with great circumspection, keeping their distance, as though they knew not what might follow. But while I prayed, their number increased; so that in a few minutes there was a pretty large congregation. I suppose the chief men of the town were there; and I spared neither rich nor poor. I almost wondered at myself, it not being usual with me to use so keen and cutting expressions: and I believe many felt that, for all their form, they were but heathens still.

Mon. 13.—I proclaimed the love of Christ to sinners, in the market-place at Morpeth. Thence we rode to Placey. The society of colliers here may be a pattern to all the societies in England. No person ever misses his band or class: they have no jar of any kind among them; but with one heart and one mind "provoke one another to love and to good works."

Thur. 16.—In the evening I preached at Sunderland. I then met the society, and told them plain, none could stay with us, unless he would part with all sin; particularly, robbing the King, selling or buying run goods; which I could no more suffer, than robbing on the highway. This I enforced on every member the next day. A few would not promise to refrain: so these I was forced to cut off. About two hundred and fifty were of a better mind.

Mon. July 4.—I took my leave of Newcastle, and about noon preached at Durham, in a pleasant meadow, near the riverside. The congregation was large, and wild enough; yet, in a short time, they were deeply attentive. Only three or four gentlemen put me in mind of the honest man at London, who was so gay and unconcerned while Dr Sherlock was preaching concerning the day of judgment: one asked, "Do you not hear what the Doctor says?" He answered, "Yes; but I am not of this parish!" Toward the close I was constrained to mention the gross ignorance I had observed in the rich and genteel people throughout the nation. On this they drew near, and showed as serious an attention as if they had been poor colliers.

Mon. 11.—It continued intensely hot; but having the wind in our faces, we received no hurt till we came to York. But the difficulty was, how to preach there, in a room which in winter used to be as hot as an oven. I cut the knot, by preaching in Blake's Square; where (the mob not being aware of us) I began and ended my discourse to a numerous congregation without the least disturbance.

Tues. 12.—I set a subscription on foot for building a more commodious room.

Mon. 25.—I left Epworth with great satisfaction, and about one preached at Clayworth. I think none was unmoved, but Michael Fenwick: who fell fast asleep under an adjoining hayrick.

Thur. 28.—About noon I preached at Woodseats: in the evening at Sheffield. I do indeed live by preaching!

How quiet is this country now, since the chief persecutors are no more seen! How many of them have been snatched away in an hour when they looked not for it! Some time since, a woman of Thorpe often swore she would wash her hands in the heart's blood of the next preacher that came. But before the next preacher came she was carried to her long home. A little before John Johnson settled at Wentworth, a stout, healthy man, who lived there, told his neighbours, "After May-day we shall have nothing but praying and preaching: but I will make noise enough to stop it." But before May-day he was silent in his grave. A servant of Lord R—— was as bitter as him, and told many lies purposely to make mischief: but before this was done, his mouth was stopped. He was drowned in one of the fish-ponds.

Mon. Aug. 8.—I took a walk in the Charter House. I wondered that all the squares and buildings, and especially the schoolboys, looked so little. But this is easily accounted for. I was little myself when I was at school, and measured all about me by myself. Accordingly, the upper boys being then bigger than myself, seemed to me very big and tall; quite contrary to what they appear now when I am taller and bigger than them. I question if this is not the real ground of the common imagination, that our forefathers, and in general men in past ages, were much larger than now: an imagination current in the world eighteen hundred years ago.

Tues. Jan. 17, 1758.—I preached at Wandsworth. A gentleman, come from America, has again opened a door in this desolate place. In the morning I preached in Mr Gilbert's house. Two negro servants of his and a mulatto appear to be much awakened. Shall not His saving health be made known to all nations?

Fri. Feb. 3.—Mr Parker (last year Mayor of Bedford) preached at the Foundery. A more artless preacher I never heard; but not destitute of pathos. I doubt not he may be of much use among honest, simple-hearted people.

Mon. 27.—Having a sermon to write against the Assizes at Bedford, I retired for a few days to Lewisham.

Hence, on *Thursday*, March 9, I rode to Bedford, and found the sermon was not to be preached till Friday. Had I known this in time, I should never have thought of preaching it; having engaged to be at Epworth on Saturday.

Fri. 10.—The congregation at St Paul's was very large and very attentive. The judge, immediately after sermon, sent me an invitation to dine with him. But having no time, I was obliged to send my excuse, and set out between one and two.

Resolving to reach Epworth at the time appointed, I set out in a post-chaise between four and five in the morning: but the frost made it so bad driving, that my companion came with the lame horses into Stamford as soon as me. The next stage I went on horseback; but I was then obliged to leave my mare, and take another post-chaise. I came to Bawtry about six. Some from Epworth had come to meet me, but were gone half an hour before I came. I knew no chaise could go the rest of the road; so it remained only to hire horses and a guide. We set out about seven, but I soon found my guide knew no more of the way than myself. However, we got pretty well to Idle-stop, about four miles from Bawtry, where we had just light to discern the river at our side, and the country covered with water. I had heard that one Richard Wright lived thereabouts, who knew the road over the moor perfectly well. Hearing one speak (for we could not see him), I called, "Who is there?" He answered, "Richard Wright." I soon agreed with him, and he quickly mounted his horse, and rode boldly forward. The north-east wind blew full in our face; and I heard them say, "It is very cold!" But neither my face, nor hands, nor feet were cold, till between nine and ten we came to Epworth: after travelling more than ninety miles, I was little more tired than when I rose in the morning.

Sun. 12.—I was much comforted at church, both morning and afternoon, by the serious behaviour of the whole congregation, so different from what it was formerly. After evening service I took my stand in the market-place, with a multitude of people from all parts. Toward the end of the sermon the rain was heavy; but it neither lessened nor disturbed the congregation.

I was apprehensive, having been at an uncommon expense, of being a little straitened for money: but after preaching, one with whom I had never exchanged a word, put a letter into my hand, in which was a bill for ten pounds. Is not "the earth the Lord's, and the fulness thereof"?

Thur. Aug. 10.—We rode through a pleasant country to Pile. We were setting out from thence when a violent shower drove us into the house again, and constrained us to talk with two or three travellers. I believe our labour was not lost; for they appeared to be greatly affected. preached at Cardiff in the evening and the next morning. We reached the New Passage about noon. But they did not tell us till half-hour after five, that the boat would not pass that night. With much difficulty I procured a small boat to carry us over, leaving our horses behind. Landing soon after six, we walked on, and between nine and ten came to Bristol.

Here I met with a trial of another kind: but this also shall be for good. On the following days was our yearly Conference, begun and ended in perfect harmony. *Thursday*, 17. I went to the cathedral to hear Mr Handel's *Messiah*. I doubt if that congregation was ever so serious at a sermon as they were during this performance. In many parts, especially several of the choruses, it exceeded my expectation.

Sun. 27.—We reached Swansea at seven, and were met by one who conducted us to his house, and thence to a kind of castle, in which was a green court, surrounded by high old walls. A large congregation assembled soon, and behaved with the utmost decency. A very uncommon blessing was among them, as uses to be among them that are simple of heart.

Mon. 28.—After preaching at Swansea in the evening, I met those who desired to join in a society, and explained to them the nature and design of it ; with which they were quite unacquainted.

Tues. 29.—I rode back to Neath, in order to put the society there (an unlicked mass) into some form. This on *Saturday* they had begged me to do ; but they seemed now to have quite forgotten it. Mr Evans, the Presbyterian minister, had turned them upside down. They looked as if they had never seen me before ; all but five or six, who were much ashamed of their brethren.

Wed. 30.—I rode on to Margam. There used to be preaching here, till Lord Mansel, dying without children, left the estate to Mr Talbot. He forbade all his tenants to receive the preachers, and so effectually put a stop to it. But he did not glory in it long. A few months after, God called him home.

Fri. Oct. 6.—I designed to go in a wherry to the Isle of Wight ; but the watermen were so extravagant in their demands, that I changed my mind, and went in the hoy : and it was well I did ; for the sea was so high, it would not have been easy for a small boat to keep above water. We landed at two, and walked on, five little miles, to Newport. The neighbouring camp had filled the town with soldiers, the most abandoned wretches whom I ever yet saw. Their whole glorying was in cursing, swearing, drunkenness, and lewdness. How gracious is God, that He does not yet send these monsters to their own place !

At five I preached in the corn-market, and at six in the morning. A few even of the soldiers attended. One of these, Benjamin Lawrence, walked with us to Wotton Bridge ; where we intended to take boat. He was in St Philip's Fort during the whole siege, concerning which I asked him many questions

Mon. 16.—I rode to Canterbury. As we came into the city, a stone flew out of the pavement and struck my mare upon the leg with such violence that she dropped down at once. I kept my seat, till, in struggling to rise, she fell again and rolled over me. When she rose I endeavoured to rise too, but found I had no use of my right leg or thigh. But an honest barber came out, lifted me up, and helped me into his shop. Feeling myself very sick, I desired a glass of cold water, which instantly gave me ease.

Tues. 17.—I found reason to rejoice over this little flock, now free from all divisions and offences. And on *Saturday* I cheerfully returned to London, after an absence of near eight months.

Mr Parker [of Bedford] informing me that Mr Berridge desired I would come to him as soon as possible, I set out for Everton on *Thursday*, November 9. I found Mr B. just taking horse, with whom I rode on, and in the evening preached at Wrestlingworth, in a large church, well filled with serious hearers.

We lodged at Mr Hickes's, the vicar, a witness of the faith which once he persecuted. The next morning I preached in his church again. In the middle of the sermon, a woman before me dropped down as dead, as one had done the night before. In a short time she came to herself, and remained deeply sensible of her want of Christ.

Hence we rode to Mr Berridge's at Everton. For many years he was seeking to be justified by his works: but a few months ago, he was thoroughly convinced that "by grace" we "are saved through faith." Immediately he began to proclaim aloud the redemption that is in Jesus; and God confirmed His own word exactly as He did at Bristol, in the beginning, by working repentance and faith in the hearers, and with the same violent outward symptoms.

I preached at six in the evening and five in the morning, and some were struck, just as at Wrestlingworth. One of these was brought into the house, with whom we spent a considerable time in prayer. I then hastened forward, and a little before it was dark, reached the Foundery.

Wed. Nov. 29.—I rode to Wandsworth, and baptized two negroes belonging to Mr Gilbert, a gentleman lately come from Antigua. One of these is deeply convinced of sin; the other rejoices in God her Saviour, and is the first African Christian I have known. But shall not our Lord, in due time, have these heathens also "for His inheritance"?

Mon. Dec. 4.—I was desired to step into the little church behind the Mansion House, commonly called St Stephen's,

Walbrook. It is nothing grand; but neat and elegant beyond expression. So that I do not wonder at the speech of the famous Italian architect, who met Lord Burlington in Italy: "My Lord, go back and see St Stephen's in London. We have not so fine a piece of architecture in Rome."

Wed. 27.—In the evening I reached Colchester.

Fri. 29.—I found the society had decreased since L—— C—— went away; and yet they had had full as good preachers. But that is not sufficient: by repeated experiments we learn, that though a man preach like an angel, he will neither collect, nor preserve a society which is collected, without visiting them from house to house.

To-day I walked all over the famous castle, perhaps the most ancient building in England. A considerable part of it is, without question, fourteen or fifteen hundred years old. It was mostly built of Roman bricks, each of which is about two inches thick, seven broad, and thirteen or fourteen long. Seat of ancient kings, British and Roman, once dreaded far and near! But what are they now? Is not "a living dog better than a dead lion"?

Tues. Feb. 27, 1759.—I walked with my brother and Mr Maxfield to L—— H——'s. After breakfast, came in Mr Whitefield, Madan, Romaine, Jones, Downing, and Venn, with some persons of quality, and a few others. Mr Whitefield, I found, was to have administered the sacrament; but he insisted upon my doing it: after which, at the request of L—— H——, I preached on 1 Cor. xiii. 13.

Sun. Mar. 18.—I administered the Lord's Supper to near two hundred communicants: so solemn a season I never remember to have known in the city of Norwich. As a considerable part of them were Dissenters, I desired every one to use what posture he judged best. Had I required them to kneel, probably half would have sat. Now all but one kneeled down.

Monday and *Tuesday* I spoke to as many of both societies, now united together, as had leisure and inclination to come. The whole number is about four hundred and twenty; of whom I do not think it improbable two hundred may continue together.

Thur. 29.—I divided the Norwich society into classes, without any distinction between them who had belonged to the Foundery or the Tabernacle.

Sun. April 1.—I met them all at six, requiring every one to show his ticket when he came in: a thing they had never heard of before. I likewise insisted on another strange regulation, that the men and women should sit apart. A third was made the same day. It had been a custom ever since the Tabernacle was built, to have the galleries full of spectators while the Lord's Supper was administered. This I judged highly improper; and therefore ordered none to be admitted, but those who desired to communicate. And I found far less difficulty than I expected, in bringing them to submit to this also.

The society now contained above five hundred and seventy members; an hundred and three of whom were in no society before, although many of them had found peace with God. I believe they would have increased to a thousand, if I could have stayed a fortnight longer. Which of these will hold fast their profession? The fowls of the air will devour some; the sun will scorch more; and others will be choked by the thorns springing up. I wonder we should ever expect that half of those who "hear the Word with joy" will bring forth fruit unto perfection.

Fri. 20.—The master of the inn at Tadcaster offering us the use of his garden, I preached to a well-behaved congregation; and about five found Mr Grimshaw and many of our brethren at Leeds. *Saturday*, 21. At half-hour past ten we reached Stainland chapel, near Elland. It is an handsome building, near the top of a mountain, and surrounded with mountains on all sides. It was filled from end to end. Mr Grimshaw read prayers, and I preached on part of the second lesson. In the room where I dressed myself were a young man and his sister, both ill of a fever. I know not that ever they heard the preaching; however, I desired we might go to prayers. They presently melted into tears.

I preached at Manchester in the evening, where we had at length a quiet audience. Wretched magistrates, who, by refusing to suppress, encouraged the rioters, had long occasioned continued tumults here: but some are now of a better spirit: and wherever magistrates desire to preserve the peace, they have sufficient power to do it.

Thur. May 17.—I inquired into a signal instance of Providence. When a coal-pit runs far under the ground, it is customary here to build a partition-wall, nearly from the shaft to within three or four yards of the end, in order to make the air circulate, which then moves down one side of the wall, turns at the end, and then moves briskly up on the other side. In a pit two miles from the town, which ran full four hundred yards under the ground, and had been long neglected, several parts of this wall were fallen down. Four men were sent down to repair it. They were about three hundred yards from the shaft, when the foul air took fire. In a moment it tore down and lose his own soul?" I was walking back through a gaping, staring crowd, when Sir Nevil came and thanked me for my sermon, to the no small amazement of his neighbours, who shrunk back as if they had seen a ghost. Thence I rode to North Scarle, the last village in Lincolnshire, ten miles short of Newark. Here a great multitude assembled from various parts.

Thurs. 30.—I preached at the Tabernacle in Norwich, to a large, rude, noisy congregation. I took knowledge what manner of teachers they had been accustomed to, and determined to mend them or end them. Accordingly, the next evening, after sermon, I reminded them of two things: the one, that it was not decent to begin talking aloud as soon as service was ended; and hurrying to and fro, as in a beargarden. The other, that it was a bad custom to gather into knots just after sermon, and turn a place of worship into a coffee-house. I therefore desired, that none would talk under that roof, but go quietly and silently away. And on *Sunday*, September 2, I had the pleasure to observe, that all went as quietly away as if they had been accustomed to it for many years.

Mon. Sept. 3.—I met the society at five, and explained the nature and use of meeting in a class. Upon inquiry, I found we have now about five hundred members. But an hundred and fifty of these do not pretend to meet at all. Of those, therefore, I make no account. They hang on but a single thread.

Fri. 14.—I returned to London. *Saturday*, 15. Having left orders for the immediate repairing of West Street chapel, I went to see what they had done, and saw cause to praise God for this also. The main timbers were so rotten, that in many places one might thrust his fingers into them. So that probably, had we delayed till spring, the whole building must have fallen to the ground.

Mon. 17.—I went to Canterbury. Two hundred soldiers, I suppose, and a whole row of officers, attended in the evening. Their number was increased the next evening, and all behaved as men fearing God.

Sun. 23.—A vast majority of the immense congregation in Moorfields were deeply serious. One such hour might convince any impartial man of the expediency of field-preaching. What building, except St Paul's church, would contain such a congregation? And if it would, what human voice could have reached them there? By repeated observations I find I can command thrice the number in the open air, that I can under a roof. And who can say the time for field-preaching is over, while: 1. Greater numbers than ever attend; 2. The converting, as well as convincing, power of God is eminently present with them?

Mon. Oct. 1.—All my leisure time, during my stay at Bristol, I employed in finishing the fourth volume of *Discourses*; probably the last which I shall publish. *Monday*, 15. I walked up to Knowle, a mile from Bristol, to see the French prisoners. Above eleven hundred of them, we were informed, were confined in that little place, without anything to lie on but a little dirty straw, or anything to cover them but a few foul thin rags, either by day or night, so that they died like rotten sheep. I was much affected, and preached in the evening on (Ex. xxiii. 9), "Thou shalt not oppress a stranger; for ye know the heart of a stranger, seeing ye were strangers in the land of Egypt." Eighteen pounds were contributed immediately, which were made up four-and-twenty the next day. With this we bought linen and woollen cloth, which were made up into shirts, waistcoats, and breeches. Some dozen of stockings were added; all which were carefully distributed, where there was the greatest want. Presently after, the Corporation of Bristol sent a large quantity of mattresses and blankets. And it was not long before contributions were set on foot at London, and in various parts of the kingdom; so that I believe from this time they were pretty well provided with all the necessaries of life.

Wednesday and *Thursday* I spent in revising and perfecting a *Treatise of Electricity*.

Sun. Nov. 4.—As I was applying those words, "They neither marry, nor are given in marriage: neither can they die any more; for they are equal to angels"; the power of God fell upon the congregation in a very uncommon manner. How seasonable! Oh how does God sweeten whatever cross we may bear for His sake!

Sat. 17.—I spent an hour agreeably and profitably with Lady G—— H——, and Sir C—— H——. It is well a few of the rich and noble are called. Oh that God would increase their number! But I should rejoice (were it the will of God), if it were done by the ministry of others. If I might choose, I should still (as I have done hitherto) preach the gospel to the poor.

Sun. Dec. 9.—I had, for the first time, a love-feast for the whole society. *Wednesday*, 12. I began reading over the Greek Testament and the notes, with my brother and several others; carefully comparing the translation with the original, and correcting or enlarging the notes as we saw occasion.

The same day I spent part of the afternoon in the British

Museum. There is a large library, a great number of curious manuscripts, many uncommon monuments of antiquity, and the whole collection of shells, butterflies, beetles, grasshoppers, etc., which the indefatigable Sir Hans Sloane, with such vast expense and labour, procured in a life of fourscore years.

Wed. 19.—I was desired to read over a Chancery bill. The occasion of it was this:—A. B. tells C. D. that one who owed him thirty pounds wanted to borrow thirty more, and asked whether he thought the eighth part of such a ship, then at sea, was sufficient security. He said he thought it was. On this A. B. lent the money. The ship came home: but, through various accidents, the eighth part yielded only twenty pounds. A. B. on this commenced a suit, to make C. D. pay him the residue of his money.

This worthy story is told in no less than an hundred and ten sheets of paper! C. D. answers, he advised to the best of his judgment; not foreseeing those accidents whereby the share which cost two hundred pounds yielded no more than twenty. This answer brought on fifteen sheets of exceptions, all which a quarter of a sheet might have contained. I desired the plaintiff and defendant to meet me the next day; both of whom were willing to stand to arbitration: and they readily agreed that C. D. should pay half his own costs, and A. B. the rest of the expense.

Sun. Jan. 13, 1760.—I preached again in West Street chapel, now enlarged, and thoroughly repaired. When I took this, eighteen years ago, I little thought the world would have borne us till now. But the right hand of the Lord hath the pre-eminence; therefore we endure unto this day.

Wed. 16.—One came to me, as she said, with a message from the Lord, to tell me, I was laying up treasures on earth, taking my ease, and minding only my eating and drinking. I told her, God knew me better; and if He had sent her, He would have sent her with a more proper message.

On *Tuesday* noon, April 1, we landed safe at Dublin.

I never saw more numerous or more serious congregations in Ireland than we had all this week. On *Easter Day*, April 6, I introduced our English custom, beginning the service at four in the morning.

Mon. April 7.—I began speaking severally to the members of the society, and was well pleased to find so great a number of them much alive to God. One consequence of this is, that the society is larger than it has been for several years: and no wonder; for where the real power of God is, it naturally spreads wider and wider.

Fri. 18.—I went with Miss F—— to see the French prisoners sent from Carrickfergus. They were surprised at hearing as good French spoke in Dublin as they could have heard in Paris, and still more at being exhorted to heart-religion, to the "faith that worketh by love."

Mon. 28.—I rode to Rathfriland, seven Irish miles from Newry, a small town built on the top of a mountain, surrounded first by a deep valley, and at a small distance by higher mountains. The Presbyterian minister had wrote to the Popish priest, to keep his people from hearing. But they would not be kept: Protestants and Papists flocked together to the meadow where I preached, and sat on the grass, still as night, while I exhorted them to "repent, and believe the gospel." The same attention appeared in the whole congregation at Terryhugan in the evening, where I spent a comfortable night in the Prophet's chamber, nine feet long, seven broad, and six high. The ceiling, floor, and walls were all of the same marble, vulgarly called clay.

Thur. May 1.—I rode to Moira. Soon after twelve, standing on a tombstone, near the church, I called a considerable number of people to "know God, and Jesus Christ whom He hath sent." We were just opposite to the Earl of Moira's house, the best finished of any I have seen in Ireland. It stands on a hill, with a large avenue in front, bounded by the church on the opposite hill. The other three sides are covered by orchards, gardens, and woods, in which are walks of various kinds.

General Flaubert, who commanded the French troops at Carrickfergus, was just gone from Lord Moira's. Major Brajelon was now there, a man of a fine person and extremely graceful behaviour. Both these affirmed, that the French were all picked men out of the King's Guards: that their commission was, to land either at Londonderry or Carrickfergus, while Monsieur Conflans landed in the south; and if they did not do this within three months, to return directly to France.

CHAPTER XI

INCREASING LABOURS

FROM SEPTEMBER 1, 1760, TO FEBRUARY 13, 1765

Mon. Sept 1, 1760.—I set out for Cornwall.

Mon. 8.—When I came to St Ives, I was determined to preach abroad; but the wind was so high, I could not stand where I had intended. But we found a little inclosure near it, one end of which was native rock, rising ten or twelve feet perpendicular, from which the ground fell with an easy descent. A jutting out of the rock, about four feet from the ground, gave me a very convenient pulpit. Here well-nigh the whole town, high and low, rich and poor, assembled together. I was afraid on *Saturday*, that the roaring of the sea, raised by the north wind, would have prevented their hearing. But God gave me so clear and strong a voice, that I believe scarce one word was lost.

Sun. 14.—At eight I chose a large ground, the sloping side of a meadow, where the congregation stood, row above row, so that all might see as well as hear.

At five I went once more into the ground at St Ives. Some of the chief of the town were now not in the skirts, but in the thickest of the people. The clear sky, the setting sun, the smooth, still water, all agreed with the state of the audience. Is anything too hard for God?

> "Thou dost the raging sea control,
>   And smooth the prospect of the deep;
> Thou mak'st the sleeping billows roll,
>   Thou mak'st the rolling billows sleep."

Sat. 20.—In the evening I took my old stand in the main street at Redruth. A multitude of people, rich and poor, calmly attended. So is the roughest become one of the quietest towns in England.

Sun. 21.—I preached in the same place at eight. At one, the day being mild and calm, we had the largest congregation of all. But it rained all the time I was preaching at Gwennap. We concluded the day with a love-feast, at which James

Roberts, a tinner of St Ives, related how God had dealt with his soul. He was one of the first in society in St Ives, but soon relapsed into his old sin, drunkenness, and wallowed in it for two years, during which time he headed the mob who pulled down the preaching-house. Not long after, he was standing with his partner at Edward May's shop when the preacher went by. His partner said, "I will tell him I am a Methodist." "Nay," said Edward, "your speech will bewray you." James felt the word as a sword, thinking in himself, "So does my speech now bewray me!" He turned and hastened home, fancying he heard the devil stepping after him all the way. For forty hours he never closed his eyes, nor tasted either meat or drink. He was then at his wit's end, and went to the window, looking to drop into hell instantly, when he heard those words, "I will be merciful to thy unrighteousness, thy sins and iniquities will I remember no more." All his load was gone; and he has now for many years walked worthy of the gospel.

On *Wednesday* evening, having (over and above meeting the societies) preached thirty times in eleven days, I found myself a little exhausted; but a day's rest set me up.

Sun. Oct. 12.—I visited the classes at Kingswood. Here only there is no increase; and yet, where was there such a prospect, till that weak man, John Cennick, confounded the poor people with strange doctrines?

In the afternoon I had appointed the children to meet at Bristol, whose parents were of the society. Thirty of them came to-day, and above fifty more on the Sunday and Thursday following. About half of these I divided into four classes, two of boys and two of girls; and appointed proper Leaders to to meet them separate. I met them altogether, twice a week, and it was not long before God began to touch some of their hearts.

Wed. 22.—Being informed that some neighbouring gentlemen had declared they would apprehend the next preacher who came to Pensford, I rode over to give them the meeting: but none appeared. It seems, the time is come at length for the Word of God to take root here also.

Fri. 24.—I visited the French prisoners at Knowle, and found many of them almost naked again. In hopes of provoking others to jealousy, I made another collection for them, and ordered the money to be laid out in linen and waistcoats, which were given to those that were most in want.

Sat. 25.—King George was gathered to his fathers. When will England have a better Prince?

Sat. Nov. 8.—I was once more brought safe to London.

I spent about a fortnight, as usual, in examining the society; a heavy, but necessary labour.

Mon. 24.—I visited as many as I could of the sick. How much better is it, when it can be done, to carry relief to the poor, than to send it! and that both for our own sake and theirs.

We observed *Friday*, December the 19th, as a day of fasting and prayer for our King and country, and the success of the gospel: and part of the answer immediately followed, in the remarkable increase of believers, and in the strengthening of those who had before attained that precious faith, "unto all patience and longsuffering with joyfulness."

Sat. 20.—In the evening I hastened back from Snowsfields, to meet the penitents (a congregation which I wish always to meet myself), and walked thither again at five in the morning.

Tues. Jan. 20, 1761.—I inquired concerning Yarmouth, a large and populous town, and as eminent, both for wickedness and ignorance, as even any seaport in England. Some had endeavoured to call them to repentance; but it was at the hazard of their lives. What could be done more? Why, last summer God sent thither the regiment in which Howell Harris was an officer. He preached every night, none daring to oppose him; and hereby a good seed was sown. Many were stirred up to seek God; and some of them now earnestly invited me to come over. I went this afternoon, and preached in the evening. The house was presently more than filled; and instead of the tumult which was expected, all were as quiet as at London.

Tues. Feb. 24.—I retired to Lewisham, and transcribed the list of the society. About an hundred and sixty I left out, to whom I can do no good at present. The number of those which now remain is two thousand three hundred and seventy-five.

Tues. Mar. 10.—We rode to Evesham, where I found the poor shattered society almost sunk into nothing. And no wonder, since they have been almost without help, till Mr Mather came. In the evening I preached in the town-hall. Both at this time, and at five in the morning, God applied His Word, and many found a desire to "strengthen the things that remained."

Mon. 23.—I hastened forward, and reached Leeds about five in the evening, where I had desired all the preachers in those parts to meet me; and an happy meeting we had both in the evening and morning. I afterwards inquired into the state of the societies in Yorkshire and Lincolnshire. I find the work of God increases on every side; but particularly in Lincolnshire, where there has been no work like this, since the time I preached at Epworth on my father's tomb.

Wed. 25.—I took horse early, breakfasted with Mr Venn, and about four in the afternoon came to Stockport. Finding the congregation waiting, I preached immediately, and then rode on to Manchester; where I rested on *Thursday*. *Friday*, 27, I rode to Bridgefield, in the midst of the Derbyshire mountains, and cried to a large congregation, "If any man thirst, let him come unto Me and drink." The next day I returned to Manchester.

Tues. April 28.—We rode partly over the mountains, partly with mountains on either hand, between which was a clear, winding river, and about four in the afternoon reached Edinburgh.

Here I met Mr Hopper, who had promised to preach in the evening, in a large room, lately an Episcopal meeting-house. *Wednesday*, 29. It being extremely cold, I preached in the same room at seven. Some of the reputable hearers cried out in amaze. "Why, this is sound doctrine! Is this he of whom Mr Wh—— used to talk so?" Talk as he will, I shall not retaliate.

I preached again in the evening, and the next day rode round by the Queensferry to Dundee; but, the wind being high, the boatman could not, at least would not, pass. Nor could we pass the next day till between nine and ten. We then rode on through Montrose to Stonehaven. Here Mr Memis met us; and on *Saturday* morning brought us to his house at Aberdeen.

In the afternoon I sent to the Principal and Regent to desire leave to preach in the College Close. This was readily granted; but as it began to rain, I was desired to go into the hall. I suppose this is full an hundred feet long, and seated all around. The congregation was large, notwithstanding the rain; and full as large at five in the morning.

Sun. May 3.—I heard two useful sermons at the kirk, one preached by the Principal of the College, the other by the Divinity Professor. A huge multitude afterwards gathered together in the College Close; and all that could hear seemed to receive the truth in love. I then added about twenty to the little society.

Mon. 4.—Before noon twenty more came to me, desiring to cast in their lot with us, and appearing to be cut to the heart.

About noon I took a walk to the King's College, in Old

Aberdeen. It has three sides of a square, handsomely built, not unlike Queen's College in Oxford. Going up to see the hall, we found a large company of ladies, with several gentlemen. They looked and spoke to one another, after which one of the gentlemen took courage and came to me. He said, "We came last night to the College Close, but could not hear, and should be extremely obliged if you would give us a short discourse here." I knew not what God might have to do ; and so began without delay, on, "God was in Christ, reconciling the world unto Himself."

In the afternoon I was walking in the library of the Marischal College, when the Principal, and the Divinity Professor, came to me ; and the latter invited me to his lodgings, where I spent an hour very agreeably. In the evening, the eagerness of the people made them ready to trample each other under foot. It was some time before they were still enough to hear ; but then they devoured every word. After preaching, Sir Archibald Grant (whom business had called to town) sent and desired to speak to me. I could not then, but promised to wait upon him, with God's leave, in my return to Edinburgh.

Tues. 5.—I accepted the Principal's invitation, and spent an hour with him at his house. I observed no stiffness at all, but the easy good breeding of a man of sense and learning. I suppose both he and all the professors, with some of the magistrates, attended in the evening. I set all the windows open ; but the hall, notwithstanding, was as hot as a bagnio. But this did not hinder either the attention of the people, or the blessing of God.

Wed. 6.—We dined at Mr Ogilvy's, one of the ministers, between whom the city is divided.

At half-hour after six I stood in the College Close, and proclaimed Christ crucified.

Thur. 7.—Leaving near ninety members in the society, I rode over to Sir A. Grant's near Monymusk, about twenty miles north-west from Aberdeen. It lies in a fruitful and pleasant valley, much of which is owing to Sir Archibald's improvements, who has ploughed up abundance of waste ground, and planted some millions of trees. His stately old house is surrounded by gardens, and rows of trees, with a clear river on one side. And about a mile from his house he has laid out a small valley into walks and gardens, on one side of which the river runs. On each side rises a steep mountain ; one rocky and bare, the other covered with trees, row above row, to the very top.

About six we went to the church. It was pretty well filled with such persons as we did not look for so near the Highlands.

But if we were surprised at their appearance, we were much more so at their singing.

Sat. 16.—About noon I preached at Warksworth.

A little above the town, on one side of the river, stand the remains of a magnificent castle. On the other side, toward the bottom of a steep hill, covered with wood, is an ancient chapel, with several apartments adjoining to it, hewn in the solid rock. The windows, the pillars, the communion-table, and several other parts are entire.

Mon. 18.—At nine I preached to a large and serious congregation at Widrington. Thence we rode to Morpeth. As it was a rainy day, they expected me to preach in the room. But observing a large covered place in the market-place, I went thither without delay. It was soon more than filled ; and many, soldiers and others, stood on the outside, notwithstanding the rain. At five I preached to the honest, simple-hearted colliers at Placey, and before sunset reached Newcastle.

Mon. June 8.—I rode over the mountains to Allandale, where I had not been for several years. After preaching and meeting the society, I took horse again, and, crossing another chain of mountains, reached Weardale before eleven.

Tues. 9.—I preached at nine, but was obliged to stand abroad, because of the multitude of people. The sun shone full in my face ; but after having spent a short time in prayer, I regarded it not. I then met the society; and came just in time to prevent their all turning Dissenters, which they were on the point of doing, being quite disgusted with the curate, whose life was no better than his doctrine.

At noon I preached in Teesdale. Most of the men are lead-miners, who a while ago were turned out of their work for following "this way." By this means many of them got into far better work ; and some time after, their old master was glad to employ them again.

We had a long stage from hence to Swaldale, where I found an earnest, loving, simple people, whom I likewise exhorted not to leave the Church, though they had not the best of ministers.

Wed. 10.—I took horse at half-hour past three, and reached Barnard Castle soon after six. I preached at eight in a ground adjoining to the town. Are these the people that a few years ago were like roaring lions ? They were now quiet as lambs ; nor could several showers drive them away till I concluded.

Tues. 23.—In the evening [at Whitby] I preached on the top of the hill, to which you ascend by an hundred ninety and one steps.

Wed. 24.—I walked round the old abbey, which, both with regard to its size (being, I judge, an hundred yards long), and the workmanship of it, is one of the finest, if not the finest, ruin in the kingdom. Hence we rode to Robin Hood's Bay, where I preached at six in the Lower Street, near the quay. In the midst of the sermon a large cat, frighted out of a chamber, leaped down upon a woman's head, and ran over the heads or shoulders of many more ; but none of them moved or cried out, any more than if it had been a butterfly.

Thur. 25.—I had a pleasant ride to Scarborough, the wind tempering the heat of the sun. I had designed to preach abroad in the evening ; but the thunder, lightning, and rain prevented : however, I stood on a balcony, and several hundreds of people stood below ; and notwithstanding the heavy rain, would not stir till I concluded.

Fri. July 3.—We returned to York, where I was desired to call upon a poor prisoner in the castle. I had formerly occasion to take notice of an hideous monster, called a Chancery Bill ; I now saw the fellow to it, called a Declaration. The plain fact was this : Some time since a man who lived near Yarm assisted others in running some brandy. His share was worth near four pounds. After he had wholly left off that bad work, and was following his own business, that of a weaver, he was arrested, and sent to York Gaol ; and, not long after, comes down a Declaration, "that Jac. Wh—— had landed a vessel laded with brandy and Geneva, at the port of London, and sold them there, whereby he was indebted to His Majesty five hundred and seventy-seven pounds and upwards." And to tell this worthy story the lawyer takes up thirteen or fourteen sheets of treble stamped paper.

O England, England ! will this reproach never be rolled away from thee ? Is there anything like this to be found, either among Papists, Turks, or heathens ? In the name of truth, justice, mercy, and common sense, I ask : 1. Why do men lie for lying sake ? Is it only to keep their hands in ? What need else, of saying it was the port of London, when every one knew the brandy was landed above three hundred miles from thence ? What a monstrous contempt of truth does this show, or rather hatred to it ! 2. Where is the justice of swelling four pounds into five hundred and seventy-seven ? 3. Where is the common sense of taking up fourteen sheets to tell a story that may be told in ten lines ? Where is the mercy of thus grinding the face of the poor ? thus sucking the blood of a poor, beggared prisoner ? Would not this be execrable villainy, if the paper and writing together were only sixpence a sheet, when they have stripped him already of his little all, and not left him fourteen groats in the world?

Sun. 5.—Believing one hindrance of the work of God in York, was the neglect of field-preaching, I preached this morning at eight, in an open place, near the city-walls. Abundance of people ran together, most of whom were deeply attentive. One or two only were angry, and threw a few stones; but it was labour lost; for none regarded them.

Sunday 12.—I had appointed to be at Haworth; but the church would not near contain the people who came from all sides: however, Mr Grimshaw had provided for this by fixing a scaffold on the outside of one of the windows, through which I went after prayers, and the people likewise all went out into the churchyard. The afternoon congregation was larger still. What has God wrought in the midst of these rough mountains!

Mon. 13.—At five I preached on the manner of waiting for "perfect love"; the rather to satisfy Mr Grimshaw, whom many had laboured to puzzle and perplex about it. So once more their bad labour was lost, and we were more united both in heart and judgment than ever.

At noon I preached in Colne, once inaccessible to the gospel; but now the yard I was in would not contain the people.

About five I preached at Padiham, another place eminent for all manner of wickedness.

Sun. 19.—I preached in Birstal room at eight. At one we had thousands, the greater part of whom were persons "fearing God and working righteousness." I rode thence to Leeds, in order to preach a funeral sermon for Mary Shent, who, after many severe conflicts, died in great peace.

I hastened back to the love-feast at Birstal. It was the first of the kind which had been there. Many were surprised when I told them, "The very design of a love-feast is a free and familiar conversation, in which every man, yea, and woman has liberty to speak whatever may be to the glory of God." Several then did speak, and not in vain: the flame ran from heart to heart, especially while one was declaring, with all simplicity, the manner wherein God, during the morning sermon (on those words, "I will, be thou clean"), had set her soul at full liberty. Two men also spoke to the same effect; and two others who had found peace with God. We then joyfully poured out our souls before God, and praised Him for His marvellous works.

Mon. 20.—I came to a full explanation with that good man Mr V——. Lord, if I must dispute, let it be with the children of the devil! Let me be at peace with Thy children!

Mon. 27.—In the afternoon I rode on to Matlock Bath.

The valley which reaches from the town to the Bath is pleasant beyond expression. In the bottom of this runs a little river, close to which a mountain rises, almost perpendicular, to an enormous height, part covered with green, part with ragged and naked rocks. On the other side, the mountain rises gradually with tufts of trees here and there. The brow on both sides is fringed with trees, which seem to answer each other.

Many of our friends were come from various parts. At six I preached standing under the hollow of a rock, on one side of a small plain; on the other side of which was a tall mountain. There were many well-dressed hearers, this being the high season; and all of them behaved well.

Sun. Aug. 2.—I had the satisfaction of hearing Mr Madan preach an excellent sermon at Haxey. At two I preached at Westwoodside, to the largest congregation I ever saw in the Isle of Axholme; and to nearly the same at Epworth Cross, as soon as the church service was ended.

Sat. 22.—I returned to London. I found the work of God swiftly increasing here. The congregations, in every place, were larger than they had been for several years.

Tues. Sept. 1.—Our Conference began, and ended on *Saturday*. After spending a fortnight more in London, and guarding both the preachers and people against running into extremes on the one hand or the other, on *Sunday*, 20, at night, I took the machine, and on *Monday*, 21, came to Bristol.

Here likewise I had the satisfaction to observe a considerable increase in the work of God.

Wed. Oct. 21.—I was desired by the condemned prisoners to give them one sermon more. And on *Thursday*, Patrick Ward, who was to die on that day, sent to request I would administer the sacrament to him. He was one-and-twenty years of age, and had scarce ever had a serious thought, till he shot the man who went to take away his gun. From that instant he felt a turn within, and never swore an oath more. His whole behaviour in prison was serious and composed: he read, prayed, and wept much; especially after one of his fellow-prisoners had found peace with God. His hope gradually increased till this day, and was much strengthened at the Lord's Supper; but still he complained, "I am not afraid, but I am not desirous, to die. I do not find that warmth in my heart: I am not sure that my sins are forgiven." He went into the cart, about twelve, in calmness, but mixed with sadness. But in a quarter of an hour, while he was wrestling with God in prayer (not seeming to know that anyone was near him), "The Holy Ghost," said he, "came upon me, and I knew that Christ was mine." From that moment his whole deportment breathed a peace and joy beyond all utterance, till, after having spent about ten minutes in private prayer, he gave the sign.

Tues. Jan. 12, 1762.—After preaching at Deptford, Welling, and Sevenoaks, on *Tuesday* and *Wednesday* I rode on to Sir Thomas l'Anson's, near Tunbridge, and, between six and seven, preached in his large parlour, which opens likewise into the hall. The plain people were all attention. If the seed be watered, surely there will be some fruit.

Monday, Feb. 15, and the following days, I spent in transcribing the list of the society. It never came up before to two thousand four hundred: now it contains above two thousand seven hundred members.

Fri. Mar. 12.—The National Fast was observed all over London with great solemnity. Surely God is well pleased even with this acknowledgment that He governs the world; and even the outward humiliation of a nation may be rewarded with outward blessings.

Fri. April 2.—It was at this time that Mr Grimshaw fell asleep.

Wed. Aug. 4.—I rode to Liverpool, where also was such a work of God as had never been known there before. We had a surprising congregation in the evening, and, as it seemed, all athirst for God. This, I found, had begun here likewise in the latter end of March; and from that time it had continually increased, till a little before I came: nine were justified in one hour. The next morning I spoke severally with those who believed they were sanctified. They were fifty-one in all: twenty-one men, twenty-one widows or married women, and nine young women or children. In one of these the change was wrought three weeks after she was justified; in three, seven days after it; in one, five days; and in Sus. Lutwich, aged fourteen, two days only. I asked Hannah Blakeley, aged eleven, "What do you want now?" She said, with amazing energy, the tears running down her cheeks, "Nothing in this world, nothing but more of my Jesus." How often "out of the mouths of babes and sucklings" dost Thou "perfect praise!"

Fri. Dec. 31.—I now stood and looked back on the past year; a year of uncommon trials and uncommon blessings. Abundance have been convinced of sin; very many have found peace with God; and in London only, I believe full two hundred have been brought into glorious liberty. And yet I have had more care and trouble in six months, than in several years preceding. What the end will be, I know not; but it is enough that God knoweth.

Mon. Jan. 17, 1763.—I rode to Lewisham, and wrote my

sermon to be preached before the Society for Reformation of Manners.

Three days I spent in the tedious work of transcribing the names of the society. I found about thirty of those who thought they were saved from sin had separated from their brethren. But above four hundred, who witnessed the same confession, seemed more united than ever.

Mon. Feb. 28.—Preaching in the evening at Spitalfields, on, "Prepare to meet thy God," I largely showed the utter absurdity of the supposition, that the world was to end that night. But notwithstanding all I could say, many were afraid to go to bed, and some wandered about in the fields, being persuaded, that, if the world did not end, at least London would be swallowed up by an earthquake. I went to my bed at my usual time, and was fast asleep about ten o'clock.

Mon. May 2, and the following days, I was fully employed in visiting the society, and settling the minds of those who had been confused and distressed by a thousand misrepresentations. Indeed, a flood of calumny and evil-speaking (as was easily foreseen) was poured out on every side. My point was still to go straight forward in the work whereto I am called.

Sun. 29.—I preached at seven in the High School yard, at Edinburgh. It being the time of the General Assembly, which drew together, not the ministers only, but abundance of the nobility and gentry, many of both sorts were present ; but abundantly more at five in the afternoon. I spake as plain as ever I did in my life. But I never knew any in Scotland offended at plain dealing. In this respect the North Britons are a pattern to all mankind.

Tues. 31.—I rode to Alnwick, and was much refreshed among a people who have not the form only, but the spirit of religion, fellowship with God, the living power of faith divine.

Wednesday, June 1. I went on to Morpeth, and preached in a ground near the town, to far the most serious congregation which I had ever seen there. At one I preached to the loving colliers in Placey, and in the evening at Newcastle.

Mon. 6.—I rode to Barnard Castle, and preached in the evening, but to such a congregation, not only with respect to number, but to seriousness and composure, as I never saw there before. I intended, after preaching, to meet the society ; but the bulk of the people were so eager to hear more, that I could not forbear letting in almost as many as the room would hold ; and it was a day of God's power : they all seemed to take the kingdom by violence, while they besieged heaven with vehement prayer.

Tues. 7.—So deep and general was the impression now made upon the people, that even at five in the morning I was obliged to preach abroad, by the numbers who flocked to hear, although the northerly wind made the air exceeding sharp. A little after preaching, one came to me who believed God had just set her soul at full liberty. She had been clearly justified long before ; but said, the change she now experienced was extremely different from what she experienced then ; as different as the noonday light from that of daybreak : that she now felt her soul all love, and quite swallowed up in God.

There is something remarkable in the manner wherein God revived His work in these parts. A few months ago the generality of people in this Circuit were exceeding lifeless. Samuel Meggot, perceiving this, advised the society at Barnard Castle to observe every Friday with fasting and prayer. The very first Friday they met together, God broke in upon them in a wonderful manner ; and His work has been increasing among them ever since. The neighbouring societies heard of this, agreed to follow the same rule, and soon experienced the same blessing. Is not the neglect of this plain duty (I mean fasting, ranked by our Lord with almsgiving and prayer) one general occasion of deadness among Christians ? Can anyone willingly neglect it, and be guiltless ?

In the evening I preached at Yarm ; but I found the good doctrine of Christian perfection had not been heard of there for some time. The wildness of our poor brethren in London has put it out of countenance above two hundred miles off ; so these strange advocates for perfection have given it a deeper wound than all its enemies together could do !

Wed. 8.—Just as I began preaching (in the open air, the room being too small even for the morning congregation) the rain began ; but it stopped in two or three minutes, I am persuaded, in answer to the prayer of faith. Incidents of the same kind I have seen abundance of times, and particularly in this journey ; and they are nothing strange to them who seriously believe " the very hairs of your head are all numbered."

Mon. 13.—Even in Epworth a few faithful servants of Satan were left, who would not leave any stone unturned to support his tottering kingdom. A kind of gentleman got a little party together, and took huge pains to disturb the congregation. He hired a company of boys to shout, and made a poor man exceeding drunk, who bawled out much ribaldry and nonsense, while he himself played the French horn. But he had little fruit of his labour. I spoke a few words to their champion, and he disappeared. The congregation was not at all disturbed, but quietly attended to the end.

Wed. 15.—I rode to Doncaster; and at ten, standing in an open place, exhorted a wild, yet civil, multitude to "seek the Lord while He might be found." Thence I went on to Leeds, and declared to a large congregation, "Now is the day of salvation." *Thursday*, 16. At five in the evening I preached at Dewsbury, and on *Friday*, 17, reached Manchester. Here I received a particular account of a remarkable incident:—An eminent drunkard of Congleton used to divert himself, whenever there was preaching there, by standing over against the house, cursing and swearing at the preacher. One evening he had a fancy to step in, and hear what the man had to say. He did so; but it made him so uneasy that he could not sleep all night. In the morning he was more uneasy still: he walked in the fields, but all in vain, till it came in his mind to go to one of his merry companions, who was always ready to abuse the Methodists. He told him how he was, and asked what he should do. "Do!" said Samuel: "go and join the society. I will; for I was never so uneasy in my life." They did so without delay. But presently David cried out, "I am sorry I joined; for I shall get drunk again, and they will turn me out." However, he stood firm for four days: on the fifth, he was persuaded by his old companions to "take one pint," and then another, and another, till one of them said, "See, here is a Methodist drunk!" David started up, and knocked him over, chair and all. He then drove the rest out of the house, caught up the landlady, carried her out, threw her into the kennel; went back to the house, broke down the door, threw it into the street, and then ran into the fields, tore his hair, and rolled up and down on the ground. In a day or two was a love-feast: he stole in, getting behind, that none might see him. While Mr Furze was at prayer, he was seized with a dreadful agony, both of body and mind. This caused many to wrestle with God for him. In a while he sprung up on his feet, stretched out his hands, and cried aloud, "All my sins are forgiven!" At the same instant, one on the other side of the room cried out, "Jesus is mine! And He has taken away all my sins." This was Samuel H. David burst through the people, caught him in his arms, and said, "Come, let us sing the Virgin Mary's song: I never could sing it before. 'My soul doth magnify the Lord, and my spirit doth rejoice in God my Saviour.'" And their following behaviour plainly showed the reality of their profession.

Mon. 20.—I preached at Maxfield about noon. As I had

not been well, and was not quite recovered, our brethren insisted on sending me in a chaise to Burslem. Between four and five I quitted the chaise, and took my horse. Presently after, hearing a cry, I looked back, and saw the chaise upside down (the wheel having violently struck against a stone), and well-nigh dashed in pieces. About seven I preached to a large congregation at Burslem: these poor potters, four years ago, were as wild and ignorant as any of the colliers in Kingswood. Lord, Thou hast power over Thy own clay !

Fri. 24.—I took horse early, and in the afternoon came once more safe to London.

Mon. Aug. 15.—I went in the one-day machine to Bath, where one of our friends from Bristol met me (as I had desired) in the afternoon, and took me thither in a post-chaise.

Thur. 18.—When we came to Brecknock, we found it was the Assize week, so that I could not have the town-hall, as before, the Court being to sit there at the very time when I had appointed to preach: so I preached at Mr James's door ; and all the people behaved as in the presence of God.

Fri. 19.—I preached near the market-place, and afterwards rode over to Trevecka. Howell Harris's house is one of the most elegant places which I have seen in Wales. The little chapel, and all things round about it, are finished in an uncommon taste, and the gardens, orchards, fish-ponds, and mount adjoining, made the place a little paradise. He thanks God for these things, and looks through them. About six-score persons are now in the family, all diligent, all constantly employed, all fearing God, and working righteousness. I preached at ten to a crowded audience, and in the evening at Brecknock again ; but to the poor only : the rich (a very few excepted) were otherwise employed.

Thur. 25.—I was more convinced than ever, that the preaching like an apostle, without joining together those that are awakened, and training them up in the ways of God, is only begetting children for the murderer. How much preaching has there been for these twenty years all over Pembrokeshire ! But no regular societies, no discipline, no order or connection ; and the consequence is, that nine in ten of the once-awakened are now faster asleep than ever.

Sat. 27.—At Swansea I preached at seven to one or two hundred people, many of whom seemed full of good desires. But as there is no society, I expect no deep or lasting work.

A man had need to be all fire, who comes into these parts, where almost every one is cold as ice : yet God is able to warm their hearts, and make rivers run in the dry places.

Sun. 28.—I preached once more in W—— church: but it was hard work.

Thence I rode to Cardiff, and found the society in as ruinous a condition as the castle. The same poison of Mysticism has well-nigh extinguished the last spark of life here also.

Wed. 31.—We reached Bristol in good time.

Sun. Sep. 4.—I preached on the quay, where multitudes attended who would not have come to the other end of the city. In the afternoon I preached near the new square. I find no other way to reach the outcasts of men. And this way God has owned, and does still own, both by the conviction and conversion of sinners.

Wed. 14.—I preached at Bath, on, "Now is the day of salvation."

Sun. 18.—I preached in the morning in Princess Street, to a numerous congregation. On *Monday* evening I gave our brethren a solemn caution, not to "love the world, neither the things of the world." This will be their grand danger: as they are industrious and frugal, they must needs increase in goods. This appears already: in London, Bristol, and most other trading towns, those who are in business have increased in substance seven-fold, some of them twenty, yea, an hundred-fold. What need, then, have these of the strongest warnings, lest they be entangled therein, and perish!

Sat. Oct. 1.—I returned to London, and found our house in ruins, great part of it being taken down, in order to a thorough repair. But as much remained as I wanted: six foot square suffices me by day or by night.

Sun. 2.—All this week I endeavoured to confirm those who had been shaken as to the important doctrine of Christian perfection, either by its wild defenders, or wise opposers, who much avail themselves of that wildness. It must needs be that such offences will come; but "woe unto him by whom the offence cometh!"

Mon. 10.—Taking Hertford in my way, I reached Norwich, and found much of the presence of God in the congregation, both this evening and the next day. On *Friday* evening I read to them all, the rules of the society, adding, "Those who are resolved to keep these rules may continue with us, and those only." I then related what I had done since I came to Norwich first, and what I would do for the time to come; particularly that I would immediately put a stop to preaching in the time of church service. I added, "For many years I have had more trouble with this society, than with half the societies in England put together With God's help, I will try you one year longer; and I hope you will bring forth better fruit."

I learned the particulars of a remarkable occurrence:—On Friday, August 19, a gentleman who was at Lisbon during the great earthquake, walking with his friend near Brighthelmstone, in Sussex, and looking south-west toward the sea, cried out, "God grant the wind may rise; otherwise we shall have an earthquake quickly. Just so the clouds whirled to and fro, and so the sky looked, that day at Lisbon." Presently the wind did rise, and brought an impetuous storm of rain and large hail. Some of the hailstones were larger than hen eggs. It moved in a line about four miles broad, making strange havoc, as it passed quite over the land, till it fell into the river, not far from Sheerness. And wherever it passed it left an hot sulphurous steam, such as almost suffocated those it reached.

Thur. Nov. 3.—I returned to London. *Saturday* 5.—I spent some time with my old friend, John Gambold. Who but Count Zinzendorf could have separated such friends as we were? Shall we never unite again?

Here I stood, and looked back on the late occurrences. Before Thomas Walsh left England, God began that great work which has continued ever since without any considerable intermission. During the whole time, many have been convinced of sin, many justified, and many backsliders healed. But the peculiar work of this season has been, what St Paul calls "the perfecting of the saints." Many persons in London, in Bristol, in York, and in various parts, both of England and Ireland, have experienced so deep and universal a change, as it had not before entered into their hearts to conceive. After a deep conviction of inbred sin, of their total fall from God, they have been so filled with faith and love (and generally in a moment), that sin vanished, and they found from that time, no pride, anger, desire, or unbelief. They could rejoice evermore, pray without ceasing, and in everything give thanks. Now, whether we call this the destruction or suspension of sin, it is a glorious work of God: such a work as, considering both the depth and extent of it, we never saw in these kingdoms before.

It is possible, some who spoke in this manner were mistaken: and it is certain, some have lost what they received. A few (very few, compared to the whole number) first gave way to enthusiasm, then to pride, next to prejudice and offence, and at last separated from their brethren. But, although this laid a huge stumbling-block in the way, still the work of God went on. Nor has it ceased to this day in any of its branches. God still convinces, justifies, sanctifies. We have lost only the dross, the enthusiasm, the prejudice, and offence. The pure gold remains, faith working by love, and, we have ground to believe, increases daily.

Dec. 1.—All the leisure hours I had in this and the following months, during the time I was in London, I spent in reading over our Works with the preachers, considering what objections had been made, and correcting whatever we judged wrong, either in the matter or expression.

Thur. Feb. 2, 1764.—I preached again in the Foundery, which had been repairing for several weeks. It is not only firm and safe (whereas before the main timbers were quite decayed), but clean and decent, and capable of receiving several hundreds more.

Mon. 6.—I opened the new chapel at Wapping, well filled with deeply attentive hearers. *Thursday,* 16. I once more took a serious walk through the tombs in Westminster Abbey. What heaps of unmeaning stone and marble! But there was one tomb which showed common sense; that beautiful figure of Mr Nightingale, endeavouring to screen his lovely wife from Death. Here indeed the marble seems to speak, and the statues appear only not alive.

Fri. 24.—I returned to London. *Wednesday,* 29. I heard *Judith,* an oratorio, performed at the Lock. Some parts of it were exceeding fine; but there are two things in all modern pieces of music, which I could never reconcile to common sense. One is, singing the same words ten times over; the other, singing different words by different persons, at one and the same time. And this, in the most solemn addresses to God, whether by way of prayer or of thanksgiving. This can never be defended by all the musicians in Europe, till reason is quite out of date.

Mon. Mar. 12.—I set out for Bristol. *Friday,* 16. I met several serious clergymen. I have long desired that there might be an open, avowed union between all who preach those fundamental truths, original sin, and justification by faith, producing inward and outward holiness; but all my endeavours have been hitherto ineffectual. God's time is not fully come

Mon. 19.—I set out for the north.

Wed. 21.—After riding about two hours and a half from Evesham, we stopped at a little village. We easily perceived, by the marks he had left, that the man of the house had been beating his wife. I took occasion from thence to speak strongly to her, concerning the hand of God, and His design in all afflictions. It seemed to be a word in season. She appeared to be not only thankful, but deeply affected.

We had an exceeding large congregation at Birmingham, in what was formerly the playhouse. Happy would it be, if all the playhouses in the kingdom were converted to so good an use. After service the mob gathered, and threw some dirt and stones at those who were going out. But it is probable they will soon be calmed, as some of them are in gaol already. A few endeavoured to make a disturbance the next evening during the preaching; but it was lost labour; the congregation would not be diverted from taking earnest heed to the things that were spoken.

Fri. 23.—I rode to Dudley, formerly a den of lions, but now as quiet as Bristol. They had just finished their preaching-house, which was thoroughly filled. I saw no trifler; but many in tears.

Sat. 31.—An odd circumstance occurred during the morning preaching [at Rotherham]. It was well only serious persons were present. An ass walked gravely in at the gate, came up to the door of the house, lifted up his head, and stood stock-still, in a posture of deep attention. Might not "the dumb beast reprove" many who have far less decency, and not much more understanding?

At noon I preached (the room being too small to contain the people) in a yard, near the bridge, in Doncaster. The wind was high and exceeding sharp, and blew all the time on the side of my head. In the afternoon I was seized with a sore throat, almost as soon as I came to Epworth: however, I preached, though with some difficulty; but afterward I could hardly speak.

Mon. April 2.—I had a day of rest.

Hence we rode to Grimsby, once the most dead, now the most lively, place in all the county.

In the evening the mayor and all the gentry of the town were present; and so was our Lord in an uncommon manner.

Thur. 5.—About eleven I preached at Elsham. The two persons who are the most zealous and active here are the steward and gardener of a gentleman, whom the minister persuaded to turn them off unless they would leave "this way." He gave them a week to consider of it; at the end of which they calmly answered, "Sir, we choose rather to want bread here, than to want 'a drop of water' hereafter." He replied, "Then follow your own conscience, so you do my business as well as formerly."

Fri. 6.—I preached at Ferry at nine in the morning, and in the evening; and, about noon, in Sir N. H.'s hall, at Gainsborough. Almost as soon as I began to speak, a cock began to crow over my head; but he was quickly dislodged, and the whole congregation, rich and poor, were quiet and attentive.

Sun. 8.—I set out for Misterton, though the common road was impassable, being all under water; but we found a way to ride round. I preached at eight, and I saw not one inattentive hearer. In our return, my mare rushing violently through a gate, struck my heel against the gatepost, and left me behind her in an instant, laid on my back at full length. She stood still till I rose and mounted again; and neither of us was hurt at all.

Tues. 10.—The wind abating, we took boat at Barton, with two such brutes as I have seldom seen. Their blasphemy, and stupid gross obscenity, were beyond all I ever heard. We first spoke to them mildly; but it had no effect. At length we were constrained to rebuke them sharply; and they kept themselves tolerably within bounds, till we landed at Hull. I preached at five, two hours sooner than was expected: by this means we had tolerable room for the greatest part of them that came; and I believe not many of them came in vain.

Tues. 17.—In consequence of repeated invitations, I rode to Helmsley. When I came, Mr Conyers was not at home; but, his housekeeper faintly asking me, I went in. By the books lying in the window and on the table, I easily perceived how he came to be so cold now, who was so warm a year ago. Not one of ours, either verse or prose, was to be seen, but several of another kind. Oh that our brethren were as zealous to make Christians as they are to make Calvinists!

He came home before dinner, and soon convinced me that the Philistines had been upon him. They had taken huge pains to prejudice him against me, and so successfully, that he did not even ask me to preach: so I had thoughts of going on; but in the afternoon he altered his purpose, and I preached in the evening to a large congregation. He seemed quite surprised; and was convinced, *for the present*, that things had been misrepresented. But how long will the conviction last? Perhaps till next month.

Wed. 18.—I called upon another serious clergyman, vicar of a little town near Pickering. He immediately told me how he had been received by warm men "to doubtful disputations." He said, this had for a time much hurt his soul; but that now the snare was broken.

Sat. 28.—I rode to Newcastle.

Sun. 29.—The ground being wet with heavy rain, I preached in the house both morning and evening. I soon found what spirit the people were of. No jar, no contention is here; but all are peaceably and lovingly striving together for the hope of the gospel. And what can hurt the Methodists, so called, but the Methodists? Only let them not fight one another, let not brother lift up sword against brother, and "no weapon formed against them shall prosper."

Wed. May 9.—I was invited to breakfast by Mr F——, a neighbouring gentleman. I found we had been schoolfellows at the Charter House: and he remembered me, though I forgot him. I spent a very agreeable hour with a serious as well as sensible man.

Fri. 18.—I received much satisfaction in conversing with the most honourable member of our society, Henry Jackson, now in the ninety-fifth or ninety-sixth year of his age. He put me in mind of that venerable man, Mr Eliot, of New England; who frequently used to say to his friends, a few years before he went to God, "My memory is gone; my understanding is gone; but I think I have more love than ever."

Wed. June 27.—I rode to Otley. In the evening we had a large congregation, at the foot of the great mountain. After preaching in the morning, I examined those who believe they are saved from sin.

Mon. July 2.—I gave a fair hearing to two of our brethren who had proved bankrupts. Such we immediately exclude from our society, unless it plainly appears not to be their own fault. Both these were in a prosperous way till they fell into that wretched trade of bill-broking, wherein no man continues long without being wholly ruined. By this means, not being sufficiently accurate in their accounts, they ran back without being sensible of it.

Tues. 3.—I was reflecting on an odd circumstance, which I cannot account for. I never relish a tune at first hearing, not till I have almost learned to sing it; and as I learn it more perfectly, I gradually lose my relish for it. I observe something similar in poetry; yea, in all the objects of imagination. I seldom relish verses at first hearing; till I have heard them over and over, they give me no pleasure; and they give me next to none when I have heard them a few times more, so as to be quite familiar. Just so a face or a picture, which does not strike me at first, becomes more pleasing as I grow more acquainted with it; but only to a certain point: for when I am too much acquainted, it is no longer pleasing. Oh, how imperfectly do we understand even the machine which we carry about us!

Sat. 21.—I rode to Bilbrook, near Wolverhampton, and preached between two and three. Thence we went on to

Madeley, an exceeding pleasant village, encompassed with trees and hills. It was a great comfort to me to converse once more with a Methodist of the old stamp, denying himself, taking up his cross, and resolved to be "altogether a Christian."

Sun. 22.—At ten Mr Fletcher read prayers, and I preached on those words in the gospel, "I am the good Shepherd: the good Shepherd layeth down his life for the sheep." The church would nothing near contain the congregation; but a window near the pulpit being taken down, those who could not come in stood in the churchyard, and I believe all could hear. The congregation, they said, used to be much smaller in the afternoon than in the morning; but I could not discern the least difference, either in number or seriousness.

Fri. 27.—We rode through a lovely vale, and over pleasant and fruitful hills, to Carmarthen. Thence, after a short bait, we went on to Pembroke, and came before I was expected; so I rested that night, having not quite recovered my journey from Shrewsbury to Roes Fair.

Tues. 31.—We set out for Glamorganshire, and rode up and down steep and stony mountains, for about five hours, to Larn. Having procured a pretty ready passage there, we went on to Lansteffan Ferry, where we were in some danger of being swallowed up in the mud before we could reach the water. Between one and two we reached Kidwelly, having been more than seven hours on horseback, in which time we could have rode round by Carmarthen with more ease both to man and beast. I have, therefore, taken my leave of these ferries; considering we save no time by crossing them (not even when we have a ready passage), and so have all the trouble, danger, and expense, clear gains. I wonder that any man of common sense, who has once made the experiment, should ever ride from Pembroke to Swansea any other way than by Carmarthen.

An honest man at Kidwelly told us there was no difficulty in riding the sands; so we rode on. In ten minutes one overtook us who used to guide persons over them; and it was well he did, or, in all probability, we had been swallowed up. The whole sands are at least ten miles over, with many streams of quicksands intermixed. But our guide was thoroughly acquainted with them, and with the road on the other side. By his help, between five and six, we came well tired to Oxwych in Gower.

Gower is a large tract of land, bounded by Brecknockshire on the north-east, the sea on the south-west, and rivers on the other sides. Here all the people talk English, and are in general the most plain, loving people in Wales. It is, therefore, no wonder that they receive "the Word with all readiness of mind."

Knowing they were scattered up and down, I had sent two persons on Sunday, that they might be there early on Monday, and so sent notice of my coming all over the country : but they came to Oxwych scarce a quarter of an hour before me ; so that the poor people had no notice at all : nor was there any to take us in ; the person with whom the preacher used to lodge being three miles out of town. After I had stayed a while in the street (for there was no public-house), a poor woman gave me house room. Having had nothing since breakfast, I was very willing to eat or drink ; but she simply told me, she had nothing in the house but a dram of gin. However, I afterwards procured a dish of tea at another house, and was much refreshed. About seven I preached to a little company, and again in the morning. They were all attention ; so that even for the sake of this handful of people I did not regret my labour.

Sun. Aug. 19.—Meeting with a pious and sensible man, who was born in the Isle of Skye, I said, "Tell me freely, did you yourself ever know a *second-sighted* man ? " He answered, after a little pause, " I have known more than one or two." I said, " But were they not deceivers ? How do you know they were really such ? " He replied, " I have been in company with them, when they dropped down as dead. Coming to themselves, they looked utterly amazed, and said, " I have been in such a place, and I saw such and such persons (perhaps fifty miles off) die in such a manner ' ; and when inquiry was made, I never could find that they were mistaken in one circumstance. But the reason why it is so hard for you to get any information concerning this is, those who have the second sight count it a great misfortune ; and it is thought a scandal to their family."

Mon. 20.—I went to Canterbury, and opened our new chapel, by preaching on, " One thing is needful." How is it that many Protestants, even in England, do not know, that no other consecration of church or chapel is allowed, much less required, in England, than the performance of public worship therein ? This is the only consecration of any church in Great Britain which is necessary, or even lawful. It is true, Archbishop Laud composed a Form of Consecration ; but it was never allowed, much less established, in England. Let this be remembered by all who talk so idly of preaching in unconsecrated places !

Mon. Sept. 24, *Tues.* 25, and *Wed.* 26 I visited the societies in Somersetshire. On the following days I met the classes in Bristol, and narrowly inquired into the character and behaviour of each person; the rather because it had been strongly affirmed that there were many disorderly walkers in the society. I found one woman and one man who, I am afraid, deserved that character. Let anyone that is more clear-sighted than me find two more, and I will thank him.

Sun. 30.—The whole society met in the evening, and jointly renewed their covenant with God, in a form recommended by Mr Richard Alleine; and many felt that God was there. It was a day of His power not to be forgotten—a day both of godly sorrow and strong consolation.

Mon. Oct. 1.—I left Bristol with joy, having seen the fruit of my labour. At noon I preached at Comb Grove to a small congregation of earnest, simple people. I had designed to preach in the evening at Bradford, in the same place I did before; but Mr. R., at whose door I then stood, had now altered his mind: so I was constrained to preach in our own room to (comparatively) an handful of people.

Tues. 2.—I breakfasted at the Devizes, with Mr B——, a black swan, an honest lawyer! Hence we rode through a most intricate road to Pewsey. I found a neighbouring gentleman had been there, moving every stone to prevent my preaching. I was informed, his first design was to raise a mob; then he would have had the churchwardens interpose; whether they intended it or no, I cannot tell; but they neither did nor said anything. The congregation filled a great part of the church, and were all deeply attentive. Surely good will be done in this place, if it be not prevented by a mixture of various doctrines.

Sun. 7.—I preached in the morning at Snowsfields, and afterwards at West Street. We had a glorious opportunity at the Lord's Supper: the rocks were broken in pieces. At five I preached in Moorfields to a huge multitude, on, "Ye are saved through faith." A little before twelve I took the machine for Norwich. *Monday,* 8. We dined at Bury, where a gentlewoman came into the coach, with whom I spent most of the afternoon in close conversation and singing praises to God.

Fri. 12.—I returned to Norwich, and inquired into the state of the society. I have seen no people in all England or Ireland so changeable as this. This society, in 1755, consisted of eighty-three members; two years after, of an hundred and thirty-four; in 1758, it was shrunk to an hundred and ten. In March, 1759, we took the Tabernacle; and within a month the society was increased to above seven hundred and sixty. But nearly five hundred of these had formerly been with James Wheatley, and having been scattered abroad, now ran together they hardly knew why. Few of them were thoroughly awakened; most deeply ignorant; all bullocks unaccustomed to the yoke, having never had any rule or order among them, but every man doing what was right in his own eyes. It was not therefore strange, that the next year, only five hundred and seven of these were left. In 1761 they were further reduced, namely, to four hundred and twelve. I cannot tell how it was, that in 1762 they were increased again to six hundred and thirty. But the moon soon changed, so that in 1763 they were shrunk to three hundred and ten. This large reduction was owing to the withdrawing the sacrament, to which they had been accustomed from the time the Tabernacle was built. They are now sunk to an hundred and seventy-four; and now probably the tide will turn again.

Sun. 14.—At seven I clearly and strongly described the height and depth of Christian holiness: and (what is strange) I could not afterward find that any one person was offended. At ten we had a congregation indeed; I trust, all of one heart. I went, as usual, to the cathedral in the afternoon, and heard a sound, practical sermon. About five our great congregation met, and (what has seldom been known) very quietly. We were equally quiet at the meeting of the society, which met now for the first time on a Sunday evening. So has God stilled the madness of the people. Are not the hearts of all men in His hand?

Mon. 15.—At the request of many, I had given notice of a watch-night. We had but an indifferent prelude: between six and seven the mob gathered in great numbers, made an huge noise, and began to throw large stones against the outward doors. But they had put themselves out of breath before eight, so that when the service begun they were all gone.

Tues. 16.—In the evening the whole congregation seemed not a little moved, while I was enforcing those solemn words, "He died for all, that they which live should not henceforth live unto themselves, but unto Him which died for them, and rose again." The same was observable, and that in a higher and higher degree, the two following evenings. If I could stay here a month, I think there would be a society little inferior to that at Bristol. But it must not be: they who will bear sound doctrine only from me, must still believe a lie.

Sun. Nov. 4.—I proposed to the Leaders, the assisting the Society for the Reformation of Manners with regard to their heavy debt. One of them asked, "Ought we not to pay our own debt first?" After some consultations, it was agreed to attempt it. The general debt of the society in London, occasioned chiefly by repairing the Foundery and chapels, and by building at Wapping and Snowsfields, was about nine hundred pounds. This I laid before the society in the evening, and desired them all to set their shoulders to the work, either by a present contribution, or by subscribing what they could pay, on the 1st of January, February, or March.

Mon. 5.—My scraps of time this week I employed in setting down my present thoughts upon a single life, which, indeed, are just the same they have been these thirty years; and the same they must be, unless I give up my Bible.

Thur. 8.—At ten (and so every morning) I met the preachers that were in town, and read over with them the *Survey of the Wisdom of God in the Creation.* Many pupils I had at the University, and I took some pains with them: but to what effect? What is become of them now? How many of them think either of their tutor or their God? But, blessed be God! I have had some pupils since, who well reward me for my labour. Now "I live"; for "ye stand fast in the Lord."

Monday, 19, and the other afternoons of this week I took up my cross, and went in person to the principal persons in our society, in every part of the town. By this means, within six days, near six hundred pounds were subscribed toward the public debt; and what was done, was done with the utmost cheerfulness. I remember but one exception: only one gentleman squeezed out ten shillings, as so many drops of blood.

Tues. Dec. 4.—I made a little excursion to Colchester. *Saturday*, 8. I saw one who, many years ago, was a "minister of God to us for good," in repressing the madness of the people —Sir John Gonson, who was near fifty years a magistrate, and has lived more than ninety. He is majestic in decay, having few wrinkles, and not stooping at all, though just dropping into the grave, having no strength, and little memory or understanding. Well might that good man, Bishop Stratford, pray, "Lord, let me not live to be useless!" And he had his desire: he was struck with a palsy in the evening, praised God all night, and died in the morning.

Monday, 10, and the three following days, I visited Canterbury, Dover, and Sandwich, and returned to London on *Friday*, 14. In the machine I read Mr Baxter's book upon apparitions. It contains several well attested accounts; but there are some which I cannot subscribe to. How hard is it to keep the middle way; not to believe too little or too much!

Sun. 16.—I buried Mrs Prior, housekeeper to Mr P., who told me, "On —— night, just at one, I rung, and said to my man coming in, 'Mrs Prior is dead. She just now came into my room, and walked round my bed.' About two the nurse came and told me she was dead. I asked at what time she died; and was answered, 'Just at one o'clock.'"

Mon. 31.—I thought it would be worth while to make an odd experiment. Remembering how surprisingly fond of music the lion at Edinburgh was, I determined to try whether this was the case with all animals of the same kind. I accordingly went to the Tower with one who plays on the German flute. He began playing near four or five lions; only one of these (the rest not seeming to regard it at all) rose up, came to the front of his den, and seemed to be all attention. Meantime, a tiger in the same den started up, leaped over the lion's back, turned and ran under his belly, leaped over him again, and so to and fro incessantly. Can we account for this by any principle of mechanism? Can we account for it at all?

Sun. Jan. 20, 1765.—I employed all my leisure hours this week in revising my letters and papers. Abundance of them I committed to the flames. Perhaps some of the rest may see the light when I am gone.

Wed. Feb. 13.—I heard *Ruth*, an oratorio, performed at Mr Madan's chapel. The sense was admirable throughout; and much of the poetry not contemptible. This, joined with exquisite music, might possibly make an impression even upon rich and honourable sinners.

CHAPTER XII

AMONG THE SOCIETIES

FROM AUGUST 14, 1765, TO MAY 5, 1768

Wed. Aug. 14, 1765.—I preached in the evening at Leeds, and the next morning rode to Huddersfield. Mr Venn having given notice on Sunday of my preaching, we had a numerous congregation. We had a warm ride from hence to Manchester; but as my day, so was my strength.

Mon. 19.—I preached in Northwich at ten, and at Manchester in the evening. Our Conference began on *Tuesday*, 20, and ended on *Friday*, 23. On *Tuesday*, 27, I rode on to Stroud, and the next morning to Bristol. After resting three or four days, on *Monday*, September 2, I set out for Cornwall. *Tuesday*, 3. I rode to Tiverton, and in the evening preached near the east end of the town to a large and quiet audience. *Wednesday*, 4. I rode on to North Tawton, a village where several of our preachers had preached occasionally. About six I went to the door of our inn; but I had hardly ended the psalm, when a clergyman came, with two or three (by courtesy of England called) gentlemen. After I had named my text, I said, "There may be some truths which concern some men only; but this concerns all mankind." The minister cried out, "That is false doctrine, that is predestination." Then the roar began, to second which they had brought an huntsman with his hounds: but the dogs were wiser than the men; for they could not bring them to make any noise at all. One of the gentlemen supplied their place. He assured us he was such, or none would have suspected it; for his language was as base, foul, and porterly, as ever was heard at Billingsgate. Dog, rascal, puppy, and the like terms, adorned almost every sentence. Finding there was no probability of a quiet hearing, I left him the field, and withdrew to my lodging.

Mon. 9.—The room would by no means contain the congregation at five in the morning. How is this town [Redruth] changed! Some years since a Methodist preacher could not safely ride through it. Now, high and low, few excepted, say, "Blessed is he that cometh in the name of the Lord."

Wed. 11.—Perceiving my voice began to fail, I resolved to preach, for a while, but twice a day. In the evening I preached in a little ground at Newlyn, to a numerous congregation. None behaved amiss but a young gentleman who seemed to understand nothing of the matter.

Thur. 12.—Coming to St Just, I learned that John Bennets had died some hours before. He was a wise and a good man, who had been above twenty years as a father to that society. A little before his death he examined each of his children concerning their abiding in the faith. Being satisfied of this, he told them, "Now I have no doubt but we shall meet again at the right hand of our Lord." He then cheerfully committed his soul to Him, and fell asleep.

Mon. 16.—We had our quarterly meeting at Redruth; and it appeared, by the accounts from all parts, that the flame which was kindled the last year, though abated, is not extinguished.

Wed. 18.—I set out for Plymouth Dock. The society at the Dock had been for some time in a miserable condition. Disputes had run so high, concerning a worthless man, that every one's sword was set, as it were, against his brother. I showed them how Satan had desired to have them, that he might sift them as wheat; and afterwards told them, that there was but one way to take,—to pass an absolute act of oblivion; not to mention, on any pretence whatever, anything that had been said or done on either side. They fully determined so to do. If they keep that resolution, God will return to them.

About this time the oldest preacher in our connection, Alexander Coats, rested from his labours. A little account of his death, one who was in the house sent me, in these words:—

"NEWCASTLE, *October* 7, 1765.

"I HAD an opportunity, the last evening, of seeing our dear, aged brother Coats. A few days before, he was sore tempted by the enemy; but near the close he had perfect peace. His faith was clear, and he found Christ precious, his portion, and his eternal all. I asked him, a little before he died, if he had 'followed cunningly devised fables.' He answered, 'No, no, no.' I then asked him whether he saw land. He said, 'Yes, I do;' and after waiting a few moments at anchor, he put into the quiet harbour."

Mon. 21.—I went in the coach to Salisbury, and on *Thursday*, 24, came to London. *Monday*, 28. I breakfasted with Mr Whitefield, who seemed to be an old, old man, being fairly worn out in his Master's service, though he has hardly seen fifty years; and yet it pleases God that I, who am now in my sixty-third year, find no disorder, no weakness, no decay, no difference from what I was at five-and-twenty; only that I have fewer teeth, and more grey hairs.

Thur. Nov. 7.—A fire broke out near the corner of Leadenhall Street, which (the wind being exceeding high) soon seized on both the corners of the street, and both the corners of Cornhill, and in a few hours destroyed above threescore houses. Yet no lives were lost. Even Mr Rutland (at whose house it began) and his whole family were preserved; part escaping through the chamber window, part over the top of the house.

Tues. Dec. 3.—I rode to Dover, and found a little company more united together than they have been for many years. Whilst several of them continued to rob the King, we seemed to be ploughing upon the sand; but since they have cut off the right hand, the Word of God sinks deep into their hearts.

Thur. 5.—I rode back to Feversham. Here I was quickly informed that the mob and the magistrates had agreed together to drive Methodism, so called, out of the town. After preaching, I told them what we had been constrained to do by the magistrate at Rolvenden; who perhaps would have been richer, by some hundred pounds, had he never meddled with the Methodists; concluding, " Since we have both God and the law on our side, if we can have peace by fair means, we had much rather; we should be exceeding glad; but if not, we will have peace."

Sat. 7.—I returned to London. *Wednesday,* 11. I had much conversation with Mr D——e, lately a Romish priest. What wonder is it, that we have so many converts to Popery, and so few to Protestantism; when the former are sure to want nothing, and the latter almost sure to starve?

Thur. 12.—I rode over to Leytonstone, and found one truly Christian family: that is, what that at Kingswood should be, and would, if it had such governors. *Friday,* 13. I examined the children, one by one. Several of them did find the love of God. One enjoys it still, and continues to walk humbly and closely with God.

Wed. 18.—Riding through the borough, all my mare's feet flew up, and she fell with my leg under her. A gentleman, stepping out, lifted me up, and helped me into his shop. I was exceeding sick, but was presently relieved by a little hartshorn and water. After resting a few minutes, I took a coach; but when I was cold, found myself much worse; being bruised on my right arm, my breast, my knee, leg, and ankle, which swelled exceedingly. However, I went on to Shoreham; where, by applying treacle twice a day, all the soreness was removed, and I recovered some strength, so as to be able to walk a little on plain ground. The Word of God does at length bear fruit here also. *Saturday*, 21. Being not yet able to ride, I returned in a chariot to London.

Sun. 22.—I was ill able to go through the service at West Street; but God provided for this also. Mr Greaves, being just ordained, came straight to the chapel, and gave me the assistance I wanted.

Thur. 26.—I should have been glad of a few days' rest, but it could not be at this busy season. However, being electrified morning and evening, my lameness mended, though but slowly.

Wed. Jan. 1, 1766.—A large congregation met in the Foundery at four o'clock, and ushered in the new year with the voice of praise and thanksgiving. In the evening we met, as usual, at the church in Spitalfields, to renew our covenant with God. This is always a refreshing season, at which some prisoners are set at liberty.

Fri. 3.—Mr B—— called upon me, now calm and in his right mind. God has repressed his furious, bitter zeal, by means of Mr Whitefield. He (Mr Whitefield) made the first breach among the Methodists: Oh that God may empower him to heal it!

Tues. 28.—Our brethren met together to consider our temporal affairs. One proposed that we should, in the first place, pay off the debt of the society, which was five hundred pounds. Towards this an hundred and seventy were subscribed immediately. At a second meeting this was enlarged to three hundred and twenty. Surely God will supply the rest.

Fri. 31.—Mr Whitefield called upon me. He breathes nothing but peace and love. Bigotry cannot stand before him, but hides its head wherever he comes.

Sun. Feb. 2.—I dined with W. Welsh, the father of the late Society for Reformation of Manners. But that excellent design is at a full stop. They have indeed convicted the wretch who, by wilful perjury, carried the cause against them in Westminster Hall; but they could never recover the expense of that suit. Lord, how long shall the ungodly triumph?

Wed. 5.—One called upon me who had been cheated out of a large fortune, and was now perishing for want of bread. I had a desire to clothe him, and send him back to his own country; but was short of money. However, I appointed him to call again in an hour. He did so; but before he came, one from whom I expected nothing less, put twenty guineas into my hand; so I ordered him to be clothed from head to foot, and sent him straight away to Dublin.

Monday, 10, and the four following days, I wrote a catalogue of the society, now reduced from eight-and-twenty hundred to about two-and-twenty. Such is the fruit of George Bell's enthusiasm, and Thomas Maxfield's gratitude!

Sun. 23.—In the evening I went to Lewisham, and finished the notes on the book of Job.

Thur. Mar. 6.—Our brethren met once more on account of the public debt. And they did not part till more than the whole (which was six hundred and ten pounds) was subscribed.

Sun. 9.—In the evening I went to Knightsbridge; and in the morning took the machine for Bristol. *Wednesday*, 12. I rode over to Kingswood; and, having told my whole mind to the masters and servants, spoke to the children in a far stronger manner than ever I did before. I will kill or cure: I will have one or the other,—a Christian school, or none at all.

Sun. 16.—I preached in Princes Street at eight, on, "Awake, thou that sleepest"; and at the Square in the evening, to a listening multitude, on, "Come, Lord Jesus!" At Kingswood we had such a congregation at ten as has not been there for several years: and I had the satisfaction to find four of our children again rejoicing in the love of God.

Mon. April 7.—I preached at Warrington, about noon, to a large congregation, rich and poor, learned and unlearned. I never spoke more plain; nor have I ever seen a congregation listen with more attention. Thence I rode to Liverpool, and thoroughly regulated the society, which had great need of it.

Thur. 10.—I looked over the wonderful deed which was lately made here; on which I observed: 1. It takes up three large skins of parchment, and so could not cost less than six guineas; whereas our own deed, transcribed by a friend, would not have cost six shillings. 2. It is verbose beyond all sense and reason; and withal so ambiguously worded, that one passage only might find matter for a suit of ten or twelve years in Chancery. 3. It everywhere calls the house a meeting-house, a name which I particularly object to. 4. It leaves no power either to the assistant or me, so much as to place or displace a steward. 5. Neither I, nor all the Conference, have power to send the same preacher two years together. To crown all, 6. If a preacher is not appointed at the Conference, the Trustees and the congregation are to choose one by most votes! And can anyone wonder I dislike this deed, which tears the Methodist discipline up by the roots?

Is it not strange, that any who have the least regard either for me or our discipline, should scruple to alter this uncouth deed?

Fri. 18.—I set out for the eastern part of Lincolnshire, and after preaching at Awkborough and Barrow in the way, came the next day to our old friends at Grimsby. It put me in mind of Purrysburg, in Georgia. It was one of the largest towns in the county: it is no bigger than a middling village, containing a small number of half-starved inhabitants, without any trade, either foreign or domestic. But this they have: they love the gospel, hardly six families excepted.

Mon. 21.—Between nine and ten I began preaching in an open place at Louth. The mob here used to be exceeding boisterous; but none now opened his mouth. How easily, when it seems Him good, does God "still the madness of the people"!

Tues. 22.—I preached to a congregation of a very different kind at Horncastle. John Hill has done more mischief here than a man of far greater talents can do good. By that unhappy division of the society, he has opened the mouths of all the gainsayers; and, to complete the scandal, he and six-and-twenty more have been dipped! "Unstable as water, thou shalt not excel!"

Wed. 23.—I preached at five; in Torrington at nine; and about two at Scotter, where the poor people now enjoy great quietness, by means of Sir N. H. About six I preached at Ferry. I do not choose to preach above twice or thrice in a day; but when I am called to do more, it is all one: I find strength according to my need.

Thur. 24.—I rode to Epworth, and the next day, through heavy rain, to Swinfleet.

Tues. 29.—I preached at noon in the new house at Thirsk, almost equal to that at Yarm: and why not quite, seeing they had the model before their eyes, and had nothing to do but to copy after it? Is it not an amazing weakness, that when they have the most beautiful pattern before them, all builders will affect to mend something? So the *je ne sçai quoi* is lost, and the second building scarce ever equals the first.

I preached at Yarm in the evening, and the next at Newcastle. I know not to what it is owing, that I have felt more weariness this spring, than I had done before for many years; unless to my fall at Christmas, which perhaps weakened the springs of my whole machine more than I was sensible of.

Thur. May 1.—I enjoyed a little rest. I do not find the least change in this respect. I love quietness and silence as well as ever; but if I am called into noise and tumult, all is well.

Sat. 24.—In the afternoon, notice having been given a week before, I went to the room at Prestonpans. And I had it all to myself; neither man, woman, nor child offered to look me in the face: so I ordered a chair to be placed in the street. Then forty or fifty crept together: but they were mere stocks and stones; no more concerned than if I had talked Greek. In the evening I preached in the new room at Edinburgh, a large and commodious building.

Mon. 26.—I spent some hours at the meeting of the National Assembly. I am very far from being of Mr Whitefield's mind, who greatly commends the solemnity of this meeting. I have seen few less solemn: I was extremely shocked at the behaviour of many of the members. Had any preacher behaved so at our Conference, he would have had no more place among us.

Mon. June 2.—I came to Dundee, wet enough. *Thursday*, 5. It being fair, we had a more numerous congregation than ever; to whom, after preaching, I took occasion to repeat most of the plausible objections which had been made to us in Scotland.

The sum of what I spoke was this:—

"I love plain dealing. Do not you? I will use it now. Bear with me.

"I hang out no false colours; but show you all I am, all I intend, all I do.

"I am a member of the Church of England; but I love good men of every church.

"My ground is the Bible. Yea, I am a Bible-bigot. I follow it in all things, both great and small.

"Therefore, 1. I always use a short private prayer, when I attend the public service of God. Do not you? Why do you not? Is not this according to the Bible?

"2. I stand, whenever I sing the praise of God in public. Does not the Bible give you plain precedents for this?

"3. I always kneel before the Lord my Maker, when I pray in public.

"4. I generally in public use the Lord's Prayer, because Christ has taught me, when I pray, to say,—.

"I advise every preacher connected with me, whether in England or Scotland, herein to tread in my steps."

Fri. 6.—We went on to Aberdeen, about seventy measured miles.

Sun. 8.—Knowing no reason why we should make God's day the shortest of the seven, I desired Joseph Thompson to preach at five. At eight I preached myself. In the afternoon

I heard a strong, close sermon, at Old Aberdeen ; and afterward preached in the College Kirk, to a very genteel, and yet serious, congregation. I then opened and enforced the way of holiness, at New Aberdeen, on a numerous congregation. *Monday*, 9. I kept a watch-night, and explained to abundance of genteel people, " One thing is needful " ; a great number of whom would not go away, till after the noon of night.

It is scarce possible to speak too plain in England ; but it is scarce possible to speak plain enough in Scotland. And if you do not, you lose all your labour, you plough upon the sand.

Mon. 16.—I took a view of one of the greatest natural curiosities in the kingdom : what is called Arthur's Seat, a small, rocky eminence, six or seven yards across, on the top of an exceeding high mountain, not far from Edinburgh. The prospect from the top of the Castle is large, but it is nothing in comparison of this. *Tuesday*, 17. I can now leave Edinburgh with comfort ; for I have fully delivered my own soul.

Wed. 18.—I set out for Glasgow. In the afternoon the rain poured down, so that we were glad to take shelter in a little house, where I soon began to talk with our host's daughter, eighteen or nineteen years old. But, to my surprise, I found her as ignorant of the nature of religion as an Hottentot. And many such I found in Scotland ; able to read, nay, and repeat the Catechism, but wholly unacquainted with true religion, yea, and all genuine morality.

Sun. 22.—At seven I was obliged to preach abroad. In the afternoon Mr Gillies was unusually close and convincing. At five I preached. In the close I enlarged upon their prejudices, and explained myself with regard to most of them. Shame, concern, and a mixture of various passions, were painted on most faces ; and I perceived the Scots, if you touch but the right key, receive as lively impressions as the English.

Mon. 23.—We rode in a mild, cool day, to Thornyhill, about sixty (measured) miles from Glasgow. Here I met with Mr Knox's *History of the Church of Scotland.* And could any man wonder, if the members of it were more fierce, sour, and bitter of spirit, than some of them are ! For what a pattern have they before them ! I know it is commonly said, " The work to be done needed such a spirit." Not so : the work of God does not, cannot need the work of the devil to forward it. And a calm, even spirit goes through rough work far better than a furious one. Although, therefore, God did use, at the time of the Reformation, some sour, overbearing, passionate men, yet He did not use them because they were such, but notwithstanding they were so. And there is no doubt, He would have used them much more, had they been of an humbler and milder spirit.

Tues. 24.—Before eight we reached Dumfries, and after a short bait pushed on in hopes of reaching Solway Frith before the sea was come in. Designing to call at an inn by the frith side, we inquired the way, and were directed to leave the main road, and go straight to the house which we saw before us. In ten minutes Duncan Wright was embogged: however, the horse plunged on, and got through. I was inclined to turn back; but Duncan telling me I needed only go a little to the left, I did so, and sunk at once to my horse's shoulders. He sprang up twice, and twice sunk again, each time deeper than before. At the third plunge he threw me on one side, and we both made shift to scramble out. I was covered with fine, soft mud, from my feet to the crown of my head; yet, blessed be God, not hurt at all. But we could not cross till between seven and eight o'clock. An honest man crossed with us, who went two miles out of his way to guide us over the sands to Skilburness; where we found a little, clean house, and passed a comfortable night.

Wed. 25.—We rode on to Whitehaven. Here I spent the rest of the week. *Sunday*, 29. I appointed the children to meet me; and desired Mr Atlay to meet them for the time to come.

Mon. 30.—About two we reached Penrith. Two of our friends guided us thence to Appleby, a county-town worthy of Ireland, containing, at least, five-and-twenty houses.

Wed. July 16.—About ten I reached Middleton, near Pickering. The church was pretty well filled.

In the evening most of the congregation at Malton were of another kind; but a whole troop of the Oxford Blues, who stood together, and were deeply serious, kept them in awe: so that all behaved decently, and many of the soldiers were present again in the morning.

Thur. 17.—In the way to Beverley, I called upon Sir Charles Hotham, and spent a comfortable hour.

Sat. 19.—I took a view of Beverley Minster, such a parish church as has scarce its fellow in England. It is a most beautiful as well as stately building, both within and without, and is kept more nicely clean than any cathedral which I have seen in the kingdom. About one I preached at Pocklington (though my strength was much exhausted), and in the evening at York.

Sun. 20.—After preaching at eight, I went to St Saviour Gate church. Towards the close of the prayers the rector sent the sexton to tell me the pulpit was at my service. I preached on the conclusion of the gospel for the day.

Sun. 27.—As Baildon church would not near contain the congregation, after the prayers were ended, I came out into the churchyard, both morning and afternoon. At Bradford there was so huge a multitude, and the rain so damped my voice, that many in the skirts of the congregation could not hear distinctly. They have just built a preaching-house, fifty-four feet square, the largest octagon we have in England; and it is the first of the kind where the roof is built with common sense, rising only a third of its breadth; yet it is as firm as any in England; nor does it at all hurt the walls. Why then does any roof rise higher? Only through want of skill, or want of honesty, in the builder.

Tues. 29.—In the evening I preached near the preaching-house at Padiham. At the close of the sermon came Mr M. His long white beard showed that his present disorder was of some continuance. In all other respects, he was quite sensible; but he told me, with much concern, "You can have no place in heaven without—a beard! Therefore, I beg, let yours grow immediately."

Wed. 30.—I rode to Rosendale; which, notwithstanding its name, is little else than a chain of mountains. *Thursday,* 31. I preached at Bacup, and then rode on to Heptonstall. The tall mountain on which it stands is quite steep and abrupt, only where the roads are made; and the deep valleys that surround it, as well as the sides of the mountains beyond, are well clothed with grass, corn, and trees. I preached with great enlargement of heart, on, "Now is the day of salvation." The renegade Methodists, first turning Calvinists, then Anabaptists, made much confusion here for a season; but as they now have taken themselves away, the poor people are in peace again.

Fri. Aug. 1.—I rode to Ewood. The last time I was here, young Mr Grimshaw received us in the same hearty manner as his father used to do; but he too is now gone into eternity! So in a few years the family is extinct! I preached at one in the meadow near the house to a numerous congregation; and we sang with one heart—

> "Let sickness blast and death devour,
>   If heaven will recompense our pains;
> Perish the grass and fade the flower,
>   Since firm the Word of God remains."

Sun. 3.—When the prayers at Haworth were ended, I preached from a little scaffold on the south side of the church, on those words in the Gospel, "Oh that thou hadst known the things that belong unto thy peace!" The communicants alone (a sight which has not been seen since Mr Grimshaw's death) filled the church.

Sun. 10.—About one I preached at Daw Green. I judged the congregation, closely wedged together, to extend forty yards one way, and about an hundred the other. Now, suppose five to stand in a yard square, they would amount to twenty thousand people. I began preaching at Leeds, between five and six, to just such another congregation. This was the hardest day's work I have had since I left London; being obliged to speak, at each place, from the beginning to the end, to the utmost extent of my voice. But my strength was as my day.

Tues. 12.—Our Conference began, and ended on Friday evening. An happier Conference we never had, nor a more profitable one.

Wed. 20.—Reached London.

It was at the earnest request of ———, whose heart God has turned again, without any expectation of mine, that I came hither so suddenly: and if no other good result from it but our firm union with Mr Whitefield, it is an abundant recompense for my labour. My brother and I conferred with him every day; and, let the honourable men do what they please, we resolved, by the grace of God, to go on, hand in hand, through honour and dishonour.

Mon. 25.—We reached Bath on *Tuesday*, in the afternoon. Many were not a little surprised, in the evening, at seeing me in the Countess of H.'s chapel.

Wed. 27.—I rode to Bristol, and the next day delivered the management of Kingswood House to stewards on whom I could depend. So I have cast an heavy load off my shoulders. Blessed be God for able and faithful men, who will do His work without any temporal reward!

Sat. 30.—We rode to Stallbridge, long the seat of war, by a senseless, insolent mob, encouraged by their betters, so called, to outrage their quiet neighbours. For what? Why, they were mad: they were Methodists. So, to bring them to their senses, they would beat their brains out. They broke their windows, leaving not one whole pane of glass, spoiled their goods, and assaulted their persons with dirt, and rotten eggs, and stones, whenever they appeared in the street. But no magistrate, though they applied to several, would show them either mercy or justice. At length they wrote to me. I ordered a lawyer to write to the rioters. He did so; but they set him at nought. We then moved the Court of King's Bench. By various artifices, they got the trial put off, from one Assizes to another, for eighteen months. But it fell so much the heavier on themselves, when they were found guilty; and, from that time, finding there is law for Methodists, they have suffered them to be at peace.

I preached near the main street, without the least disturbance, to a large and attentive congregation.

Mon. Sept. 1.—I came to Plymouth Dock, where, after heavy storms, there is now a calm.

Thur. 4.—At noon I preached in Truro. I was in hopes, when Mr Walker died, the enmity in those who were called his people would have died also. But it is not so: they still look upon us as rank heretics, and will have no fellowship with us.

Fri. 5.—I preached near Helstone, to an exceeding large and serious congregation. What a surprising change is wrought here also, within a few years, where a Methodist preacher could hardly go through the street without a shower of stones!

Fri. 12.—I rode to St Hilary, and in the evening preached near the new house, on, "Awake, thou that sleepest." In returning to my lodging, it being dark, my horse was just stepping into a tin-pit, when an honest man caught him by the bridle, and turned his head the other way.

Thur. 18.—I rode to Collumpton, preached at six, and then went on to Tiverton. *Friday,* 19, came a messenger from Jo. Magor, dangerously ill at Sidmouth, four or five and twenty miles off, to tell me he could not die in peace till he had seen me. So the next morning, after preaching, I set out, spent an hour with him, by which he was exceedingly refreshed, and returned to Tiverton time enough to rest a little before the evening preaching.

Tues. 23.—At eleven I preached to a large and serious congregation at Lymsham Green. When I concluded, a clergyman began to entertain the people with a dispute concerning lay-preachers. In the instant began a violent shower; so they left him to himself. But it was fair again in the afternoon, and we had a pleasant ride to Bristol.

Sun. Oct. 5.—At eight I administered the sacrament at Lady H.'s chapel in Bath.

Several evenings this week I preached at Bristol on the education of children. Some answered all by that poor, lame, miserable shift, "Oh, he has no children of his own!" But many of a nobler spirit, owned the truth, and pleaded guilty before God.

Thur. 9.—I waited on the good old Bishop of Londonderry, and spent two or three hours in useful conversation.

Fri. 31.—At my return to London, I found it needful to hasten to Leytonstone; but I came too late. Miss Lewen died the day before, after an illness of five days. Some hours before, she witnessed that good confession—

> "Nature's last agony is o'er,
> And cruel sin subsists no more."

A while after, she cried out earnestly, "Do you not see Him? There He is! Glory! glory! glory! I shall be with Him for ever—for ever—for ever!"

So died Margaret Lewen! a pattern to all young women of fortune in England: a real Bible Christian. So she "rests from her labours, and her works do follow her."

Sat. Nov. 1.—"God, who hath knit together His elect in one communion and fellowship," gave us a solemn season at West Street (as usual) in praising Him for all His saints. On this day in particular, I commonly find the truth of these words:—

> "The church triumphant in His love,
> Their mighty joys we know:
> They praise the Lamb in hymns above,
> And we in hymns below."

Sun. Jan. 11, 1767.—I made a push for the lending-stock; speaking more strongly than ever I had done before. The effect was, that it was raised from about fifty, to one hundred and twenty pounds.

Wed. 21.—I had a conversation with an ingenious man, who proved to a demonstration, that it was the duty of every man that could, to be "clothed in purple and fine linen," and to "fare sumptuously every day"; and that he would do abundantly more good hereby than he could do by "feeding the hungry and clothing the naked." Oh the depth of human understanding! What may not a man believe if he will?

Thur. Aug. 6.—I reached Newcastle. *Saturday,* 8. At the request of Mr Whitaker, of New England, I preached, and afterwards made a collection for the Indian schools in America. A large sum of money is now collected; but will money convert heathens? Find preachers of David Brainerd's spirit, and nothing can stand before them; but without this, what will gold or silver do? No more than lead or iron. They have indeed sent thousands to hell; but never yet brought a soul to heaven.

Wed. 12.—I took coach. The next day we reached Grantham, and London about seven on *Friday* evening; having run, that day, an hundred and ten miles. On the road

I read over Seller's *History of Palmyra*, and Norden's *Travels into Egypt and Abyssinia*; two as dry and unsatisfying books as ever I read in my life.

Tues. 18.—I met in conference with our assistants and a select number of preachers. To these were added, on *Thursday* and *Friday*, Mr Whitefield, Howell Harris, and many stewards and local preachers. Love and harmony reigned from the beginning to the end; but we have all need of more love and holiness; and, in order thereto, of crying continually, " Lord, increase our faith !"

Wed. Sept. 2.—Upon inquiry, I found the work of God in Pembrokeshire had been exceedingly hindered, chiefly by Mr Davies's preachers, who had continually inveighed against ours, and thereby frightened abundance of people from hearing, or coming near them. This had sometimes provoked them to retort, which always made a bad matter worse. The advice, therefore, which I gave them was: 1. Let all the people sacredly abstain from backbiting, tale-bearing, evil-speaking. 2. Let all our preachers abstain from returning railing for railing, either in public or in private; as well as from disputing. 3. Let them never preach controversy, but plain, practical, and experimental religion.

Fri. 25.—I was desired to preach at Freshford; but the people durst not come to the house, because of the smallpox, of which Joseph Allan, " an Israelite indeed," had died the day before. So they placed a table near the churchyard. But I had no sooner begun to speak, than the bells began to ring, by the procurement of a neighbouring gentleman. However, it was labour lost; for my voice prevailed, and the people heard me distinctly: nay, a person extremely deaf, who had not been able to hear a sermon for several years, told his neighbours, with great joy, that he had heard and understood all, from the beginning to the end.

Sat. 26.—I was informed, between twelve and one, that Mrs B[lackwell] was dying. Judging I had no time to lose, about one I left Bristol, and about seven on *Sunday* morning came to London. Learning there that she was better, I stayed to preach and administer the sacrament at the chapel, and then hastened on, and spent a solemn and profitable hour at Lewisham. I preached again at West Street chapel in the afternoon, and made a collection for the poor, as I had done in the morning. Soon after I took chaise again, and on *Monday*, about noon, came to Bristol.

Wed. 30.—I preached to a large and very serious congregation on Redcliff Hill. This is the way to overturn Satan's kingdom. In field-preaching, more than any other means, God is found of them that sought Him not. By this, death, heaven, and hell, come to the ears, if not the hearts, of them that "care for none of these things."

Fri. Nov. 20.—I preached to the condemned felons in Newgate, on, "To-day shalt thou be with Me in paradise." All of them were struck, and melted into tears: who knows but some of them may "reap in joy"?

In the evening I preached at Leytonstone. How good would it be for me to be here, not twice in a year, but in a month! So it appears to me: but God is wiser than man. When it is really best, will He not bring it to pass?

Mon. 23.—I went to Canterbury. Here I met with the *Life of Mahomet*, wrote, I suppose, by the Count de Boulanvilliers. Whoever the author is, he is a very pert, shallow, self-conceited coxcomb, remarkable for nothing but his immense assurance and thorough contempt of Christianity. And the book is a dull, ill-digested romance, supported by no authorities at all; whereas Dean Prideaux (a writer of ten times his sense) cites his authorities for everything he advances.

Every evening this week I preached at Norwich, to a quiet, well-behaved congregation. Our friends, the mob, seem to have taken their leave; and so have triflers: all that remain seem to be deeply serious. But how easily are even these turned out of the way! One of our old members, about a year ago, left the society, and never heard the preaching since, because Mr Lincoln said, "Mr Wesley and all his followers would go to hell together!" However, on *Tuesday* night he ventured to the house once more; and God met him there, and revealed His Son in his heart.

I had appointed to be at Sheerness on *Wednesday*, December 16th. Accordingly, I took horse between five and six, and came thither between five and six in the evening. At half an hour after six, I began reading prayers (the Governor of the fort having given me the use of the chapel), and afterwards preached.

Such a town as many of these live in is scarce to be found again in England. In the dock adjoining to the fort there are six old men-of-war. These are divided into small tenements, forty, fifty, or sixty in a ship, with little chimneys and windows; and each of these contains a family. In one of them, where we called, a man and his wife, and six little children lived. And yet all the ship was sweet and tolerably clean; sweeter than most sailing ships I have been in. *Saturday*, 19. I returned to London.

J.W.J.—22

Mon. Jan. 4, 1768.—At my leisure hours this week, I read Dr Priestley's ingenious book on Electricity. He seems to have accurately collected and well digested all that is known on that curious subject. But how little is that all ! Indeed the use of it we know; at least, in some good degree. We know it is a thousand medicines in one : in particular, that it is the most efficacious medicine in nervous disorders of every kind, which has ever yet been discovered. But if we aim at theory, we know nothing. We are soon—

"Lost and bewildered in the fruitless search."

Mon. 11.—This week I spent my scraps of time in reading Mr Wodrow's *History of the Sufferings of the Church of Scotland*. It would transcend belief, but that the vouchers are too authentic to admit of any exception. Oh what a blessed Governor was that good-natured man, so called, King Charles the Second ! Bloody Queen Mary was a lamb, a mere dove, in comparison of him !

Mon. Feb. 8.—I met with a surprising poem, entitled, " Choheleth ; or, the Preacher." It is a paraphrase, in tolerable verse, on the Book of Ecclesiastes. I really think the author of it (a Turkey merchant), understands both the difficult expressions, and the connection of the whole, better than any other either ancient or modern writer whom I have seen. He was at Lisbon during the great earthquake, just then sitting in his night-gown and slippers. Before he could dress himself, part of the house he was in fell, and blocked him up. By this means his life was saved ; for all who had run out were dashed in pieces by the falling houses.

Thur. 18.—Having been importunately pressed thereto, I rode (through a keen east wind) to Chatham. About six in the evening I preached at the barracks, in what they call the church. It is a large room, in which the chaplain reads prayers, and preaches now and then. It was soon as hot as an oven, through the multitude of people ; some hundreds of whom were soldiers : and they were "all ear," as Mr Boston says, scarce allowing themselves to breathe. Even between five and six the next morning the room was warm enough. I suppose upwards of two hundred soldiers were a part of the audience. Many of these are already warring a good warfare, knowing in whom they have believed.

Mon. Mar. 14.—I set out on my northern journey. *Tuesday*, 15. About noon I preached at Painswick, and in the evening at Gloucester. The mob here was for a considerable time both noisy and mischievous. But an honest magistrate, taking the

matter in hand quickly, tamed the beasts of the people. So
may any magistrate, if he will; so that wherever a mob continues any time, all they do is to be imputed not so much to the
rabble as to the justices.

Wed. 16.—About nine I preached at Cheltenham,—a quiet,
comfortable place; though it would not have been so, if either
the rector or the Anabaptist minister could have prevented it.
Both these have blown the trumpet with their might; but the
people had no ears to hear. The difficulty [at Worcester] was,
where to preach. No room was large enough to contain the
people; and it was too cold for them to stand abroad. At length
we went to a friend's, near the town, whose barn was larger
than many churches. Nothing is wanting here but a commodious house: and will not God provide this also?

Fri. 18.—The vicar of Pebworth had given notice in the
church on Sunday, that I was to preach there on Friday. But
the squire of the parish said, "It is contrary to the canons"
(wise squire!), "and it shall not be." So I preached about a
mile from it, at Broadmarston, by the side of Mr Eden's house.

Sat. 19.—We rode to Birmingham. The tumults which
subsisted here so many years are now wholly suppressed by a
resolute magistrate. After preaching, I was pleased to see a
venerable monument of antiquity, George Bridgins, in the one
hundred and seventh year of his age. He can still walk to
the preaching, and retains his senses and understanding
tolerably well.

Tues. 22.—I read over a small book, *Poems*, by Miss
Whately, a farmer's daughter. She had little advantage from
education, but an astonishing genius. Some of her elegies I
think quite equal to Mr Gray's. If she had had proper helps
for a few years, I question whether she would not have excelled
any female poet that ever yet appeared in England.

Mon. 28.—I met the stewards of the several societies at
Manchester. The times of outward distress are now over: God
has given us plenty of all things.

Wed. 30.—I rode to a little town called New Mills, in the
High Peak of Derbyshire. I preached at noon in their large
new chapel, which (in consideration that preaching-houses have
need of air) has a casement in every window, three inches
square! That is the custom of the country!

Sun. May 1.—I preached in the new room [Aberdeen]; in
the afternoon at the College Kirk, in Old Aberdeen. At six,
knowing our house could not contain the congregation, I
preached in the Castle Gate, on the paved stones. A large
number of people were all attention; but there were many rude,

stupid creatures round about them, who knew as little of reason as of religion; I never saw such brutes in Scotland before. One of them threw a potato, which fell on my arm: I turned to them; and some were ashamed.

Mon. 2.—I set out early from Aberdeen, and about noon preached in Brechin. After sermon, the provost desired to see me, and said, "Sir, my son had epileptic fits from his infancy: Dr Ogylvie prescribed for him many times, and at length told me he could do no more. I desired Mr Blair last Monday to speak to you. On Tuesday morning my son said to his mother, he had just been dreaming that his fits were gone, and he was perfectly well. Soon after I gave him the drops you advised: he is perfectly well, and has not had one fit since." In the evening I preached to a large congregation at Dundee. They heard attentively, but seemed to feel nothing. The next evening I spoke more strongly, and to their hearts rather than their understanding; and I believe a few felt the Word of God sharp as a two-edged sword.

Thur. 5.—We rode through the pleasant and fruitful Carse of Gowry, a plain, fifteen or sixteen miles long, between the river Tay and the mountains, very thick inhabited, to Perth. In the afternoon we walked over to the royal palace at Scone. It is a large old house, delightfully situated, but swiftly running to ruin. Yet there are a few good pictures, and some fine tapestry left, in what they call the Queen's and the King's chambers. And what is far more curious, there is a bed and a set of hangings, in the (once) royal apartment, which was wrought by poor Queen Mary, while she was imprisoned in the castle of Lochleven. It is some of the finest needlework I ever saw, and plainly shows both her exquisite skill and unwearied industry.

CHAPTER XIII

REAPING THE HARVEST

FROM MAY 14, 1768, TO JULY 31, 1770

Saturday, May 14, 1768.—I walked once more through Holyrood House, a noble pile of building: but the greatest part of it left to itself, and so (like the palace at Scone) swiftly running to ruin. The tapestry is dirty, and quite faded; the fine ceilings dropping down; and many of the pictures in the gallery torn or cut through. This was the work of good General Hawley's soldiers (like General, like men!), who, after running away from the Scots at Falkirk, revenged themselves on the harmless canvas!

Sun. 15.—At eight I preached in the High School yard; and I believe not a few of the hearers were cut to the heart. Between twelve and one a far larger congregation assembled on the Castle Hill; and I believe my voice commanded them all, while I opened and enforced those awful words, " I saw the dead, small and great, stand before God." In the evening our house was sufficiently crowded, even with the rich and honourable.

Mon. 16.—I preached in the evening at Dunbar, near the shore, to an unusually large congregation.

Fri. 20.—I went on in reading that fine book, Bishop Butler's *Analogy*. But I doubt it is too hard for most of those for whom it is chiefly intended. Freethinkers, so called, are seldom close thinkers. They will not be at the pains of reading such a book at this. One that would profit them must dilute his sense, or they will neither swallow nor digest it.

It is true that the English in general, and indeed most of the men of learning in Europe, have given up all accounts of witches and apparitions, as mere old wives' fables. I am sorry for it; and I willingly take this opportunity of entering my solemn protest against this violent compliment which so many that believe the Bible pay to those who do not believe it. I owe them no such service. I take knowledge, these are at the bottom of the outcry which has been raised, and with such insolence spread throughout the nation, in direct opposition not only to the Bible but to the suffrage of the wisest and best of men in all ages and nations.

Wed. June 1.—I preached in Teesdale. The sun was scorching hot when I began, but was soon covered with clouds. Many of the militia were present at Barnard Castle in the evening, and behaved with decency. I was well pleased to lodge at a gentleman's, an old schoolfellow, half a mile from the town. What a dream are the fifty or sixty years that have slipped away since we were at the Charter House!

Thur. 2.—I preached, at noon, at a farmer's house, near Brough, in Westmoreland. The sun was hot enough, but some shady trees covered both me and most of the congregation. A little bird perched on one of them, and sung, without intermission, from the beginning of the service unto the end.

Fri. 3.—I rode to Richmond, intending to preach near the house of one of our friends; but some of the chief of the town sent to desire me to preach in the market-place. The Yorkshire militia were all there, just returned from their exercise: and a more rude rabble-rout I never saw; without sense, decency, or good manners.

In running down one of the mountains yesterday, I had got a sprain in my thigh: it was rather worse to-day; but as I rode to Barnard Castle, the sun shone so hot upon it, that, before I came to the town, it was quite well. In the evening the commanding officer gave orders there should be no exercise, that all the Durham militia (what a contrast!) might be at liberty to attend the preaching. Accordingly, we had a little army of officers as well as soldiers; and all behaved well. A large number of them were present at five in the morning. I have not found so deep and lively a work in any other part of the kingdom, as runs through the whole Circuit, particularly in the vales that wind between these horrid mountains. I returned to Newcastle in the evening.

Sat. Aug. 13.—We reached Bristol between eleven and twelve.

Sun. 14.—Hearing my wife was dangerously ill, I took chaise immediately, and reached the Foundery before one in the morning. Finding the fever was turned, and the danger over, about two I set out again, and in the afternoon came (not at all tired) to Bristol.

Our Conference began on *Tuesday*, 16, and ended on *Friday*, 19. Oh, what can we do for more labourers? We can only cry to "the Lord of the harvest."

Mon. 22.—I rode through impetuous rain to Weston, a village near Bridgewater. A while ago the people here were lions; but now they are become lambs.

Mon. 29.—I rode to St Columb, intending to preach there but finding no place that was tolerably convenient, I was going to take horse, when one offered me the use of his meadow close to the town.

Tues. 30.—At Redruth I found the people gathered from all parts; and God gave a loud call to the backsliders. Indeed there was need; for T. Rankin left between three and four hundred members in the society, and I found an hundred and ten!

Wed. 31.—I met the children, a work which will exercise the talents of the most able preachers in England.

Fri. Sept. 2.—I preached at noon to an earnest company at Zennor, and in the evening to a far larger at St Just. Here being informed that one of our sisters in the next parish, Morva, who entertained the preachers formerly, was now decrepit, and had not heard a sermon for many years, I went on *Saturday*, 3, at noon, to Alice Daniel's, and preached near the house, on, "They who shall be accounted worthy to obtain that world, and the resurrection from the dead, are equal unto the angels, and are the children of God, being the children of the resurrection." I have always thought there is something venerable in persons worn out with age; especially when they retain their understanding, and walk in the ways of God.

Fri. 16.—I rode, through heavy rain, to Polperro. Here the room over which we were to lodge being filled with pilchards and conger-eels, the perfume was too potent for me; so that I was not sorry when one of our friends invited me to lodge at her house. Soon after I began to preach, heavy rain began; yet none went away till the whole service was ended.

Sat. 17.—When we came to Crimble Passage, we were at a full stop. The boatmen told us the storm was so high, that it was not possible to pass: however, at length we persuaded them to venture out; and we did not ship one sea till we got over.

Sun. 18.—Between one and two I began preaching on the quay in Plymouth. Notwithstanding the rain, abundance of people stood to hear. But one silly man talked without ceasing, till I desired the people to open to the right and left, and let me look him in the face. They did so. He pulled off his hat, and quietly went away.

Sat. Oct. 22.—I was much surprised in reading an *Essay on Music*, wrote by one who is a thorough master of the subject, to find that the music of the ancients was as simple as that of the Methodists; that their music wholly consisted of melody, or the arrangement of single notes; that what is now called harmony, singing in parts, the whole of counterpoint and fugues, is quite novel, being never known in the world till the popedom of Leo the Tenth. He further observes, that as the singing different words by different persons at the very same time necessarily prevents attention to the sense, so it frequently destroys melody for the sake of harmony ; meantime it destroys the very end of music, which is to affect the passions.

Fri. 28.—I returned to London.

Wed. Nov. 30.—I rode to Dover, and came in just before a violent storm began. It did not hinder the people. Many were obliged to go away after the house was filled. What a desire to hear runs through all the seaport towns wherever we come ! Surely God is besieging this nation, and attacking it at all the entrances !

Thur. Dec. 1.—I made an odd observation here, which I recommend to all our preachers. The people of Canterbury have been so often reproved (and frequently without a cause), for being dead and cold, that it has utterly discouraged them, and made them cold as stones. How delicate a thing is it to reprove ! To do it well requires more than human wisdom.

Wed. 14.—I saw the Westminster scholars act the *Adelphi* of Terence ; an entertainment not unworthy of a Christian. Oh how do these heathens shame us ! Their very comedies contain both excellent sense, the liveliest pictures of men and manners, and so fine strokes of genuine morality, as are seldom found in the writings of Christians.

In the latter end of the month I took some pains in reading over Dr Young's *Night Thoughts*, leaving out the indifferent lines, correcting many of the rest, and explaining the hard words, in order to make that noble work more useful to all, and more intelligible to ordinary readers.

Mon. Jan. 9, 1769.—I spent a comfortable and profitable hour with Mr Whitefield, in calling to mind the former times, and the manner wherein God prepared us for a work which it had not then entered into our hearts to conceive.

Mon. Feb. 6.—I spent an hour with a venerable woman, near ninety years of age, who retains her health, her senses, her understanding, and even her memory, to a good degree. In the last century she belonged to my grandfather Annesley's congregation, at whose house her father and she used to dine every Thursday; and whom she remembers to have frequently seen in his study, at the top of the house, with his window open, and without any fire, winter or summer. He lived seventy-seven years, and would probably have lived longer, had he not began water-drinking at seventy.

Mon. 27.—I had one more agreeable conversation with my

old friend and fellow-labourer, George Whitefield. His soul appeared to be vigorous still, but his body was sinking apace ; and unless God interposes with His mighty hand, he must soon finish his labours.

Sun. Mar. 5.—After preaching at Spitalfields in the morning, and at West Street in the afternoon, I went to Brentford ; on *Monday*, to Hungerford ; and the next day, to Bath. On the road, I read over Dr Campbell's excellent answer to David Hume's insolent book against miracles ; and Dr Brown's keen *Animadversions of the Characteristics of Lord Shaftesbury*,— another lively, half-thinking writer.

Wed. 8.—I preached at Bristol, and met the society. The next three days I examined them, as usual, one by one.

Mon. 13.—I set out northward.

Tues. 14.—After preaching to a large congregation at five, we rode toward Tewkesbury ; notice having been given of my preaching about noon at a house a mile from the town. But we could not get to it ; the floods were so high ; so I intended to go straight to Worcester. But one informing me, a congregation from all parts was waiting, we set out another way, and waded through the water. This congregation too seemed quite earnest ; so that I did not regret my labour. But the going and coming was hard work, so that I was a little tired before we came to Worcester.

Tues. 21.—I went to Parkgate, and, about eleven, embarked on board the *King George*.

On *Thursday*, *Friday*, and *Saturday*, I laboured to allay the ferment which still remained in the [Dublin] society. I heard the preachers face to face, once and again, and endeavoured to remove their little misunderstandings.

Mon. April 17.—In the evening, and twice on *Tuesday*, I preached to a genteel yet serious audience, in Mr M'Gough's avenue, at Armagh. But God only can reach the heart. *Wednesday*, 19. As it rained, I chose rather to preach in M'Gough's yard. The rain increasing, we retired into one of his buildings. This was the first time that I preached in a stable ; and I believe more good was done by this than all the other sermons I have preached at Armagh.

We took horse about ten, being desired to call at Kinnard (ten or eleven miles out of the way), where a little society had been lately formed, who were much alive to God. At the town-end, I was met by a messenger from Archdeacon C——e, who desired I would take a bed with him ; and soon after by another, who told me, the archdeacon desired I would alight at his door. I did so ; and found an old friend whom I had not seen for four or five and thirty years. He received me with the most cordial affection; and, after a time, said, "We have been building a new church, which my neighbours expected me to open; but if you please to do it, it will be as well." Hearing the bell, the people flocked together from all parts of the town, and "received the Word with all readiness of mind."

Wed. 26.—Being to preach at Brickfield, four or five (English) miles from Derry, I chose walking, to show these poor indolent creatures how to use their own feet. Finding the bulk of the hearers quite senseless, I spoke as strongly as I could, on, "Where their worm dieth not, and the fire is not quenched." But I did not perceive they were at all affected. God only can raise the dead.

Thur. May 4.—I found near Swadlinbar, as artless, as earnest, and as loving a people as even at Tonny-lommon. About six I preached at the town's end, the very Papists appearing as attentive as the Protestants; and I doubt not thousands of these would soon be zealous Christians, were it not for their wretched priests, who will not enter into the kingdom of God themselves, and diligently hinder those that would.

Sat. June 17.—I finished *Historic Doubts on the Life and Reign of Richard the Third*. What an amazing monster, both in body and mind, have our historians and poets painted him! And yet I think Mr Walpole makes it more clear than one could expect at this distance of time: 1. That he was not only not remarkably deformed, but, on the contrary, remarkably handsome. 2. That his queen, whom he entirely loved, died a natural death. 3. That his nephew, Edward the Fifth, did so too; there being no shadow of proof to the contrary. 4. That his other nephew, Richard, was the very person whom Henry the Seventh murdered, after constraining him to call himself Perkin Warbeck. 5. That the death of his brother, the Duke of Clarence, was the sole act, not of him, but Edward the Fourth. 6. That he had no hand at all in the murder of Henry the Sixth, any more than of his son. And, lastly, that he was clear of all blame as to the execution of Lord Hastings; as well as of Rivers, Grey, and Vaughan. What a surprising thing is it, then, that all our historians should have so readily swallowed the account of that wretch who "killed, and also took possession" of the throne; and blundered on, one after another! Only it is to be observed, for fifty years no one could contradict that account, but at the peril of his head.

Mon. July 3.—I rode to Coolylough (where was the quarterly meeting), and preached at eleven, and in the evening. While we were singing, I was surprised to see the horses from all parts of the ground gathering about us. Is it true then that horses, as well as lions and tigers, have an ear for music?

Sat. 15.—I crossed the country to my old pupil, Mr Morgan's, and in the afternoon returned to Dublin.

All the following week we had a remarkable blessing, both at the morning and evening service. On *Wednesday* and *Thursday* we had our little Conference, at which most of the preachers in the kingdom were present. We agreed to set apart Friday, the 21st, for a day of fasting and prayer. At every meeting, particularly the last, our Lord refreshed us in an uncommon manner.

Sun. 23.—At nine I preached in the Royal Square at the barracks, on the dead, small and great, standing before God. An huge multitude soon gathered together, and listened with deep attention. Many of the soldiers were among them. By what means but field-preaching could we have reached these poor souls?

Mon. 24.—After preaching in the evening, I went on board the packet, and the next afternoon landed at Holyhead.

Fri. 28.—I rode to Manchester. As we were pretty well tired, our friends there insisted on my going on in a chaise; so in the morning, *Saturday*, 29, we set out. When we were on the brow of the hill above Ripponden, suddenly the saddle-horse fell, with the driver under him; and both lay without motion. The shaft-horse then boggled and turned short toward the edge of the precipice; but presently the driver and horse rose up unhurt, and we went on safe to Leeds.

Sun. 30.—Mr Crook being out of order, I read prayers and preached in Hunslet church, both morning and afternoon. At five I preached at Leeds; and on *Monday*, 31, prepared all things for the ensuing Conference. *Tuesday*, August 1, it began; and a more loving one we never had. On *Thursday* I mentioned the case of our brethren at New York, who had built the first Methodist preaching-house in America, and were in great want of money, but much more of preachers. Two of our preachers, Richard Boardman and Joseph Pillmoor, willingly offered themselves for the service; by whom we determined to send them fifty pounds, as a token of our brotherly love.

I gave a second reading to that lively book, *Mr Newton's Account of his own Experience.* There is something very extraordinary therein; but one may a   * for it without a jot of predestination. I doubt not but ..., .. ,." as Colonel Gardiner's conversion, was an answer to his mother's prayers.

Wed. 23.—I went on to Trevecka. Here we found a concourse of people from all parts, come to celebrate the

Countess of Huntingdon's birthday, and the anniversary of her school, which was opened on the twenty-fourth of August last year. I preached in the evening, to as many as her chapel could well contain; which is extremely neat, or rather, elegant; as is the dining-room, the school, and all the house. About nine Howell Harris desired me to give a short exhortation to his family. I did so; and then went back to my Lady's, and laid me down in peace.

Thur. 24.—I administered the Lord's Supper to the family. At ten the public service began. Mr Fletcher preached an exceeding lively sermon in the court, the chapel being far too small. After him, Mr William Williams preached in Welsh, till between one and two o'clock. At two we dined. Meantime, a large number of people had baskets of bread and meat carried to them in the court. At three I took my turn there, then Mr Fletcher, and, about five, the congregation was dismissed. Between seven and eight the love-feast began, at which I believe many were comforted. In the evening several of us retired into the neighbouring wood, which is exceeding pleasantly laid out in walks; one of which leads to a little mount, raised in the midst of a meadow, that commands a delightful prospect. This is Howell Harris's work, who has likewise greatly enlarged and beautified his house; so that, with the gardens, orchards, walks, and pieces of water that surround it, it is a kind of little paradise.

Sun. 27.—After preaching at Kingswood and Bristol, I rode to Cross, to lessen the next day's journey. *Monday*, 28. I rode to Tiverton; on *Tuesday*, to Launceston.

Last week I read over, as I rode, great part of Homer's *Odyssey*. I always imagined it was, like Milton's *Paradise Regained*,

"The last faint effort of an expiring Muse."

But how was I mistaken! How far has Homer's latter poem the pre-eminence over the former! It is not, indeed, without its blemishes; among which, perhaps, one might reckon his making Ulysses swim nine days and nine nights without sustenance; the incredible manner of his escape from Polyphemus (unless the goat was as strong as an ox), and the introducing Minerva at every turn, without any *dignus vindice nodus*.[1] But his numerous beauties make large amends for these. Was ever man so happy in his descriptions, so exact and consistent in his characters, and so natural in telling a story! He likewise continually inserts the finest strokes of

---

[1] "Difficult point, that requires a serious solution."—ED.

morality (which I cannot find in Virgil); on all occasions
recommending the fear of God, with justice, mercy, and truth. In
this only he is inconsistent with himself: he makes his hero say,

"Wisdom never lies;"

and,
> "Him, on whate'er pretence, that lies can tell,
> My soul abhors him as the gates of hell."

Meanwhile, he himself, on the slightest pretence, tells deliberate
lies over and over; nay, and is highly commended for so doing,
even by the goddess of Wisdom!

Wed. Sept. 6.—This afternoon I went to the top of Brent
Hill: I know not I ever before saw such a prospect. Westward,
one may see to the mouth of the Bristol Channel; and the three
other ways, as far as the eye can reach. And most of the land
which you see is well cultivated, well wooded, and well watered.

Tues. 12.—I inquired into the state of Kingswood School.
The grievance now is the number of children. Instead of thirty
(as I desired), we have near fifty; whereby our masters are
burdened. And it is scarce possible to keep them in so exact
order as we might do a smaller number. However, this still comes
nearer a Christian school than any I know in the kingdom.

Tues. 19.—Between twelve and one, I preached at Freshford; and on White's Hill, near Bradford, in the evening. By
this means many had an opportunity of hearing, who would not
have come to the room. I had designed to preach there again
the next evening; but a gentleman in the town desired me to
preach at his door. The beasts of the people were tolerably
quiet till I had nearly finished my sermon. They then lifted up
their voice, especially one, called a gentleman, who had filled his
pocket with rotten eggs: but, a young man coming unawares,
clapped his hands on each side, and mashed them all at once.
In an instant he was perfume all over; though it was not so
sweet as balsam.

Tues. Oct. 17.—Having appointed to preach in Oxford at
ten, I was under some difficulty. I did not like to preach in the
Dissenting meeting-house; and I did not see how to avoid it.
But the proprietors cut the knot for me, by locking up the doors.
So I preached in James Mears's garden; and to such a
congregation as I had not had in Oxford since I preached in
St Mary's church.

Tues. 24.—Between six and seven I preached at Northampton; and it was an awful season.

This evening there was such an Aurora Borealis as I never
saw before: the colours, both the white, the flame-colour, and
the scarlet, were so exceeding strong and beautiful. But they

were awful too : so that abundance of people were frighted into many good resolutions.

Thur. Nov. 2.—We went to Yarmouth, a cold, dead, uncomfortable place.

In the coach, going and coming, I read several volumes of Mr Guthrie's ingenious *History of Scotland* : I suppose, as impartial an one as any to be found, and as much to be depended upon. I never read any writer before who gave me so much light into the real character of that odd mixture, King James the First; nor into that of Mary Queen of Scots, so totally misrepresented by Buchanan, Queen Elizabeth's pensioner, and her other hireling writers ; and not much less, by Dr Robertson. Them he effectually exposes, showing how grossly they contradict matter of fact, and one another. He likewise points out the many and great mistakes of Dr R., such as seem to imply either great inattention or great partiality. Upon the whole, that much-injured Queen appears to have been far the greatest woman of that age, exquisitely beautiful in her person, of a fine address, of a deep, unaffected piety, and of a stronger understanding even in youth than Queen Elizabeth had at threescore. And probably the despair wherein Queen Elizabeth died was owing to her death, rather than that of Lord Essex.

Tues. Dec. 26.—I read the letters from our preachers in America, informing us that God had begun a glorious work there ; that both in New York and Philadelphia multitudes flock to hear, and behave with the deepest seriousness ; and that the society in each place already contains above an hundred members.

Thur. Feb. 8, 1770.—I went to Wandsworth. Every one thought no good could be done here ; we had tried for above twenty years. Very few would even give us the hearing ; and the few that did, seemed little the better for it. But all on a sudden, crowds flock to hear ; many are cut to the heart ; many filled with peace and joy in believing ; many long for the whole image of God.

Fri. 23.—I was desired to hear Mr Leoni sing at the Jewish synagogue. I never before saw a Jewish congregation behave so decently. Indeed the place itself is so solemn, that it might strike an awe upon those who have any thought of God.

Wed. 28.—I sat down to read and seriously consider some of the writings of Baron Swedenborg. I began with huge prejudice in his favour, knowing him to be a pious man, one of a strong understanding, of much learning, and one who thoroughly believed himself. But I could not hold out long. Any one of his visions puts his real character out of doubt He is one of the most ingenious, lively, entertaining madmen, that ever set pen to paper. But his waking dreams are so wild, so far remote both from Scripture and common-sense, that one might as easily swallow the stories of *Tom Thumb* or *Jack the Giant-Killer*.

Mon. Mar. 19.—I rode to Craidley. In the following days I went on slowly, through Staffordshire and Cheshire, to Manchester. In this journey, as well as in many others, I observed a mistake that almost universally prevails; and I desire all travellers to take good notice of it, which may save them both from trouble and danger. Near thirty years ago, I was thinking, " How is it that no horse ever stumbles while I am reading?" (History, poetry, and philosophy I commonly read on horseback, having other employment at other times.) No account can possibly be given but this: because then I throw the reins on his neck. I then set myself to observe; and I aver, that in riding above an hundred thousand miles, I scarce ever remember any horse (except two, that would fall head over heels any way) to fall, or make a considerable stumble, while I rode with a slack rein. To fancy, therefore, that a tight rein prevents stumbling is a capital blunder. I have repeated the trial more frequently than most men in the kingdom can do. A slack rein will prevent stumbling if anything will. But in some horses nothing can.

Wed. April 25.—Taking horse at five, we rode to Dunkeld, the first considerable town in the Highlands. We were agreeably surprised; a pleasanter situation cannot be easily imagined. Afterwards we went some miles on a smooth, delightful road, hanging over the river Tay; and then went on, winding through the mountains, to the castle of Blair. The mountains, for the next twenty miles, were much higher, and covered with snow. In the evening we came to Dalwhinny, the dearest inn I have met with in North Britain. In the morning we were informed, so much snow had fallen in the night, that we could get no farther. And, indeed, three young women, attempting to cross the mountain to Blair, were swallowed up in the snow. However, we resolved, with God's help, to go as far as we could. But, about noon, we were at a full stop; the snow, driving together on the top of the mountain, had quite blocked up the road. We dismounted, and, striking out of the road warily, sometimes to the left, sometimes to the right, with many stumbles, but no hurt, we got on to Dalmagarry, and before sunset, to Inverness.

Fri. 27.— I breakfasted with the senior minister, Mr M'Kenzie, a pious and friendly man. At six in the evening I began preaching in the church, and with very uncommon liberty of spirit. At seven in the morning I preached in the library, a large commodious room ; but it would not contain the congregation : many were constrained to go away. Afterwards I rode over to Fort George, a very regular fortification, capable of containing four thousand men. As I was just taking horse, the commanding officer sent word, I was welcome to preach. But it was a little too late: I had then but just time to ride back to Inverness.

Sun. 29.—At seven, the benches being removed, the library contained us tolerably well; and, I am persuaded, God shook the hearts of many outside Christians. I preached in the church at five in the afternoon. Mr Helton designed to preach abroad at seven ; but the ministers desired he would preach in the church, which he did, to a large and attentive congregation. Many followed us from the church to our lodgings, with whom I spent some time in prayer, and then advised them, as many as could, to meet together, and spend an hour every evening in prayer and useful conversation.

Mon. 30.—We set out in a fine morning. A little before we reached Nairn, we were met by a messenger from the minister, Mr Dunbar ; who desired, I would breakfast with him, and give them a sermon in his church. Afterwards we hastened to Elgin, through a pleasant and well cultivated country. When we set out from hence, the rain began, and poured down till we came to the Spey, the most impetuous river I ever saw. Finding the large boat was in no haste to move, I stepped into a small one, just going off. It whirled us over the stream almost in a minute. I waited at the inn at Fochabers (dark and dirty enough in all reason), till our friends overtook me with the horses. The outside of the inn at Keith was of the same hue, and promised us no great things. But we were agreeably disappointed. We found plenty of everything, and so dried ourselves at leisure.

Tues. May 1.—I rode on to Aberdeen, and spent the rest of the week there.

Sun. 6.—At seven in the evening I preached at Arbroath, properly Aberbrothwick. The whole town seems moved.

Tues. 8.—I took a view of the small remains of the abbey. I know nothing like it in all North Britain. I paced it, and found it an hundred yards long. The breadth is proportionable. Part of the west end, which is still standing, shows it was full as high as Westminster Abbey. The south end of the cross-aisle likewise is standing, near the top of which is a large circular window. The zealous Reformers, they told us, burnt this down. God deliver us from reforming mobs !

I have seen no town in Scotland which increases so fast,

or which is built with so much common sense, as this. Two entire new streets, and part of a third, have been built within these two years. They run parallel with each other, and have a row of gardens between them. So that every house has a garden; and thus both health and convenience are consulted.

Fri. 11.—I went forward to Edinburgh. *Saturday*, 12. I received but a melancholy account of the state of things here. The congregations were nearly as usual; but the society which, when I was here before, consisted of above an hundred and sixty members, was now shrunk to about fifty. Such is the fruit of a single preacher's staying a whole year in one place ! together with the labours of good Mr Townshend.

Mon. 14.—After ten years' inquiry, I have learned what are the Highlands of Scotland. Some told me, " The Highlands begin when you cross the Tay"; others, "when you cross the North Esk"; and others, "when you cross the river Spey": but all of them missed the mark. For the truth of the matter is, the Highlands are bounded by no river at all, but by cairns, or heaps of stones laid in a row, south-west and north-east, from sea to sea. These formerly divided the kingdom of the Picts from that of the Caledonians, which included all the country north of the cairns; several whereof are still remaining. It takes in Argyllshire, most of Perthshire, Morayshire, with all the north-west counties. This is called the Highlands, because a considerable part of it (though not the whole) is mountainous. But it is not more mountainous than North Wales, nor than many parts of England and Ireland; nor do I believe it has any mountain higher than Snowdon Hill, or the Skiddaw in Cumberland. Talking Erse, therefore, is not the thing that distinguishes these from the Lowlands. Neither is this or that river; both the Tay, the Esk, and the Spey running through the Highlands, not south of them.

Thur. 17.—At five in the morning I took a solemn leave of our friends at Edinburgh.

Sat. 26.—We went by water to North Biddick. In returning, as we were four large boats in company, we made

"The mountains and vales His praises rebound."

So is even the water-language now changed.

Fri. June 15.—I was agreeably surprised to find the whole road from Thirsk to Stokesley, which used to be extremely bad, better than most turnpikes. The gentlemen had exerted themselves, and raised money enough to mend it effectually. So they had done for several hundred miles in Scotland, and throughout all Connaught in Ireland; and so they undoubtedly might do throughout all England, without saddling the poor people with the vile imposition of turnpikes for ever.

Sat. 16.—I found our preacher, James Brownfield, had just set up for himself. The reasons he gave for leaving the Methodists were: 1. That they went to church; 2. That they held perfection. I earnestly desired our society to leave him to God, and say nothing about him, good or bad.

Thur. 28.—I rode to Mr Sutcliffe's at Hoohole: a lovely valley, encompassed with high mountains. I stood on the smooth grass before his house (which stands on a gently-rising ground), and all the people on the slope before me. It was a glorious opportunity. I trust many " came boldly to the throne," and found " grace to help in time of need."

I can hardly believe that I am this day entered into the sixty-eighth year of my age. How marvellous are the ways of God! How has He kept me even from a child! From ten to thirteen or fourteen, I had little but bread to eat, and not great plenty of that. I believe this was so far from hurting me, that it laid the foundation of lasting health. When I grew up, in consequence of reading Dr Cheyne, I chose to eat sparingly, and drink water. This was another great means of continuing my health, till I was about seven-and-twenty. I then began spitting of blood, which continued several years. A warm climate cured this. I was afterwards brought to the brink of death by a fever; but it left me healthier than before. Eleven years after, I was in the third stage of a consumption; in three months it pleased God to remove this also. Since that time I have known neither pain nor sickness, and am now healthier than I was forty years ago. This hath God wrought!

Thur. July 5.—I preached at six at Daw Green, near Dewsbury. All things contributed to make it a refreshing season; the gently-declining sun, the stillness of the evening, the beauty of the meadows and fields, through which

" The smooth clear ' river drew its sinuous train ' " ;

the opposite hills and woods, and the earnestness of the people, covering the top of the hill on which we stood; and above all, the Day-spring from on high, the consolation of the Holy One!

Sat. 7.—I rode to Miss Bosanquet's. Her family is still a pattern, and a general blessing, to the country.

Tues. 31.—In the evening I preached in the Castle-yard at Leicester, to a multitude of awakened and unawakened. One feeble attempt was made to disturb them: a man was sent to cry fresh salmon at a little distance; but he might as well have spared the pains, for none took the least notice of him.

CHAPTER XIV

THE HONOURED GUEST

FROM NOVEMBER 10, 1770, TO DECEMBER 2, 1775

Sat., Nov. 10, 1770.—I had the melancholy news of Mr Whitefield's death confirmed by his executors, who desired me to preach his funeral sermon on Sunday, the 18th. In order to write this, I retired to Lewisham on *Monday*; and on *Sunday* following, went to the chapel in Tottenham-court Road. An immense multitude was gathered together from all corners of the town. I was at first afraid that a great part of the congregation would not be able to hear; but it pleased God so to strengthen my voice, that even those at the door heard distinctly. It was an awful season; all were still as night; most appeared to be deeply affected; and an impression was made on many, which one would hope will not speedily be effaced.

The time appointed for my beginning at the Tabernacle was half-hour after five; but it was quite filled at three; so I began at four. At first the noise was exceeding great; but it ceased when I began to speak; and my voice was again so strengthened that all who were within could hear, unless an accidental noise hindered here or there for a few moments.

Fri. 23.—Being desired by the Trustees of the Tabernacle at Greenwich to preach Mr Whitefield's funeral sermon there, I went over to-day for that purpose; but neither would this house contain the congregation.

Wed. Jan. 2, 1771.—I preached in the evening, at Deptford, a kind of funeral sermon for Mr Whitefield. In every place I wish to show all possible respect to the memory of that great and good man.

Wed. 23.—For what cause I know not to this day, —— set out for Newcastle, purposing "never to return." *Non eam reliqui: non dimisi: non revocabo.*[1]

---

[1] "I did not desert her: I did not send her away: I will never recall her."—ED.

Fri. 25.—I revised and transcribed my Will, declaring as simply, as plainly, and as briefly as I could, nothing more nor nothing else, but "what I would have done with the worldly goods which I leave behind me."

Thur. April 11.—I preached at Loughan and Athlone.

Sun. 14.—I designed to preach abroad; but the storm drove us into the house. This house was built and given, with the ground on which it stands, by a single gentleman.

Sat. Dec. 21.—I met an old friend, James Hutton, whom I had not seen for five-and-twenty years. I felt this made no difference; my heart was quite open; his seemed to be the same; and we conversed just as we did in 1738, when we met in Fetter Lane.

Monday, 23, and so all the following days, when I was not particularly engaged, I spent an hour in the morning with our preachers, as I used to do with my pupils at Oxford.

Mon. 30.—At my brother's request, I sat again for my picture. This melancholy employment always reminds me of that natural reflection—

"Behold what frailty we in man may see!
His shadow is less given to change than he."

Tues. Jan. 14, 1772.—I spent an agreeable hour with Dr S——, the oldest acquaintance I now have. He is the greatest genius in little things, that ever fell under my notice. Almost everything about him is of his own invention, either in whole or in part. Even his fire-screen, his lamps of various sorts, his inkhorn, his very save-all. I really believe, were he seriously to set about it, he could invent the best mouse-trap that ever was in the world.

Wed. Feb. 12.—I read a book, published by an honest Quaker, on that execrable sum of all villainies, commonly called the Slave Trade. I read of nothing like it in the heathen world, whether ancient or modern: and it infinitely exceeds, in every instance of barbarity, whatever Christian slaves suffer in Mahometan countries.

Fri. 14.—I began to execute a design, which had long been in my thoughts, to print as accurate an edition of my works, as a bookseller would do. Surely I ought to be as exact for God's sake, as he would be for money.

Fri. 21.—I met several of my friends, who had begun a subscription to prevent my riding on horseback; which I cannot do quite so well, since a hurt which I got some months ago. If they continue it, well; if not, I shall have strength according to my need.

Mon. April 6.—In the afternoon I drank tea at Am. O.

But how was I shocked! The children that used to cling about me, and drink in every word, had been at a boarding-school. There they had unlearned all religion, and even seriousness; and had learned pride, vanity, affectation, and whatever could guard them against the knowledge and love of God. Methodist parents, who would send your girls headlong to hell, send them to a fashionable boarding-school!

Thur. May 7.—I took Thomas Cherry away with me; but it was too late; he will hardly recover. Let all observe (that no more preachers may murder themselves), here is another martyr to screaming!

Tues. 12.—I preached at Ormiston, ten miles south of Edinburgh, to a large and deeply serious congregation. I dined at the minister's, a sensible man, who heartily bid us God-speed. But he soon changed his mind: Lord H——n informing him that he had received a letter from Lady H——n, assuring him that we were "dreadful heretics, to whom no countenance should be given." It is a pity! Should not the children of God leave the devil to do his own work?

Thur. 21.—I went to the Bass, which, in the horrid reign of Charles the Second, was the prison of those venerable men who suffered the loss of all things for a good conscience. It is a high rock surrounded by the sea, two or three miles in circumference, and about two miles from the shore. The strong east wind made the water so rough, that the boat could hardly live: and when we came to the only landing-place (the other sides being quite perpendicular), it was with much difficulty that we got up, climbing on our hands and knees. The castle, as one may judge by what remains, was utterly inaccessible. The walls of the chapel, and of the Governor's house, are tolerably entire. The garden walls are still seen near the top of the rock, with the well in the midst of it. And round the walls there are spots of grass, that feed eighteen or twenty sheep. But the proper natives of the island are Solund geese, a bird about the size of a Muscovy duck, which breed by thousands, from generation to generation, on the sides of the rock. It is peculiar to these, that they lay but one egg, which they do not sit upon at all, but keep it under one foot (as we saw with our eyes), till it is hatched. How many prayers did the holy men confined here offer up, in that evil day! And how many thanksgivings should we return, for all the liberty, civil and religious, which we enjoy!

Fri. 22.—We took a view of the famous Roman camp, lying on a mountain, two or three miles from the town. It is encompassed with two broad and deep ditches, and is not easy of approach on any side. Here lay General Leslie with his army while Cromwell was starving below. He had no way to escape; but the enthusiastic fury of the Scots delivered him. When they marched into the valley to swallow him up, he mowed them down like grass.

Tues. June 2.—We rode to New Orygan in Teesdale. The people were deeply attentive; but, I think, not deeply affected. From the top of the next enormous mountain, we had a view of Weardale. It is a lovely prospect. The green gently-rising meadows and fields, on both sides of the little river, clear as crystal, were sprinkled over with innumerable little houses; three in four of which (if not nine in ten) are sprung up since the Methodists came hither. Since that time, the beasts are turned into men, and the wilderness into a fruitful field.

Wed. 3.—I desired to speak with those who believed God had saved them from inward sin. I closely examined them, twenty in all, ten men, eight women, and two children. Of one man, and one or two women, I stood in doubt. The experience of the rest was clear; particularly that of the children, Margaret Spenser, aged fourteen, and Sally Blackburn, a year younger. But what a contrast was there between them! Sally Blackburn was all calmness; her look, her speech, her whole carriage was as sedate, as if she had lived threescore years. On the contrary, Peggy was all fire; her eyes sparkled; her very features spoke; her whole face was all alive; and she looked as if she was just ready to take wing for heaven! Lord, let neither of these live to dishonour thee! Rather take them unspotted to Thyself!

Thur. 4.—At five I took my leave of this blessed people. I was a little surprised, in looking attentively upon them, to observe so many beautiful faces as I never saw before in one congregation; many of the children in particular, twelve or fourteen of whom (chiefly boys) sat full in my view. But I allow, much more might be owing to grace than nature, to the heaven within, that shone outward.

Before I give a more particular account of this work of God, it may be well to look back to the very beginning of it. In this part of Weardale, the people in general are employed in the lead mines. In the year 1749 Mr Hopper and John Brown came and preached among them. But it made no impression; none opposed, and none asked them to eat or drink. Mr H., nevertheless, made them several visits in the ensuing spring and summer. Towards autumn four found peace with God, and agreed to meet together. At Christmas two of the exhorters in Allandale determined to visit Weardale. Before they entered it, they kneeled down on the snow, and earnestly besought the

Lord that He would incline some person, who was worthy, to receive them into his house. At the first house where they called they were bid welcome, and they stayed there four days. Their word was with power, so that many were convinced, and some converted to God. One of these exhorters was Jacob Rowell. They continued their visits, at intervals, all winter. In the beginning of summer, about twenty lively, steady people were joined together. From that time they gradually increased to thirty-five, and continued about that number for ten years. There was then a remarkable revival among them, by means of Samuel Meggot; so that they increased to eighty; but, four years since, they were reduced to sixty-three. From that time they increased again, and were, in August, an hundred and twenty.

In two respects, this society has always been peculiarly remarkable: the one, they have been the most liberal in providing everything needful for the preachers: the other, they have been particularly careful with regard to marriage. They have in general married with each other; and that not for the sake of money, but virtue. Hence, having been yoke-fellows in grace before, they more easily bear the yoke of marriage, and assist each other in training up their children; and God has eminently blessed them therein. For in most of their families, the greatest part of the children above ten years old are converted to God. So that to several among them one may say, as St Paul to Timothy, "The faith which dwelt first in thy grandmother, and thy mother, I am persuaded is in thee also." It was observable, too, that their Leaders were upright men, alive to God, and having an uncommon gift in prayer. This was increased by their continual exercise of it. The preachers were there but once a fortnight. But though they had neither preacher nor exhorter, they met every night for singing and prayer.

Last summer the work of God revived, and gradually increased till the end of November. Then God began to make bare His arm in an extraordinary manner. Those who were strangers to God, felt, as it were, a sword in their bones, constraining them to roar aloud. Those who knew God were filled with joy unspeakable, and were almost equally loud in praise and thanksgiving. The convictions that seized the unawakened were generally exceeding deep, so that their cries drowned every other voice, and no other means could be used than the speaking to the distressed, one by one, and encouraging them to lay hold on Christ. And this has not been in vain. Many that were either on their knees, or prostrate on the ground, have suddenly started up, and their very countenance showed that the Comforter was come. Immediately these began to go about from one to another of them that were still in distress, praising God, and exhorting them without delay to come to so gracious a Saviour. Many, who to that hour appeared quite unconcerned, were thereby cut to the heart, and suddenly filled with such anguish of soul as extorted loud and bitter cries. By such a succession of persons mourning and rejoicing, they have been frequently detained, so that they could not part till ten or eleven at night, nay, sometimes, not till four in the morning.

Such a work, it is true, in many respects, was that at Everton some years since; yet not in all, as will fully appear, if we consider a few more circumstances of this:—

"Forty-three of these are children, thirty of whom are rejoicing in the love of God. The chief instrument God has used among these is Jane Salkeld, a school-mistress, a young woman that is a pattern to all that believe. A few of her children are, Phebe Teatherstone, nine years and an half old, a child of uncommon understanding; Hannah Watson, ten years old, full of faith and love; Aaron Ridson, not eleven years old, but wise and staid as a man; Sarah Smith, eight years and an half old, but as serious as a woman of fifty; Sarah Morris, fourteen years of age, is as a mother among them, always serious, always watching over the rest, and building them up in love."

Tues. July 14.—I preached at Sheffield; *Thursday*, 16, at Hathenham; and *Friday*, 17, at Hatfield. Here, some time since, a justice levied a fine on a local preacher, on pretence of the Conventicle Act. So did a justice in Kent, three or four years ago; but it cost him some hundred pounds for his pains.

The next day I rested at Epworth.

Fri. Aug. 14.—About noon, at the request of my old friend Howell Harris, I preached at Trevecka, on the strait gate; and we found our hearts knit together as at the beginning. He said, "I have borne with those pert, ignorant young men, vulgarly called students, till I cannot in conscience bear any longer. They preach barefaced reprobation, and so broad Antinomianism, that I have been constrained to oppose them to the face, even in the public congregation." It is no wonder they should preach thus. What better can be expected from raw lads of little understanding, little learning, and no experience?

Fri. 21.—I preached again about eight, and then rode back to Harford. After dinner we hasted to the Passage; but the watermen were not in haste to fetch us over; so I sat down on a convenient stone, and finished the little tract I had in hand. However, I got to Pembroke in time, and preached in the townhall, where we had a solemn and comfortable opportunity.

In this journey [Kent] I read over Sir John Dalrymple's *Memoirs of the Revolution.*

Fri. Jan. 1, 1773.—We (as usual) solemnly renewed our covenant with God. *Monday,* 4. I began revising my letters and papers. One of them was wrote above an hundred and fifty years ago (in 1619), I suppose, by my grandfather's father, to her he was to marry in a few days. Several were wrote by my brothers and me when at school, many while we were at the University; abundantly testifying (if it be worth knowing) what was our aim from our youth up.

Tues. Feb. 2.—Captain Webb preached at the Foundery. I admire the wisdom of God, in still raising up various preachers, according to the various tastes of men. The captain is all life and fire: therefore, although he is not deep or regular, yet many who would not hear a better preacher, flock together to hear him. And many are convinced under his preaching; some justified; a few built up in love.

Wed. July 21.— We had our quarterly meeting at London; at which I was surprised to find, that our income does not yet answer our expense. We were again near two hundred pounds bad. My private account I find still worse. I have laboured as much as many writers; and all my labour has gained me, in seventy years, a debt of five or six hundred pounds.

Sat. Aug. 28.—I returned to Bristol.

Fri. Sept. 10.—I went over to Kingswood, and inquired into the present state of the children. I found part of them had walked closely with God; part had not, and were in heaviness. Hearing in the evening that they were got to prayer by themselves in the school, I went down; but, not being willing to disturb them, stood at the window. Two or three had gone in first; then more and more, till above thirty were gathered together. Such a sight I never saw before nor since.

Sun. 12.—Four of Miss Owen's children desired leave to partake of the Lord's Supper. I talked with them severally, and found they were all still rejoicing in the love of God. And they confirmed the account, that there was only one of their whole number who was unaffected on Monday: but all the rest could then say with confidence, "Lord, Thou knowest that I love Thee." I suppose such a visitation of children has not been known in England these hundred years. In so marvellous a manner, "out of the mouths of babes and sucklings" God has "perfected praise"!

Wed. 29.—After preaching at Pensford, I went to Publow, and in the morning spent a little time with the lovely children. Those of them who were lately affected do not appear to have lost anything of what they had received; and some of them were clearly gaining ground, and advancing in the faith which works by love.

Tues. Jan. 11, 1774.—I began at the east end of the town to visit the society from house to house. I know no branch of the pastoral office which is of greater importance than this. But it is so grievous to flesh and blood, that I can prevail on few, even of our preachers, to undertake it.

Tues. Mar. 29.—At Newcastle-under-Lyme, where I was invited by the mayor, a serious, sensible man, to lodge at his house. I was desired (our room being but small) to preach in the market-place. Abundance of people were soon gathered together, who surprised me not a little, by mistaking the tune, and striking up the March in *Judas Maccabeus*. Many of them had admirable voices, and tolerable skill. I know not when I have heard so agreeable a sound: it was indeed the voice of melody. But we had one jarring string: a drunken gentleman was a little noisy, till he was carried away.

Fri. April 15.—I preached at a preaching-house just built at Chowbent, which was lately a den of lions; but they are all now quiet as lambs. So they were the next day at the new house, near Bury.

Sun. 17.—I rode to Halifax. Such a country church I never saw before. I suppose, except York Minster, there is none in the county so large. Yet it would not near contain the congregation.

While I was at dinner at Dr Leigh's, one came from Huddersfield to tell me the vicar was willing I should preach in the church. Dr Leigh lending me his servant and his horse, I set out immediately; and, riding fast, came into the church while the vicar was reading the Psalms. It was well the people had no notice of my preaching, till I came into the town: they quickly filled the church. I did not spare them, but fully delivered my own soul.

Mon. 18.—The minister of Heptonstall sent me word that I was welcome to preach in his church. It was with difficulty we got up the steep mountain; and when we were upon it, the wind was ready to bear us away. The church was filled, not with curious but serious hearers. No others would face so furious a storm. At the Ewood, in the evening, we had the usual blessing.

Tues. 19.—Mrs Holmes, who has been some years confined

to her bed, sent, and desired I would preach at her house. As
I stood in the passage, both she could hear, and all that stood
in the adjoining rooms.

Wed. June 1.—I went on to Edinburgh, and the next day
examined the society one by one. I was agreeably surprised.
They have fairly profited since I was here last. Such a number
of persons having sound Christian experience I never found
in this society before. I preached in the evening to a very
elegant congregation, and yet with great enlargement of heart.
Saturday, 4, I found uncommon liberty at Edinburgh in applying
Ezekiel's vision of the dry bones. As I was walking home,
two men followed me, one of whom said, "Sir, you are my
prisoner. I have a warrant from the Sheriff to carry you to
the Tolbooth." At first I thought he jested ; but finding the
thing was serious, I desired one or two of our friends to go up
with me. When we were safe lodged in a house adjoining to
the Tolbooth, I desired the officer to let me see his warrant.
I found the prosecutor was one George Sutherland, once
a member of the society. He had deposed, "That Hugh
Saunderson, one of John Wesley's preachers, had taken from
his wife one hundred pounds in money, and upwards of thirty
pounds in goods ; and had, besides that, terrified her into
madness ; so that, through the want of her help, and the loss
of business, he was damaged five hundred pounds."

Before the Sheriff, Archibald Cockburn, Esq., he had
deposed, "That the said John Wesley and Hugh Saunderson,
to evade her pursuit, were preparing to fly the country ; and
therefore he desired his warrant to search for, seize, and
incarcerate them in the Tolbooth, till they should find security
for their appearance." To this request the Sheriff had assented,
and given his warrant for that purpose.

But why does he incarcerate John Wesley? Nothing is
laid against him, less or more. Hugh Saunderson preaches
in connection with him. What then? Was not the Sheriff
strangely overseen?

Mr Sutherland furiously insisted that the officer should
carry us to the Tolbooth without delay. However, he waited
till two or three of our friends came, and gave a bond for our
appearance on the 24th instant. Mr S. did appear, the cause
was heard, and the prosecutor fined one thousand pounds.

Sat. 11.—I set out for the Dales. About noon I preached
at Wolsingham, and in the evening near the preaching-house
in Weardale.

Sun. 12.—The rain drove us into the house, both morning
and afternoon. Afterwards I met the poor remains of the select

society; but neither of my two lovely children, neither Peggy Spence nor Sally Blackburn, were there. Indeed a whole row of such I had seen before; but three in four of them were now as careless as ever. In the evening I sent for Peggy Spence and Sally Blackburn. Peggy came, and I found she had wellnigh regained her ground, walking in the light, and having a lively hope of recovering all that she had lost. Sally flatly refused to come, and then ran out of doors. Being found at length, after a flood of tears, she was brought almost by force. But I could not get one look, and hardly a word, from her. She seemed to have no hope left: yet she is not out of God's reach.

I now inquired into the causes of that grievous decay in the vast work of God, which was here two years since; and I found several causes had concurred: 1. Not one of the preachers that succeeded was capable of being a nursing-father to the new-born children. 2. Jane Salkeld, one great instrument of the work, marrying, was debarred from meeting the young ones; and there being none left who so naturally cared for them, they fell heaps upon heaps. 3. Most of the liveliest in the society were the single men and women; and several of these in a little time contracted an inordinate affection for each other; whereby they so grieved the Holy Spirit of God, that He in great measure departed from them. 4. Men arose among ourselves, who undervalued the work of God, and called the great work of sanctification a delusion. By this they grieved some, and angered others; so that both the one and the other were much weakened. 5. Hence, the love of many waxing cold, the preachers were discouraged; and jealousies, heart-burnings, evil surmisings, were multiplied more and more. There is now a little revival: God grant it may increase!

Mon. 20.—About nine I set out for Horsley, with Mr Hopper and Mr Smith. I took Mrs Smith and her two little girls, in the chaise with me. About two miles from the town, just on the brow of the hill, on a sudden both the horses set out, without any visible cause, and flew down the hill, like an arrow out of a bow. In a minute John fell off the coach-box The horses then went on full speed, sometimes to the edge of the ditch on the right, sometimes on the left. A cart came up against them: they avoided it as exactly as if the man had been on the box. A narrow bridge was at the foot of the hill. They went directly over the middle of it. They ran up the next hill with the same speed; many persons meeting us, but getting out of the way. Near the top of the hill was a gate, which led into a farmer's yard. It stood open. They turned short, and run through it, without touching the gate on one side or the post on the other. I thought, "However, the gate which is on the other side of the yard, and is shut, will stop them": but they rushed through it, as if it had been a cobweb, and galloped on through the cornfield. The little girls cried out, "Grandpapa, save us!" I told them, "Nothing will hurt you: do not be afraid"; feeling no more fear or care (blessed be God!) than if I had been sitting in my study. The horses ran on, till they came to the edge of a steep precipice. Just then Mr Smith, who could not overtake us before, galloped in between. They stopped in a moment. Had they gone on ever so little, he and we must have gone down together!

I am persuaded both evil and good angels had a large share in this transaction: how large we do not know now; but we shall know hereafter.

Tues. 28.—This being my birthday, the first day of my seventy-second year, I was considering, How is this, that I find just the same strength as I did thirty years ago? That my sight is considerably better now, and my nerves firmer, than they were then? That I have none of the infirmities of old age, and have lost several I had in my youth? The grand cause is, the good pleasure of God, who doeth whatsoever pleaseth Him. The chief means are: 1. My constantly rising at four, for about fifty years. 2. My generally preaching at five in the morning; one of the most healthy exercises in the world. 3. My never travelling less, by sea or land, than four thousand five hundred miles in a year.

Mon. Oct. 3, and on *Tuesday* and *Wednesday*, I examined the society [at Bristol].

Thur. 6.—I met those of our society who had votes in the ensuing election, and advised them: 1. To vote, without fee or reward, for the person they judged most worthy; 2. To speak no evil of the person they voted against; and, 3. To take care their spirits were not sharpened against those that voted on the other side.

Sun. 9.—The evening being fair and mild, I preached in the new square. It was a fruitful season:—

"Soft fell the word, as flew the air;"

even "as the rain into a fleece of wool." Many such seasons we have had lately: almost every day one and another has found peace, particularly young persons and children. Shall not they be a blessing in the rising generation? In the evening we had a solemn opportunity of renewing our covenant with

God; a means of grace which I wonder has been so seldom used either in Romish or Protestant churches!

Monday, 31, and the following days, I visited the societies near London. *Friday*, Nov. 4. In the afternoon John Downes (who had preached with us many years) was saying, " I felt such a love to the people at West Street, that I could be content to die with them. I do not find myself very well; but I must be with them this evening." He went thither, and began preaching on, " Come unto Me, ye that are weary and heavy-laden." After speaking ten or twelve minutes, he sunk down and spake no more, till his spirit returned to God.

I suppose he was by nature full as great a genius as Sir Isaac Newton. I will mention but two or three instances of it:—When he was at school, learning algebra, he came one day to his master, and said, " Sir, I can prove this proposition a better way than it is proved in the book." His master thought it could not be; but upon trial, acknowledged it to be so. Some time after, his father sent him to Newcastle with a clock, which was to be mended. He observed the clock-maker's tools, and the manner how he took it in pieces, and put it together again; and when he came home, first made himself tools, and then made a clock, which went as true as any in the town. I suppose such strength of genius as this has scarce been known in Europe before.

Another proof of it was this:—Thirty years ago, while I was shaving, he was whittling the top of a stick: I asked, " What are you doing?" He answered, " I am taking your face, which I intend to engrave on a copper-plate." Accordingly, without any instruction, he first made himself tools, and then engraved the plate. The second picture which he engraved, was that which was prefixed to the *Notes upon the New Testament*. Such another instance, I suppose, not all England, or perhaps Europe can produce.

For several months past, he had far deeper communion with God, than ever he had had in his life; and for some days he had been frequently saying, " I am so happy, that I scarce know how to live. I enjoy such fellowship with God, as I thought could not be had on this side heaven." And having now finished his course of fifty-two years, after a long conflict with pain, sickness, and poverty, he gloriously rested from his labours, and entered into the joy of his Lord.

Sun. 13.—After a day of much labour, at my usual time (half-hour past nine), I lay down to rest. I told my servants, " I must rise at three, the Norwich coach setting out at four." Hearing one of them knock, though sooner than I expected,

I rose and dressed myself; but afterwards, looking at my
watch, I found it was but half-past ten. While I was considering what to do, I heard a confused sound of many voices
below: and looking out at the window towards the yard, I saw
it was as light as day. Meantime, many large flakes of fire
were continually flying about the house; all the upper part of
which was built of wood, which was near as dry as tinder. A
large deal-yard, at a very small distance from us, was all in a
light fire; from which the north-west wind drove the flames
directly upon the Foundery; and there was no probability of
help, for no water could be found. Perceiving I could be of
no use, I took my Diary and my papers, and retired to a friend's
house. I had no fear; committing the matter into God's hands,
and knowing He would do whatever was best. Immediately
the wind turned about from north-west to south-east; and our
pump supplied the engines with abundance of water; so that
in a little more than two hours, all the danger was over.

About six, on *Sunday*, April 2 [1775], we landed at Dunleary;
and between nine and ten reached Whitefriar Street. *Sunday*, 9.
The good old Dean of St Patrick's desired me to come within
the rails, and assist him at the Lord's Supper. This also was a
means of removing much prejudice from those who were zealous
for the Church. *Monday*, 10. I began my tour through the
kingdom.

Wed. 26.—I went on to Waterford, where the rain drove us
into the preaching-house—the most foul, horrid, miserable hole
which I have seen since I left England. The next day I got
into the open air, and a large congregation attended. I had
designed to set out early in the morning; but doubting if I
should ever have such another opportunity (the major of the
Highland regiment standing behind me, with several of his
officers, many of the soldiers before me, and the sentinel at
the entrance of the court), I gave notice of preaching at ten
the next morning, and at four in the afternoon.

Wed. May 17.—I examined the society at Limerick, containing now an hundred and one persons, seven less than they
were two years ago. I a little wonder at this; considering
the scandal of the cross is well-nigh ceased here, through the
wise and steady behaviour of our brethren. But they want
zeal; they are not fervent in spirit: therefore, they cannot
increase.

Wed. 31.—We hastened to Dargbridge, and found a large
congregation waiting. They appeared, one and all, to be
deeply serious. Indeed there is a wonderful reformation
spreading throughout this whole country, for several miles

round. Outward wickedness is gone; and many, young and old, witness that the kingdom of God is within them.

Thur. June 1.—I reached Londonderry. June 4. (Being *Whit-Sunday.*) The bishop preached a judicious, useful sermon, on the blasphemy of the Holy Ghost. *Tuesday*, 6. He invited me to dinner; and told me, "I know you do not love our hours, and will therefore order dinner to be on table between two and three o'clock." We had a piece of boiled beef, and an English pudding. This is true good breeding. The bishop is entirely easy and unaffected in his whole behaviour, exemplary in all parts of public worship, and plenteous in good works.

Fri. 9.—I lodged at a gentleman's, who showed me a flower, which he called a gummy-cystus. It blooms in the morning, with a large, beautiful, snow-white flower; but every flower dies in the evening. New flowers blow and fall every day. Does not this short-lived flower answer to that short-lived animal, the ephemeron fly?

Tues. 13.—I was not very well in the morning, but supposed it would soon go off. In the afternoon, the weather being extremely hot, I lay down on the grass, in Mr Lark's orchard at Cockhill. This I had been accustomed to do for forty years, and never remember to have been hurt by it: only I never before lay on my face; in which posture I fell asleep. I waked a little, and but a little, out of order, and preached with ease to a multitude of people. Afterwards I was a good deal worse. In going on to Derryanvil, I wondered what was the matter, that I could not attend to what I was reading; no, not for three minutes together; but my thoughts were perpetually shifting. Yet, all the time I was preaching in the evening, (although I stood in the open air, with the wind whistling round my head), my mind was as composed as ever. *Friday*, 16. In going to Lurgan, I was again surprised that I could not fix my attention on what I read: yet, while I was preaching in the evening, on the Parade, I found my mind perfectly composed; although it rained a great part of the time, which did not well agree with my head. *Saturday*, 17. I was persuaded to send for Dr Laws, a sensible and skilful physician.

I was now at a full stand, whether to aim at Lisburn, or to push forward for Dublin. But my friends doubting whether I could bear so long a journey, I went straight to Derryaghy; a gentleman's seat, on the side of a hill, three miles beyond Lisburn. Here nature sunk, and I took my bed. My memory faded, as well as my strength, and well-nigh my understanding.

AUG. 1775] **The Honoured Guest** 361

Only those words ran in my mind, when I saw Miss Gayer on one side of the bed, looking at her mother on the other—

> "She sat, like Patience on a monument,
> Smiling at grief."

But still I had no thirst, no difficulty of breathing, no pain, from head to foot.

I can give no account of what followed for two or three days, being more dead than alive. Only I remember it was difficult for me to speak, my throat being exceeding dry. But Joseph Bradford tells me I said on *Wednesday*, "It will be determined before this time to-morrow."

In the night of *Thursday*, 22, Joseph Bradford came to me with a cup, and said, "Sir, you must take this." I thought, "I will, if I can swallow, to please him; for it will neither do me harm nor good." Immediately it set me a vomiting; my heart began to beat, and my pulse to play again; and from that hour the extremity of the symptoms abated. The next day I sat up several hours, and walked four or five times across the room. On *Saturday* I sat up all day, and walked across the room many times, without any weariness; on *Sunday* I came downstairs, and sat several hours in the parlour; on *Monday* I walked out before the house; on *Tuesday* I took an airing in the chaise; and on *Wednesday*, trusting in God, to the astonishment of my friends, I set out for Dublin.

Tues. July 4.—Finding myself a little stronger, I preached for the first time; and I believe most could hear. I preached on *Thursday* again; and my voice was clear, though weak. So on *Sunday* I ventured to preach twice, and found no weariness at all. *Monday*, 10. I began my regular course of preaching, morning and evening.

Tues. Aug. 1.—Our Conference began. Having received several letters, intimating that many of the preachers were utterly unqualified for the work, having neither grace nor gifts sufficient for it, I determined to examine this weighty charge with all possible exactness. In order to this, I read those letters to all the Conference; and begged that every one would freely propose and enforce whatever objection he had to anyone. The objections proposed were considered at large: in two or three difficult cases, committees were appointed for that purpose. In consequence of this, we were all fully convinced that the charge advanced was without foundation; that God has really sent those labourers into His vineyard, and has qualified them for the work: and we were all more closely united together than we have been for many years.

J.W.J.—24

Sat. Nov. 11.—I made some additions to the *Calm Address to our American Colonies*. Need any one ask from what motive this was wrote? Let him look round: England is in a flame! a flame of malice and rage against the King, and almost all that are in authority under him. I labour to put out this flame. Ought not every true patriot to do the same? If hireling writers on either side judge of me by themselves, that I cannot help.

CHAPTER XV

NEW PREACHING-HOUSES

FROM JANUARY 14, 1776, TO AUGUST 8, 1779

Sun. Jan. 14, 1776.—As I was going to West Street chapel, one of the chaise-springs suddenly snapped asunder; but the horses instantly stopping, I stepped out without the least inconvenience.

At all my vacant hours in this and the following week, I endeavoured to finish the *Concise History of England*. I am sensible it must give offence, as in many parts I am quite singular; particularly with regard to those greatly injured characters, Richard III., and Mary Queen of Scots. But I must speak as I think; although still waiting for, and willing to receive, better information.

Sun. 28.—I was desired to preach a charity sermon in Allhallows church, Lombard Street. In the year 1735, about forty years ago, I preached in this church, at the earnest request of the churchwardens, to a numerous congregation, who came, like me, with an intent to hear Dr Heylyn. This was the first time that, having no notes about me, I preached extempore.

Fri. Mar. 1.—As we cannot depend on having the Foundery long, we met to consult about building a new chapel. Our petition to the city for a piece of ground lies before their committee; but when we shall get any further, I know not: so I determined to begin my Circuit as usual; but promised to return whenever I should receive notice that our petition was granted.

Sun. April 7.—On *Easter Day* the preaching-house at Manchester contained the congregation pretty well at seven in the morning; but in the afternoon I was obliged to be abroad, thousands upon thousands flocking together. I stood in a convenient place, almost over against the Infirmary, and exhorted a listening multitude to "live unto Him who died for them and rose again."

Tues. 30.—In the evening I preached in a kind of square, at Colne, to a multitude of people, all drinking in the Word. I scarce ever saw a congregation wherein men, women, and children stood in such a posture : and this in the town wherein, thirty years ago, no Methodist could show his head ! The first that preached here was John Jane, who was innocently riding through the town, when the zealous mob pulled him off his horse, and put him in the stocks. He seized the opportunity, and vehemently exhorted them "to flee from the wrath to come."

Mon. May 6.—After preaching at Cockermouth and Wigton, I went on to Carlisle, and preached to a very serious congregation. Here I saw a very extraordinary genius, a man blind from four years of age, who could wind worsted, weave flowered plush on an engine and loom of his own making ; who wove his own name in plush, and made his own clothes, and his own tools of every sort. Some years ago, being shut up in the organ-loft at church, he felt every part of it, and afterwards made an organ for himself, which, judges say, is an exceeding good one. He then taught himself to play upon it psalm-tunes, anthems, voluntaries, or anything which he heard. I heard him play several tunes with great accuracy, and a complex voluntary : I suppose all Europe can hardly produce such another instance. His name is Joseph Strong. But what is he the better for all this, if he is still "without God in the world"?

Thur. 16.—I attended an ordination at Arbroath. The service lasted about four hours ; but it did not strike me. It was doubtless very grave ; but I thought it was very dull.

Fri. 17.—I reached Aberdeen in good time. *Saturday,* 18. I read over Dr Johnson's *Tour to the Western Isles.* It is a very curious book, wrote with admirable sense, and, I think, great fidelity ; although, in some respects, he is thought to bear hard on the nation, which I am satisfied he never intended.

Fri. 24.—I returned to Arbroath, and lodged at Provost Grey's. So, for a time, we are in honour ! I have hardly seen such another place in the three kingdoms, as this is at present. Hitherto there is no opposer at all, but every one seems to bid us God-speed !

Mon. 27.—I paid a visit to St Andrews, once the largest city in the kingdom. It was eight times as large as it is now, and a place of very great trade : but the sea rushing from the north-east, gradually destroyed the harbour and trade together ; in consequence of which, whole streets (that were) are now meadows and gardens. Three broad, straight, handsome streets remain, all pointing at the old cathedral ; which, by the ruins, appears to have been above three hundred feet long, and proportionably broad and high : so that it seems to have exceeded York Minster, and to have at least equalled any cathedral in England. Another church, afterwards used in its stead, bears date 1124. A steeple, standing near the cathedral, is thought to have stood thirteen hundred years.

Fri. June 28.—I am seventy-three years old, and far abler to preach than I was at three-and-twenty. What natural means has God used to produce so wonderful an effect? 1. Continual exercise and change of air, by travelling above four thousand miles in a year. 2. Constant rising at four. 3. The ability, if ever I want, to sleep immediately. 4. The never losing a night's sleep in my life. 5. Two violent fevers, and two deep consumptions. These, it is true, were rough medicines : but they were of admirable service ; causing my flesh to come again as the flesh of a little child. May I add, lastly, evenness of temper? I *feel* and *grieve* ; but, by the grace of God, I *fret* at nothing. But still "the help that is done upon earth, He doeth it Himself." And this He doeth in answer to many prayers.

Thur. July 18.—I preached at Nottingham ; and, having no time to lose, took chaise at noon, and the next evening, *Friday*, 19, met the committee at the Foundery.

Fri. Aug. 2.—We made our first subscription toward building a new chapel ; and at this, and the two following meetings, above a thousand pounds were cheerfully subscribed.

Sun. 4.—Many of the preachers being come to town, I enforced that solemn caution, in the Epistle for the day, "Let him that standeth take heed lest he fall." And God applied it to many hearts. In the afternoon I preached in Moorfields to thousands, on Acts ii. 32, "This Jesus hath God raised up, whereof we all are witnesses."

Tues. 6.—Our Conference began, and ended on *Friday*, 9, which we observed with fasting and prayer, as well for our own nation as for our brethren in America. In several Conferences, we have had great love and unity ; but in this there was, over and above, such a general seriousness and solemnity of spirit as we scarcely have had before. *Sunday*, 11. About half an hour after four I set out ; and at half an hour after eleven on *Monday*, came to Bristol.

I found Mr Fletcher a little better, and proposed his taking a journey with me to Cornwall ; nothing being so likely to restore his health, as a journey of four or five hundred miles : but his physician would in nowise consent ; so I gave up the point.

Tues. 13.—I preached at Taunton, and afterwards went

with Mr Brown to Kingston. The large, old parsonage house is pleasantly situated close to the churchyard, just fit for a contemplative man. Here I found a clergyman, Dr Coke, late Gentleman Commoner of Jesus College in Oxford, who came twenty miles on purpose. I had much conversation with him; and an union then began, which I trust shall never end.

Tues. 27.—About noon I preached in the piazza, adjoining to the coinage-hall in Truro. In the evening I preached in an open space at Mevagissey, to most of the inhabitants of the town; where I saw a very rare thing,—men swiftly increasing in substance, and yet not decreasing in holiness.

Mon. Sept. 2.—In my way to Exeter, I read over an ingenious tract, containing some observations which I never saw before. In particular, that if corn sells for twice as much now as it did at the time of the Revolution, it is in effect no dearer than it was then, because we have now twice as much money; that if other things sell now for twice as much as they did then, corn ought to do so too; that though the price of all things increases as money increases, yet they are really no dearer than they were before; and, lastly, that to petition Parliament to alter these things, is to put them upon impossibilities, and can answer no end but that of inflaming the people against their governors.

On *Saturday*, 7, I went on to Bristol.

Mon. 9.—I began, what I had long intended, visiting the society from house to house, setting apart at least two hours in a day for that purpose. I was surprised to find the simplicity with which one and all spoke, both of their temporal and spiritual state. Nor could I easily have known, by any other means, how great a work God has wrought among them. I found exceeding little to reprove; but much to praise God for. And I observed one thing, which I did not expect:—In visiting all the families, without Lawford Gate, by far the poorest about the city, I did not find so much as one person who was out of work.

Fri. Nov. 29.—We considered the several plans which were offered for the new chapel [London]. Having agreed upon one, we desired a surveyor to draw out the particulars, with an estimate of the expense. We then ordered proposals to be drawn up for those who were willing to undertake any part of the building.

Friday, December 13, was the national fast. It was observed not only throughout the city, but (I was afterwards informed) throughout the nation, with the utmost solemnity. I shall not wonder if God should now interpose and send us prosperity, since, at length, we are not too proud to acknowledge "there is a God that judgeth the earth."

Tues. 31.—We concluded the year with solemn praise to God for continuing His great work in our land. It has never been intermitted one year or one month, since the year 1738; in which my brother and I began to preach that strange doctrine of salvation by faith.

Wed. Jan. 1, 1777.—We met, as usual, to renew our covenant with God.

Mon. 13.—I took the opportunity of spending an hour every morning with the preachers, as I did with my pupils at Oxford. And we endeavoured not only to increase each other's knowledge, but "to provoke one another to love and to good works."

Wed. 15.—I began visiting those of our society who lived in Bethnal Green hamlet. Many of them I found in such poverty as few can conceive without seeing it. Oh, why do not all the rich that fear God constantly visit the poor! Can they spend part of their spare time better? Certainly not. So they will find in that day when "every man shall receive his own reward according to his own labour."

Such another scene I saw the next day, in visiting another part of the society. I have not found any such distress, no, not in the prison of Newgate. One poor man was just creeping out of his sick bed, to his ragged wife and three little children; who were more than half naked, and the very picture of famine; when one bringing in a loaf of bread, they all ran, seized upon it, and tore it in pieces in an instant. Who would not rejoice that there is another world?

Mon. Feb. 3.—Hearing there was some disturbance at Bristol, occasioned by men whose tongues were set on fire against the Government, I went down in the diligence, and on *Tuesday* evening strongly enforced those solemn words, "Put them in mind to be subject to principalities and powers, to speak evil of no man."

Finding the repeated attempts to set fire to the city had occasioned a general consternation, on *Wednesday*, 5, I opened and applied those words to a crowded audience: "Is there any evil in the city, and the Lord hath not done it?" On *Thursday* I wrote *A calm Address to the Inhabitants of England*.

Sat. 15.—At the third message, I took up my cross, and went to see Dr Dodd, in the Compter. I was greatly surprised. He seemed, though deeply affected, yet thoroughly resigned to the will of God. Mrs Dodd likewise behaved with the utmost propriety. I doubt not, God will bring good out of this evil. *Tuesday*, 18. I visited him again, and found him still in a desirable state of mind; calmly giving himself up to whatever God should determine concerning him.

Sun. Mar. 2.—Being a warm sunshiny day, I preached in Moorfields, in the evening. There were thousands upon thousands; and all were still as night. Not only violence and rioting, but even scoffing at field-preachers is now over.

Sun. 16.—I preached at St. Werburgh's, the first church I ever preached in at Bristol. I had desired my friends not to come thither, but to leave room for strangers. By this means the church was well filled, but not overmuch crowded; which gives occasion to them that seek occasion. as it is a real inconvenience to the parishioners.

Mon. April 14.—I preached about noon at Warrington, and in the evening at Liverpool; where many large ships are now laid up in the docks, which had been employed for many years in buying or stealing poor Africans, and selling them in America for slaves. The men-butchers have now nothing to do at this laudable occupation. Since the American war broke out, there is no demand for human cattle So the men of Africa, as well as Europe, may enjoy their native liberty.

Monday, 21, was the day appointed for laying the foundation of the new chapel. The rain befriended us much, by keeping away thousands who purposed to be there. But there were still such multitudes, that it was with great difficulty I got through them, to lay the first stone. Upon this was a plate of brass (covered with another stone), on which was engraved, "This was laid by Mr John Wesley, on April 1, 1777." Probably this will be seen no more, by any human eye; but will remain there, till the earth and the works thereof are burned up.

Sun. 27.—The sun breaking out, I snatched the opportunity of preaching to many thousands in Moorfields.

Tues. May 20.—I met the committee for building, which indeed was my chief business at London. We consulted together on several articles, and were confidently persuaded that He who had incited us to begin, would enable us to finish.

Sat. 24.—My brother and I paid another visit to Dr Dodd, and spent a melancholy and useful hour. He appears, so far as man can judge, to be a true, evangelical penitent.

Fri. 30.—I went on to Whitehaven, where I found a little vessel waiting for me. After preaching in the evening, I went on board about eight o'clock, and before eight in the morning landed at Douglas, in the Isle of Man.

Douglas exceedingly resembles Newlyn in Cornwall; both

in its situation, form, and buildings; only it is much larger, and has a few houses equal to most in Penzance. As soon as we landed, I was challenged by Mr Booth, who had seen me in Ireland, and whose brother has been for many years a member of the society in Coolylough. A chaise was provided to carry me to Castletown. I was greatly surprised at the country. All the way from Douglas to Castletown it is as pleasant and as well cultivated as most parts of England, with many gentlemen's seats. Castletown a good deal resembles Galway; only it is not so large. At six I preached near the castle, I believe, to all the inhabitants of the town. Two or three gay young women showed they knew nothing about religion; all the rest were deeply serious. Afterwards I spent an hour very agreeably at Mrs Wood's, the widow of the late Governor. I was much pressed to stay a little longer at Castletown; but my time was fixed.

Sun. June 1.—At six I preached in our own room; and, to my surprise, saw all the gentlewomen there. Young as well as old were now deeply affected, and would fain have had me stayed, were it but an hour or two; but I was forced to hasten away, in order to be at Peel town before the service began.

Mr Corbett said, he would gladly have asked me to preach, but that the bishop had forbidden him; who had also forbidden all his clergy to admit any Methodist preacher to the Lord's Supper. But is any clergyman obliged, either in law or conscience, to obey such a prohibition? By no means. The *will* even of the King does not bind any *English* subject, unless it be seconded by an express law. How much less the will of a bishop? "But did not you take an oath to obey him?" No, nor any clergyman in the three kingdoms. This is a mere vulgar error. Shame that it should prevail almost universally.

Mon. 2.—A more loving, simple-hearted people than this I never saw. And no wonder; for they have but six Papists, and no Dissenters, in the island. It is supposed to contain near thirty thousand people, remarkably courteous and humane. Ever since smuggling was suppressed, they diligently cultivate their land: and they have a large herring fishery, so that the country improves daily.

Wed. 25.—I saw Dr Dodd for the last time. He was in exactly such a temper as I wished. He never at any time expressed the least murmuring or resentment at anyone; but entirely and calmly gave himself up to the will of God. Such a prisoner I scarce ever saw before; much less, such a condemned malefactor. I should think, none could converse with him without acknowledging that God is with him.

Fri. Aug. 1.—I desired as many as could to join together in fasting and prayer, that God would restore the spirit of love and of a sound mind, to the poor deluded rebels in America.

Tues. 5.—Our yearly Conference began. I now particularly inquired (as that report had been spread far and wide) of every assistant, " Have you reason to believe, from your own observation, that the Methodists are a fallen people? Is there a decay or an increase in the work of God where you have been? Are the societies in general more dead, or more alive to God, than they were some years ago?" The almost universal answer was, " If we must 'know them by their fruits,' there is no decay in the work of God among the people in general. The societies are not dead to God : they are as much alive as they have been for many years. And we look on this report as a mere device of Satan, to make our hands hang down."

"But how can this question be decided?" You, and you, can judge no farther than you see. You cannot judge of one part by another ; of the people of London, suppose, by those of Bristol. And none but myself has an opportunity of seeing them throughout the three kingdoms.

But to come to a short issue. In most places, the Methodists are still a poor, despised people, labouring under reproach, and many inconveniences ; therefore, wherever the power of God is not, they decrease. By this, then, you may form a sure judgment. Do the Methodists in general decrease in number? Then they decrease in grace ; they are a fallen, or, at least, a falling people. But they do not decrease in number ; they continually increase ; therefore, they are not a fallen people.

Tues. 19.—I went forward to Taunton, with Dr Coke, who, being dismissed from his curacy, has bid adieu to his honourable name, and determined to cast in his lot with us.

Sat. Sept. 27.—Having abundance of letters from Dublin, informing me that the society there was in the utmost confusion, by reason of some of the chief members, whom the preachers had thought it needful to exclude from the society ; and finding all I could write was not sufficient to stop the growing evil, I saw but one way remaining, to go myself, and that as soon as possible.

Mon. Oct. 6.—At ten I met the contending parties ; the preachers on one hand, and the excluded members on the other ; I heard them at large, and they pleaded their several causes with earnestness and calmness too. At the desire of the members lately excluded, I now drew up the short state of the case ; but I could in no wise pacify them : they were all civil, nay, it seemed, affectionate to me ; but they could never forgive the preachers that had expelled them : so that I could not desire them to return into the society ; they could only remain friends at a distance.

Sat. 11.—I visited many, sick and well, and endeavoured to confirm them in their love towards each other. I was more and more convinced that God had sent me at this time to heal the breach of His people.

Sun. Nov. 23.—I preached in Lewisham church, for the benefit of the Humane Society, instituted for the sake of those who seem to be drowned, strangled, or killed by any sudden stroke. It is a glorious design ; in consequence of which many have been recovered that must otherwise have inevitably perished.

Mon. 24.—I spent the afternoon at Mr Blackwell's, with the B—— of ——. His whole behaviour was worthy of a Christian bishop ; easy, affable, courteous ; and yet all his conversation spoke the dignity which was suitable to his character.

Having been many times desired, for near forty years, to publish a magazine, I at length complied ; and now began to collect materials for it. If it once begin, I incline to think it will not end but with my life.

Sat. Dec. 13.—Being strongly urged to lay the first stone of the house which was going to be built at Bath, on *Sunday*, 14, after preaching at West Street chapel in the morning, and at St Paul's, Shadwell, in the afternoon, I went to Brentford. I preached at six ; and, taking chaise at twelve, on *Monday*, 15, easily reached Bath in the afternoon.

Just at this time there was a combination among many of the post-chaise drivers on the Bath road, especially those that drove in the night, to deliver their passengers into each other's hands. One driver stopped at the spot they had appointed, where another waited to attack the chaise. In consequence of this, many were robbed ; but I had a good Protector still. I have travelled all roads, by day and by night, for these forty years, and never was interrupted yet.

Tues. Feb. 17, 1778.—I wrote *A serious Address to the Inhabitants of England*, with regard to the present state of the nation,—so strangely misrepresented both by ignorant and designing men,—to remove, if possible, the apprehensions which have been so diligently spread, as if it were on the brink of ruin.

Friday, 27, was the day appointed for the national fast ; and it was observed with due solemnity. All shops were shut up ; all was quiet in the streets ; all places of public worship were crowded ; no food was served up in the King's house till five o'clock in the evening. Thus far, at least, we acknowledge God may direct our paths.

Wed. Mar. 4.—I went to Bristol. I found the panic had spread hither also, as if the nation were on the brink of ruin. Strange that those who love God should be so frightened at shadows! I can compare this only to the alarm which spread through the nation in King William's time, that on that very night the Irish Papists were to cut the throats of all the Protestants in England.

Mon. 9.—On this and the following days I visited the society, and found a good increase. This year, I myself (which I have seldom done) chose the preachers for Bristol; and these were plain men; and likely to do more good than has been done in one year, for these twenty years.

Mon. 16.—I took a cheerful leave of our friends at Bristol, and set out once more for Ireland.

Tues. Aug. 4.—Our Conference began: so large a number of preachers never met at a Conference before. I preached, morning and evening, till *Thursday* night: then my voice began to fail; so I desired two of our preachers to supply my place the next day. On *Saturday* the Conference ended.

Mon. 17.—Dr Coke, my brother, and I, took coach for Bristol; and early on *Thursday*, 20, I set out for Cornwall.

Sun. 23.—At seven I preached in our room, and at one on the quay, at Plymouth. The common people behaved well; but I was shocked at the stupidity and ill-breeding of several officers, who kept walking and talking together all the time with the most perfect unconcern. We had no such Gallios in the evening at the Dock, though the congregation was four times as large. Surely this is an understanding people; may their love be equal to their knowledge!

Mon. 24.—In the way to Medros, Mr Furz gave me a strange relation, which was afterwards confirmed by eye and ear witnesses:—In July, 1748, Martin Hoskins, of Sithney, being in a violent passion, was struck raving mad, and obliged to be chained down to the floor. Charles Sk—— went to see him. He cried out, "Who are thou? Hast thou faith? No; thou art afraid." Charles felt an inexpressible shock, and was raving mad himself. He continued so for several days, till some agreed to keep a day of fasting and prayer. His lunacy then ended as suddenly as it began. But what was peculiarly remarkable was, while he was ill, Martin was quite well: as soon as he was well, Martin was as ill as ever.

Thence I went on to Redruth, Helstone, and Penzance. On *Thursday*, 27, in the evening I preached in the market-place, at St Just. Very few of our old society are now left: the far greater part of them are in Abraham's bosom. But the new generation are of the same spirit; serious, earnest, devoted to God; and particularly remarkable for simplicity and Christian sincerity.

Fri. 28.—The stewards of the societies met at St Ives,—a company of pious, sensible men. I rejoiced to find that peace and love prevailed through the whole Circuit. Those who styled themselves My Lady's Preachers, who screamed, and railed, and threatened to swallow us up, are vanished away. I cannot learn that they have made one convert;—a plain proof that God did not send them.

Sun. 30.—About five I preached in the amphitheatre at Gwennap, it was believed, to four-and-twenty thousand. Afterwards I spent a solemn hour with the society, and slept in peace.

Tues. Sept. 1.—I went to Tiverton. I was musing here on what I heard a good man say long since,—"Once in seven years I burn all my sermons; for it is a shame if I cannot write better sermons now than I did seven years ago." Whatever others can do, I really cannot. I cannot write a better sermon on the Good Steward, than I did seven years ago: I cannot write a better on the Great Assize, than I did twenty years ago: I cannot write a better on the Use of Money, than I did near thirty years ago: nay, I know not that I can write a better on the Circumcision of the Heart, than I did five-and-forty years ago. Perhaps, indeed, I may have read five or six hundred books more than I had then, and may know a little more history, or natural philosophy, than I did; but I am not sensible that this has made any essential addition to my knowledge in divinity. Forty years ago I knew and preached every Christian doctrine which I preach now.

Sunday, Nov. 1, was the day appointed for opening the new chapel in the City Road. It is perfectly neat, but not fine; and contains far more people than the Foundery: I believe, together with the morning chapel, as many as the Tabernacle. Many were afraid that the multitudes, crowding from all parts, would have occasioned much disturbance. But they were happily disappointed: there was none at all: all was quietness, decency, and order. I preached on part of Solomon's Prayer at the Dedication of the Temple; and both in the morning and afternoon (when I preached on the hundred forty and four thousand standing with the Lamb on Mount Zion) God was eminently present in the midst of the congregation.

Sun. 29.—I was desired to preach a charity sermon in St Luke's church, Old Street. I doubt whether it was ever so crowded before; and the fear of God seemed to possess the whole audience. In the afternoon I preached at the new chapel; and at seven, in St Margaret's, Rood Lane; full as much crowded as St Luke's. Is then the scandal of the cross ceased?

Fri. Dec. 11.—I preached at Lambeth, in the chapel newly prepared by Mr Edwards, whose wife has seventy-five boarders. Miss Owen, at Publow, takes only twenty, thinking she cannot do her duty to any more.

Sun. 20.—I buried what was mortal of honest Silas Told. For many years he attended the malefactors in Newgate, without fee or reward; and I suppose no man for this hundred years has been so successful in that melancholy office. God had given him peculiar talents for it; and he had amazing success therein. The greatest part of those whom he attended died in peace, and many of them in the triumph of faith.

Fri. 25.—(Being *Christmas Day.*) Our service began at four, as usual, in the new chapel. I expected Mr Richardson to read prayers at West Street chapel, but he did not come; so I read prayers myself, and preached, and administered the sacrament to several hundred people. In the afternoon I preached at the new chapel, thoroughly filled in every corner; and in the evening at St Sepulchre's, one of the largest parish churches in London. It was warm enough, being sufficiently filled; yet I felt no weakness or weariness, but was stronger after I had preached my fourth sermon, than I was after the first.

Fri. Jan. 1, 1779.—At length we have a house capable of containing the whole society. We met there this evening to renew our covenant with God; and we never met on that solemn occasion without a peculiar blessing.

Tues. 12.—I dined and drank tea with four German ministers. I could not but admire the wisdom of those that appointed them. They seem to consider not only the essential points, their sense and piety, but even those smaller things, the good breeding, the address, yea, the persons of those they send into foreign countries.

Wednesday, Feb. 10, was a national fast. So solemn a one I never saw before. From one end of the city to the other, there was scarce anyone seen in the streets. All places of public worship were crowded in an uncommon degree; and an unusual awe sat on most faces. I preached on the words of God to Abraham, interceding for Sodom, "I will not destroy the city for his sake."

Thur. Mar. 11.—I opened the new chapel at Bath. It is about half as large as that at London, and built nearly upon the same model.

Mon. 15.—I began my tour through England and Scotland;

the lovely weather continuing, such as the oldest man alive had not seen before, for January, February, and half of March.

Thur. July 22.—I took coach for London. I was nobly attended: behind the coach were ten convicted felons, loudly blaspheming and rattling their chains; by my side sat a man with a loaded blunderbuss, and another upon the coach.

Sun. 25.—Both the chapels were full enough. On *Monday*, I retired to Lewisham to write. *Tuesday*, August 3. Our Conference began; which continued and ended in peace and love. *Sunday*, 8. I was at West Street in the morning, and at the new chapel in the evening, when I took a solemn leave of the affectionate congregation. This was the last night which I spent at the Foundery. What hath God wrought there in one-and-forty years!

CHAPTER XVI

THE PASSING OF THE OLD METHODISTS

FROM AUGUST 9, 1779, TO JULY 24, 1782

Mon. Aug. 9, 1779.—I set out for Wales, with my brother and his family. *Thursday*, 12. We went on to Monmouth, where the late storm is blown over.

Fri. 13.—As I was going down a steep pair of stairs, my foot slipped, and I fell down several steps. Falling on the edge of one of them, it broke the case of an almanac, which was in my pocket, all to pieces. The edge of another stair met my right buckle, and snapped the steel chape of it in two; but I was not hurt. So doth our good Master give His angels charge over us! In the evening I preached at Brecknock; and, leaving my brother there, on *Saturday*, 14, went forward to Carmarthen.

Fri. 20.—Many of us met at noon, and spent a solemn hour in intercession for our King and country.

Sat. 21.—I went to Pembroke. Understanding that a large number of American prisoners were here, in the evening I took my stand over against the place where they were confined; so that they all could hear distinctly. Many of them seemed much affected. Oh that God may set their souls at liberty!

Mon. 23.—I came once more to Carmarthen. Finding the people here (as indeed in every place) under a deep consternation through the terrible reports which flew on every side, I cried aloud in the market-place, "Say ye unto the righteous, it shall be well with him." God made it a word in season to them, and many were no longer afraid.

Thur. 26.—I preached at five, and again at eleven. I think this was the happiest time of all. The poor and the rich seemed to be equally affected. Oh how are the times changed at Cowbridge, since the people compassed the house where I was, and poured in stones from every quarter! But my strength was then according to my day; and (blessed be God!) so it is still.

Mon. 29.—I set out for the west, and in the evening preached at Taunton.

A gentleman, just come from Plymouth, gave us a very remarkable account:—"For two days the combined fleets of France and Spain lay at the mouth of the harbour. They might have entered it with perfect ease. The wind was fair; there was no fleet to oppose them; and the island, which is the grand security of the place, being incapable of giving them any hindrance; for there was scarce any garrison, and the few men that were there had no wadding at all, and but two rounds of powder." But had they not cannon? Yes, in abundance; but only two of them were mounted! Why then did they not go in, destroy the dock, and burn or at least plunder the town? I believe they could hardly tell themselves. —The plain reason was, the bridle of God was in their teeth; and He had said, "Hitherto shall ye come, and no farther."

Sat. Sept. 4.—I returned to Bristol.

Fri. Oct. 8.—This night I lodged in the new house at London. How many more nights have I to spend there?

Sat. Nov. 13.—I had the pleasure of an hour's conversation with Mr G., one of the members of the first Congress in America. He unfolded a strange tale indeed! How has poor K. G. been betrayed on every side! But this is our comfort: there is One higher than they. And he will command all things to work together for good.

Mon. Dec. 13.—I retired to Lewisham, and settled the society book. Fifty-seven members of the society have died this year; and none of them "as a fool dieth." An hundred and seventy have left the society. Such are the fruits of senseless prejudice.

Tues. Jan. 18, 1780.—Receiving more and more accounts of the increase of Popery, I believed it my duty to write a letter concerning it, which was afterwards inserted in the public papers. Many were grievously offended; but I cannot help it: I must follow my own conscience.

Sat. 22.—I spent an hour or two very agreeably in Sir Ashton Lever's Museum. It does not equal the British Museum in size; nor is it constructed on so large a plan: as it contains no manuscripts, no books, no antiquities, nor any remarkable works of art. But I believe, for natural curiosities, it is not excelled by any museum in Europe; and all the beasts, birds, reptiles, and insects are admirably well ranged and preserved: so that if you saw many of them elsewhere, you would imagine they were alive! The hippopotamus, in particular, looks as fierce as if he was just coming out of the river; and the old lion appears as formidable now as when he was stalking in the Tower.

Wed. April 12.—In the evening I preached in the new house at Leeds. *Thursday*, 13. I opened the new house at Hunslet. On *Friday* I preached at Woodhouse. *Sunday*, 16. Our house at Leeds was full at eight; yet every one heard distinctly. In the afternoon I preached at the old church; but a considerable part of the people could not hear. Indeed, the church is remarkably ill constructed. Had it been built with common sense, all that were in it, and even more, might have heard every word.

Wed. 19.—I went to Otley; but Mr Ritchie was dead before I came. But he had first witnessed a good confession. One telling him, "You will be better soon"; he replied, "I cannot be better; for I have God in my heart. I am happy, happy, happy in His love."

Mr Wilson, the vicar, after a little hesitation, consented that I should preach his funeral sermon: this I did to-day. The text he had chosen was, "To you that believe, He is precious."

Fri. May 5.—Notice having been given, without my knowledge, of my preaching at Ninthead, all the lead-miners that could, got together; and I declared to them, "All things are ready." After riding over another enormous mountain, I preached at Gamblesby (as I did about thirty years ago) to a large congregation of rich and poor. The chief man of the town was formerly a local preacher, but now keeps his carriage. Has he increased in holiness as well as in wealth? If not, he has made a poor exchange.

Thur. 11.—I reached Newcastle; and on *Friday*, 12, went to Sunderland. Many of our friends prosper in the world. I wish their souls may prosper also.

Mon. 15.—I set out for Scotland.

Fri. 19.—I preached at Joppa, a settlement of colliers, three miles from Edinburgh. Some months ago, as some of them were cursing and swearing, one of our local preachers going by reproved them. One of them followed after him, and begged he would give them a sermon. He did so several times. Afterwards the travelling preachers went, and a few quickly agreed to meet together. Some of these now know in whom they have believed, and walk worthy of their profession.

Sun. 21.—The rain hindered me from preaching at noon upon the Castle Hill. In the evening the house was well filled, and I was enabled to speak strong words. But I am not a preacher for the people of Edinburgh. Hugh Saunderson and Michael Fenwick are more to their taste.

Wed. 31.—I went to Mr Parker's at Shincliff, near Durham. The congregation being far too large to get into the house, I stood near his door. It seemed as if the whole village were ready to receive the truth in the love thereof. Perhaps their earnestness may provoke the people of Durham to jealousy.

Tues. June 6.—An arch news-writer published a paragraph to-day, probably designed for wit, concerning the large pension which the famous Wesley received for defending the King. This so increased the congregation in the evening, that scores were obliged to go away.

Sun. 11.—I preached at Kirton, about eight, to a very large and very serious congregation. Only before me stood one, something like a gentleman, with his hat on even at prayer. I could scarce help telling him a story :—In Jamaica, a negro passing by the Governor, pulled off his hat; so did the Governor; at which one expressing his surprise, he said, "Sir, I should be ashamed if a negro had more good manners than the Governor of Jamaica."

Mon. 12.—About eleven I preached at Newton-upon-Trent, to a large and very genteel congregation. Thence we went to Newark : but our friends were divided as to the place where I should preach. At length they found a convenient place, covered on three sides, and on the fourth open to the street. It contained two or three thousand people well, who appeared to hear as for life. Only one big man, exceeding drunk, was very noisy and turbulent, till his wife (*fortissima Tyndaridarum !*[1]) seized him by the collar, gave him two or three hearty boxes on the ear, and dragged him away like a calf. But, at length, he got out of her hands, crept in among the people, and stood as quiet as a lamb.

Tues. 13.—I accepted of an invitation from a gentleman at Lincoln, in which I had not set my foot for upwards of fifty years. At six in the evening I preached in the castle-yard, to a large and attentive congregation. Will God have a people here also ?

Fri. 16.—We went on to Boston, the largest town in the county, except Lincoln. From the top of the steeple (which I suppose is by far the highest tower in the kingdom) we had a view not only of all the town, but of all the adjacent country. Formerly this town was in the fens ; but the fens are vanished away : great part of them is turned into pasture, and part into arable land. At six the house contained the congregation, all of whom behaved in a most decent manner. How different from those wild beasts with whom Mr Mitchell and Mr Mather

[1] " The bravest Amazonian of her race."—ED.

had to do ! *Sat.* 17. The house was pretty well filled in the morning, and many were much affected. A gentleman who was there invited me to dinner, and offered me the use of his paddock ; but the wind was so exceeding high, that I could not preach abroad, as I did when I was here before, just six-and-twenty years ago ; and Mr Thompson, a friendly Anabaptist, offering me the use of his large meeting-house, I willingly accepted the offer. I preached to most of the chief persons in the town, on 1 Cor. xiii. 1-3 ; and many of them seemed utterly amazed.

Tues. 20.—After preaching at Tealby, I went on to Grimsby, where I am still more at home than at any place in the east of Lincolnshire ; though scarce any of our first members remain : they are all safe lodged in Abraham's bosom. But here is still a loving people, though a little disturbed by the Calvinists, who seize on every halting soul as their own lawful prey.

Sun. 25.—At Belton, Sir William Anderson, the rector, having sent an express order to his curate, he did not dare to gainsay. So at ten I began reading prayers to such a congregation as I apprehend hardly ever assembled in this church before. I preached on Luke viii. 18, part of the second lesson. Not a breath was heard ; all was still "as summer's noontide air" ; and I believe our Lord then sowed seed in many hearts which will bring forth fruit to perfection.

Mon. July 17.—My brother and I set out for Bath.

Mon. 24.—I went on to Bristol. While I was at Bath, I narrowly observed and considered the celebrated cartoons ; the three first in particular. What a poor designer was one of the finest painters in the world ! 1. Here are two men in a boat ; each of them more than half as long as the boat itself. 2. Our Lord, saying to Peter, "Feed My sheep," points to three or four sheep standing by Him. 3. While Peter and John heal the lame man, two naked boys stand by them. For what ! Oh, pity that so fine a painter should be utterly without common sense !

In the evening I saw one of the greatest curiosities in the vegetable creation—the Nightly Cereus. About four in the afternoon, the dry stem began to swell ; about six, it gradually opened ; and about eight, it was in its full glory. I think the inner part of this flower, which was snow-white, was about five inches diameter ; the yellow rays which surrounded it, I judged, were in diameter nine or ten inches. About twelve it began to droop, being covered with a cold sweat ; at four it died away.

The people at Bath were still upon my mind : so on *Thursday*, 27, I went over again ; and God was with us of a truth, whenever we assembled together. Surely God is healing the breaches of this poor, shattered people.

Sun. Oct. 1.—I preached, as usual, morning and evening at the room. About two I preached a funeral sermon at Kingswood, for that blessed saint, Bathsheba Hall, a pattern for many years of zealously doing and patiently suffering the will of God. In the evening about seven hundred of us joined in solemnly renewing our covenant with God.

Mon. Nov. 20.—I went on to Chatham, and finding the society groaning under a large debt, advised them to open a weekly subscription. The same advice I gave to the society at Sheerness. This advice they all cheerfully followed, and with good effect. On *Friday*, 24, we agreed to follow the same example at London ; and in one year we paid off one thousand four hundred pounds.

Sun. Dec. 10.—I began reading and explaining to the society the large minutes of the Conference. I desire to do all things openly and above-board. I would have all the world, and especially all of our society, see not only all the steps we take, but the reasons why we take them.

Sat. 16.—Having a second message from Lord George Gordon, earnestly desiring to see me, I wrote a line to Lord Stormont, who, on *Monday*, 18, sent me a warrant to see him. On *Tuesday*, 19, I spent an hour with him, at his apartment in the Tower. Our conversation turned upon Popery and religion. He seemed to be well acquainted with the Bible ; and had abundance of other books, enough to furnish a study. I was agreeably surprised to find he did not complain of any person or thing ; and cannot but hope, his confinement will take a right turn, and prove a lasting blessing to him.

Fri. 29.—I saw the indictment of the Grand Jury against Lord George Gordon. I stood aghast! What a shocking insult upon truth and common sense ! But it is the usual form. The more is the shame. Why will not the Parliament remove this scandal from our nation ?

Sat. 30.—Waking between one and two in the morning, I observed a bright light shine upon the chapel. I easily concluded there was a fire near ; probably in the adjoining timber-yard. If so, I knew it would soon lay us in ashes. I first called all the family to prayer ; then going out, we found the fire about a hundred yards off, and had broke out while the wind was south. But a sailor cried out, "Avast ! Avast ! the wind is turned in a moment !" So it did, to the west, while we were at prayer, and so drove the flame from us. We then thankfully returned, and I rested well the residue of the night.

Thur. Jan. 25, 1781.—I spent an agreeable hour at a concert of my nephews. But I was a little out of my element among lords and ladies. I love plain music and plain company best.

Wed. Mar. 28.—Burslem. How is the whole face of this country changed in about twenty years! Since the potteries were introduced, inhabitants have continually flowed in from every side. Hence the wilderness is literally become a fruitful field. Houses, villages, towns, have sprung up. And the country is not more improved than the people. The Word of God has had free course among them. Sinners are daily awakened and converted to God ; and believers grow in the knowledge of Christ

After preaching at Congleton, Macclesfield, and Stockport, in my way, on *Friday*, 30, I opened the new chapel at Manchester, about the size of that in London.

Sun. April 1.—I began reading prayers at ten o'clock. Our country friends flocked in from all sides. At the Communion was such a sight as I am persuaded was never seen at Manchester before : eleven or twelve hundred communicants at once ; and all of them fearing God.

Tues. 3.—I took a solemn leave of our affectionate friends here, and went on to Bolton. The society here are true, original Methodists. They are not conformed to the world, either in its maxims, its spirit, or its fashions ; but are simple followers of the Lamb : consequently they increase both in grace and number.

Wed. 4.—I went over to Wigan, and preached a funeral sermon for Betty Brown, one of the first members of this society ; one of whom, John Layland, gave me the following artless account of her :—" She met with us in a class about twenty years, even to the Sunday before her death, which was on Friday, March 2. Going to market that day in good health, she returned (as she often did) without her husband, ate her supper, and went to bed. About midnight he came and found her body ; but the spirit was fled ! Her love for God, for His cause, and for her brethren and sisters, was truly remarkable. So was her pity for backsliders. At home and abroad she was continually intent on one thing.

" She was the beloved of God, the delight of His children, a dread to wicked men, and a torment to devils."

Fri. 6.—I went to Alpraham, and preached the funeral sermon of good old sister Crawley. She had been indeed a mother in Israel ; a pattern of all good works. *Saturday*, 7. At noon, I preached at Preston-on-the-Hill ; and in the evening at Warrington. *Sunday*, 8. The service was at the usual hours. I came just in time to put a stop to a bad custom, which was creeping in here : a few men, who had fine voices, sang a Psalm which no one knew, in a tune fit for an opera, wherein three, four, or five persons sung different words at the same time !

Tues. May 8.—In the evening I preached in the town-hall at Cardiff : but the congregation was almost wholly new. The far greater part of the old society, Ann Jenkins, Thomas Glascot, Arthur Price, Jane Haswell, Nancy Newell, and a long train, are gone hence, and are no more seen. And how few are followers of them, as they were of Christ!

Mon. 14.—Before I reached Monmouth, one met and informed me, that Mr C., a Justice of the Peace, one of the greatest men in the town, desired I would take a bed at his house. Of consequence, all the rabble of the town were as quiet as lambs ; and we had a comfortable opportunity both night and morning. Surely this is the Lord's doing !

Thur. 17.— I preached at Whitchurch and Nantwich. *Sunday,* 20. I found much enlargement in applying to a numerous congregation the lovely account given by St James of " pure religion and undefiled." In the afternoon I preached a funeral sermon for Mary Charlton, an Israelite indeed. From the hour that she first knew the pardoning love of God, she never lost sight of it for a moment. Eleven years ago, she believed that God had cleansed her from all sin ; and she showed that she had not believed in vain, by her holy and unblamable conversation.

Sun. Aug. 5.—At the old church in Leeds we had eighteen clergymen, and about eleven hundred communicants. I preached there at three ; the church was thoroughly filled ; and I believe most could hear, while I explained the " new covenant," which God has now made with the Israel of God.

Mon. 6.—I desired Mr Fletcher, Dr Coke, and four more of our brethren, to meet every evening, that we might consult together on any difficulty that occurred. On *Tuesday* our Conference began, at which were present about seventy preachers, whom I had severally invited to come and assist me with their advice, in carrying on the great work of God. *Wednesday,* 8. I desired Mr Fletcher to preach. I do not wonder he should be so popular ; not only because he preaches with all his might, but because the power of God attends both his preaching and prayer. On *Monday* and *Tuesday* we finished the remaining business of the Conference, and ended it with solemn prayer and thanksgiving.

Wed. 15.—I went to Sheffield. In the afternoon I took

a view of the chapel lately built by the Duke of Norfolk. One may safely say, there is none like it in the three kingdoms ; nor, I suppose, in the world. It is a stone building, an octagon, about eighty feet diameter. A cupola, which is at a great height, gives some, but not much, light. A little more is given by four small windows which are under the galleries. The pulpit is movable ; it rolls upon wheels ; and is shifted once a quarter, that all the pews may face it in their turns : I presume the first contrivance of the kind in Europe.

After preaching in the evening to a crowded audience, and exhorting the society to brotherly love, I took chaise with Dr Coke ; and travelling day and night, the next evening came to London.

Sun. Sept. 2.—About five in the evening I preached at Gwennap. I believe two or three and twenty thousand were present ; and I believe God enabled me so to speak, that even those who stood farthest off could hear distinctly. I think this is my *ne plus ultra.* I shall scarce see a larger congregation, till we meet in the air.

On *Wednesday,* 5, about noon, I preached at Taunton. I believe it my duty to relate here what some will esteem a most notable instance of enthusiasm. Be it so or not, I aver the plain fact. In an hour after we left Taunton, one of the chaise-horses was on a sudden so lame, that he could hardly set his foot to the ground. It being impossible to procure any human help, I knew of no remedy but prayer. Immediately the lameness was gone, and he went just as he did before. In the evening I preached at South Brent ; and the next day went on to Bristol.

Fri. 7.—I went over to Kingswood, and made a particular inquiry into the management of the school. I found some of the rules had not been observed at all ; particularly that of rising in the morning. Surely Satan has a peculiar spite at this school ! What trouble has it cost me for above these thirty years ! I can plan ; but who will execute ? I know not ; God help me !

Fri. 28.—About noon I preached at Keynsham ; and not without hopes of doing good even here.

Fri. Nov. 2.—I returned to London.

Mon. 5.—I began visiting the classes, and found a considerable increase in the society. This I impute chiefly to a small company of young persons, who have kept a prayer-meeting at five every morning. In the following week, I visited most of the country societies, and found them increasing rather than decreasing.

Mon. Jan. 14, 1782.—Being informed, that, through the ill conduct of the preachers, things were in much disorder at Colchester, I went down, hoping to "strengthen the things which remained, that were ready to die. I found that part of the class Leaders were dead, and the rest had left the society; the bands were totally dissolved; morning preaching was given up; and hardly any, except on Sunday, attended the evening preaching. This evening, however, we had a very large congregation, to whom I proclaimed "the terrors of the Lord." I then told them I would immediately restore the morning preaching: and the next morning I suppose an hundred attended. In the daytime I visited as many as I possibly could, in all quarters of the town. I then inquired, who were proper and willing to meet in band; and who were fittest for Leaders, either of bands or classes. The congregation this evening was larger than the last; and many again put their hands to the plough.

March 29.—(Being *Good Friday*.) I came to Macclesfield just time enough to assist Mr Simpson in the laborious service of the day. I preached for him morning and afternoon; and we administered the sacrament to about thirteen hundred persons. While we were administering, I heard a low, soft, solemn sound, just like that of an Æolian harp. It continued five or six minutes, and so affected many that they could not refrain from tears. It then gradually died away. Strange that no other organist (that I know) should think of this. In the evening I preached at our room. Here was that harmony which art cannot imitate.

Tues. April 2.—About ten I preached at New Mills, to as simple a people as those at Chapel. Perceiving they had suffered much by not having the doctrine of perfection clearly explained, I preached expressly on the head; and spoke to the same effect on meeting the society. The spirits of many greatly revived: and they are now "going on unto perfection." I found it needful to press the same thing at Stockport in the evening.

Fri. 5.—About one I preached at Oldham; and was surprised to see all the street lined with little children; and such children as I never saw till now. Before preaching they only ran round me and before me; but after it, a whole troop, boys and girls, closed me in, and would not be content till I shook each of them by the hand. Being then asked to visit a dying woman, I no sooner entered the room, than both she and her companions were in such an emotion as I have seldom seen. Some laughed; some cried; all were so transported that they could hardly speak. Oh how much better is it to go to the poor, than to the rich ; and to the house of mourning, than to the house of feasting !

Sat. May 11.—About noon I preached at Doncaster ; and in the evening at Epworth. I found the accounts I had received of the work of God here, were not at all exaggerated. Here is a little country town, containing a little more than eight or nine hundred grown people ; and there has been such a work among them, as we have not seen in so short a time either at Leeds, Bristol, or London.

Tues. 14.—Some years ago four factories for spinning and weaving were set up at Epworth. In these a large number of young women, and boys and girls, were employed. The whole conversation of these was profane and loose to the last degree. But some of these stumbling in at the prayer-meeting were suddenly cut to the heart. These never rested till they had gained their companions. The whole scene was changed. In three of the factories, no more lewdness or profaneness were found ; for God had put a new song in their mouth, and blasphemies were turned to praise. Those three I visited to-day, and found religion had taken deep root in them. No trifling word was heard among them, and they watch over each other in love.

Wed. 15.—I set out for the other side of Lincolnshire. *Thursday*, 16. I preached in the new house at Barrow. I was well pleased to meet with my old fellow-traveller, Charles Delamotte, here. He gave me an invitation to lodge at his house, which I willingly accepted of. He seemed to be just the same as when we lodged together five-and-forty years ago. Only he complained of the infirmities of old age, which, through the mercy of God, I know nothing of.

Fri. 31.—As I lodged with Lady Maxwell at Saughton Hall (a good old mansion-house, three miles from Edinburgh), she desired me to give a short discourse to a few of her poor neighbours. I did so, at four in the afternoon, on the story of Dives and Lazarus. About seven I preached in our house at Edinburgh, and fully delivered my own soul. *Saturday*, June 1. I spent a little time with forty poor children, whom Lady Maxwell keeps at school. They are swiftly brought forward in reading and writing, and learn the principles of religion. But I observe in them all the *ambitiosa paupertas*.[1] Be they ever so poor, they must have a scrap of finery. Many of them have not a shoe to their foot : but the girl in rags is not without her ruffles.

Fri. June 28.—I entered into my eightieth year ; but,

[1] " The love of finery among the poor."—ED.

blessed be God, my time is not "labour and sorrow." I find no more pain or bodily infirmities than at five-and-twenty. This I still impute : 1. To the power of God, fitting me for what He calls me to. 2. To my still travelling four or five thousand miles a year. 3. To my sleeping, night or day, whenever I want it. 4. To my rising at a set hour. And, 5. To my constant preaching, particularly in the morning.

Sat. July 20.—We reached London. All the following week the congregations were uncommonly large. *Wednesday*, 24. My brother and I paid our last visit to Lewisham, and spent a few pensive hours with the relict of our good friend, Mr Blackwell. We took one more walk round the garden and meadow, which he took so much pains to improve. Upwards of forty years this has been my place of retirement, when I could spare two or three days from London. In that time, first Mrs Sparrow went to rest; then Mrs Dewall; then good Mrs Blackwell; now Mr Blackwell himself. Who can tell how soon we may follow them?

CHAPTER XVII

"*MY REMNANT OF DAYS*"

FROM SEPTEMBER 6, 1782, TO OCTOBER 24, 1790

Friday, Sept. 6, 1782.—In the afternoon we went on to Bristol.

Sun. 8.—My brother read prayers, and I preached to a very uncommon congregation. But a far more numerous one met near King's Square in the evening; on whom I strongly enforced, "Ye cannot serve God and mammon." Permit me to observe here, how you may distinguish a genuine small Field's Bible from a spurious one: the genuine reads here, "Ye *can* serve God and mammon." In the spurious, the "not" is supplied.

Sun. Nov. 24.—I preached at St Clement's in the Strand (the largest church I ever preached in at London, except, perhaps, St Sepulchre's), to an immense congregation.

Fri. Jan. 10, 1783.—I paid one more visit to Mr Perronet, now in his ninetieth year. I do not know so venerable a man. His understanding is little, if at all, impaired; and his heart seems to be all love.

Fri. Feb. 21.—At our yearly meeting for that purpose, we examined our yearly accounts, and found the money received (just answering the expense) was upwards of three thousand pounds a year. But that is nothing to me: what I receive of it is neither more nor less than thirty pounds.

Tues. July 29.—Our Conference [at Bristol] began, at which two important points were considered: first, the case of Birstal house; and, secondly, the state of Kingswood School. With regard to the former, our brethren earnestly desired that I would go to Birstal myself, believing this would be the most effectual way of bringing the Trustees to reason. With regard to the latter, we all agreed, that either the school should cease, or the rules of it be punctually observed: particularly, that the children should never play; and that a master should be always present with them.

Wed. Sept. 3.—I consulted the preachers, how it was best to proceed with the Trustees of Birstal house, to prevail upon them to settle it on the Methodist plan. They all advised me to begin by preaching there. Accordingly, I preached on *Thursday* evening, and met the society. I preached again in the morning. *Friday,* 5. About nine I met the nineteen Trustees ; and, after exhorting them to peace and love, said, " All that I desire is, that this house may be settled on the Methodist plan ; and the same clause may be inserted in your deed which is inserted in the deed of the new chapel in London : viz. ' In case the doctrine or practice of any preacher should, in the opinion of the major part of the Trustees, be not conformable to Mr W——'s *Sermons,* and *Notes on the New Testament,* on representing this another preacher shall be sent within three months.'"

Five of the Trustees were willing to accept of our first proposals ; the rest were not willing.

Although I could not obtain the end proposed ; and, in that respect, had only my labour for my pains ; yet I do not at all repent of my journey : I have done my part ; let others bear their own burden. Going back nearly the same way I came, on *Saturday,* 13, I reached Bristol. I had likewise good reward for my labour, in the recovery of my health, by a journey of five or six hundred miles.

Fri. 26.—Observing the deep poverty of many of our brethren, I determined to do what I could for their relief. I spoke severally to some that were in good circumstances, and received about forty pounds. Next I inquired who were in the most pressing want, and visited them at their own houses. I was surprised to find no murmuring spirits among them, but many that were truly happy in God ; and all of them appeared to be exceeding thankful for the scanty relief which they received.

Fri. Oct. 10.—I went to Winchester, and had the pleasure of dining with Mr Lowth, and supping with Mrs Blackwell.

Sat. Nov. 1. I returned to London.

When I was at Sevenoaks I made an odd remark. In the year 1769, I weighed a hundred and twenty-two pounds. In 1783, I weighed not a pound more or less. I doubt whether such another instance is to be found in Great Britain.

Thur. Dec. 18.—I spent two hours with that great man, Dr Johnson, who is sinking into the grave by a gentle decay. *Saturday,* 27. I dined at Mr Awbrey's, with Mr Wynantz, son of the Dutch merchant at whose house I met with Peter Böhler and his brethren, forty-five years ago.

Mon. Jan. 12, 1784.—Desiring to help some that were in pressing want, but not having any money left, I believed it was not improper, in such a case, to desire help from God. A few hours after, one from whom I expected nothing less, put ten pounds into my hands.

Wed. 21.—Being vehemently accused, by a well-meaning man, of very many things, particularly of covetousness and uncourteousness, I referred the matter to three of our brethren. Truly, in these articles, " I know nothing by myself. But He that judgeth me is the Lord."

Sat. Feb. 14.—I desired all our preachers to meet, and consider thoroughly the proposal of sending missionaries to the East Indies. After the matter had been fully considered, we were unanimous in our judgment, that we have no call thither yet, no invitation, no providential opening of any kind.

Fri. Mar. 5.—I talked at large with our masters in Kingswood School, who are now just such as I wished for. At length the rules of the house are punctually observed, and the children are all in good order.

The next week I visited the classes at Bristol. *Friday*, 12, being at Samuel Rayner's, in Bradford, I was convinced of two vulgar errors : the one, that nightingales will not live in cages ; the other, that they only sing a month or two in the year. He has now three nightingales in cages ; and they sing almost all day long, from November to August.

Mon. April 5.—I was surprised, when I came to Chester, to find that there also morning preaching was quite left off, for this worthy reason : " Because the people will not come, or, at least, not in the winter." If so, the Methodists are a fallen people. Here is proof. They have " lost their first love "; and they never will or can recover it, till they " do the first works."

As soon as I set foot in Georgia, I began preaching at five in the morning ; and every communicant, that is, every serious person in the town, constantly attended throughout the year : I mean, came every morning, winter and summer, unless in the case of sickness. They did so till I left the province. In the year 1738, when God began His great work in England, I began preaching at the same hour, winter and summer, and never wanted a congregation. If they will not attend now, they have lost their zeal ; and then, it cannot be denied, they are a fallen people.

And, in the meantime, we are labouring to secure the preaching-houses to the next generation ! In the name of God, let us, if possible, secure the present generation from drawing back to perdition ! Let all the preachers that are still alive to

God join together as one man, fast and pray, lift up their voice as a trumpet, be instant, in season, out of season, to convince them they are fallen; and exhort them instantly to "repent, and do the first works": this in particular,—rising in the morning, without which neither their souls nor bodies can long remain in health.

Mon. 19.—I went on to Ambleside; where, as I was sitting down to supper, I was informed, notice had been given of my preaching, and that the congregation was waiting. I would not disappoint them; but preached immediately on salvation by faith. Among them were a gentleman and his wife, who gave me a remarkable relation. She said she had often heard her mother relate, what an intimate acquaintance had told her, that her husband was concerned in the Rebellion of 1745. He was tried at Carlisle, and found guilty. The evening before he was to die, sitting and musing in her chair, she fell fast asleep. She dreamed, one came to her, and said, "Go to such a part of the wall, and among the loose stones you will find a key, which you must carry to your husband." She waked; but, thinking it a common dream, paid no attention to it. Presently she fell asleep again, and dreamed the very same dream. She started up, put on her cloak and hat, and went to that part of the wall, and among the loose stones found a key. Having, with some difficulty, procured admission into the gaol, she gave this to her husband. It opened the door of his cell, as well as the lock of the prison door. So at midnight he escaped for life.

Tues. May 4.—I reached Aberdeen between four and five in the afternoon. *Wednesday,* 5. I found the morning preaching had been long discontinued; yet the bands and the select society were kept up. But many were faint and weak for want of morning preaching and prayer-meetings, of which I found scarce any traces in Scotland.

In the evening I talked largely with the preachers, and showed them the hurt it did both to them and the people, for any one preacher to stay six or eight weeks together in one place. Neither can he find matter for preaching every morning and evening, nor will the people come to hear him. Hence he grows cold by lying in bed, and so do the people. Whereas if he never stays more than a fortnight together in one place, he may find matter enough, and the people will gladly hear him. They immediately drew up such a plan for this Circuit, which they determined to pursue.

Thur. 6.—We set out immediately after preaching and reached Old Meldrum about ten. A servant of Lady Banff's was waiting for us there, who desired I would take post-horses to Fort Glen. All the family received us with the most cordial affection. At seven I preached to a small congregation, all of whom were seriously attentive, and some, I believe, deeply affected.

Wed. 12.—I dined once more at Sir Lodowick Grant's, whom likewise I scarce expected to see any more. His lady is lately gone to rest, and he seems to be swiftly following her. A church being offered me at Elgin in the evening, I had a multitude of hearers. I do not despair of good being done even here provided the preachers be "sons of thunder."

Tues. June 8.—I came to Stockton-upon-Tees. Here I found an uncommon work of God among the children. Many of them from six to fourteen were under serious impressions, and earnestly desirous to save their souls. There were upwards of sixty who constantly came to be examined, and appeared to be greatly awakened. I preached at noon, on, "The kingdom of heaven is at hand"; and the people seemed to feel every word. As soon as I came down from the desk, I was enclosed by a body of children; one of whom, and another, sunk down upon their knees, until they were all kneeling: so I kneeled down myself, and began praying for them. Abundance of people ran back into the house. The fire kindled, and ran from heart to heart, till few, if any, were unaffected. Is not this a new thing in the earth? God begins His work in children. Thus it has been also in Cornwall, Manchester, and Epworth. Thus the flame spreads to those of riper years; till at length they all know Him, and praise Him from the least unto the greatest.

Having procured an easier horse, I rode over the great mountain into Weardale. But I found not my old host: good Stephen Watson was removed to Abraham's bosom. So was that mother in Israel, Jane Nattres (before, Salkeld); the great instrument of that amazing work among the children. But God is with them still: most of the Leaders and many of the people are much alive to God; as we found in the evening, when we had such a shower of grace as I have seldom known.

Wed. 16.—The morning congregation filled the house. Indeed the society here [Whitby] may be a pattern to all in England. They despise all ornaments but good works, together with a meek and quiet spirit. I did not see a ruffle, no, nor a fashionable cap, among them; though many of them are in easy circumstances.

Sat. 26.—I rode to Epworth, which I still love beyond most places in the world.

Thur. Aug. 26.—On the road I read over Voltaire's memoirs

JAN. 1785]   "My Remnant of Days"   393

of himself. Certainly never was a more consummate coxcomb! But even his character is less horrid than that of his royal hero! Surely so unnatural a brute never disgraced a throne before.

What a pity that his father had not beheaded him in his youth, and saved him from all this sin and shame!

Tues. 31.—Dr Coke, Mr Whatcoat, and Mr Vasey, came down from London, in order to embark for America.

Wed. Sept. 1.—Being now clear in my own mind, I took a step which I had long weighed in my mind, and appointed Mr Whatcoat and Mr Vasey to go and serve the desolate sheep in America. *Thursday*, 2. I added to them three more; which, I verily believe, will be much to the glory of God.

Thur. 30.—I had a long conversation with John M'Geary, one of our American preachers, just come to England. He gave a pleasing account of the work of God there, continually increasing, and vehemently importuned me to pay one more visit to America before I die. Nay, I shall pay no more visits to new worlds, till I go to the world of spirits.

Sat. Nov. 20.—At three in the morning two or three men broke into our house, through the kitchen window. Thence they came up into the parlour, and broke open Mr Moore's bureau, where they found two or three pounds: the night before I had prevented his leaving there seventy pounds, which he had just received. They next broke open the cupboard, and took away some silver spoons. Just at this time the alarum, which Mr Moore, by mistake, had set for half-past three (instead of four), went off, as it usually did, with a thundering noise. At this the thieves ran away with all speed; though their work was not half done; and the whole damage which we sustained scarce amounted to six pounds.

Sun. Dec. 26.—I preached the condemned criminals' sermon in Newgate. Forty-seven were under sentence of death. While they were coming in, there was something very awful in the clink of their chains. But no sound was heard, either from them or the crowded audience, after the text was named, "There is joy in heaven over one sinner that repenteth, more than over ninety and nine just persons, that need not repentance." The power of the Lord was eminently present, and most of the prisoners were in tears. A few days after, twenty of them died at once, five of whom died in peace. I could not but greatly approve of the spirit and behaviour of Mr Villette, the ordinary; and I rejoiced to hear, that it was the same on all similar occasions.

Tues. Jan. 4, 1785.—At this season we usually distribute coals and bread among the poor of the society. But I now considered, they wanted clothes, as well as food. So on this, and the four following days, I walked through the town, and begged two hundred pounds, in order to clothe them that needed it most. But it was hard work, as most of the streets were filled with melting snow, which often lay ankle deep ; so that my feet were steeped in snow-water nearly from morning till evening : I held it out pretty well till *Saturday* evening ; but I was laid up with a violent flux, which increased every hour, till, at six in the morning, Dr Whitehead called upon me. His first draught made me quite easy ; and three or four more perfected the cure. If he lives some years, I expect he will be one of the most eminent physicians in Europe.

Thur. April 24.—I was now considering how strangely the grain of mustard-seed, planted about fifty years ago, has grown up. It has spread through all Great Britain and Ireland; the Isle of Wight, and the Isle of Man ; then to America, from the Leeward Islands, through the whole continent, into Canada and Newfoundland. And the societies, in all these parts, walk by one rule, knowing religion is holy tempers ; and striving to worship God, not in form only, but likewise "in spirit and in truth."

Thur. May 5.—Before I came half-way to Cork, I was met by about thirty horsemen. We dined at Middleton, and then rode on through a pleasant, well-cultivated country to Cork.

Fri. 6.—I made an exact inquiry into the state of the society. I found the number was about four hundred, many of whom were greatly in earnest. Many children, chiefly girls, were indisputably justified ; some of them were likewise sanctified, and were patterns of all holiness.

But how shall we keep up the flame that is now kindled, not only in Cork, but in many parts of the nation? Not by sitting still ; but by stirring up the gift of God that is in them ; by uninterrupted watchfulness ; by warning every one, and exhorting every one ; by besieging the throne with all the powers of prayer : and, after all, some will, and some will not, improve the grace which they have received. Therefore there must be a falling away. We are not to be discouraged at this ; but to do all that in us lies to-day, leaving the morrow to God.

Sat. 7.—On this day that venerable saint, Mr Perronet, desired his granddaughter, Miss Briggs, who attended him day and night, to go out into the garden, and take a little air. He was reading, and hearing her read, the three last chapters of Isaiah. When she returned, he was in a kind of ecstasy ; the tears running down his cheeks, from a deep sense of the glorious things which were shortly to come to pass. He continued unspeakably happy that day, and on Sunday was, if possible, happier still. And indeed heaven seemed to be as it were opened to all that were round about him. When he was in bed, she went into his room to see if anything was wanting ; and as she stood at the feet of the bed, he smiled, and broke out, "God bless thee, my dear child, and all that belongs to thee ! Yea, He will bless thee !" Which he earnestly repeated many times, till she left the room. When she went in, the next morning, Monday, 9, his spirit was returned to God.

So ended the holy and happy life of Mr Vincent Perronet, in the ninety-second year of his age. I follow hard after him in years, being now in the eighty-second year of my age. Oh that I may follow him in holiness ; and that my last end may be like his !

Wed. 18.—Learning that a little girl had sat up all night, and then walked two miles to see me, I took her into the chaise ; and was surprised to find her continually rejoicing in God. In the afternoon we went on to Ballinrobe.

Mon. Aug. 1.—Having, with a few select friends, weighed the matter thoroughly, I yielded to their judgment, and set apart three of our well-tried preachers, John Pawson, Thomas Hanby, and Joseph Taylor, to minister in Scotland ; and I trust God will bless their ministrations, and show that He has sent them. *Wednesday*, 3. Our peaceful Conference ended, the God of power having presided over all our consultations.

Fri. Sept. 26.—In the evening I preached in the market-place at St Ives, to almost the whole town. This was the first place in Cornwall where we preached, and where Satan fought fiercely for his kingdom ; but now all is peace. I found old John Nance had rested from his labours. Some months since, sitting behind the preacher, in the pulpit, he sunk down, was carried out, and fell asleep !

Sat. 27.—About nine I preached at the copper-works, near the Hayle, in the new preaching-house. I suppose such another is not in England, nor in Europe, nor in the world. It is round, and all the walls are brass ; that is, brazen slugs. It seems nothing can destroy this, till heaven and earth pass away.

Fri. Oct. 4.—I returned to London. *Sunday*, 6. I preached a funeral sermon for that great and good man, Mr Fletcher ; and most of the congregation felt that God was in the midst of them. In the afternoon I buried the remains of Judith Perry, a lovely young woman, snatched away at eighteen ; but she was ripe for the Bridegroom, and went to meet Him in the full triumph of faith. *Sunday*, 13. I preached at Shoreditch church.

Mon. Dec. 5, and so the whole week, I spent every hour I

could spare, in the unpleasing but necessary work of going through the town, and begging for the poor men who had been employed in finishing the new chapel. It is true, I am not obliged to do this ; but if I do it not, nobody else will.

Tues. Jan. 24, 1786.—I was desired to go and hear the King deliver his speech in the House of Lords. But how agreeably was I surprised ! He pronounced every word with exact propriety. I much doubt whether there be any other King in Europe, that is so just and natural a speaker.

Mon. Mar. 13.—I left Bristol, taking Mr Bradburn with me ; as I judged a change of place and of objects would be a means of calming his mind, deeply affected with the loss of a beloved wife.

Thur. May 11.—In my way hither [Penrith], I looked over Lord Bacon's *Ten Centuries of Experiments.* Many of them are extremely curious; and many may be highly useful. Afterwards I read Dr Anderson's *Account of the Hebrides.* How accurate and sensible a writer ! But how clearly does he show that, through the ill-judged salt [duty], the herring-fishery there, which might be of great advantage, is so effectually destroyed, that the King's revenue therefrom is annihilated ; yea, that it generally, at least frequently, turns out some thousand pounds worse than nothing !

Sun. June 25.—I preached at Misterton. I was grieved to see so small a congregation at Haxey church. It was not so when Mr Harle lived here. Oh what a curse in this poor land are pluralities and non-residence ! But these are evils that God alone can cure.

Wed. 28.—I entered into the eighty-third year of my age. I am a wonder to myself. It is now twelve years since I have felt any such sensation as weariness. I am never tired (such is the goodness of God !), either with writing, preaching, or travelling. One natural cause undoubtedly is, my continual exercise and change of air. How the latter contributes to health I know not ; but certainly it does.

Tues. July 25.—Our Conference began : about eighty preachers attended. We met every day at six and nine in the morning, and at two in the afternoon. On *Tuesday* and on *Wednesday* morning the characters of the preachers were considered, whether already admitted or not. On *Thursday* in the afternoon we permitted any of the society to be present, and weighed what was said about separating from the Church : but we all determined to continue therein, without one dissenting voice ; and I doubt not but this determination will stand, at least till I am removed into a better world.

Sat. Aug. 12.—Mr Williams, minister of the Episcopal church, and Mr Scott, minister of the Scotch church, both welcomed me to Holland.

Mon. 14.—Taking boat at eight, we went at our ease through one of the pleasantest summer countries in Europe, and reached the Hague between twelve and one. Being determined to lodge at no more inns, I went with brother Ferguson to his own lodging, and passed a quiet and comfortable night.

Tues. 15.—Making the experiment when we took boat, I found I could write as well in the boat as in my study: so from this hour I continued writing whenever I was on board. What mode of travelling is to be compared with this? About noon we called on Professor Roers, at Leyden, a very sensible and conversible man: as he spoke Latin very fluently, I could willingly have spent some hours with him; but I had appointed to be at Amsterdam in the evening.

Thur. 17.—In the afternoon we met a little company in the town who seemed to be truly alive to God: one Miss Rouquet in particular, whose least recommendation was, that she could speak both Dutch, French, and English. She spent the evening at Miss Falconberg's, the chief gentlewoman in the town. Here we supped. The manner was particular: no tablecloth was used, but plates, with knives and forks, and napkins, to each person, and fifteen or sixteen small ones; on which were bread, butter, cheese, slices of hung beef, cakes, pancakes, and fruit of various kinds. To these were added music on an excellent organ, one of the sweetest tones I ever heard.

Having seen all the friends I proposed to see, on *Thursday*, 24, I took my leave of this loving people, and the pleasant city of Amsterdam, very probably for ever; and, setting out at seven in the morning, between two and three in the afternoon came to Utrecht. Mr Vanrocy, the gentleman who had engaged me to lodge, sent a coach to wait for me at my landing; and received me with the courtesy and cordiality of an old Yorkshire Methodist.

Mon. 28.—We took boat at seven.

Sun. Sept. 3.—When we had been twenty-four hours on board, we were scarce come a third of our way. I judged we should not get on unless I preached; which I therefore did, between two and three in the afternoon, on, "It is appointed unto men once to die"; and I believe all were affected, for the present. Afterwards, we had a fair wind for several hours; but it then fell dead calm again. This did not last long; for as soon as prayer was over, a fresh breeze sprung up, and brought us into the bay.

Mon. 25.—I now applied myself in earnest to the writing of Mr Fletcher's *Life*, having procured the best materials I could. To this I dedicated all the time I could spare, till November, from five in the morning till eight at night. These are my studying hours; I cannot write longer in a day without hurting my eyes.

Mon. Oct. 2.—I went to Chatham, and had much comfort with the loving, serious congregation in the evening, as well as at five in the morning. *Tuesday*, 3. We then ran down, with a fair, pleasant wind, to Sheerness. The preaching-house here is now finished, but by means never heard of. The building was undertaken a few months since, by a little handful of men, without any probable means of finishing it. But God so moved the hearts of the people in the dock, that even those who did not pretend to any religion, carpenters, shipwrights, labourers, ran up, at all their vacant hours, and worked with all their might, without any pay. By this means a large square house was soon elegantly finished, both within and without; and it is the neatest building, next to the new chapel in London, of any in the south of England.

Tues. 24.—I met the classes at Deptford, and was vehemently importuned to order the Sunday service in our room at the same time with that of the church. It is easy to see that this would be a formal separation from the Church. We fixed both our morning and evening service, all over England, at such hours as not to interfere with the Church; with this very design,—that those of the Church, if they chose it, might attend both the one and the other. But to fix it at the same hour, is obliging them to separate either from the Church or us; and this I judge to be not only inexpedient, but totally unlawful for me to do.

Sun. Nov. 5.—I buried the remains of John Cowmeadow, another martyr to loud and long preaching. To save his life, if possible, when he was half dead, I took him to travel with me. But it was too late: he revived a little, but soon relapsed; and after a few months died in peace. He had the ornament of a meek and quiet spirit, and was of an exemplary behaviour.

Tues. Dec. 5.—All the time I could save to the end of the week I spent in transcribing the society: a dull, but necessary, work, which I have taken upon myself once a year for near these fifty years.

Fri. Feb. 9, 1787.—Being earnestly desired by our brethren at Newark, one hundred and twenty-four miles from London, to come and open their new house, I took the mail-coach in the evening, and reached Newark the next day about four in the afternoon.

Sun. 11.—I preached in the new house at nine,—a lightsome, cheerful building, and gave notice of preaching at five in the afternoon. But it was not long before I received a message from the mayor, to desire me to begin preaching a little later, that himself and several of the aldermen might the more conveniently attend. God opened my mouth to speak strong words, and the hearts of many to receive them.

Thur. 15.—I preached at Deptford, and was agreeably surprised to find the threatening storm blown over, and all our brethren at peace and love with each other.

Thur. March 8.—I went on to Bristol; and the same afternoon Mrs Fletcher came thither from Madeley. The work of God has much increased in Bristol since I was here last, especially among the young men, many of whom are a pattern to all the society.

Sat. 10.—I had the pleasure of an hour's conversation with Mrs Fletcher. She appears to be swiftly growing in grace, and ripening for a better world. I encouraged her to do all the good she could during her short stay in Bristol. Accordingly she met, in the following week, as many of the classes as her time and strength would permit; and her words were as fire, conveying both light and heat to the hearts of all that heard her.

Wed. 21.—We had a numerous congregation at Gloucester, on whom I strongly enforced the great salvation. About eleven I had the satisfaction of spending an hour with the bishop; a sensible, candid, and, I hope, pious man. The palace in which he lives (once the priory) is a venerable place, quite retired and elegant, though not splendid; the chapel, in particular, fitted up by good Bishop Benson.

Finding prejudice was now laid asleep, the tide running the contrary way, our friends thought it time to prepare for building their preaching-house: and a hundred pounds are already subscribed.

Fri. 23.—In the evening I opened the new house at Wolverhampton, nearly as large as that at Newcastle-upon-Tyne. It would not near contain the people, though they were wedged together as close as possible.

Thur. 29.—About twelve I preached at Lane-end. Here we entered into the country which seems to be all on fire,—that which borders on Burslem on every side: preachers and people provoking one another to love and good works, in such a manner as was never seen before. In the evening I preached at Burslem. Observing the people flocking together, I began half an hour before the appointed time. But, notwithstanding this, the house would not contain one-half of the congregation: so, while I was preaching in the house to all that could get in, John Broadbent preached in a yard to the rest. The love-feast followed: but such a one as I have not known for many years. While the two or three first spoke, the power of God so fell upon all that were present, some praying, and others giving thanks, that their voices could scarce be heard: and two or three were speaking at a time, till I gently advised them to speak one at a time; and they did so, with amazing energy.

Fri. 30.—I had appointed to preach at five in the morning; but soon after four I was saluted by a concert of music, both vocal and instrumental, at our gate, making the air ring with a hymn to the tune of Judas Maccabeus: it was a good prelude. So I began almost half an hour before five; yet the house was crowded both above and below. I strongly, but very tenderly, enforced that caution, "Let him that standeth take heed lest he fall."

Sat. 31.—I went on to Macclesfield, and found a people still alive to God, in spite of swiftly increasing riches. If they continue so, it will be the only instance I have known, in above half a century. I warned them in the strongest terms I could.

Thur. June 21.—In the afternoon it pleased God to bring us safe to Dublin, when we had been absent a little over two months.

Tues. 26.—We were agreeably surprised with the arrival of Dr Coke, who came from Philadelphia in nine-and-twenty days, and gave us a pleasing account of the work of God in America. *Thursday*, 28. I had the pleasure of a conversation with Mr Howard, I think one of the greatest men in Europe. Nothing but the mighty power of God can enable him to go through his difficult and dangerous employments. But what can hurt us, if God is on our side?

Sat. 30.—I desired all our preachers to meet me, and consider the state of our brethren in America, who have been terribly frightened at their own shadow, as if the English preachers were just going to enslave them. I believe that fear is now over, and they are more aware of Satan's devices.

Fri. July 27.—I was invited to breakfast at Bury, by Mr Peel, a calico-printer; who, a few years ago, began with five hundred pounds, and is now supposed to have gained fifty thousand pounds. Oh, what a miracle if he lose not his soul!

Thence we went to Bolton. Here are eight hundred poor children taught in our Sunday schools, by about eighty masters, who receive no pay but what they are to receive from their Great Master. About a hundred of them (part boys and part girls) are taught to sing; and they sang so true, that, all singing together, there seemed to be but one voice. The house was thoroughly filled, while I explained and applied the first commandment. In the evening, many of the children still hovering round the house, I desired forty or fifty to come in and sing—

"Vital spark of heavenly flame."

Although some of them were silent, not being able to sing for tears; yet the harmony was such as I believe could not be equalled in the King's chapel.

Mon. Aug. 13.—We set out from Yarmouth with a fair wind; but it soon turned against us, and blew so hard that in the afternoon we were glad to put in at Swanage. I found we had still a little society here. I had not seen them for thirteen years, and had no thought of seeing them now; but God does all things well. In the evening I preached in the Presbyterian meeting-house, not often, I believe, so well filled; and afterwards passed half an hour very agreeably with the minister, in the parsonage-house, which he rents, a neat, retired house, with a delightful garden. Thence we adjourned to the house of our old brother Collins, and between eight and nine went on board.

Tues. 14.—Sailing on, with a fair wind, we fully expected to reach Guernsey in the afternoon; but the wind turning contrary, and blowing hard, we found it would be impossible. We then judged it best to put in at the Isle of Alderney; but we were very near being shipwrecked in the bay. When we were in the middle of the rocks, with the sea rippling all round us, the wind totally failed. Had this continued, we must have struck upon one or other of the rocks; so we went to prayer, and the wind sprang up instantly. About sunset we landed; and, though we had five beds in the same room, slept in peace.

Sat. 18.—Dr Coke and I dined at the Governor's [Guernsey]. I was well pleased to find other company. We conversed seriously, for upwards of an hour, with a sensible, well-bred, agreeable man. In the evening I preached to the largest congregation I have seen here.

Sun. 19.—Joseph Bradford preached at six in the morning, at Montplaisir les Terres, to a numerous congregation. I preached at half an hour past eight. At ten I went to the

French church. At five we had the largest congregation of all; of whom I took a solemn and affectionate leave.

Mon. 20.—We embarked between three and four in the morning, in a very small, inconvenient sloop, and not a swift sailer; so that we were seven hours in sailing what is called seven leagues. About eleven we landed at St Helier, and went straight to Mr Brackenbury's house.

Thur. 23.—I rode to St Mary's, five or six miles from St Helier, through shady, pleasant lanes. None at the house could speak English, but I had interpreters enough. In the evening our large room was thoroughly filled: I preached on, "By grace are ye saved, through faith." Mr Brackenbury interpreted sentence by sentence; and God owned His Word, though delivered in so awkward a manner; but especially in prayer: I prayed in English, and Mr B. in French.

The houses here are exactly like those in the interior parts of Wales, equal to the best farmers' houses in Lincolnshire; and the people in general are far better behaved than our country farmers in England.

Tues. 28.—Being still detained by contrary winds, I preached at six in the evening to a larger congregation than ever, in the assembly-room. It conveniently contains five or six hundred people. Most of the gentry were present; and I believe felt that God was there in an uncommon degree. Being still detained, I preached there again the next evening, to a larger congregation than ever. I now judged, I had fully delivered my own soul: and in the morning, the wind serving for Guernsey, and not for Southampton, I returned thither not unwillingly; since it was not by my choice, but by the great providence of God: for in the afternoon I was offered the use of the assembly-room; a spacious chamber in the market-place, which would contain at least thrice as many as our former room. I willingly accepted the offer, and preached at six to such a congregation as I had not seen here before.

Mon. Oct. 29.—I looked over all the manuscripts which I had collected for the Magazine, destroyed what I did not think worth publishing, and corrected the rest. *Tuesday*, 30. I went down to Miss Harvey's, at Hinxworth, in Hertfordshire. Mr Simeon, from Cambridge, met me there; who breathes the very spirit of Mr Fletcher. The chapel was quite crowded in the evening.

Sat. Nov. 3.—I had a long conversation with Mr Clulow, on that execrable Act, called the Conventicle Act. After consulting the Act of Toleration, with that of the fourteenth of Queen Anne, we were both clearly convinced, that it was the safest way to license all our chapels, and all our travelling preachers, not as Dissenters, but simply "Preachers of the Gospel"; and that no justice, or bench of justices, has any authority to refuse licensing either the house or the preachers.

Thur. 29.—I preached at Mr Edwards's, in Lambeth. How wonderfully does God fit people for their work! Here Mrs Edwards, a person of no extraordinary natural abilities, teaches near a hundred children, and keeps them in as good, if not better, order, than most schoolmistresses in the kingdom!

Fri. 30.—I met the committee, to consider the state of our temporal circumstances. We are still running backward. Some way must be found to make our income answer our expenses.

Sun. Dec. 9.—I went down at half-hour past five, but found no preacher in the chapel, though we had three or four in the house; so I preached myself. Afterwards, inquiring why none of my family attended the morning preaching, they said, it was because they sat up too late. I resolved to put a stop to this; and therefore ordered, that, 1. Every one under my roof should go to bed at nine; that, 2. Every one might attend the morning preaching: and so they have done ever since.

Tues. 18.—I retired to Newington, and hid myself for almost three days. *Friday*, 21. The committee proposed to me, 1. That families of men and women should sit together in both chapels; 2. That every one who took a pew should have it as his own: thus overthrowing, at one blow, the discipline which I have been establishing for fifty years!

Sat. 22.—I yielded to the importunity of a painter, and sat an hour and a half, in all, for my picture. I think it was the best that ever was taken; but what is the picture of a man above fourscore?

Mon. 24.—We had another meeting of the committee; who, after a calm and loving consultation, judged it best, 1. That the men and women should sit separate still; and, 2. That none should claim any pew as his own, either in the new chapel, or in West Street.

Feb. 25, 1788.—I took a solemn leave of the congregation at West Street, by applying once more what I had enforced fifty years before, "By grace are ye saved, through faith." At the following meeting, the presence of God, in a marvellous manner, filled the place. The next evening we had a very numerous congregation at the new chapel, to which I declared the whole counsel of God. I seemed now to have finished my work in London. If I see it again, well; if not, I pray God to raise up others, that will be more faithful and more successful in His work!

Mon. March 3.—I went on to Bristol, and, having two or three quiet days, finished my sermon upon Conscience. On *Tuesday* I gave notice of my design to preach on Thursday evening, upon (what is now the general topic) Slavery. In consequence of this, on *Thursday*, the house from end to end was filled with high and low, rich and poor. I preached on that ancient prophecy, "God shall enlarge Japheth. And he shall dwell in the tents of Shem; and Canaan shall be his servant." About the middle of the discourse, while there was on every side attention still as night, a vehement noise arose, none could tell why, and shot like lightning through the whole congregation. The terror and confusion were inexpressible. You might have imagined it was a city taken by storm. The people rushed upon each other with the utmost violence; the benches were broken in pieces: and nine-tenths of the congregation appeared to be struck with the same panic. In about six minutes the storm ceased, almost as suddenly as it rose; and, all being calm, I went on without the least interruption.

It was the strangest incident of the kind I ever remember; and I believe none can account for it, without supposing some preternatural influence. Satan fought, lest his kingdom should be delivered up. We set *Friday* apart as a day of fasting and prayer, that God would remember those poor outcasts of men; and (what seems impossible with men, considering the wealth and power of their oppressors) make a way for them to escape, and break their chains in sunder.

Sun. 16.—I was invited by the Mayor, Mr Edger, to preach in his chapel, and afterwards to dine with him at the Mansion House. Most of the aldermen were at church, and a multitude of high and low; to whom I explained and applied that awful passage of Scripture,—the history of Dives and Lazarus.

Mon. 17.—I began my northern journey, in a mild, lovely morning.

Wed. 19.—About noon I preached at Tewkesbury, where also, notwithstanding the market, the house was overfilled; and the people were deeply attentive.

We went to Worcester in the afternoon, where also the house is far too small for the congregation. The Methodists here have by well-doing utterly put to silence the ignorance of foolish men; so that they are now abundantly more in danger by honour than by dishonour.

Sat. 22.—In the evening we had a Sunday congregation at Birmingham. Here there is a glorious increase of the work of God. The society is risen to above eight hundred, so that it is at present inferior to none in England, except those in London and Bristol.

Wed. 26.—I went on to Wednesbury, the mother-society of Staffordshire. But few of the old standers are left : I think but three, out of three hundred and fifteen.

Thur. 27.—About noon I preached at Dudley, and with much liberty of spirit : but with far more at Wolverhampton in the evening ; the new house being sufficiently crowded. What a den of lions was this town for many years ! But now, it seems, the last will be first. *Friday,* 28. We came to our dear friends at Madeley. Mrs Fletcher's health is surprisingly mended ; and one might take her nephew for a believer of seven years' standing ; he seems so well established in the faith of the gospel. The congregation was surprisingly large in the evening ; and great was their solemn joy, while I applied, "When Christ who is our life shall appear, then shall ye also appear with Him in glory."

Thur. April 3.—I crossed over to Leek, where for many years we seemed to be ploughing upon the sand ; but, at length, the fruit appears.

Sat. 19.—We went on to Bolton, where I preached in the evening in one of the most elegant houses in the kingdom, and to one of the liveliest congregations. And this I must avow, there is not such a set of singers in any of the Methodist congregations in the three kingdoms. There cannot be ; for we have near a hundred such trebles, boys and girls, selected out of our Sunday schools, and accurately taught, as are not found together in any chapel, cathedral, or music-room within the four seas. Besides, the spirit with which they all sing, and the beauty of many of them, so suits the melody, that I defy any to exceed it ; except the singing of angels in our Father's house.

Sun. 20.—At eight, and at one, the house was thoroughly filled. About three I met between nine hundred and a thousand of the children belonging to our Sunday schools. I never saw such a sight before. They were all exactly clean, as well as plain, in their apparel. All were serious and well-behaved. Many, both boys and girls, had as beautiful faces as, I believe, England or Europe can afford. When they all sung together, and none of them out of tune, the melody was beyond that of any theatre ; and, what is the best of all, many of them truly fear God, and some rejoice in His salvation. These are a pattern to all the town. Their usual diversion is to visit the poor that are sick (sometimes six, or eight, or ten together), to exhort, comfort, and pray with them. Frequently ten or more of them get together to sing and pray by themselves; sometimes thirty or forty; and are so earnestly engaged, alternately singing, praying, and crying, that they know not how to part.

Fri. May 16.—Our new preaching-house [Glasgow] will, I believe, contain about as many as the chapel at Bath. But oh, the difference! It has the pulpit on one side; and has exactly the look of a Presbyterian meeting-house. It is the very sister of our house at Brentford. Perhaps an omen of what will be when I am gone.

Sun. 18.—I preached at eleven on the Parable of the Sower; at half-past two on Ps. l. 23; and in the evening on, "Now abideth faith, hope, love; these three." I subjoined a short account of Methodism, particularly insisting on the circumstances,—There is no other religious society under heaven which requires nothing of men in order to their admission into it, but a desire to save their souls. Look all around you, you cannot be admitted into the Church, or society of the Presbyterians, Anabaptists, Quakers, or any others, unless you hold the same opinions with them, and adhere to the same mode of worship.

The Methodists alone do not insist on your holding this or that opinion; but they think, and let think. Neither do they impose any particular mode of worship; but you may continue to worship in your former manner, be it what it may. Now, I do not know any other religious society, either ancient or modern, wherein such liberty of conscience is now allowed, or has been allowed, since the age of the apostles. Here is our glorying; and a glorying peculiar to us. What society shares it with us?

Sat. 24.—About one we reached Alnwick. I was a little surprised at the new preaching-house (in which I preached in the evening), exactly resembling the meeting-house we hire at Brentford. Had they no eyes? Or had they never seen any English house? But the scarecrow must now stand without remedy.

Sun. 25.—This was the day on which all the Nonjuring congregations in Scotland began, by common agreement, to pray in all their public worship for King George and his family. I preached at nine, at two, and at half-past five; the last time on the Gospel for the day (the history of Dives and Lazarus), with much enlargement of spirit.

Thur. June 5.—Desiring to pay one more visit to the loving society in Weardale, I set out early, and drove through wonderful roads to Walsingham: a town near the entrance of the vale. I could not preach abroad, because of the storm; and the house would not near contain the people. However, as many crowded in as could : the rest got near the door or windows ; and surely the willing mind was accepted.

Sat. 28.—I this day enter on my eighty-fifth year: and what cause have I to praise God, as for a thousand spiritual blessings, so for bodily blessings also! How little have I suffered yet by "the rush of numerous years"! It is true, I am not so agile as I was in times past. I do not run or walk so fast as I did ; my sight is a little decayed ; my left eye is grown dim, and hardly serves me to read ; I have daily some pain in the ball of my right eye, as also in my right temple (occasioned by a blow received some months since), and in my right shoulder and arm, which I impute partly to a sprain and partly to the rheumatism. I find likewise some decay in my memory, with regard to names and things lately past ; but not at all with regard to what I have read or heard twenty, forty, or sixty years ago ; neither do I find any decay in my hearing, smell, taste, or appetite (though I want but a third part of the food I did once) ; nor do I feel any such thing as weariness, either in travelling or preaching : and I am not conscious of any decay in writing sermons ; which I do as readily, and I believe as correctly, as ever.

To what cause can I impute this, that I am as I am ? First, doubtless, to the power of God, fitting me for the work to which I am called, as long as He pleases to continue me therein ; and, next, subordinately to this, to the prayers of His children.

May we not impute it as inferior means—

1. To my constant exercise and change of air ?

2. To my never having lost a night's sleep, sick or well, at land or at sea, since I was born ?

3. To my having sleep at command ; so that whenever I feel myself almost worn out, I call it, and it comes, day or night ?

4. To my having constantly, for above sixty years, risen at four in the morning ?

5. To my constant preaching at five in the morning, for above fifty years ?

6. To my having had so little pain in my life ; and so little sorrow, or anxious care ?

Even now, though I find pain daily in my eye, or temple, or arm ; yet it is never violent, and seldom lasts many minutes at a time.

Whether or not this is sent to give me warning that I am shortly to quit this tabernacle, I do not know ; but be it one way or the other, I have only to say—

> "My remnant of days
> I spend to His praise
> Who died the whole world to redeem;
> Be they many or few,
> My days are His due,
> And they all are devoted to Him!"

Sun. July 6.—I came to Epworth before the church service began; and was glad to observe the seriousness with which Mr Gibson read prayers, and preached a plain useful sermon; but was sorry to see scarce twenty communicants, half of whom came on my account. I was informed likewise, that scarce fifty persons used to attend the Sunday service. What can be done to remedy this sore evil?

I fain would prevent the members here from leaving the Church; but I cannot do it. As Mr G. is not a pious man, but rather an enemy to piety, who frequently preaches against the truth, and those that hold and love it, I cannot with all my influence persuade them either to hear him, or to attend the sacrament administered by him. If I cannot carry this point even while I live, who then can do it when I die? And the case of Epworth is the case of every church, where the minister neither loves nor preaches the gospel. The Methodists will not attend his ministrations. What then is to be done?

Fri. 11.—We set out early for Derby. About nine, within about a mile of the Peacock, suddenly the axletree of my chaise snapped asunder, and the carriage over-turned. The horses stood still till Jenny Smith and I crept out at the forewindows. The broken glass cut one of my gloves a little, but did us no other damage. I soon procured another chaise, and went on to Derby, where I preached in the evening; and at five in the morning on *Saturday*, 12; and then went on to Nottingham.

Saturday, 19. I spent an hour in Chesterfield Street, with my widowed sister and her children. They all seemed inclined to make the right use of the late providential dispensation.

I preached at the new chapel every evening during the Conference, which continued nine days, beginning on *Tuesday*, July 29, and ending on *Wednesday*, August 6: and we found the time little enough; being obliged to pass over many things very briefly, which deserved a fuller consideration.

One of the most important points considered at this Conference, was that of leaving the Church. The sum of a long conversation was: 1. That, in a course of fifty years, we had neither premeditately nor willingly varied from it in one article either of doctrine or discipline. 2. That we were not yet conscious of varying from it in any point of doctrine. 3. That we have in a course of years, out of necessity, not choice, slowly and warily varied in some points of discipline, by preaching in the fields, by extemporary prayer, by employing lay preachers, by forming and regulating societies, and by holding yearly Conferences. But we did none of these things till we were convinced we could no longer omit them, but at the peril of our souls.

Wed. Aug. 6.—Our Conference ended, as it began, in great peace. We kept this day as a fast, meeting at five, nine, and one, for prayer; and concluding the day with a solemn watch-night.

Wed. Sept. 3.—I made a little beginning of some account of my brother's life. Perhaps I may not live to finish it. Then let it fall into some better hands!

Sat. 6.—I walked over to Mr Henderson's, at Hannam, and thence to Bristol. But my friends, more kind than wise, would scarce suffer it. It seemed so sad a thing to walk five or six miles! I am ashamed, that a Methodist preacher, in tolerable health, should make any difficulty of this.

Sat. 20.—I met the Trustees for the new room; who were all willing to add a codicil to the deed of trust, in order to ascertain to the Conference (after me) the sole right of appointing the preachers in it.

Fri. Oct. 10.—I appointed a committee for auditing my accounts, and superintending the business of the Book-room; which, I doubt not, will be managed in a very different manner from what it has been hitherto.

Wed. Dec. 10, and the following days, I corrected my brother's posthumous poems; being short Psalms (some few excepted), [hymns] on the four Gospels, and the Acts of the Apostles. They make five volumes in quarto, containing eighteen or nineteen hundred pages. They were finished April 25, 1765.

Many of these are little, if any, inferior to his former poems, having the same justness and strength of thought, with the same beauty of expression; yea, the same keenness of wit on proper occasions, as bright and piercing as ever.

Mon. 15.—In the evening I preached at Miss Teulon's school in Highgate. I think it was the coldest night I ever remember.

This week I dedicated to the reading over my brother's works. They are short poems on the Psalms, the four Gospels, and the Acts of the Apostles. Some are bad; some mean; some most excellently good: they give the true sense of

Scripture, always in good English, generally in good verse; many of them are equal to most, if not to any, he ever wrote; but some still savour of that poisonous mysticism, with which we were both not a little tainted before we went to America. This gave a gloomy cast, first to his mind, and then to many of his verses: this made him frequently describe religion as a melancholy thing: this so often sounded in his ears, "To the desert!" and strongly persuaded in favour of solitude.

Mon. Jan. 5, 1789.—At the earnest desire of Mrs T——, I once more sat for my picture. Mr Romney is a painter indeed. He struck off an exact likeness at once; and did more in one hour than Sir Joshua did in ten.

Fri. 9.—I left no money to anyone in my will, because I had none. But now considering, that, whenever I am removed, money will soon arise by sale of books, I added a few legacies by a codicil, to be paid as soon as may be. But I would fain do a little good while I live; for who can tell what will come after him?

Tues. 20.—I retired in order to finish my year's accounts. If possible I must be a better economist; for instead of having anything beforehand, I am now considerably in debt: but this I do not like. I would fain settle even my accounts before I die.

Sunday, March 1, was a solemn day indeed. The new chapel was sufficiently crowded both morning and afternoon; and few that expected a parting blessing, were disappointed of their hope. At seven in the evening I took the mail-coach; and having three of our brethren, we spent a comfortable night, partly in sound sleep, and partly in singing praise to God. It will now quickly be seen whether they who prophesied some time since, that I should not outlive this month, be sent of God or not. One way or the other, it is my care to be always ready.

Fri. 27.—We went on to Holyhead; and at eight in the evening went on board the Claremont packet. The wind stood fair three or four hours: it then turned against us, and blew hard. I do not remember I was ever so sick at sea before; but this was little to the cramp which held most of the night with little intermission. All *Saturday* we were beating to and fro, and gaining little ground; and I was so ill, throughout the day, as to be fit for nothing; but I slept well in the night, and about eight in the morning, *Sunday*, 29, came safe to Dublin quay.

I went straight up to the new room. We had a numerous congregation, and as serious as if we had been at West Street.

I preached on the sickness and recovery of King Hezekiah and King George; and great was our rejoicing. I really took knowledge of the change which God has wrought in this congregation within a few years. A great part of them were light and airy; now almost all appear as serious as death. *Monday*, 30. I began preaching at five in the morning; and the congregation, both then and the following mornings, was far larger in proportion than those at London. Meanwhile I had letter upon letter concerning the Sunday service; but I could not give any answer till I had made a full inquiry both into the occasion and the effects of it. The occasion was this :—About two years ago it was complained, that few of our society attended the church on Sunday; most of them either sitting at home, or going on Sunday morning to some Dissenting meeting. Hereby many of them were hurt, and inclined to separate from the Church. To prevent this, it was proposed to have service at the room; which I consented to, on condition that they would attend St Patrick's every first Sunday in the month. The effect was: 1. That they went no more to the meetings. 2. That three times more went to St Patrick's (perhaps six times) in six or twelve months, than had done for ten or twenty years before. Observe! This is done, not to prepare for, but to prevent, a separation from the Church.

Sun. April 5.—I preached in the new room at seven. At eleven I went to the cathedral. I desired those of our society who did not go to their parish churches, would go with me to St Patrick's. Many of them did so. It was said, the number of communicants was about five hundred ; more than went there in the whole year before the Methodists were known in Ireland.

Mon. 6.—To-day, and for some days following, I was so overborne with letters, that I had hardly time to do anything but to read and answer them. *Wednesday*, 8. I visited and administered the sacrament to our poor widows; four-and-twenty of whom are tolerably provided for in our widows' house. The frowardness and stubbornness of some of these was, for a time, a grievous trial to the rest ; but this is past : they are all now of a better spirit, and adorn the doctrine of God our Saviour.

Saturday, 18, was a day of peace. *Sunday*, 19. The commanding officer sending to offer me the use of any part of the barracks, I preached at five in the riding-house, a very spacious building, to a multitude of people, on, " Believe on the Lord Jesus Christ, and thou shalt be saved." I think the Word did not fall to the ground.

Fri. May 1.—We went to Capoquin. The rain preventing my preaching abroad, I accepted of a very large room which was offered me in the barracks. As we went up the street, we had a very numerous retinue, hallooing and shouting with all their might; but the sentinel keeping out the mob, we had a quiet congregation within. A Popish gentleman inviting me to lodge at his house, I spent a comfortable evening.

Mon. June 8.—We went on to Belfast. I had at first thought of preaching in the linen-hall; but the weather being very uncertain, I went to the heads of the large meeting-house, to desire the use of it, which they granted in the most obliging manner. It is the completest place of public worship I have ever seen. It is of an oval form; as I judge by my eye, a hundred feet long, and seventy or eighty broad. It is very lofty, and has two rows of large windows; so that it is as light as our new chapel in London: and the rows of pillars, with every other part, are so finely proportioned, that it is beautiful in the highest degree.

The house was so crowded both within and without (and indeed with some of the most respectable persons in the town), that it was with the utmost difficulty I got in; but I then found I went not up without the Lord. Great was my liberty of speech among them; great was our glorying the Lord: so that I gave notice, contrary to my first design, of my intending to preach there again in the morning; but soon after, the sexton sent me word, it must not be; for the crowds had damaged the house, and some of them had broke off and carried away the silver which was on the Bible in the pulpit: so I desired one of our preachers to preach in our little house, and left Belfast early in the morning.

Fri. 19.—About eleven I preached in the streets at Swords; and in the afternoon reached Dublin.

Sun. 21.—I preached and administered the Lord's Supper; in the conclusion of which

"The o'erwhelming power of grace divine

overshadowed the congregation On *Monday, Tuesday,* and *Wednesday* I visited the classes; now containing a little above a thousand members, after I had excluded about a hundred. *Thursday,* 25. I went on to Mrs Tighe's, at Rosanna, near Wicklow, an exceeding pleasant seat, deeply embosomed in woods on every side. In the evening I preached in the great hall, to about a hundred very genteel persons.

Sat. 27.—We returned to Dublin by the glen of the Downs, much resembling that which lies north above Keswick Water. All this country is remarkably fruitful and pleasant; having, in many parts, a fine sea, as well as land, prospect.

Sun. 28.—In the conclusion of the morning service, we had a remarkable blessing; and the same in the evening, moving the whole congregation as the heart of one man.

This day I enter on my eighty-sixth year. I now find I grow old: 1. My sight is decayed; so that I cannot read a small print, unless in a strong light. 2. My strength is decayed; so that I walk much slower than I did some years since. 3. My memory of names, whether of persons or places, is decayed; till I stop a little to recollect them. What I should be afraid of, is, if I took thought for the morrow, that my body should weigh down my mind; and create either stubbornness, by the decrease of my understanding; or peevishness, by the increase of bodily infirmities: but Thou shalt answer for me, O Lord my God.

Fri. July 3.—Our little Conference began in Dublin, and ended *Tuesday*, 7. On this I observe: 1. I never had between forty and fifty such preachers together in Ireland before; all of them, we had reason to hope, alive to God, and earnestly devoted to His service. 2. I never saw such a number of preachers before, so unanimous in all points, particularly as to leaving the Church; which none of them had the least thought of. It is no wonder that there has been this year so large an increase of the society.

Sun. 12.—At seven I preached in Marlborough Street, where (though it rained all the morning) we had a full congregation of serious people. We met at the new room at half-hour past nine; and truly God was with us. We had never so many communicants before; but as my day, so was my strength. About two we left Dublin, and hastened down to the ship; the *Princess Royal*, of Parkgate; the neatest and most elegant packet I ever saw. But the wind failing, we did not get out of the bay till about twelve. We had exceeding agreeable company; and I slept as well as if I had been in my own bed. *Monday*, 13. The sea being smooth, I shut myself up in my chaise, and read over the Life of the famous Mr George F——, one of the most extraordinary men (if we may call him a man) that has lived for many centuries. I never heard before of so cool, deliberate, relentless a murderer! And yet from the breaking of the rope at his execution, which gave him two hours of vehement prayer, there is room to hope he found mercy at last.

In the evening we sang a hymn upon deck, which soon drew all the company about us. I then, without any delay, began preaching on, "It is appointed unto men once to die." I believe all were a little affected for the present. We were then constrained to slacken sail, and to lie by for some hours, not having water to pass the bar : however, we landed between four and five in the morning, *Tuesday*, 14 ; and, after resting an hour, I went to Chester. I lodged at T. Briscoe's : a lovely family indeed ; just such another as Miss B.'s at Keynsham. The children, indeed, are not quite so genteel, but full as much awakened ; and, I think, the most loving I ever saw.

Tues. 28.—[Leeds] The Conference began : about a hundred preachers were present, and never was our Master more eminently present with us. The case of separation from the Church was largely considered, and we were all unanimous against it. *Saturday*, August 1. We considered the case of Dewsbury House, which the self-elected Trustees have robbed us of. The point they contended for was this,—that they should have a right of rejecting any preachers they disapproved of. But this, we saw, would destroy itinerancy. So they chose J. A. for a preacher, who adopted W. E. for his curate. Nothing remained but to build another preaching-house, towards which we subscribed two hundred and six pounds on the spot.

Sat. Aug. 8.—I settled all my temporal business, and, in particular, chose a new person to prepare the *Arminian Magazine* ; being obliged, however unwillingly, to drop Mr O——, for only these two reasons : 1. The errata are insufferable ; I have borne them for these twelve years, but can bear them no longer. 2. Several pieces are inserted without my knowledge, both in prose and verse. I must try whether these things cannot be amended for the short residue of my life.

Tues. 18.—In the afternoon, as we could not pass by the common road, we procured leave to drive round by some fields, and got to Falmouth in good time. The last time I was here, above forty years ago, I was taken prisoner by an immense mob, gaping and roaring like lions : but how is the tide turned ! High and low now lined the street, from one end of the town to the other, out of stark love and kindness, gaping and staring as if the King were going by. In the evening I preached on the smooth top of the hill, at a small distance from the sea, to the largest congregation I have ever seen in Cornwall, except in or near Redruth. And such a time I have not known before, since I returned from Ireland. God moved wonderfully on the hearts of the people, who all seemed to know the day of their visitation.

Wed. 19.—I preached at noon in the High Street in Helstone, to the largest and most serious congregation which I ever remember to have seen there. *Thursday*, 20. I went on to St Just, and preached in the evening to a lovely congregation, many of whom have not left their first love. *Friday*, 21. About eleven I preached at Newlyn, and in the evening at Penzance; at both places I was obliged to preach abroad. *Saturday*, 22. I crossed over to Redruth, and at six preached to a huge multitude, as usual, from the steps of the market-house. The Word seemed to sink deep into every heart. I know not that ever I spent such a week in Cornwall before.

Sun. 23.—I preached there again in the morning, and in the evening at the amphitheatre; I suppose, for the last time; for my voice cannot now command the still increasing multitude. It was supposed they were now more than five-and-twenty thousand. I think it scarce possible that all should hear.

Mon. 24.—Calling at Marazion in my way to Penzance, where I had promised to preach once more, the house was filled in a few minutes, so that I could not refrain from preaching a short sermon; and God was there of a truth. We had a rainy afternoon; so I was obliged to preach in the new preaching-house, considerably the largest, and, in many respects, far the best, in Cornwall.

Tues. 25.—I went to St Ives, and preached, as usual, on one side of the market-place. Well-nigh all the town attended, and with all possible seriousness. Surely forty years' labour has not been in vain here.

Fri. Sept. 11.—I went over to Kingswood: sweet recess! where everything is now just as I wish. But

"Man was not born in shades to lie!"

Let us work now: we shall rest by-and-by. *Saturday*, 12. I spent some time with the children; all of whom behaved well: several are much awakened, and a few rejoicing in the favour of God.

Sun. 27.—I preached at the new room, morning and evening, and in the afternoon at Temple church; but it was full as much as I could do. I doubt I must not hereafter attempt to preach more than twice a day.

Thur. Oct. 8.—I set out early, and in the afternoon we were brought to London.

I am now as well, by the good providence of God, as I am likely to be while I live. My sight is so decayed that I cannot well read by candle-light; but I can write as well as ever: and my strength is much lessened, so that I cannot easily preach above twice a day. But, I bless God, my memory is not much decayed; and my understanding is as clear as it has been these fifty years.

Tues. 27.—I went on to Witney. Here I found a lively people, many of whom were hungering and thirsting after righteousness. Of what use to a whole community may one person be, even a woman, that is full of faith and love! The Lord strengthen thy heart, and fully prepare thee for every good word and work!

Thur. 29.—I returned to Oxford; and as notice had been given, though without my knowledge, of my preaching at noon, I did so, on, "There is one God," to a very serious congregation; but in the evening such a multitude of people pressed in, that they hindered one another from hearing. I know not when we have had so noisy a congregation; so that by their eagerness to hear they defeated their own purpose.

Fri. 30.—In my way to Wycombe, I spent an hour at Mr Smyth's, in Cudsden. He has ten children, from eighteen to a year or two old; but all under government: so that I met the very picture of my father's family. What a wretched steward was he, who influenced Lord H—— to put away such a tenant! *Saturday*, 31. We came safe and well to London.

Sun. Nov. 1.—Being *All-Saints' Day*, a day that I peculiarly love, I preached on Rev. vii. 1; and we rejoiced with solemn joy. *Monday*, 2. Miss H. met me at Hatfield, and took me on to Hinxworth.

Sun. Dec. 27.—I preached in St. Luke's, our parish church, in the afternoon, to a very numerous congregation, on, "The Spirit and the Bride say, Come." So are the tables turned, that I have now more invitations to preach in churches than I can accept of.

Mon. 28.—I retired to Peckham; and at leisure hours read part of a very pretty trifle,—the *Life of Mrs Bellamy*. Surely never did any, since John Dryden, study more

"To make vice pleasing, and damnation shine,"

than this lively and elegant writer. She has a fine imagination; a strong understanding; an easy style, improved by much reading; a fine benevolent temper; and every qualification that could consist with a total ignorance of God. But God was not in all her thoughts. Abundance of anecdotes she inserts, which may be true or false. One of them, concerning Mr Garrick, is curious. She says, "When he was taking ship for England, a lady presented him with a parcel, which she desired him not to open till he was at sea. When he did, he found Wesley's Hymns, which he immediately threw overboard." I cannot believe it. I think Mr G. had more sense. He knew my brother well; and he knew him to be not only far superior in learning, but in poetry, to Mr Thomson, and all his theatrical writers put together: none of them can equal him, either in strong, nervous sense, or purity and elegance of language. The musical compositions of his sons are not more excellent than the poetical ones of their father.

Fri. Jan. 1, 1790.—I am now an old man, decayed from head to foot. My eyes are dim ; my right hand shakes much ; my mouth is hot and dry every morning ; I have a lingering fever almost every day ; my motion is weak and slow. However, blessed be God, I do not slack my labour ; I can preach and write still.

Sat. 2.—I preached at Snowsfields to the largest congregation I have seen there this year, on, " I am not ashamed of the gospel of Christ." *Sunday* 3. I suppose near two thousand met at the new chapel to renew their covenant with God ; a scriptural means of grace which is now almost everywhere forgotten, except among the Methodists.

Fri. 29.—We had our general quarterly meeting, whereby it appeared, that the society received and expended about three thousand pounds a year : but our expense still exceeded our income. *Saturday*, 30. I began meeting the classes, which took up this day and all the next week.

Sun. Feb. 21.—I preached to the children at the new chapel ; and I believe not in vain. *Monday*, 22. I submitted to importunity, and once more sat for my picture. I could scarce believe myself !—the picture of one in his eighty-seventh year.

Sunday, March 14, was a comfortable day. In the morning I met the Strangers' Society, instituted wholly for the relief, not of our society, but for poor, sick, friendless strangers. I do not know that I ever heard or read of such an institution till within a few years ago. So this also is one of the fruits of Methodism.

Wed. 17.—In the way to Tewkesbury, at the earnest desire of Samuel Vernon, I called on him and his five daughters (all grown up), who are lately joined to that society ; all of whom are now in great earnest, and bid fair to adorn the gospel of God our Saviour.

Mon. 22.—I went on to our old friends at Wednesbury, where the work of God greatly revives. Business has exceedingly decreased, and most of them have left the town. So much the more have the poor grown in grace, and laid up treasure in heaven. But we were at a great loss in the evening. I could not preach abroad after sunset, and the house would not near contain the people.

Wed. 24.—We rode to Madeley, through a pleasant rain which did not hinder the church from being thoroughly filled ; and, I believe, all who had spiritual discernment perceived that it was filled with the presence of God. *Friday*, 26. I finished my sermon on the Wedding Garment; perhaps the last that I shall write. My eyes are now waxed dim; my natural force is abated. However, while I can, I would fain do a little for God before I drop into the dust.

Mon. April 5.—Calling at Altringham, I was desired to speak a few words to the people in the new chapel; but almost as soon as I got thither, the house was filled; and soon after, more than filled. About twelve I preached in the chapel at Northwich, to a large and very lively congregation; and, in the evening, met once more with our old affectionate friends at Chester.

Here I met with one of the most extraordinary phenomena that I ever saw, or heard of:—Mr Sellers has in his yard a large Newfoundland dog, and an old raven. These have fallen deeply in love with each other, and never desire to be apart. The bird has learned the bark of the dog, so that few can distinguish them. She is inconsolable when he goes out; and, if he stays out a day or two, she will get up all the bones and scraps she can, and hoard them up for him till he comes back.

Wed. June 2.—We set out early, and reached Carlisle about noon. The work a little increases here: a small handful of people stand firm; and those that opposed are broken to pieces. Our house would not near contain the congregation; and the Word of God was with power. *Thursday*, 3. We rode to Hexham, through one of the pleasantest countries that I have lately seen. The road lay (from Haisle) on the side of a fruitful mountain, shaded with trees, and sloping down to a clear river; which ran between ours and another fruitful mountain, well wooded and improved. At Hexham they have lately built a convenient preaching-house; but it is too small already. Here is a loving people, much alive to God, and consequently increasing daily. *Friday*, 4. We reached Newcastle. In this and Kingswood house, were I to do my own will, I should choose to spend the short remainder of my days. But it cannot be; this is not my rest. This and the next evening we had a numerous congregation; and the people seemed much alive.

Mon. 7.—I transcribed the stations of the preachers. *Tuesday*, 8. I wrote a form for settling the preaching-houses, without any superfluous words, which shall be used for the time to come, verbatim, for all the houses to which I contribute anything. I will no more encourage that villainous tautology of lawyers, which is the scandal of our nation. In the evening

I preached to the children of our Sunday school ; six or seven
hundred of whom were present. None of our masters or
mistresses teach for pay: they seek a reward that man
cannot give.

Wed. 9.—Having despatched all the business I had to do
here, in the evening I took a solemn leave of this lovely people;
perhaps never to see them more in this life ; and set out early
in the morning.

Sun. 13.—In the morning I preached a charity sermon in
Monkwearmouth church, for the Sunday school ; which has
already cleared the streets of all the children that used to play
there on a Sunday from morning to evening.

Fri. 18.—I preached at Stokesley in the morning ; and then
went on to Whitby. It was very providential, that part of the
adjoining mountain fell down, and demolished our old preaching-house, with many houses besides ; by which means we
have one of the most beautiful chapels in Great Britain, finely
situated on the steep side of the mountain.

Mon. 21.—Being importuned by our friends at Malton to
call there (it being but about thirty miles out of the way), I set
out early, to prevent the heat of the day. Calling at Pickering,
some of the society soon found me out, with whom I went to
the preaching-house ; which was full enough in a few minutes'
time. So was the house at Malton, in the evening ; where I
found the society more loving and united together than they
had been for many years.

Tues. 22.—I crossed over to Scarborough. The congregation in the evening was unusually small, being not yet recovered
from the blessed fruits of the election.

Mon. 28.—This day I enter into my eighty-eighth year.
For above eighty-six years I found none of the infirmities of
old age ; my eyes did not wax dim, neither was my natural
strength abated : but last August I found almost a sudden
change. My eyes were so dim, that no glasses would help me.
My strength likewise now quite forsook me ; and probably will
not return in this world. But I feel no pain from head to foot ;
only it seems nature is exhausted ; and, humanly speaking,
will sink more and more, till

"The weary springs of life stand still at last."

Tues. 29.—I crossed over through Epworth to Owstone, and
passed a comfortable day with many of the preachers. This,
which was one of the last societies in the Circuit, is now become
first, in grace, as well as number. The new preaching-house
not being able to contain one-half of the congregation, I

preached abroad in the calm, mild evening ; and I believe God applied His Word to many hearts.

Thur. July 1.—I went to Lincoln. After dinner we took a walk in and round the minster ; which I really think is more elegant than that at York, in various parts of the structure, as well as in its admirable situation. The new house was thoroughly filled in the evening, and with hearers uncommonly serious. There seems to be a remarkable difference between the people of Lincoln, and those of York. They have not so much fire and vigour of spirit ; but far more mildness and gentleness ; by means of which, if they had the same outward helps, they would probably excel their neighbours.

Some miles short of Lincoln, our post-boy stopped at an inn on the road, to give his horses a little water. As soon as we went in, the innkeeper burst into tears, as did his wife; wringing her hands, and weeping bitterly. "What !" he said, "are you come into my house ! My father is John Lester of Epworth." I found both he and his wife had been of our society. We spent some time in prayer together ; and I trust not in vain.

Sat. 3.—I reached Epworth, and, after preaching in the evening, met the society ; and reminded them of what they were some years ago, and what they are now ; scarce retaining the shadow of their former zeal and activity in all the ways of God.

Sun. 4.—I went over to Misterton, where likewise the work of God was exceedingly decayed. The house being far too small to contain the multitude of people, I stood under a spreading tree ; and strongly exhorted them to "strengthen the things that remained," which were "ready to die." Thence I hastened back to Epworth ; but I could not reach it till the Church service was begun. It was observed, Mr Gibson read the prayers with unusual solemnity ; and I believe he was not displeased to see five times as many at church, and ten times as many at the Lord's Table, as usual. As soon as the afternoon service ended, I began in the market-place to press that awful question, "How shall we escape, if we neglect so great salvation ?" on such a congregation as was never seen at Epworth before.

Fri. Aug. 27.—I returned to Bristol.

Sun. 29.—Mr Baddiley being gone to the north, and Mr Collins being engaged elsewhere, I had none to assist in the service, and could not read the prayers myself; so I was obliged to shorten the service, which brought the prayers, sermon, and Lord's Supper, within the compass of three hours. I preached in the afternoon near King's Square ; and the hearts of the people bowed down before the Lord.

Tues. 31.—William Kingston, the man born without arms, came to see me of his own accord. Some time since he received a clear sense of the favour of God ; but after some months he was persuaded by some of his old companions to join in a favourite diversion, whereby he lost sight of God, and gave up all he had gained : but God now touched his heart again, and he is once more in earnest to save his soul. He is of a middling height and size, has a pleasing look and voice, and an easy, agreeable behaviour. At breakfast he shook off his shoes, which are made on purpose, took the teacup between his toes, and the toast with his other foot. He likewise writes a fair hand, and does most things with his feet which we do with our hands.

Sat. Sept. 4.—I went on to Bath, and preached in the evening to a serious, but small congregation, for want of notice. *Sunday*, 5. This day I cut off that vile custom, I know not when or how it began, of preaching three times a day by the same preacher to the same congregation ; enough to weary out both the bodies and minds of the speaker, as well as his hearers.

Monday, 13, and the three following days, I met the classes of the society, which contains nine hundred and forty-four members. Still I complain of false musters. It was told in London that this society contained above a thousand members; and yet it falls so far short of a thousand. There is altogether a fault in this matter.

Thur. 16.—I saw a pelican. Is it not strange that we have no true account or picture of this bird ? It is one of the most beautiful in nature ; being indeed a large swan, almost twice as big as a tame one ; snow-white, and elegantly shaped. Only its neck is three-quarters of a yard long, and capable of being so distended as to contain two gallons of liquid or solid. She builds her nest in some wood, not far from a river ; from which she daily brings a quantity of fish to her young ; this she carries in her neck (the only pouch which she had), and then divides it among her young ; and hence is fabricated the idle tale of her feeding them with her blood.

Fri. 17.—I went over to Thornbury, and preached at noon to a very large and deeply serious congregation. In the evening we had a solemn watch-night at Kingswood. *Saturday*, 18. I called upon Mr Easterbrook, ill of a disorder which no physician understands, and which it seems God alone can cure. He is a pattern to all Bristol, and indeed to all England ; having beside his other incessant labours, which never were intermitted, preached in every house in his parish !

Monday, 20, and the next day, I read over the King of

Sweden's tract upon the "Balance of Power in Europe." If it be really his, he is certainly one of the most sensible, as well as one of the bravest, princes in Europe; and if his account be true, what a woman is the Czarina! But still God is over all!

Wed. 22.—I preached once more in Temple church, on "All things are possible to him that believeth."

Sat. 25.—Mr Hay, the Presbyterian minister of Lewensmead meeting, came to desire me to let him have the use of our preaching-house on Sundays, at those hours when we did not use it ourselves (near ten in the morning and two in the afternoon), while his house was rebuilding. To this I willingly consented, and he preached an excellent sermon there the next day at two. I preached at five in the morning to more than the house would well contain.

Thur. 30. It being a lovely morning, we went in a wherry, through Cowes harbour, to Newport; one of the pleasantest, neatest, and most elegant towns in the King's dominions.

Sat. Oct. 2.—Setting out, as usual, at two, we came to Cobham between ten and eleven; and found a party of our friends from London ready to receive us. We walked an hour in the gardens; but the innkeeper informed us, strangers were not admitted, unless on Tuesday and Friday. However, hearing Mr Hopkins was at home, I sent in my name, and desired that favour; which was immediately granted. We spent an hour very agreeably in those lovely walks. In the afternoon we went on to London.

Sunday, 3, was indeed a comfortable day. I preached at the new chapel, morning and evening, with great enlargement of spirit. At the love-feast which followed, great was our rejoicing; many declared what God had done for their souls; and many were filled with consolation.

Having answered my letters, and finished my other little business for the present, on *Tuesday*, 5, I went to Rye. Though the warning was short, the congregation was exceeding large, and behaved with remarkable seriousness. While our people mixed with the Calvinists here, we were always perplexed, and gained no ground; but since they kept to themselves, they have continually increased in grace as well as in number. I was now informed how signally God had overtaken that wretch who murdered Mr Haddock some years since. Being lately overtaken by Captain Bray in one of the King's cutters, he made a desperate resistance: and even when boarded, fought still, and drew a pistol at Captain Bray; who then hewed him in pieces with his cutlass.

Thur. 7.—I went over to that poor skeleton of ancient

Winchelsea. It is beautifully situated on the top of a steep hill, and was regularly built in broad streets, crossing each other, and encompassing a very large square; in the midst of which was a large church, now in ruins. I stood under a large tree, on the side of it, and called to most of the inhabitants of the town, "The kingdom of heaven is at hand; repent, and believe the gospel." It seemed as if all that heard were, for the present, almost persuaded to be Christians.

In the evening I preached once more at Rye; and the Word did not fall to the ground. In the morning we left this loving, well united people, and dined at Sevenoaks. After dinner, we spent an hour in the Duke of Dorset's house. I could not but observe some change for the worse here. The silk covers are removed from several of the pictures, particularly that of Count Ugolino and his sons; and it is placed in a worse light; so that I could hardly discern the little boy that, when he saw his father gnawing his own arm for anguish, cried out, "Papa, if you are hungry, do not eat your own arm, but mine." The preaching-house was filled in the evening with people, and with the presence of God.

Sat. 9.—We returned to London.

Wed. 13.—I preached at Norwich; but the house would in no wise contain the congregation. How wonderfully is the tide turned! I am become an honourable man at Norwich. God has at length made our enemies to be at peace with us; and scarce any but Antinomians open their mouth against us.

Thurs. 14.—I went to Yarmouth; and, at length, found a society in peace, and much united together. In the evening the congregation was too large to get into the preaching-house; yet they were far less noisy than usual. After supper a little company went to prayer, and the power of God fell upon us; especially when a young woman broke out into prayer, to the surprise and comfort of us all. *Friday*, 15. I went to Lowestoft, to a steady, loving, well-united society. The more strange it is, that they neither increase nor decrease in number. *Saturday*, 16. I preached at Loddon about one; and at six in Norwich. *Sunday*, 17. At seven I administered the Lord's Supper to about one hundred and fifty persons, near twice as many as we had last year. I take knowledge, that the last year's preachers were in earnest. Afterwards we went to our own parish church; although there was no sermon there, nor at any of the thirty-six churches in the town, save the cathedral, and St Peter's. I preached at two. When I had done, Mr Horne called upon me, who preached at the cathedral in the morning: an agreeable man, both in temper and person;

and, I believe, much alive to God. At half an hour after five I preached again, to as many as the house would contain ; and even those that could not get in stayed more quiet and silent than ever I saw them before. Indeed they all seemed to know that God was there ; and I have no doubt but He will revive His work here also.

Mon. 18.—No coach going out for Lynn to-day, I was obliged to take a post-chaise. But at Dereham no horses were to be had ; so we were obliged to take the same horses to Swaffham. A congregation was ready here, that filled the house, and seemed quite ready to receive instruction. But here neither could we procure any post-horses ; so that we were obliged to take a single-horse chaise. The wind, with mizzling rain, came full in our faces ; and we had nothing to screen us from it ; so that I was thoroughly chilled from head to foot before I came to Lynn. But I soon forgot this little inconvenience ; for which the earnestness of the congregation made me large amends.

Tues. 19.—In the evening all the clergymen in the town, except one, who was lame, were present at the preaching. They are all prejudiced in favour of the Methodists ; as indeed are most of the townsmen ; who give a fair proof by contributing so much to our Sunday schools ; so that there is near twenty pounds in hand. *Wednesday*, 20. I had appointed to preach at Diss, a town near Scoleton ; but the difficulty was, where I could preach. The minister was willing I should preach in the church ; but feared offending the bishop, who, going up to London, was within a few miles of the town. But a gentleman asking the bishop whether he had any objection to it, was answered, " None at all." I think this church is one of the largest in this county. I suppose it has not been so filled these hundred years. This evening and the next I preached at Bury, to a deeply attentive congregation, many of whom know in whom they have believed. So that here we have not lost all our labour. *Friday*, 22. We returned to London.

Sun. 24.—I explained, to a numerous congregation in Spitalfields church, " the whole armour of God." St Paul's, Shadwell, was still more crowded in the afternoon, while I enforced that important truth, " One thing is needful " ; and I hope many, even then, resolved to choose the better part.

INDEX

Abbé Paris, 239.
Aberdare, 233, 243.
Aberdeen, 292, 332, 364, 391.
Abergavenny, 85, 117.
Acomb, 203.
Adams, Mr., 172.
Aghrim, 220.
Alderney, 401.
Aldersgate Street, 51, 61.
Alemouth, 223.
Allandale, 202, 294.
Allhallows Church, 363.
All Saints' Day, 231, 274.
Alnwick, 223, 264, 299, 406.
Alpraham, 238.
Alstone Moor, 235.
Altringham, 42, 173, 418.
Ambleside, 391.
Amsterdam, 397.
Anderson, Sir William, 380.
Anglesey, 244.
Annesley, Dr. Samuel, 81.
Appleby, 323.
Arbroath, 364.
Archbishop of Canterbury, 125.
—— of Dublin, 219.
Assembly, General, of the Church of Scotland, 321
Athlone, 216.
Avon, 99.
Axholme, 297.

Back Lane, Bristol, 67.
Bacup, 324.
Baddeley, 420.
Baildon, 226, 324.

Baldock, 198.
Baldon Ferry, 243.
Baldwin Street, 67, 70.
Bands, in Bristol, 106.
—— in Kingswood, 102.
Banff, Lady, 391.
Baptist Mills, 66.
Barkswell, 144.
Barley Hall, 146.
Barnard Castle, 294.
Barnborough, 224.
Barnstaple, 183.
Barrow, 320.
Barrowford, 226.
Barton, 307.
Bath, 67, 78, 120, 140, 302, 374, 421.
Bearfield, 87.
Bear Yard, London, 61.
Bedford, 275, 277.
Bedford, Rev. Mr., 61.
Beercrocomb, 194.
Beeston, 128.
Belfast, 412.
Belinger, Mr., 17, 21.
Bennet, Rev. Mr., 174, 183, 194.
Bennet, John, 168, 173, 230, 237.
Bennets, John, 316.
Benson, Bishop of Gloucester, 399.
Berridge, 280.
Bertholdsdorf, 59.
Berwick, 223.
Bethnal Green, 367.
Beverley, 284, 323.
Bexley, 103.

Index

Biddick, 345.
Birmingham, 41, 190, 222, 239, 306, 331, 404.
Birstal, 127, 139, 146, 204, 237, 296, 389.
Bishops, 189.
Blackheath, 76.
Blackwell, Mr. E., 371.
—— Mrs., 328.
Blair Castle, 343.
Blanchland, 202.
Blewbury, 191.
Blow, William, 156.
Boardman, 339.
Bocardo, 63.
Bodleian Library, 112.
Bohler, Peter, 39, 40, 44, 46, 53, 107.
Bolton, 229, 237, 382, 401, 405.

Camborne, 207, 272.
Cambridge, 402.
Camelford, 194.
Canterbury, 240, 275, 281, 285, 310, 329, 336.
Capoquin, 412.
Cardiff, 86, 116, 144, 233, 243, 278, 302, 383.
Carlisle, 364, 391.
Carmarthen, 309, 376.
Carnarvon, 209.
Carrickfergus, 288.
Carse of Gowry, 332.
Castletown, 369.
Causton, Mr., 12, 22, 31.
Cawley, Richard, 238.
Cennick, Mr., 105, 250, 290.
Chancery Bill, 129, 295.
Charlestown, 16, 21, 33.
Charlton, 267.
Charter House, 308.
Chatham, 330, 381, 398.
Chelsea, 114, 123, 231.
Cheltenham, 321.
Chertsey, 241.
Chester, 259, 262, 269, 273, 390.
Chippenham, 123, 266.
Chowbent, 354.
Chowden, 141, 145.

City Road, 373.
Clara, 217, 219.
Clayton, 42, 157, 192, 255.
Clayworth, 276.
Clifton, 69, 189.
Cobham, 422.
Cockermouth, 364.
Cockhill, 360.
Coke, Dr., 370, 372, 383, 384, 393, 400, 401.
Colbeck, Mr. T., 226.
Colchester, 280, 385.
Coleby, Mr., 168.
Colen, 56.
Collins, 181, 420.
Colne, 296, 363.
Conference, 205, 267, 279, 361, 365, 381, 396, 408, 409, 413, 414
Congleton, 382.
Connam, 209.
Coningsby, 222, 256.
Connaught, 217.
Coolylough, 200, 338, 369.
Cope, General, 184.
Corbett, Rev. Mr., 369.
Cork, 260, 394.
Coventry, 131.
Cowbridge, 144, 376.
Cowes, 8, 9.
Cowmeadow, John, 398.
Cownley, Mr., 234.
Cowper, Miss, 131.
Craidley, 343.
Crowan, 174.
Cubert, 272.
Culloden, 195.

Dannabull, 243.
Dargbridge, 359
Darien, 19, 20.
Darlaston, 151, 152, 160, 161, 163.
Darlington, 172.
Davy-Hulme, 238, 263.
Decknatel, 56.
Delamotte, 7, 17, 18, 33, 386.
Deptford, 82, 106, 298, 347, 398, 399.
Derby, 408.

Index

Dereham, 424.
Dettingen, 159.
Devizes, 197, 311.
Dewsbury, 346.
Dober, Martin, 12, 59.
Dodd, Dr., 367, 368, 369.
Doddridge, Dr., 183.
Doncaster, 187, 301.
Donnington Park, 131, 139.
Douglas, 369.
Dover, 317, 336.
Downes, John, 166, 167, 190, 358.
Dresden, 58.
Drury Lane, 103, 122.
Dublin, 191, 221, 287, 339, 360, 370, 400, 410, 412, 413.
Dublin, Archbishop of, 210, 251.
Dudley, 238, 306.
Dumfries, 323.
Dummer, 53, 65.
Dunbar, Mr., 344.
Dundee, 292, 321.
Dunkeld, 343.
Dunleary, 359.
Durham, 168, 258, 276, 283, 379.

Eccleshill, 226.
Eckerhausen, 57.
Edger, Mr., 404.
Edinburgh, 186, 188, 263, 293, 299, 314, 321, 322, 345, 355, 386, 392, 408, 420.
Edwards, Mr., of Lambeth, 374, 403.
Elgin, 392.
Ellison, Rev. Mr., 185.
Elsham, 305.
Enfield Chase, 110.
Ephrem Syrus, 18, 201.
Epworth, 129, 155, 157, 167, 173, 187, 199, 222, 251, 254, 276, 277, 278, 297, 300, 352, 386, 392, 408, 420.
Eustick, 174, 177.
Evans, Mr., 279.
Everton, 280.
Evesham, 131, 134, 291, 305.
Ewood, 258, 324, 354.
Exeter, 91, 366.

Falmouth, 179, 271, 414.
Fenwick, Michael, 276, 378.
Fenwick, William, 172.
Fenwick, Mrs., 189.
Ferry, 167.
Ferry Bridge, 187.
Fetter Lane, 65, 75, 81, 82, 90, 92, 99, 108.
Feversham, 307.
Fishponds, 78, 84.
Flanders, 267.
Flaubert, General, 288.
Fletcher, Rev. John, 275, 309, 340, 365, 385, 395, 398.
Fletcher, Mrs., 399.
Fonmon Castle, 116, 144, 167, 183.
Fort Argyle, 19.
Fort Glen, 392.
Foundery, 100, 102, 105, 134, 189, 240, 241, 254, 274, 277, 281, 305, 334, 353, 365, 375.
Fox, Mr., 41, 42.
Francke, Professor, 57.
Frederica, 13, 14, 15.
Freshford, 328, 341.
Furz, Mr., 372.

Gainsborough, 285, 306.
Gambold, Rev. John, 39, 106, 112, 304.
Garth, 215, 233.
Gateshead and Gateshead Fell, 185, 187, 202, 283.
Gilbert, Mr, 277.
Gins, 235.
Glasgow, 263, 322, 405.
Glass, Mr., 187.
Gloucester, 79, 330, 399.
Goodshaw, 229.
Gordon, Lord George, 381.
Graham, Colonel, 196.
Grampound, 193.
Grant, Sir Archibald, 293.
—— Sir Lodowick, 392.
Grantham, 198, 199, 327.
Great St. Helen's Church, 40.
Greaves, Rev. Mr., 110.
Greenfield, Edward, 176.

Griffith, Robert, 245.
Grimsby, 199, 259, 306, 380.
Grimshaw, Rev. William, 226, 282, 296, 298.
Guernsey, 401, 402.
Gwennap, 175, 176, 181, 193, 194, 207, 271, 289, 373.
Gwynne, Miss Sarah, 233.

Hackney, 268.
Haddock, Mr., 422.
Haime, John, 195, 263.
Hainton, 256.
Halifax, 128, 168, 354.
Hall, Rev. Mr., 63, 107, 136.
—— Bathsheba, 381.
Halle, 57.
Handy, Mr., 220.
Hannam, 409.
Hannam, Mount, 66, 67, 85.
Harle, Mr., 396.
Harris, Howell, 174, 240, 352.
Harrison, John, 129.
Hatfield, 198, 416.
Hatside, 236.
Haworth, 264, 266, 296, 324.
Haxey, 129, 130, 297, 396.
Haxey Car, 199.
Hayes, 240.
Hayfield, 230.
Heally, John, 143.
Hedgeford, 43.
Helmsley, 307.
Helstone, 194, 271, 272, 372, 414.
Helton, Mr., 344.
Hemmington, 111
Hensingham, 235.
Heptonstall, 228, 258, 264, 324, 354.
Hermsdorf, Mr., 58.
Hernhuth, 38.
Hertford, 303.
Hexham, 202, 419.
Hibbaldstow, 130.
Hide, Mr., 206.
Highgate, 409.
Hinden, 204.
Hinely Hill, 234.
Hinxworth, 416.

Hird, Mark, 8, 15.
—— Thomas, 8, 15.
Hitchins, Thomas, 194.
Holyhead, 216, 243, 339, 410.
Holyrood House, 333.
Hoohole, 346.
Hoole, Rev. Mr., 42.
Hopper, Mr. Christopher, 236.
Horncastle, 320.
Horsley, 202, 356.
Howe, Mr. 111.
Huddersfield, 315, 354.
Hull, 156, 256.
Hungerford, 97, 135, 337.
Hunslet, 339, 378.
Huntingdon, Lady, 340.
Husk, General, 186.
Hutchins, Mr., 63.
Hutton, Mr. James, 45, 169. 348.

Ingham, Rev. Benjamin, 7, 8, 17, 18, 55, 63, 99, 127.
Ireland, 372.
Ishel, Degory, 166.
Isham, Dr., 253.
Islington, 62, 75.

Jena, 57.
Jenkins, Herbert, 193.
—— Abraham, 215.
Johnson, Dr., 389.
Jones, Mr. William, 246.
—— James, 160.
Joppa, 378.

Keelman's Hospital, 136.
Keighley, 226, 269.
Keith, 344.
Kelso, 275.
Kempis, Thomas à, 47.
Kendal, 257.
Kennington Common, 77, 81, 103, 128.
Kensington, 147.
Keswick, 235.
Keynsham, 384.
Kidwelly, 309.
Killcock, 219.
Killdorrery, 248.

Index

Kinchen, 41, 43.
King George II., 184, 186.
Kingston (Somerset), 366.
Kingswood, 66, 78, 89, 91, 94, 102, 104, 105, 117, 120, 134, 135, 136, 137, 141, 147, 150, 170, 189, 191, 205, 209, 231, 233, 234, 290, 302, 317, 353, 381, 384, 415, 421.
—— School, 221, 242, 265, 340, 341.
Kington, 193.
Kirton, 167, 379.
Knaresborough, 128.
Knightsbridge, 240, 319.
Knowle, 287.

Lambeth, 81, 374, 403.
Lancaster, John, 232.
Land's End, 147, 148, 149.
Lane, Mr., 151, 155.
Laneast, 174, 194, 424.
Lane End, 399.
Lanhithel, 97.
Lanzufried, 192, 215.
—— Church, 215.
Larn, 309.
Larwood, 199.
Laseby, 199.
Launceston, 150, 164, 340.
Law, Rev. W., 8.
Leeds, 128, 157, 158, 188, 189, 270, 291, 339, 378, 383.
Leicester, 275, 346.
Leigh, 265, 274.
Leoni, 342.
Lewen, Miss, 327.
Lewensmead, 422.
Lewisham, 197, 211, 239, 266, 277, 291, 298, 328, 347, 371, 377, 387.
Leytonstone, 327, 329.
Limerick, 251, 359.
Lincoln, 167, 379, 420.
Linner, Michael, 60.
Liverpool, 269, 298.
London, 183, 188, 191, 211, 234, 239, 242, 265, 290, 297, 303, 305, 327, 329, 336, 353, 368.

Londonderry, 360.
Looe, 193.
Louth, 320, 389.
Lunell, Mr., 210.
Lyddel, John, 187.

Macclesfield, 382, 385, 400.
Machynlleth, 215.
Mackford, Mr., 228.
Madan, Mr., 297.
M'Geary, Mr., John, 393.
M'Kenzie, Mr., 343.
Madeley, 309, 399, 417.
Maesmennys, 144, 233.
Malmesbury, 92, 99.
Manchester, 41, 204, 255, 258, 259, 263, 269, 282, 292, 301, 343, 363, 382, 392.
Marazion, 174, 175, 415.
Margam, 279.
Marienborn, 57.
Markfield, 111, 112, 131, 146, 159, 183.
Marsden, 189.
Marylebone Fields, 99, 108.
Mather, Mr., 379.
Matlock Bath, 296.
Maxfield, Mr., 175, 281, 301.
Maxwell, Lady, 386.
Medros, 372.
Memis, Mr., 292.
Mentz, 57.
Middleton, 323.
Midgley, 229.
Mill Town, 173.
Minehead, 183.
Minories, 61.
Misterton, 307, 396, 420.
Moira, 288.
Monkwearmouth, 419.
Monmouth, 376, 383.
Montrose, 292.
Moore, Mr., 393.
Moorfields, 77, 81, 128, 264, 273, 368,
More, Mr., 128.
Morgan, Mr. Jenkin, 243.
Morpeth, 222, 276, 294, 299.
Morva, 147.

Mount Melick, 247.
Muncy, Jane, 113.

Nairn, 344.
Nance, John, 177, 395.
Nantwich, 262, 383.
Nash, 74.
Naylor, Mary, 141.
Neath, 193, 279.
Nelson, John, 126, 139, 148, 203, 204, 264, 269.
Newark, 141, 199, 398.
Newbury, 191, 197.
Newcastle, 136, 141, 145, 156, 168, 171, 183, 188, 200, 224, 307, 327, 399.
Newgate, 66, 68, 77, 96, 134, 185, 232, 242, 367, 374, 393.
Newington, 188, 211, 239.
Newlands, 202.
Newlyn, 208, 272, 316, 415.
New Mills, 385.
New Passage, 155, 243, 278.
Newport, 86, 116, 279.
Newport Pagnell, 146.
Newry, 288.
Newton-upon-Trent, 379.
Nicholas Street, Bristol, 72.
Ninthead, 300.
Nitschman, David, 12.
Northallerton, 172, 270.
Northampton, 101, 110, 126, 136, 183, 341.
Northwich, 418.
Norton, 167.
Norwich, 274, 281, 303, 311, 329.
Nottingham, 111, 146, 155, 158, 190, 365, 408.

Ogbrook, 110.
Ogilvy, Mr., 293.
Oglethorpe, Mr., 9, 11, 12, 18.
Oldham, 385.
Old Sarum, 267.
Osmotherly, 172, 200, 203.
Otley, 308, 378.
Oulton, 225.
Ouston, or Owstone, 129, 419.

Oxford, 7, 40, 43, 61, 62, 83, 92, 93, 99, 113, 124, 134, 144, 169, 233, 341, 348, 416.
Oxlee, Mr. William, 97.
Oxwych, 310.

Padiham, 296.
Painswick, 131, 144.
Parker, Mr., 259, 275, 277, 379.
Parks, Joan, 154.
Pawson, Rev. John, 395.
Paxton, Andrew, 196.
Peacock, Robert, 201.
Pearce, John, 272.
Pebworth, 331.
Peel, Isle of Man, 369.
—— Mr., 400.
Pembrock, Alderman, 248.
Pembroke, 309, 376.
Pendennis Castle, 271.
Penrith, 323.
Penruddock Moor, 235.
Penryn, 271.
Pensford, 68, 124, 354.
Penzance, 175, 208, 369, 372, 415.
Pepusch, Dr., 221.
Perronet, Mr., 388, 394, 395.
Perry, Judith, 395.
Persehouse, Mr., 151, 155.
Peters, Sarah, 231.
Philips, Rev. Mr., 144.
Philipstown, 217.
Phœnix Park, 210.
Pickering, 307, 419.
Piers, Rev. Henry, 168, 191.
Pill, 273.
Placey, 142, 143, 276, 294.
Plaistow, 82.
Plymouth, 193, 205, 265, 316, 326, 335, 377.
Pocklington, 323.
Pontefract, 190.
Pontypool, 85, 86, 116.
Porkellis, 194.
Port Royal, 16, 32.
Potten, 198.
Preston-on-the-Hill, 382.
Pretender, The, 183, 188.
Prichard, Mr. William, 243, 246.

Probis, Mr., 194.
Publow, 374.
Purrysburg, 32, 320.

Queensferry, 292.

Ratcliffe Square, 133.
Rathfriland, 288.
Rayner, Samuel, 390.
Reading, 65, 95, 331.
Redruth, 271, 289, 316, 335, 372, 414.
Renton, 203.
Richards, Mr., 135, 212.
Richardson, Rev. Mr., 374.
Richmond (Yorkshire), 334.
Riddel, 138.
Ridley, Mr., 129, 183.
Ripley, 131.
Robin Hood's Bay, 264, 294.
Rochdale, 237.
Roers, Professor, 397.
Rogers, Dr., 29.
Romley, Rev. Mr., 129, 139, 187.
Romney, Mr., 410.
Rosanna, 412.
Rose Green, 73, 78.
Rosendale, 204, 324.
Rotterdam, 55.
Roughlee, 204, 226, 228, 258.
Rowell, Jacob, 34, 351.
Runwick, 83.
Rutty, Dr., 218.
Rye, 422.

Salford, 42, 402.
Salisbury, 40, 55.
Sandgate, 127.
Sandhutton, 143, 170, 187.
Sandwich, 313.
Saughton Hall, 386.
Saunderson, Hugh, 378.
Savannah, 11, 12, 14, 16, 49.
Scarborough, 295, 419.
Scone, 332.
Scot, Francis, 225.
Scotter, 329.
Sennan, 147.
Servetus, Michael, 112.

Seven Dials, 145, 274.
Sevenoaks, 195, 298, 389, 423.
Seward, Mr., 99.
Shadwell, 371, 424.
Shaftesbury, 251.
Sheerness, 329, 381.
Sheffield, 131, 139, 146, 167, 183, 187, 190, 256, 276, 352, 383.
Shepherd, Mr., 181, 190, 191.
Shepton, 214.
Shincliff, 379.
Shipton, 200.
Shipston, 41.
Shore, 204.
Shoreditch, 395.
Shoreham, 168, 239.
Simmonds, 7.
Simeon, Mr., 402.
Sitch, William, 154.
Sithney, 194, 207, 372.
Skelton, 248.
Skidoway, 13.
Skircoat Green, 225.
Slater, Edward, 154.
Slaton, Thomas, 203.
Smith, Mrs., 356.
Solway Firth, 323.
Spen, 224.
Spitalfields, 64, 242, 252, 271, 299, 424.
St. Agnes, 207.
St. Andrew's, 39.
St. Ann's, 42, 46, 241.
St. Bartholomew, 221.
St. Catherine Cree, 40.
St. Clement's, Strand, 62.
St. Columb, 194, 335.
St. Eath, 174.
St. George's-in-the-East, 61.
St. Helen's, 8.
St. Helier, 402.
St. Ives, 175, 176, 182, 193, 206, 207, 265, 289, 373, 395, 415.
St. John's, Clerkenwell, 61.
St. John's, Wapping, 40.
St. Just, 148, 176, 177, 182, 208, 316.
St. Mary's, 148, 402.
St. Mary Week, 194.

St. Michael's Mount, 175.
St. Patrick, 218, 411.
St. Paul's, 277.
St. Peter's, 423.
Stafford, 41.
Stallbridge, 425.
Stamford, 198, 278.
Stanley, 83,
Stephenson, Mr., 138, 171.
Stewart, Mr., 65.
Sticklepath, 150.
Stithians, 176, 182.
Stockport, 173, 382, 385.
Stockton and Stockton-upon-Tees, 392.
Stokesley, 419,
Stone, William, 214.
Stonehouse, Rev. Mr., 46.
Stonsey Gate, 204.
Stormont, Lord, 301.
Strong, Joseph, 364.
Sullivan, Daniel, of Cork, 234.
Sunderland, 189, 224, 276, 283.
Sutcliffe, Mr., 346.
Swaftham, 424.
Swanage, 401.
Swansea, 279, 302.
Swedenborg, Baron, 342.

Tadcaster, 282.
Tanfield Leigh, 137, 138, 141, 146.
Tannabull, 215.
Taunton, 209, 267, 365, 370, 377, 384.
Taylor, David, 130.
—— John, 126, 129.
Tealby, 380.
Teesdale, 294, 334.
Telchig, Mr., 52.
Tennent, Gilbert, 268.
Terdinny, 208.
Tetney, 199.
Tewkesbury, 337, 404, 417.
Thirsk, 200, 194, 320.
Thomas, Mr., 180.
—— Howell, 243.
Thompson, Mr., 21, 174, 183, 194, 380.
Thornbury, 79, 421.

Three-cornered Down, 147.
Timmins, Stephen, 190.
Tipton Green, 162, 173.
Tiverton, 90, 91, 326, 340, 373.
Todmorden, 229, 258, 269.
Told, Silas, 374.
Tomkins, Mr., 174.
Torrington, 320.
Trefollwin, 243, 246.
Trembath, Mr., 187, 193, 212.
Trent, 155.
Tresmere, 174.
Trevecka, 302, 339, 352.
Trevonan, 182.
Trewint, 164, 183.
Trezilla, 181.
Trezuthan Downs, 148.
Trounce, Mr., 182.
Trowbridge, 267.
Truro, 271, 326, 366.
Tuggle, 224.
Tullamore, 219.
Tunbridge, 298.

Usk, 85, 86.
Utrecht, 397.
Uutfass, 56.

Vanrocy, Mr., 397.
Vasey, Mr., 393.
Venn, Rev. Mr., 292.
Villette, Mr., 393.
Villear, 195.

Wakefield, 225.
Wales, 104, 113, 144, 376.
Walker, Rev. Mr., 271.
—— Francis, 183.
Walsal, 151, 154, 162, 163.
Walsh, Mr. Thomas, 264, 274, 275, 304.
Wandsworth, 277, 280, 342.
Wapping, 40, 76, 274, 305, 313.
Ward, Francis, 145, 150, 154.
Warrington, 269, 319, 368, 382
Waterford, 359.
Wattevil, Baron, 55.
Weardale, 294, 392, 406.
Weaver's Hall, 66, 68.

Webb, Captain, 353.
Wednesbury, 139, 143, 145, 150, 151, 152, 160, 161, 162, 163, 173, 190, 222, 238, 405, 417.
Wells, 80.
Wensley Dale, 157.
Wentworth, General, 187.
Wesley, Charles, 7, 63, 65, 234.
—— Susannah, Mrs., 132.
Westminster, 62, 241.
West Street Chapel, 189, 240, 285, 287, 319, 327, 374, 375, 403, 410.
Whatcoat, Mr., 393.
Whitby, 264, 294, 392, 419.
Whitchurch, 383.
White, John, 274.
Whitefield, Rev. George, 76, 105, 107, 125, 236, 240, 265, 273, 321, 316, 325, 328, 336, 347.
Whitehaven, 234, 236, 323, 368.
Whitehead, Dr., 394.
Whitelamb, Rev. Mr., 130.
Wick, 197, 198.
Wickham, 258.
Widdop, 204, 228.
Widrington, 223, 294.
Wigan, 382.
Wigton, 364.

Williams, Mr., 116, 137.
Williamson, Rev. Mr., 27, 270.
Wilson, Mr., 378.
Winchester, 389.
Windsor, 95, 134, 211.
Witham, 43.
Witney, 415.
Wolf, Mr., 53.
Wolsingham, 406.
Wolverhampton, 308, 399, 405.
Wood, Mr., 162.
—— Mrs., 369.
Woodseat, 276.
Worcester, 337, 404.
Wrangle, 256.
Wright, Richard, 278.
Wroote, 130.
Wycombe, 90, 195, 416.
Wynantz, Mr., 389.

Yarm, 295, 300, 320.
Yarmouth, 291, 342, 423.
York, 203, 264, 270, 276, 295, 296, 323.
Young, Robert, 171.
Ysselstein, 55.

Zennor, 148, 208.

DATE DUE

WITHDRAWN
from
Funderburg Library